Lecture Notes in Computer Science   11533

Commenced Publication in 1973
Founding and Former Series Editors:
Gerhard Goos, Juris Hartmanis, and Jan van Leeuwen

More information about this series at http://www.springer.com/series/7408

Hanne Riis Nielson · Emilio Tuosto (Eds.)

Coordination Models and Languages

21st IFIP WG 6.1 International Conference, COORDINATION 2019
Held as Part of the 14th International Federated Conference
on Distributed Computing Techniques, DisCoTec 2019
Kongens Lyngby, Denmark, June 17–21, 2019
Proceedings

 Springer

Editors
Hanne Riis Nielson ⓘ
Technical University of Denmark
Kongens Lyngby, Denmark

Emilio Tuosto ⓘ
Gran Sasso Science Institute
L'Aquila, Italy

University of Leicester
Leicester, UK

ISSN 0302-9743   ISSN 1611-3349   (electronic)
Lecture Notes in Computer Science
ISBN 978-3-030-22396-0   ISBN 978-3-030-22397-7   (eBook)
https://doi.org/10.1007/978-3-030-22397-7

LNCS Sublibrary: SL2 – Programming and Software Engineering

This Springer imprint is published by the registered company Springer Nature Switzerland AG
The registered company address is: Gewerbestrasse 11, 6330 Cham, Switzerland

Foreword

The 14th International Federated Conference on Distributed Computing Techniques (DisCoTec) took place in Kongens Lyngby, Denmark, during June 17–21, 2019. It was organized by the Department of Applied Mathematics and Computer Science at the Technical University of Denmark.

The DisCoTec series is one of the major events sponsored by the International Federation for Information Processing (IFIP). It comprised three conferences:

– COORDINATION, the IFIP WG 6.1 21st International Conference on Coordination Models and Languages
– DAIS, the IFIP WG 6.1 19th International Conference on Distributed Applications and Interoperable Systems
– FORTE, the IFIP WG 6.1 39th International Conference on Formal Techniques for Distributed Objects, Components and Systems

Together, these conferences cover a broad spectrum of distributed computing subjects, ranging from theoretical foundations and formal description techniques to systems research issues.

In addition to the individual sessions of each conference, the event included several plenary sessions that gathered attendants from the three conferences. This year, the general chair and the DisCoTec Steering Committee joined the three DisCoTec conferences in the selection and nomination of the plenary keynote speakers, whose number was accordingly increased from the traditional three to five. The five keynote speakers and the title of their talks are listed below:

– Prof. David Basin (ETH Zürich, Switzerland) – "Security Protocols: Model Checking Standards"
– Dr. Anne-Marie Kermarrec (Inria Rennes, France) – "Making Sense of Fast Big Data"
– Prof. Marta Kwiatkowska (University of Oxford, UK) – "Versatile Quantitative Modelling: Verification, Synthesis and Data Inference for Cyber-Physical Systems"
– Prof. Silvio Micali (MIT, USA) – "ALGORAND – The Distributed Ledger for the Borderless Economy"
– Prof. Martin Wirsing (LMU, Germany) – "Toward Formally Designing Collective Adaptive Systems"

As is traditional in DisCoTec, an additional joint session with the best papers from each conference was organized. The best papers were:

– "Representing Dependencies in Event Structures" by G. Michele Pinna (Coordination)
– "FOUGERE: User-Centric Location Privacy in Mobile Crowdsourcing Apps" by Lakhdar Meftah, Romain Rouvoy and Isabelle Chrisment (DAIS)

- "Psi-Calculi Revisited: Connectivity and Compositionality" by Johannes Åman Pohjola (FORTE)

Associated with the federated event were also two satellite events that took place:

- ICE, the 12th International Workshop on Interaction and Concurrency Experience
- DisCoRail, the First International Workshop on Distributed Computing in Future Railway Systems

I would like to thank the Program Committee chairs of the different events for their help and cooperation during the preparation of the conference, and the Steering Committee and Advisory Boards of DisCoTec and their conferences for their guidance and support. The organization of DisCoTec 2019 was only possible thanks to the dedicated work of the Organizing Committee, including Francisco "Kiko" Fernández Reyes and Francesco Tiezzi (publicity chairs), Maurice ter Beek, Valerio Schiavoni, and Andrea Vandin (workshop chairs), Ann-Cathrin Dunker (logistics and finances), as well as all the students and colleagues who volunteered their time to help. Finally, I would like to thank IFIP WG 6.1 for sponsoring this event, Springer's *Lecture Notes in Computer Science* team for their support and sponsorship, EasyChair for providing the reviewing infrastructure, the Nordic IoT Hub for their sponsorship, and the Technical University of Denmark for providing meeting rooms and additional support.

June 2019   Alberto Lluch Lafuente

Preface

This volume contains the papers presented at COORDINATION 2019 held in Lyngby during June 17–21, 2019, as part of the federated DisCoTeC conference. Continuing a tradition started in 1996, the proceedings of COORDINATION 2019 are published in Springer's *Lecture Notes in Computer Science* (LNCS). The conference's main topics of interest are related to architectures, models, and languages for the specification and verification of coordination mechanisms of modern information systems. The separation of concerns between coordination and computation is key to cope with the complexity of modern systems which involve concurrency, distribution, mobility, adaptiveness, and reconfigurability. In fact, the identification of suitable coordination mechanisms allows us to cleanly separate local behavior from communication, increase modularity, simplify reasoning, and ultimately enhancing software development.

The Program Committee (PC) of COORDINATION 2019 consisted of 28 prominent researchers from 14 different countries. A total of 35 abstracts were submitted to the conference and 15 papers were selected among the 25 actual submissions. Each submission was assessed by at least three reviewers and this process was supplemented by an in-depth discussion phase during which the merits of all the papers were considered. The contributions published in this volume were selected according to their quality, originality, clarity, and relevance. The program also includes the invited talk of Prof. Martin Wirsing from the Ludwig-Maximilians-Universität München, Germany; a short abstract of Martin's speech entitled "Machine-Learning Techniques for Systematically Engineering Adaptive Systems" is included in these proceedings.

Many people contributed to the success of COORDINATION 2019. We first of all would like to thank the authors for submitting high-quality papers. We also thank the PC members for their effort and time to read and discuss the papers. The reviews and the comments were very thorough and constructive. The use of external reviewers, whom we also thank, has been very limited to the few cases where specific expertise was required.

This edition of the conference has been enriched by the organization of a "tool track" and three special topics. We are grateful to Omar Inverso and Hugo Torres Vieira, who took care of identifying an innovative reviewing process whereby tool papers were selected according to the combination of an extended abstract and a short video demonstration, after which full papers were produced to be included in these proceedings. A special thank you also goes to the PC members who identified new topics aiming to connect coordination to other research areas. In particular we thank Laura Bocchi for suggesting the topic "From Coordination to Verification and Back," Chiara Bodei and Hugo Torres Vieira for the topic "Exploring the Frontiers Between Coordination and Control Systems," and Jean-Marie Jaquet for the topic "Coordination of Emerging Parallel/Distributed Architectures." As a result of the efforts of these PC members, COORDINATION 2019 had one session dedicated to the emerging topics and two sessions dedicated to tool papers.

Furthermore, we wish to thank the Steering Committee of Coordination and the Steering Board of DisCoTeC for their support. The organization of COORDINATION 2019 would have been much harder without the assistance of the Organizing Committee; we are indeed very grateful to Alberto Lluch Lafuente, the general chair of DisCoTeC 2019, and to the publicity chairs, Kiko Fernández-Reyes and Francesco Tiezzi. It was also a pleasure to collaborate with the other members of the Scientific Committee: José Orlando Pereira, Jorge A. Pérez, Laura Ricci, and Nobuko Yoshida.

We are indebted to the conference attendees for keeping this research community lively and interactive, and ultimately ensuring the success of this conference series.

Emilio Tuosto thanks the GSSI for the financial support provided.

Finally, we thank the providers of the EasyChair conference management system, whose facilities greatly helped us run the review process and facilitate the preparation of the proceedings. With respect to the latter, we also warmly thank Anna Kramer, from Springer, for her help in producing the proceedings.

May 2019   Hanne Riis Nielson
                                                                 Emilio Tuosto

Organization

Program Committee Chairs

Hanne Riis Nielson   DTU COMPUTE, Denmark
Emilio Tuosto   Gran Sasso Science Institute, Italy and University
     of Leicester, UK

Steering Committee

Gul Agha   University of Illinois at Urbana Champaign, USA
Farhad Arbab   CWI and Leiden University, The Netherlands
Rocco De Nicola   IMT, School for Advanced Studies, Italy
Giovanna di Marzo   Université de Genève, Switzerland
  Serugendo
Tom Holvoet   KU Leuven, Belgium
Jean-Marie Jacquet   University of Namur, Belgium
Christine Julien   The University of Texas at Austin, USA
Eva Kühn   Vienna University of Technology, Austria
Alberto Lluch Lafuente   Technical University of Denmark, Denmark
Michele Loreti   University of Camerino, Italy
Mieke Massink   ISTI CNR, Italy
Wolfgang De Meuter   Vrije Universiteit Brussels, Belgium
José Proença   University of Minho, Portugal
Rosario Pugliese   Università di Firenze, Italy
Hanne Riis Nielson   DTU Compute, Denmark
Marjan Sirjani   Reykjavik University, Iceland
Carolyn Talcott   SRI International, California, USA
Emilio Tuosto   GSSI, Italy and University of Leicester, UK
Vasco T. Vasconcelos   University of Lisbon, Portugal
Gianluigi Zavattaro (Chair)   University of Bologna, Italy
Mirko Viroli   University of Bologna, Italy

Program Committee

Stephanie Balzer   Carnegie Mellon University, USA
Simon Bliudze   Inria, France
Laura Bocchi   University of Kent, UK
Chiara Bodei   University of Pisa, Italy
Roberto Bruni   University of Pisa, Italy
Giovanna Di Marzo   Université de Genève, Switzerland
  Serugendo
Fatemeh Ghassemi   University of Tehran, Iran

Elisa Gonzalez Boix	VUB, Belgium
Roberto Guanciale	KTH, Sweden
Ludovic Henrio	CNRS, France
Thomas Hildebrandt	University of Copenhagen, Denmark
Omar Inverso	Gran Sasso Science Institute, Italy
Jean-Marie Jacquet	University of Namur, Belgium
Eva Kühn	Vienna University of Technology, Austria
Michele Loreti	University of Camerino, Italy
Mieke Massink	CNR-ISTI, Italy
Hernan Melgratti	Universidad de Buenos Aires, Argentina
Claudio Antares Mezzina	University of Leicester, UK
Rumyana Neykova	Brunel University London, UK
Luca Padovani	University of Turin, Italy
Danilo Pianini	University of Bologna, Italy
Christian W. Probst	Unitec Institute of Technology, New Zealand
Rene Rydhof Hansen	Aalborg University, Denmark
Gwen Salaün	University of Grenoble Alpes, France
Meng Sun	Peking University, China
Carolyn Talcott	SRI International, USA
Hugo Torres Vieira	IMT School for Advanced Studies Lucca, Italy
Takuo Watanabe	Tokyo Institute of Technology, Japan

Additional Reviewers

Vincenzo Ciancia
Stefan Crass
Letterio Galletta
Gerson Joskowicz
Diego Latella
Yi Li
Frank Pfenning
Xiyue Zhang

Machine-Learning Techniques for Systematically Engineering Adaptive Systems (Invited Talk)

Martin Wirsing

Ludwig-Maximilians-Universität München, München, Germany

Abstract. Many modern software systems are distributed and have to cope at runtime with dynamically changing environments and possibly also with new requirements [3]. Examples of such adaptive systems are autonomous robots, robot swarms and also socio-technical systems such as smart city or smart health care applications. The ASCENS project [1] has developed foundations for building adaptive systems in a way that combines software engineering approaches with the assurance about functional and non-functional properties provided by formal methods and the flexibility, low management overhead, and optimal utilisation of resources promised by autonomic, self-aware systems.

In this talk we review the engineering approach of ASCENS and by integrating machine learning techniques we complement it to "AISCENS." The ASCENS life cycle for developing autonomous and adaptive systems is presented and it is illustrated with two complementary approaches: the development of a swarm of robots using "classical" software design methods [4] and the use of simulation-based online planning for autonomously adapting the behaviour of a robot [2]. In addition, a new machine learning approach for synthesizing agent policies from hard and soft requirements is presented and the performance-safety tradeoff for such requirements is discussed.

References

1. ASCENS: Autonomic Component Ensembles. Integrated Project, 2010-10-01 - 2015-03-31, Grant agreement no: 257414, EU 7th Framework Programme. http://www.ascens-ist.eu/. Accessed 25 Apr 2019
2. Belzner, L., Hennicker, R., Wirsing, M.: Onplan: a framework for simulation-based online planning. In: Braga, C., Ölveczky, P.C. (eds.) FACS 2015. LNCS, vol. 9539, pp. 1–30. Springer, Cham (2015). https://doi.org/10.1007/978-3-319-28934-2_1
3. Jähnichen, S., De Nicola, R., Wirsing, M.: The meaning of adaptation: mastering the unforeseen? In: Margaria, T., Steffen, B. (eds.) ISoLA 2018. LNCS, vol. 11246, pp. 109–117. Springer, Cham (2018). https://doi.org/10.1007/978-3-030-03424-5_8
4. Wirsing, M., Hölzl, M.M., Koch, N., Mayer, P. (eds.): Software Engineering for Collective Autonomic Systems - The ASCENS Approach. LNCS, vol. 8998. Springer, Cham (2015). https://doi.org/10.1007/978-3-319-16310-9

In cooperation with Lenz Belzner, Thomas Gabor, Rolf Hennicker, and Alexander Knapp.

Contents

Coordination Patterns

Tools (2)

Computational Models

Representing Dependencies in Event Structures

G. Michele Pinna[(⊠)]

Dipartimento di Matematica e Informatica, Università di Cagliari, Cagliari, Italy
gmpinna@unica.it

Abstract. Event Structures where the causality may change dynamically have been introduced recently. In this kind of Event Structures the changes in the set of the causes of an event are triggered by modifiers that may add or remove dependencies, thus making the happening of an event contextual. Still the focus is always on the dependencies of the event. In this paper we promote the idea that the *context* determined by the modifiers plays a major rôle, and the context itself determines not only the causes but also what causality should be. Modifiers are then used to understand when an event (or a set of events) can be added to a configuration, together with a set of events modeling dependencies, which will play a less important rôle. We show that most of the notions of Event Structure presented in literature can be translated into this new kind of Event Structure, preserving the main notion, namely the one of configuration.

1 Introduction

The notion of causality is an intriguing one. In the sequential case, the intuition behind it is almost trivial: if the activity e depends on the activity e′, then to happen the activity e needs that e′ has already happened. This is easily represented in Petri nets [24], the transition e′ *produces* a token that is *consumed* by the transition e (the net N′). The dependency is testified by the observation that the activity e′ always precedes the activity e. However this intuition does not reflect other possibilities. If we abandon the sequential case and move toward possibly loosely cooperating system the notion of causality become involved. Consider the case of a Petri net with inhibitor arcs [13] where the precondition of the transition e′ inhibits the transition e (the net N). The latter to happens needs that the transition e′ happens first, and the *observation* testifies that the activity e needs that e′ has already happened, though resources are not exchanged between e′ and e. In both cases the observation that the event e′ must happen first leads to state that e′ precedes e and this can be well represented with a partial order relation among events.

Work partially funded by RAS (Regione Autonoma della Sardegna) - L.R. 7/2007 - Project SardCoin, CUP: F72F16003030002).

H. Riis Nielson and E. Tuosto (Eds.): COORDINATION 2019, LNCS 11533, pp. 3–18, 2019.
https://doi.org/10.1007/978-3-030-22397-7_1

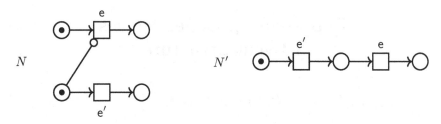

This quite simple discussion suggests that the notion of causality may have many facets. In fact, if the dependencies are modeled just with a well founded partial order, inhibitor arcs can be used to model these dependencies, but the notion of partial order does not capture precisely the subtleties that are connected to the notion of causality.

To represent the semantics of concurrent systems the notion of *event structure* plays a prominent role. Event structures have been introduced in [18] and [27] and since then have been considered as a cornerstone. The idea is simple: the activities of a system are the *events* and their relationships are specified somehow, *e.g.* with a partial order modeling the *enabling* and a predicate expressing when activities are *coherent* or not. Starting from this idea many authors have faced the problem of adapting this notion to many different situations which have as a target the attempt to represent faithfully various situations. This has triggered many different approaches. In [11] and [12] *causal automata* are discussed, with the idea that the conditions under which an event may happen are specified by a suitable logic formula, in [10] and [9] it is argued that a partial order may be not enough or may be, in some situation, a too rigid notion, and this idea is used also in [21] and [22] where the notion of *event automata* is introduced, and it is used also in [20] where an enabling/disabling relation for event automata is discussed. Looking at the enabling relation, both *bundle event structures* [15] and *dual event structures* [16] provide a notion of enabling capturing *or*-causality (the former exclusive *or*-causality and the latter non exclusive *or*-causality). *Asymmetric event structures* [6] introduces a weaker notion of causality which models contextual arcs in Petri nets, or in the case *circular event structures* [7] the enabling notion is tailored to model also *circular dependencies*. In *flow event structures* [8] the partial order is required to hold only in configurations. Finally we mention the approaches aiming at modeling the possibility that the dependencies of an event may change either by dropping some of them or by adding new ones [1]. This short and incomplete discussion (the event structures spectrum is rather broad) should point out the variety of approaches present in literature. It should be also observed that the majority of the approaches model causality with a relation that can be reduced to a partial order, hence causality is represented stating what are the events that should have happened before.

In this paper we introduce yet another notion of event structure. Triggered by recent works on *adding* or *subtracting* dependencies among events based on the fact that apparently unrelated events have happened [1,3], we argue that rather than focussing on how to model these enrichment or/and impoverishment, it is much more natural to focus on the context on which an event takes place. In fact it is a context that can determine the proper dependencies that are applicable at the state where the event should take place and the context holds, and the context can also be used as well to forbid that the event is added to the state. This new relation resembles the one used in *inhibitor* event structures [5], but it differs in the way the contexts are determined. In the case of inhibitor event structures the presence of a certain event (the inhibiting context) was used to require that another one was present as well (representing the trigger able to remove the inhibition). Here the flavour is different as it is more prescriptive: it is required that exactly a set of events is present and if this happens then also another one should be present as well. It should be stressed that triggers and contexts may exchange their role. Consider again the two nets depicted before, we may have that in both cases the trigger is determined by the happening of the event e' and the context is the empty set, but we can consider as context the event e' and the trigger as the empty set. This simple relation, which we will call *context-dependency* relation, suffices to cover the various notions presented in literature. It is worth observing that determining the context and the triggers associated to it is quite similar to trying to understand the dependencies. Consider the net N'' below.

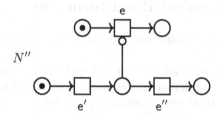

Here e may be added either to the empty set or to a set containing both e' and e''. The context containing e' only leads to require that the event e'' is present (in the spirit of the relation for inhibitor event structures), making e dependent on e''. However we could also have chosen to focus on contexts only and in this case the context containing just e' is ruled out among the contexts in which, together with some others dependencies, e may take place, and in this case the two contexts are $\emptyset$ and $\{e', e''\}$. As hinted above, it will turn out that the context plays a more relevant role with respect to the dependencies, as the context can be seen positively (it specifies under which conditions an event can be added, together with the dependency) or negatively (it specifies under which conditions an event can be added, and in this case the event cannot be added simply stipulating that it depends on itself).

In this paper we will focus on event structures where the change of state is always triggered by the happening of a single event, hence we will not consider steps (*i.e.* non empty and finite subsets of events), and where the states (configurations) are finite, though not always explicitly assumed. However the generalization to steps is straightforward.

Organization of the Paper: In the next section we will introduce and discuss the new brand of event structure. In Sect. 3 we will review and briefly analyze some notions of event structures presented in literature, namely *prime* event structure [27], *relaxed prime* event structure and *dynamic causality* event structure [1], *inhibitor* event structure [5] and event structure for *resolvable conflicts* [26], and, in Sect. 4, we show that the each event structure presented in Sect. 3 can be translated into this new kind of event structure. We will recall also the notion *event automata* which will can used to compare the various notions of event structure. We will end the paper with some conclusions and we will give some hints for further developments.

Notation: Let A be a set, with let ρ we denote a sequence of elements belonging to A, and with ϵ we denote the empty sequence. With $\overline{\rho}$ we denote the set of elements of A appearing in ρ. Thus $\overline{\rho} = \emptyset$ if $\rho = \epsilon$ and $\overline{a\rho'} = \{a\} \cup \overline{\rho'}$ if $\rho = a\rho'$. Given a sequence $\rho = a_1 \cdots a_n$ with $len(\rho)$ we denote its length, with ρ_0 we sometime denote sequence ϵ and, if $len(\rho) \geq 1$, for each $1 \leq i \leq len(\rho)$ with ρ_i we denote the sequence $a_1 \cdots a_i$. Let A be a set, with 2^A we denote the subsets of A and with 2^A_{fin} the finite subsets of A.

2   Context-Dependent Event Structure

We introduce yet another notion of event structure, which is the main contribution of the paper.

We start recalling what an *event* is and we introduce the notion of *configuration*. An event is an atomic individual action which is able to change the state of a system. Event structures in particular are intended to model *concurrent systems* by defining relationships among events such as *causality* and *conflict*, establishing the conditions on which a certain event can be added to a state. The *state* of a system modeled by an event structure is a *subset* of events (those happened so far), and this set of events is called *configuration*. States can be enriched by adding other information beside the one represented by the events that have determined the state, either adding information on the relationship among the various events in the state, *e.g.* adding dependencies among them (the state is then a partial order, [25]) or adding suitable information to the whole state.

We pursue this idea that the happening of an event depends on a set of modifiers (the *context*) and on a set of *real* dependencies, which are activated by the set of modifiers.

We recall that in this paper we will consider only *unlabelled* event structures. To simplify the presentation we retain the classic binary conflict relation. Given a subset $X \subseteq E$ of events and a conflict relation $\#$, which is an irreflexive and symmetric relation, we say that X is *conflict free* iff $\forall e, e' \in X$ it holds that $\neg(e \# e')$.

Definition 1. *A* context-dependent event structure *(CDES) is a triple* $E = (E, \#, \gg)$ *where*

- E *is a set of* events,
- $\# \subseteq E \times E$ *is an irreflexive and symmetric relation, called* conflict relation, *and*
- $\gg \subseteq 2^A \times E$, *where* $A \subseteq 2^E_{fin} \times 2^E_{fin}$, *is a relation, called the* context-dependency relation *(*CD-*relation), which is such that for each* $Z \gg e$ *it holds that*
  - $Z \neq \emptyset$, *and*
  - *for each* $(X, Y) \in Z$ *it holds that* X *and* Y *are conflict-free.*
  Each element of the CD-*relation* $\gg$ *is called* entry.

The CD-relation models, for each event, which are the possible contexts in which the event may happen (the first component of each pair) and for each context which are the events that have to be occurred (the second component). We stipulate that dependencies and contexts are formed by non conflicting events, though this is not strictly needed, as the relation can model also conflicts. How this relation is used will become clear in the notion of enabling of an event. We have to determine, for each $Z \gg e$, which of the contexts X_i should be considered. To do so we define the *context* associated to each entry of the CD-relation. Given $Z \gg e$, where $Z = \{(X_1, Y_1), \ldots, (X_n, Y_n)\}$, with $\mathrm{CXT}(Z)$ we denote the set of events $\bigcup_{i=1}^{|Z|} X_i$, and this is the one regarding $Z \gg e$.

Definition 2. *Let* $E = (E, \#, \gg)$ *be a* CDES *and* $C \subseteq E$ *be a subset of events. Then the event* $e \notin C$ *is* enabled *at* C, *denoted with* $C[e\rangle$, *if for each* $Z \gg e$, *with* $Z = \{(X_1, Y_1), \ldots, (X_n, Y_n)\}$, *there is a pair* $(X_i, Y_i) \in Z$ *such that* $\mathrm{CXT}(Z) \cap C = X_i$ *and* $Y_i \subseteq C$.

Observe that requiring the non emptiness of the set Z in $Z \gg e$ guarantees that an event e may be enabled at some subset of events. The CD-relation could be used to express conflicts: $e \# e'$ could be modeled by adding $\{((\{e\}, \{e'\}))\} \gg e'$ and $\{((\{e'\}, \{e\}))\} \gg e$ to the $\gg$ relation, and the presence of just one of them would model the asymmetric conflict. The conflicts modeled in this way are *persistent*.

Definition 3. *Let* $E = (E, \#, \gg)$ *be a* CDES. *Let* C *be a subset of* E. *We say that* C *is a* configuration *of the* CDES E *iff there exists a sequence of distinct events* $\rho = e_1 \cdots e_n \cdots$ *over* E *such that*

- $\overline{\rho} = C$,
- $\overline{\rho}$ *is conflict-free, and*
- $\forall 1 \leq i \leq len(\rho).\ \overline{\rho}_{i-1}[e_i\rangle.$

Denoting with $\mathrm{Conf}_{\mathrm{CDES}}(E)$ the set of configurations of a CDES, we introduce the relation among configurations. Given two configurations C and C' of a CDES such that $C \cup \{e_{n+1}\} = C'$, we stipulate that $C \mapsto_{\mathrm{CDES}} C'$ iff $C[e_{n+1}\rangle$.

We illustrate this new kind of event structure with some examples.

Example 1. Consider three events a, b and c. All the events are singularly enabled but a and b are in conflict unless c has not happened (we will see later that this are called *resolvable* conflicts). Hence for the event a we stipulate

$$\{(\emptyset, \emptyset), (\{c\}, \emptyset), (\{b\}, \{c\})\} \gg a$$

that should be interpreted as follows: if the context is $\emptyset$ or $\{c\}$ then a is enabled without any further condition (the Y are the empty set), if the context is $\{b\}$ then also $\{c\}$ should be present. The set $\mathrm{CxT}(\{(\emptyset, \emptyset), (\{c\}, \emptyset), (\{b\}, \{c\})\})$ is $\{b, c\}$.

Similarly, for the event b we stipulate

$$\{(\emptyset, \emptyset), (\{c\}, \emptyset), (\{a\}, \{c\})\} \gg b$$

which is justified as above and finally for the event c we stipulate

$$\{(\emptyset, \emptyset), (\{a\}, \emptyset), (\{b\}, \emptyset)\} \gg c$$

namely any context allows to add the event.

Below we depict the configurations and how they are related.

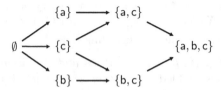

Example 2. Consider three events a, b and c, and assume that c depends on a unless the event b has occurred, and in this case this dependency is removed. Thus there is a classic causality between a and c, but it can dropped if b occurs. Clearly a and b are always enabled. The CD-relation is $\{(\emptyset, \emptyset)\} \gg a$, $\{(\emptyset, \emptyset)\} \gg b$ and $\{(\emptyset, \{a\}), (\{b\}, \emptyset)\} \gg c$.

Example 3. Consider three events a, b and c, and assume that c depends on a just when the event b has occurred, and in this case this dependency is added, otherwise it may happen without Thus the classic causality relation between a and c is added if b occurs. Again a and b are always enabled. The CD-relation is $\{(\emptyset, \emptyset)\} \gg a$, $\{(\emptyset, \emptyset)\} \gg b$ and $\{(\emptyset, \emptyset), (\{b\}, \{a\})\} \gg c$.

These examples should clarify how the CD-relation is used and its *expressivity*.

3   Event Structures

We have introduced a new notion of event structure that we should confront with the others presented in literature (at least some of them). Therefore we review some of the various definitions of event structures.

Prime Event Structures: Prime event structures are one among the first proposed and the most widely studied [27], especially for the connections with *prime algebraic domains* and *causal nets*. The dependencies among events are modeled using a *partial order* relation, the incompatibility among events is modeled using a symmetric and irreflexive relation, the conflict relation, and it is required that the conflict relation is inherited along the partial order.

Definition 4. *A* prime event structure (PES) *is a triple* $P = (E, \leq, \#)$, *where (a)* E *is a set of* events, *(b)* $\leq \subseteq E \times E$ *is a well founded* partial order *called* causality relation, *(c)* $\# \subseteq E \times E$ *is an irreflexive and symmetric relation, called* conflict relation, *such that* $e \# e' \leq e'' \Rightarrow e \# e''$, *and (c)* $\leq \cap \# = \emptyset$.

Given an event $e \in E$, with $\lfloor e \rfloor$ we denote the set $\{e' \mid e' \leq e\}$, and the requirement that the partial order is well founded implies that for each $e \in E$, the set $\lfloor e \rfloor$ is finite. We say that C is a *configuration* of the PES P iff C is conflict free and for each $e \in C$ it holds that $\lfloor e \rfloor \subseteq C$. The set of configuration of a PES is denoted with $\mathsf{Conf}_{\mathrm{PES}}(P)$. Clearly $(\mathsf{Conf}_{\mathrm{PES}}(P), \subseteq)$ is a partial order. With $\mapsto_{\mathrm{PES}}$ we denote the relation over $\mathsf{Conf}_{\mathrm{PES}}(P) \times \mathsf{Conf}_{\mathrm{PES}}(P)$ defined as $C \mapsto_{\mathrm{PES}} C'$ iff $C \subset C'$ and $C' = C \cup \{e\}$ for some $e \in E$.

Relaxed Prime Event Structures: Some of the requirements of a PES, the one on the dependencies among events (here called enabling) and the ore regarding the conflicts among events (which does not need to be saturated), can be relaxed yielding a *relaxed* prime event structure [1,3]. In this definition the events that must be *present* in a state to allow the execution of another one are the events in a (finite) subset called *immediate causes* and often denoted with ic.

Definition 5. *A* relaxed *prime event structure (*rPES*) is a triple* $(E, \rightarrow, \#)$, *where (a)* E *is a set of* events, *(b)* $\rightarrow \subseteq E \times E$ *is the* enabling relation *such that* $\forall e \in E$ *the set* $\mathrm{ic}(e) = \{e' \mid e' \rightarrow e\}$ *is finite, and (c)* $\# \subseteq E \times E$ *is an irreflexive and symmetric* conflict relation.

The intuition is that the $\rightarrow$ relation plays the role of the causality relation and the conflict relation models conflicts among events, as before. The immediate causes can be seen as a mapping $\mathrm{ic} \colon E \rightarrow 2^E_{fin}$. Let $T = (E, \rightarrow, \#)$ be a rPES. Let C be a subset of E. We say that C is a *configuration* of the rPES T iff there exists a sequence of distinct events $\rho = e_1 \cdots e_n \cdots$ over E such that $\overline{\rho} = C$, $\overline{\rho}$ is *conflict free*, and for each $1 \leq i \leq len(\rho)$. $\mathrm{ic}(e_i) \subseteq \overline{\rho_{i-1}}$. The set of configuration of a rPES is denoted with $\mathsf{Conf}_{r\mathrm{PES}}(T)$. In rPES the emphasis is put on the existence of an ordering in which the events are added to a configuration, and this will be valid for many of the kinds of event structures. $(\mathsf{Conf}_{r\mathrm{PES}}(T), \subseteq)$ is a partial order. With $\mapsto_{r\mathrm{PES}}$ we denote the relation over $\mathsf{Conf}_{r\mathrm{PES}}(T) \times \mathsf{Conf}_{r\mathrm{PES}}(T)$ defined as $C \mapsto_{r\mathrm{PES}} C'$ iff $C \subset C'$ and $C' = C \cup \{e\}$ for some $e \in E$.

A PES is also a rPES: the causality relation is the enabling relation and the conflict relation is the same one. e is added to a configuration C when its causes are in C and no conflict arises. Given a rPES $T = (E, \rightarrow, \#)$, it is not difficult to see that $(E, \rightarrow^*, \hat{\#})$ is a PES, where $\rightarrow^*$ is the reflexive and transitive closure of

$\rightarrow$ and $\hat{\#}$ is obtained by $\#$ stipulating that $\# \subseteq \hat{\#}$ and it is closed with respect to $\rightarrow^*$, *i.e.* if e $\hat{\#}$ e$'$ $\rightarrow^*$ e$''$ then e $\hat{\#}$ e$''$. Indeed, the fact that $\rightarrow^*$ is a partial order is guaranteed by the fact that each event is executable, that $\rightarrow^*$ is well founded is implied by the finiteness of causes for each event e $\in$ E and $\hat{\#}$ is the semantic closure of $\#$: no new conflict is introduced.

Dynamic Causality Event Structures: We now review a notion of event structure where causality may change [1,3]. The idea is to enrich a rPES with two relations, one modeling the shrinking causality (some dependencies are dropped) and the other the growing causality (some dependencies are added). The shrinking and the growing causality relations are ternary relations stipulating that the happening of a specific event (the *modifier*) allows to drop or add a specific cause (the contribution) for another event (the *target*).

We illustrate these relations with the aid of a number of auxiliary subsets of events associated to these relations. Let E be a set of events. A *shrinking causality* relation is a ternary relation $\lhd \subseteq E \times E \times E$, and the elements of this relation are denoted with e$'$ $\lhd$ [e $\rightarrow$ e$''$]. Given e$'$ $\lhd$ [e $\rightarrow$ e$''$], e$'$ is called *modifier*, e$''$ *target* and e *contribution*. ShrMod(e$''$) = {e$'$ | e$'$ $\lhd$ [e $\rightarrow$ e$''$]} is the set of modifiers for a given target e$''$ and Drop(e$'$, e$''$) = {e | e$'$ $\lhd$ [e $\rightarrow$ e$''$]} is the set of contributions for a given modifier e$'$ and a given target e$''$. Let H be a finite subset of E and let e be an event, we define the set dc$(H, e) = \bigcup_{e' \in H \cap \text{ShrMod}(e)} \text{Drop}(e', e)$ as the set of *dropped* causes with respect to H for the event e. A *growing causality* relation is a ternary relation $\blacktriangleright \subseteq E \times E \times E$, and the elements of this relation are denoted as e$'$ $\blacktriangleright$ [e $\rightarrow$ e$''$] Given e$'$ $\blacktriangleright$ [e $\rightarrow$ e$''$], e$'$ is called *modifier*, e$''$ *target* and e *contribution*. GroMod(e$''$) = {e$'$ | e$'$ $\blacktriangleright$ [e $\rightarrow$ e$''$]} is the set of modifiers for a given target e$''$ and Add(e$'$, e$''$) = {e | e$'$ $\blacktriangleright$ [e $\rightarrow$ e$''$]} is the set of contributions for a given modifier e$'$ and a given target e$''$. Let H be a finite subset of E and let e be an event, we define the set ac$(H, e) = \bigcup_{e' \in H \cap \text{GroMod}(e)} \text{Add}(e', e)$ as the set of *added* causes with respect to H for the event e. The two relation of shrinking and growing causality give the functions dc$: 2_{fin}^E \times E \rightarrow 2_{fin}^E$. and ac$: 2_{fin}^E \times E \rightarrow 2_{fin}^E$.

Definition 6. *A* dynamic causality event structure (DCES) *is a quintuple $D = (E, \rightarrow, \#, \lhd, \blacktriangleright)$, where $(E, \rightarrow, \#)$ is a rPES, $\lhd \subseteq E \times E \times E$ is the shrinking causality relation, $\blacktriangleright \subseteq E \times E \times E$ is the growing causality relation, and are such that for all e, e$'$, e$'' \in E$*

1. e$'$ $\lhd$ [e $\rightarrow$ e$''$] $\wedge$ $\nexists$e$''' \in$ E. e$'''$ $\blacktriangleright$ [e $\rightarrow$ e$''$] $\Longrightarrow$ e $\rightarrow$ e$''$,
2. e$'$ $\blacktriangleright$ [e $\rightarrow$ e$''$] $\wedge$ $\nexists$e$''' \in$ E.e$'''$ $\lhd$ [e $\rightarrow$ e$''$] $\Longrightarrow$ $\neg$(e $\rightarrow$ e$''$),
3. e$'$ $\blacktriangleright$ [e $\rightarrow$ e$''$] $\Longrightarrow$ $\neg$(e$'$ $\lhd$ [e $\rightarrow$ e$''$]), *and*
4. $\forall$e, e$' \in$ E. $\nexists$e$''$, e$''' \in$ E. e$''$ $\lhd$ [e $\rightarrow$ e$'$] *and* e$'''$ $\blacktriangleright$ [e $\rightarrow$ e$'$].

For further comments on this definition we refer to [1] and [3]. It should be observed, however, that the definition we consider here is slightly less general of the one presented there, as we add a further condition, the last one, which is defined in [2] and does not allow that the same contribution can be added and removed by two different modifiers. These are called in [2] *single state dynamic causality event structures* and rule out the fact that some causality (or absence of) depends on the order of modifiers. Conditions 1 and 2 simply state that in the case of the shrinking relation the dependency should be present, and in the case of the growing the dependency should be absent; condition 3 says that if a dependency is added then it cannot be removed, or a removed dependency cannot be added, and the final condition express the fact that two modifiers, one growing and the other shrinking, cannot act on the same dependency. Clearly a DCES where $\lhd$ and $\blacktriangleright$ are empty is a rPES.

Let $D = (\mathsf{E}, \rightarrow, \#, \lhd, \blacktriangleright)$ be a DCES. Let C be a subset of E. We say that C is a *configuration* of the DCES iff there exists a sequence of distinct events $\rho = \mathsf{e}_1 \cdots \mathsf{e}_n$ over E such that (a) $\overline{\rho} = C$, (b) $\overline{\rho}$ is conflict-free, and (c) $\forall 1 \leq i \leq len(\rho)$. $((ic(\mathsf{e}_i) \cup ac(\overline{\rho_{i-1}}, \mathsf{e}_i)) \setminus dc(\overline{\rho_{i-1}}, \mathsf{e}_i)) \subseteq \overline{\rho_{i-1}}$. The set of configuration of a DCES is denoted with $\mathrm{Conf}_{\mathrm{DCES}}(D)$.

With $\mapsto_{\mathrm{DCES}}$ we denote the relation over $\mathrm{Conf}_{\mathrm{DCES}}(D) \times \mathrm{Conf}_{\mathrm{DCES}}(D)$ defined as $C \mapsto_{\mathrm{DCES}} C'$ iff $C \subset C'$, $C' = C \cup \{\mathsf{e}\}$ for some $\mathsf{e} \in \mathsf{E}$ and $((ic(\mathsf{e}) \cup ac(C, \mathsf{e})) \setminus dc(C, \mathsf{e})) \subseteq C$.

Example 4. Consider the set of events $\{\mathsf{a}, \mathsf{b}, \mathsf{c}, \mathsf{d}, \mathsf{e}\}$, with $\mathsf{b} \rightarrow \mathsf{c}$, $\mathsf{a} \lhd [\mathsf{b} \rightarrow \mathsf{c}]$, $\mathsf{d} \blacktriangleright [\mathsf{e} \rightarrow \mathsf{c}]$, $\mathsf{a} \# \mathsf{e}$ and $\mathsf{d} \# \mathsf{b}$. a and d are the modifiers for the target c, the happening of a has the effect that the cause b may be dropped, and the one of d that the cause e should be added for c. If the prefix of the trace is bc (the target c is executed before of one of its modifiers a and d) then the final part of the trace is any either a or e, and as $\mathsf{d} \# \mathsf{b}$ we have that d cannot be added. If the modifier a is executed before c then we have the traces ac (as the immediate cause b of c is dropped by a) followed by b or d, and if the modifier d is executed, then before adding c, we need e (the modifier d add the immediate cause e for c), and in this case we cannot add b for sure as it is in conflict with d or a as it is in conflict with e. If both modifiers a and d happen, then the event c is permanently disabled, as it needs the contribution e (growing cause) which is in conflict with a. Below are shown the configurations of this DCES and the $\mapsto_{\mathrm{DCES}}$ relation.

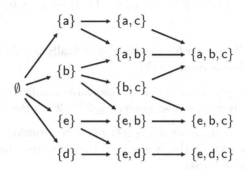

A shrinking event structure (SES) is a DCES where the ▶ relation is empty and a growing event structure (GES) is a DCES where the ◁ relation is empty.

Inhibitor Event Structures: Inhibitor event structure [5] are equipped with a relation $\vdash\!\!\circ\ \subseteq 2_1^E \times E \times 2_{fin}^E$ allowing to model conflicts (even asymmetric) as well as temporary inhibitions. With 2_1^E we denote the subsets of events with cardinality at most one (the empty set or singletons). The intuition behind this relation is the following: given $\vdash\!\!\circ(a, e, A)$, the event e is enabled at a configuration is whenever the configuration contains the set a, then its intersection with A is non empty. Hence the event in a non empty a *inhibits* the happening of e unless some event in A has happened as well. We stipulate that given $\vdash\!\!\circ(a, e, A)$ the events in A are pairwise conflicting (denoted with $\#(A)$). Two events e and e' are in conflict if $\vdash\!\!\circ(\{e'\}, e, \emptyset)$ and $\vdash\!\!\circ(\{e\}, e', \emptyset)$. An *or-causality* relation $<$ is definable stipulating that $A < e$ if $\vdash\!\!\circ(\emptyset, e, A)$, and that if $A < e$ and $B < e'$ for some $e' \in A$ then also $B < e$. This relation should be interpreted as follows: $A < e$ means that if e is present, then also an event in A should be present.

Definition 7. *An* inhibitor event structure *(IES) is a pair $I = (E, \vdash\!\!\circ)$, where E is a set of* events *and $\vdash\!\!\circ\ \subseteq 2_1^E \times E \times 2_{fin}^E$ is a relation such that for each $\vdash\!\!\circ(a, e, A)$ it holds that $\#(A)$ and $a \cup A \neq \emptyset$.*

We briefly recall the intuition: consider an event e and a triple in the $\vdash\!\!\circ$ relation $\vdash\!\!\circ(a, e, A)$. Then e can be added provided that if the event in a is present also one in A should be present. Let $I = (E, \vdash\!\!\circ)$ be an IES. Let C be a subset of E. We say that C is a *configuration* of the IES I iff there exists a sequence of distinct events $\rho = e_1 \cdots e_n \cdots$ over E such that $\overline{\rho} = C$ and for each $i \leq n$, for each $\vdash\!\!\circ(a, e_i, A)$, it holds that $a \subseteq \overline{\rho_{i-1}} \Rightarrow \overline{\rho_{i-1}} \cap A \neq \emptyset$. The set of configuration of a IES is denoted with $\mathsf{Conf}_{IES}(I)$. With $\mapsto_{IES}$ we denote the relation over $\mathsf{Conf}_{IES}(I) \times \mathsf{Conf}_{IES}(D)$ defined as $C \mapsto_{IES} C'$ iff $C \subset C'$ and $C' = C \cup \{e\}$ for some $e \in E$.

Example 5. Consider three events a, b and c, $\vdash\!\!\circ(\{a\}, c, \{b\})$ and $\vdash\!\!\circ(\emptyset, b, \{a\})$. The maximal event traces are cab and abc. The event c is inhibited when the event a has occurred unless the event b has occurred as well. The configurations are $\emptyset$, $\{a\}$, $\{c\}$, $\{a, b\}$, $\{a, c\}$ and $\{a, b, c\}$ and are reached as follows: $\emptyset \mapsto_{IES} \{a\}$, $\emptyset \mapsto_{IES} \{c\}$, $\{a\} \mapsto_{IES} \{a, b\}$, $\{c\} \mapsto_{IES} \{a, c\}$, $\{a, b\} \mapsto_{IES} \{a, b, c\}$ and $\{a, c\} \mapsto_{IES} \{a, b, c\}$.

Event Structures with Resolvable Conflicts: We finally recall the notion of event structure with resolvable conflicts [26].

Definition 8. *An* event structure with resolvable conflicts *(RCES) is the pair $R = (E, \vdash)$ where E is a set of events and $\vdash\ \subseteq 2^E \times 2^E$ is the enabling relation.*

No restriction is posed on the enabling relation. The intuition is that stipulating $X \vdash Y$ one state that for all the events in Y to occur, also the events in the set X should have occurred first.

The *single event* transition relation $\leadsto\ \subseteq 2^E \times 2^E$ of a RCES $R = (E, \vdash)$ is given by $X \leadsto Y \Leftrightarrow (X \subseteq Y \wedge |Y \setminus X| \leq 1 \wedge \forall Z \subseteq Y. \exists W \subseteq X. W \vdash Z)$.

With this notion it is possible to define what a configuration is: it is a subset X of events such that $X \leadsto X$. The requirement that $X \leadsto X$ implies that each subset of events is enabled in the configuration. Let $R = (\mathsf{E}, \vdash)$ be a RCES. Let C be a subset of E. We say that C is a *configuration* of the IES I iff there exists a sequence of distinct events $\rho = \mathsf{e}_1 \cdots \mathsf{e}_n \cdots$ over E such that for each $1 \leq i \leq len(\rho)$ it holds that $\overline{\rho_{i-1}}$ and $\overline{\rho_i}$ are configurations, and $\overline{\rho_{i-1}} \leadsto \overline{\rho_i}$. The set of configuration of a RCES is denoted with $\mathsf{Conf}_{\mathrm{RCES}}(R)$.

Given two configurations C and C' of a RCES, such that $C \cup \{\mathsf{e}_{n+1}\} = C'$ and $C \leadsto C$, we stipulate again that $\overline{\rho} \mapsto_{\mathrm{DCES}} \overline{\rho'}$, defining a relation over $\mathsf{Conf}_{\mathrm{RCES}}(R) \times \mathsf{Conf}_{\mathrm{RCES}}(R)$. Observe that the enabling relation $\vdash$ is used not only to state under which condition an event may happen but also to stipulate when an event is *deducible* from a set of events, justifying also the deduction symbol used for this relation. Observe also that $\mapsto_{\mathrm{RCES}}$ is essentially $\leadsto$.

Example 6. Consider three events a, b and c, and $\emptyset \vdash X$ where $X \subseteq \{\mathsf{a}, \mathsf{b}, \mathsf{c}\}$ with $X \neq \{\mathsf{a}, \mathsf{b}\}$ and $\{\mathsf{c}\} \vdash \{\mathsf{a}, \mathsf{b}\}$. The intuition is that all the events are singularly enabled but a and b are in conflict unless c has not happened. In fact $\{\mathsf{a}, \mathsf{b}\}$ is not a configuration as taking $\{\mathsf{a}, \mathsf{b}\}$ as the $Z \subseteq \{\mathsf{a}, \mathsf{b}\}$ of the notion of single event transition relation, there is no subset of $\{\mathsf{a}, \mathsf{b}\}$ enabling these two events.

The configurations and how they are reached are those of the Example 1.

4   Embedding and Comparing Event Structures

We now show that each of the event structure we have seen so far can be seen as a CDES, and also how to compare them. For the sake of simplicity, we will consider event structures where each event e is *executable*, namely that there is at least a configuration containing it.

Comparing Event Structures: We start by devising how we can compare two event structures of any kind. The intuition is obvious: two event structures are equivalent iff they have the same configurations and the $\mapsto$ relations defined on configurations coincide. We recall the notion of *event automaton* [22].

Definition 9. *Let E be a set of events. An* event automaton over E *(ea) is the tuple $\mathcal{E} = \langle \mathsf{E}, \mathsf{S}, \mapsto, s_0 \rangle$ such that*

- $\mathsf{S} \subseteq 2^{\mathsf{E}}$, *and*
- $\mapsto \subseteq \mathsf{S} \times \mathsf{S}$ *is such that $s \mapsto s'$ implies that $s \subset s'$.*

$s_0 \in \mathsf{S}$ *is the initial state.*

Event automata can easily express configurations of any kind of event structure, provided that for each kind a way to reach a configuration from another is given. The kind of event structure is ranged over by $\mu, \mu' \in \{\mathrm{PES}, r\mathrm{PES}, \mathrm{DCES}, \mathrm{IES}, \mathrm{RCES}, \mathrm{CDES}\}$.

Theorem 1. *Let X be an event structure of kind μ over the set of events E. Then $\mathcal{G}_\mu(X) = \langle \mathsf{E}, \mathsf{Conf}_\mu(X), \mapsto_\mu, \emptyset \rangle$ is an event automaton.*

Using event automata we can decide when two event structures are equivalent.

Definition 10. *Let X and Y be event structures over the same set of events E of kind μ and μ' respectively. We say that X and Y are* equivalent*, denoted with $X \equiv Y$, iff $\mathcal{G}_\mu(X) = \mathcal{G}_{\mu'}(Y)$.*

The expressivity is explicitly studied in [1] and [3]. Informally a kind of event structure is more expressive with respect to another, when there is a configuration of the former that cannot be a configuration of the latter, whatever is done with the various relations among events. Incomparable means that neither one is more expressive than the other or the vice versa. We shortly summarize part of these findings, when considering finite configurations. PES and rPES are equally expressive, whereas SES and GES are strictly more expressive than rPES, and are incomparable one with respect to the other. These two are both less expressive than DCES and RCES, which are incomparable. The relative expressivity of other kinds of event structure has not been investigated.

Embedding Event Structures into CDES: We prove now a more general result, namely that given any *event automaton* $\mathcal{E}$, which is obtained by the configurations of any kind of event structure, it is possible to obtain a CDES whose configurations are precisely the ones of the event automaton $\mathcal{E}$. We start identifying, in an ea, the events that are in *conflict*. The conflict relation we obtain is a *semantic* conflict relation: two events are in conflict iff they never appear together in a state.

Definition 11. *Let $\mathcal{E} = \langle \mathsf{E}, \mathsf{S}, \mapsto, s_0 \rangle$ be an ea. We define a symmetric and irreflexive conflict relation $\#_{\mathsf{ea}}$ as follows: $\mathsf{e} \#_{\mathsf{ea}} \mathsf{e}'$ iff for each $s \in \mathsf{S}$. $\{\mathsf{e}, \mathsf{e}'\} \not\subseteq s$.*

In order to obtain the CD-relation we need some further definitions. Fixed an event e, the first one identifies the states where this event can be added, and the second one identifies the states where the event cannot be added.

Definition 12. *Let $\mathcal{E} = \langle \mathsf{E}, \mathsf{S}, \mapsto, s_0 \rangle$ be an ea. To each event $\mathsf{e} \in \mathsf{E}$ we associate the subset of events $\{s \in \mathsf{S} \mid s \cup \{\mathsf{e}\} \in \mathsf{S} \ \wedge \ s \mapsto s \cup \{\mathsf{e}\}\}$, which we denote with $\mathcal{C}(\mathcal{E}, \mathsf{e})$.*

Definition 13. *Let $\mathcal{E} = \langle \mathsf{E}, \mathsf{S}, \mapsto, s_0 \rangle$ be an ea. To each event $\mathsf{e} \in \mathsf{E}$ we associate the set of configuration $\{s \in \mathsf{S} \mid s \cup \{\mathsf{e}\} \notin \mathsf{S}\}$, which we denote with $\mathcal{I}(\mathcal{E}, \mathsf{e})$.*

Definition 12 characterizes when an event is enabled giving the *allowing* context, whereas the Definition 13 gives the context where the event cannot be added, and it is called *negative* context. These two sets are used to obtain the CD-relation.

Theorem 2. *Let $\mathcal{E} = \langle \mathsf{E}, \mathsf{S}, \mapsto, s_0 \rangle$ be an ea. Then $\mathcal{F}_{\mathsf{ea}}(\mathcal{E}) = (\mathsf{E}, \#, \gg)$ is a* CDES*, where $\#$ is the relation $\#_{\mathsf{ea}}$ of Definition 11, and for each $\mathsf{e} \in \mathsf{E}$ we have $\{(X, \emptyset) \mid X \in \mathcal{C}(\mathcal{E}, \mathsf{e})\} \cup \{(X, \{\mathsf{e}\}) \mid X \in \mathcal{I}(\mathcal{E}, \mathsf{e})\} \gg \mathsf{e}$. Furthermore $\mathcal{E} \equiv \mathcal{G}_{\mathrm{CDES}}(\mathcal{F}_{\mathsf{ea}}(\mathcal{E}))$.*

The theorem has a main consequence, namely that event automata and CDES are equally expressive.

Example 7. Consider the RCES of the Example 6. The associated event automaton is the one depicted in the Example 1. It has no conflict as all the three events are present in a configuration together. The associated CD-relation, obtained using Definition 12 and Definition 13, is the following one, which is a little different from the one devised in the Example 1 as here it is obtained from an event automaton. $\{(\emptyset, \emptyset), (\{c\}, \emptyset), (\{c, b\}, \emptyset), (\{b\}, \{a\})\} \gg$ a because the set $\mathcal{C}(\mathsf{Conf}_{\mathrm{RCES}}(R), \mathsf{a})$ contains the sets $\emptyset$, $\{c\}$ and $\{c, b\}$, whereas the set of the *negative context* $\mathcal{I}(\mathsf{Conf}_{\mathrm{RCES}}(R), \mathsf{a})$ contains just $\{b\}$, the one $\{(\emptyset, \emptyset), (\{c\}, \emptyset), (\{a, b\}, \emptyset), (\{a\}, \{b\})\} \gg$ b as $\mathcal{C}(\mathsf{Conf}_{\mathrm{RCES}}(R), \mathsf{b})$ contains the sets $\emptyset$, $\{c\}$ and $\{a, c\}$, $\mathcal{I}(\mathsf{Conf}_{\mathrm{RCES}}(R), \mathsf{b})$ contains $\{a\}$, and finally $\{(\emptyset, \emptyset), (\{a\}, \emptyset), (\{b\}, \emptyset)\} \gg$ c as $\mathcal{C}(\mathsf{Conf}_{\mathrm{RCES}}(R), \mathsf{c})$ contains the sets $\emptyset$, $\{a\}$ and $\{b\}$, and $\mathcal{I}(\mathsf{Conf}_{\mathrm{RCES}}(R), \mathsf{c})$ is the empty set.

As a consequence of the Theorem 2 we have the following result.

Corollary 1. *Let X be an event structure of type μ and let $\mathcal{G}_\mu(X)$ be the associated* ea. *Then $\mathcal{F}_{\mathsf{ea}}(\mathcal{G}_\mu(X))$ is* CDES, *and $X \equiv \mathcal{F}_{\mathsf{ea}}(\mathcal{G}_\mu(X))$.*

The construction identifies properly the *context* in which an event is allowed to happen, and this context becomes the main ingredient of the CD-relation, as the construction does not give the *causes* but just the context. If on the one hand this suggests that the context, rather than the causal dependencies, is the relevant ingredient, on the other hand it is less informative with respect to the usual causality definitions.

We review some kind of event structures, showing that a more informative CD-relation can be indeed obtained. We will focus only on few of them.

PES: In this case the idea is that causes of an event are just the set of events that should be present in the configuration.

Proposition 1. *Let $P = (\mathsf{E}, \leq, \#)$ be a* PES. *Then $\mathcal{F}_{\mathrm{PES}}(P) = (\mathsf{E}, \#, \gg)$ is a* CDES, *where $\{(\emptyset, \lfloor \mathsf{e} \rfloor \setminus \{\mathsf{e}\})\} \gg \mathsf{e}$ for each $\mathsf{e} \in \mathsf{E}$. Furthermore $P \equiv \mathcal{F}_{\mathrm{PES}}(P)$.*

This is not the unique way to associate to the causality relation $\leq$ of a PES the $\gg$ relation: one alternative would have been to add $\{(\emptyset, \{\mathsf{e}'\})\} \gg \mathsf{e}$ for each $\mathsf{e}' < \mathsf{e}$ and another one would be $\{(\lfloor \mathsf{e} \rfloor \setminus \{\mathsf{e}\}, \emptyset)\} \gg \mathsf{e}$ showing that the events causally before e are indeed the context allowing the event e to happen.

Example 8. Consider the PES $(\{\mathsf{a}, \mathsf{b}, \mathsf{c}\}, \leq, \#)$ where $\mathsf{a} \leq \mathsf{b}$ (we omit the reflexive part of the $\leq$ relation), $\mathsf{a} \# \mathsf{c}$ and $\mathsf{b} \# \mathsf{c}$. The event traces are ϵ, a, ab and c, and the associated configurations are $\emptyset$, $\{\mathsf{a}\}$, $\{\mathsf{a}, \mathsf{b}\}$ and $\{\mathsf{c}\}$ (the $\mapsto_{\mathrm{PES}}$ relation is obvious). The conflict relation is the same and the CD-relation is $\{(\emptyset, \emptyset)\} \gg \mathsf{a}$, $\{(\emptyset, \emptyset)\} \gg \mathsf{c}$ and $\{(\emptyset, \{\mathsf{a}\})\} \gg \mathsf{b}$. As noticed before we could have stipulated also $\{(\{\mathsf{a}\}, \emptyset)\} \gg \mathsf{b}$ instead of $\{(\emptyset, \{\mathsf{a}\})\} \gg \mathsf{b}$ obtaining the same set of configurations and the same transition graph.

DCES: The intuition in this case consists in mixing the two approaches above.

Proposition 2. *Let $D = (\mathsf{E}, \#, \rightarrow, \lhd, \blacktriangleright)$ be a* DCES. *$\mathcal{F}_{\mathrm{DCES}}(D) = (\mathsf{E}, \#, \gg)$ is a* CDES *where the relation $\gg$ is defined as $\{(X, (\mathsf{ic}(\mathsf{e}) \setminus (\bigcup_{\mathsf{e}' \in X} \mathsf{Drop}(\mathsf{e}', \mathsf{e}))) \cup$*

$\bigcup_{e' \in X} \mathsf{Add}(e', e)) \mid X \subseteq \mathsf{GroMod}(e) \cup \mathsf{ShrMod}(e) \gg e$ *for each* $e \in E$. *Furthermore* $D \equiv \mathcal{F}_{\mathrm{DCES}}(G)$.

Example 9. Concerning the DCES of the Example 4, the conflict relation is the one of the DCES whereas the CD-relation is $\{(\emptyset, \emptyset)\} \gg$ a, $\{(\emptyset, \emptyset)\} \gg$ b, $\{(\emptyset, \emptyset)\} \gg$ e, $\{(\emptyset, \emptyset)\} \gg$ d and for c we have $\{(\emptyset, \{b\}), (\{a\}, \emptyset), (\{d\}, \{b, e\}), (\{a, d\}, \{e\})\} \gg$ c.

IES: In the case of IES there are two main observations: one, there is no conflict relation, and second, though there is some similarity between the $\vdash\!\circ$ relation and the $\gg$ relation, there is also a quite subtle difference. When adding an event e to a configuration of an IES, and we have $\vdash\!\circ(a, e, A)$, one would simply add the pairs $(a, \{e'\})$ for each $e' \in A$ (as the events in A are pairwise conflicting) but this does not work in the case A is the empty set, as it has a different meaning in the $\vdash\!\circ$ relation with respect to the $\gg$ relation. In the former, it means that the event in a inhibits the event e, whereas in the latter the pair $(a, \emptyset)$ simply says that if the context a is present then there is no further event needed. Taking into account these differences, the translation is fairly simple. We first define the conflict relation and then the relation $\gg$, which is almost the same as the $\vdash\!\circ$ relation.

Proposition 3. *Let* $I = (E, \vdash\!\circ)$ *be an* IES. $\mathcal{F}_{\mathrm{IES}}(I) = (E, \#, \gg)$ *is a* CDES, *where* e $\#$ e' *iff* $\vdash\!\circ(\{e\}, e', \emptyset)$ *and* $\vdash\!\circ(\{e'\}, e, \emptyset)$, *and for each* $e \in E$, *if* $\vdash\!\circ(a, e, A)$ *and* $A \neq \emptyset$ *then* $\{(\emptyset, \emptyset)\} \cup \{(a, \{e'\}) \mid e' \in A\} \gg e$, *if* $\vdash\!\circ(a, e, A)$ *and* $A = \emptyset$ *then* $\{(a, \{e\})\} \gg e$. *Furthermore* $I \equiv \mathcal{F}_{\mathrm{IES}}(I)$.

Example 10. The IES of the Example 5 induces the empty conflict relation, and the CD-relation is $\{(\emptyset, \emptyset)\} \gg$ a, $\{(\emptyset, \{a\})\} \gg$ b and $\{(\emptyset, \emptyset), (\{a\}, \{b\})\} \gg$ c.

Higher Order Causality: The comparison with event structures with higher-order dynamics of [14] is done indirectly, as these are equivalent to event structures with resolvable conflicts. In this approach the relations $\triangleleft$ and $\blacktriangleright$ are generalized to take into account set of modifiers, targets and contributions. The drawback is that the happening of an event implies a recalculation of these relation, similarly to what it is done in causal automata. In fact it is fairly obvious that given one simple step transition graph (meaning that a configuration is reached by another one adding just one event), it is always possible to obtain a CDES.

5   Conclusion

In this paper we have introduced a new brand of event structure where the main relation, the CD-relation, models the various conditions under which an event can be added to a subset of events. The relation is now defined as $\gg \subseteq 2^A \times E$, where $A \subseteq 2^E \times 2^E$, thus it stipulates for each event which are the context-dependency pairs, but it can be easily generalized to subsets of events modeling precisely, when events happen together (as it is done in [23] or [26]). The focus is on the contexts in which an event can be added, which may change, rather that modeling the dependencies and how these may change. Here the choice is whether it is better to focus on dependencies (and how they may change) or on the context. The advantage of the latter is its generality, whereas the former may be useful in pointing out relations among events.

It should be clear that this kind of event structures is capable of modeling the same enabling situation for an event in various way, and it could be interesting to understand if there could be an informative way canonically. In fact, the canonical relation just focus on all the contexts in which an event can be added, and the dependency set is less informative. Thus finding a way to identify minimal contexts together with a set of dependencies may be useful, similarly to what it has been discussed when associating PES to CDES.

It remains to stress that CDES can be generalized not only allowing steps but also representing contexts in a richer way. Here we have considered contexts as subset of events, but they can have a richer structure. This would allow to characterize more precisely contexts, allowing, for instance, to drop the last requirement we have placed on DCES, as in this case the order in which the modifiers appear may influence the dependencies. Finally we observe that the idea of context is not new, for instance they have been considered in [17] or in [4], and a comparison with these should be considered.

In this paper we have considered various event structures, still some interesting notions remained out of the scope of this paper, like reversible event structures [19], but we are confident that our approach can be used also in the reversibility setting.

References

1. Arbach, Y., Karcher, D., Peters, K., Nestmann, U.: Dynamic causality in event structures. In: Graf, S., Viswanathan, M. (eds.) FORTE 2015. LNCS, vol. 9039, pp. 83–97. Springer, Cham (2015). https://doi.org/10.1007/978-3-319-19195-9_6
2. Arbach, Y., Karcher, D., Peters, K., Nestmann, U.: Dynamic causality in event structures (technical report). CoRR abs/1504.00512 (2015)
3. Arbach, Y., Karcher, D.S., Peters, K., Nestmann, U.: Dynamic causality in event structures. Logical Methods Comput. Sci. **14**(1), 1–17 (2018)
4. Baldan, P., Bracciali, A., Bruni, R.: A semantic framework for open processes. Theor. Comput. Sci. **389**(3), 446–483 (2007)
5. Baldan, P., Busi, N., Corradini, A., Pinna, G.M.: Domain and event structure semantics for Petri nets with read and inhibitor arcs. Theor. Comput. Sci. **323**(1–3), 129–189 (2004)
6. Baldan, P., Corradini, A., Montanari, U.: Contextual Petri nets, asymmetric event structures and processes. Inf. Comput. **171**(1), 1–49 (2001)
7. Bartoletti, M., Cimoli, T., Pinna, G.M., Zunino, R.: Circular causality in event structures. Fundam. Inform. **134**(3–4), 219–259 (2014)
8. Boudol, G.: Flow event structures and flow nets. In: Guessarian, I. (ed.) LITP 1990. LNCS, vol. 469, pp. 62–95. Springer, Heidelberg (1990). https://doi.org/10.1007/3-540-53479-2_4

9. Gaifman, H.: Modeling concurrency by partial orders and nonlinear transition systems. In: de Bakker, J.W., de Roever, W.-P., Rozenberg, G. (eds.) REX 1988. LNCS, vol. 354, pp. 467–488. Springer, Heidelberg (1989). https://doi.org/10.1007/BFb0013031

10. Gaifman, H., Pratt, V.R.: Partial order models of concurrency and the computation of functions. In: Gries, D. (ed.) LICS 1987 Conference Proceedings, pp. 72–85. IEEE Computer Society (1987)

11. Gunawardena, J.: Geometric logic, causality and event structures. In: Baeten, J.C.M., Groote, J.F. (eds.) CONCUR 1991. LNCS, vol. 527, pp. 266–280. Springer, Heidelberg (1991). https://doi.org/10.1007/3-540-54430-5_94

12. Gunawardena, J.: Causal automata. Theor. Comput. Sci. **101**(2), 265–288 (1992)

13. Janicki, R., Koutny, M.: Semantics of inhibitor nets. Inf. Comput. **123**, 1–16 (1995)

14. Karcher, D.S., Nestmann, U.: Higher-order dynamics in event structures. In: Leucker, M., Rueda, C., Valencia, F.D. (eds.) ICTAC 2015. LNCS, vol. 9399, pp. 258–271. Springer, Cham (2015). https://doi.org/10.1007/978-3-319-25150-9_16

15. Langerak, R.: Bundle event structures: a non-interleaving semantics for LOTOS. In: Diaz, M., Groz, R. (eds.) FORTE 1992 Conference Proceedings. IFIP Transactions, vol. C-10, pp. 331–346. North-Holland (1992)

16. Langerak, R., Brinksma, E., Katoen, J.-P.: Causal ambiguity and partial orders in event structures. In: Mazurkiewicz, A., Winkowski, J. (eds.) CONCUR 1997. LNCS, vol. 1243, pp. 317–331. Springer, Heidelberg (1997). https://doi.org/10.1007/3-540-63141-0_22

17. Leifer, J.J., Milner, R.: Transition systems, link graphs and petri nets. Math. Struct. Comput. Sci. **16**(6), 989–1047 (2006)

18. Nielsen, M., Plotkin, G., Winskel, G.: Petri nets, event structures and domains, part 1. Theor. Comput. Sci. **13**, 85–108 (1981)

19. Phillips, I., Ulidowski, I.: Reversibility and asymmetric conflict in event structures. J. Logic Algebraic Methods Program. **84**(6), 781–805 (2015)

20. Pinna, G.M.: Event structures with disabling/enabling relation and event automata. Fundam. Inform. **73**(3), 409–430 (2006)

21. Pinna, G.M., Poigné, A.: On the nature of events. In: Havel, I.M., Koubek, V. (eds.) MFCS 1992. LNCS, vol. 629, pp. 430–441. Springer, Heidelberg (1992). https://doi.org/10.1007/3-540-55808-X_42

22. Pinna, G.M., Poigné, A.: On the nature of events: another perspective in concurrency. Theor. Comput. Sci. **138**(2), 425–454 (1995)

23. Pinna, G.M., Saba, A.: Modeling dependencies and simultaneity in membrane system computations. Theor. Comput. Sci. **431**, 13–39 (2012)

24. Reisig, W.: Petri Nets: An Introduction. EACTS Monographs on Theoretical Computer Science. Springer, Heidelberg (1985). https://doi.org/10.1007/978-3-642-69968-9

25. Rensink, A.: Posets for configurations!. In: Cleaveland, W.R. (ed.) CONCUR 1992. LNCS, vol. 630, pp. 269–285. Springer, Heidelberg (1992). https://doi.org/10.1007/BFb0084797

26. van Glabbeek, R., Plotkin, G.: Event structures for resolvable conflict. In: Fiala, J., Koubek, V., Kratochvíl, J. (eds.) MFCS 2004. LNCS, vol. 3153, pp. 550–561. Springer, Heidelberg (2004). https://doi.org/10.1007/978-3-540-28629-5_42

27. Winskel, G.: Event structures. In: Brauer, W., Reisig, W., Rozenberg, G. (eds.) ACPN 1986. LNCS, vol. 255, pp. 325–392. Springer, Heidelberg (1987). https://doi.org/10.1007/3-540-17906-2_31

Reversing P/T Nets

Hernán Melgratti[1]([⊠]), Claudio Antares Mezzina[2,3]([⊠]), and Irek Ulidowski[2]([⊠])

[1] University of Buenos Aires - Conicet, Buenos Aires, Argentina
`hmelgra@dc.uba.ar`
[2] University of Leicester, Leicester, England
`iu3@leicester.ac.uk`
[3] Dipartimento di Scienze Pure e Applicate, Università di Urbino, Urbino, Italy
`claudio.mezzina@uniurb.it`

Abstract. Petri Nets are a well-known model of concurrency and provide an ideal setting for the study of fundamental aspects in concurrent systems. Despite their simplicity, they still lack a satisfactory causally reversible semantics. We develop such semantics for Place/Transitions Petri Nets (P/T nets) based on two observations. Firstly, a net that explicitly expresses causality and conflict among events, e.g., an occurrence net, can be straightforwardly reversed by adding reversal for each of its transitions. Secondly, the standard unfolding construction associates a P/T net with an occurrence net that preserves all of its computation. Consequently, the reversible semantics of a P/T net can be obtained as the reversible semantics of its unfolding. We show that such reversible behaviour can be expressed as a finite net whose tokens are coloured by causal histories. Colours in our encoding resemble the causal memories that are typical in reversible process calculi.

1 Introduction

Reversible computing is attracting interest for its applications in many fields including hardware design and quantum computing [30], the modelling of biochemical reactions [12,25,26], parallel discrete event simulation [27] and program reversing for debugging [8,11,16].

A model for reversible computation features two computation flows: the standard forward direction and the reverse one, which allows to reach back any past state of the computation. Reversibility is well understood in a sequential setting in which executions are totally ordered sets of events (see [17]): a sequential computation can be reversed by successively undoing the last not yet undone event. Reversibility becomes more challenging in a concurrent setting because there is no natural way for totally ordering events. Often concurrency models account for the causal dependencies among events, which are reflected as a partial order. Reversing an execution consisting of a partially ordered set of events reduces to successively undoing one of the maximal events not yet undone. This is at the basis of the *causally-consistent reversibility* [6,15,23], which relates reversibility

© IFIP International Federation for Information Processing 2019
Published by Springer Nature Switzerland AG 2019
H. Riis Nielson and E. Tuosto (Eds.): COORDINATION 2019, LNCS 11533, pp. 19–36, 2019.
https://doi.org/10.1007/978-3-030-22397-7_2

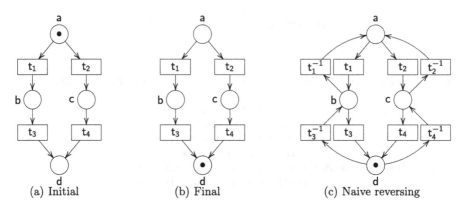

(a) Initial   (b) Final   (c) Naive reversing

Fig. 1. Backward conflict and naive reversing.

with causality. Intuitively, this notion stipulates that any event can be undone provided that all its consequences, if any, are undone beforehand. Reversibility in distributed systems such as in checkpoint/rollback protocols [29] and in transactions [7,13] can be modelled by causal-consistent reversibility. The interplay between reversibility and concurrency has been widely studied in process calculi [4,6,14,19,23], event structures [5,9,24,28] and lately Petri Nets [1,21]. Despite being a very basic model of concurrency, Petri nets still lack a satisfactory causally-consistent reversible semantics. For instance, no current models are able to handle cyclic nets.

A key point when reversing computation in Petri nets is to handle backward conflicts, i.e., the fact that a token can be generated in a place because of different causes. Consider the net in Fig. 1(a) showing the initial state of a system that can either perform t_1 followed by t_3, or t_2 followed by t_4. The final state of a complete computation is depicted in Fig. 1(b). The information in that state is not enough to deduce whether the token in d has been produced because of t_3 or t_4. Even worse, if we "naively" reverse the net by just adding transitions in the reverse direction, as shown in Fig. 1(c), the reverse transition will do more than undoing the computation. In fact, the token in d can be put back either in b or c regardless of the previous computation.

Analogous problems arise when a net is cyclic. Previous approaches [1,21] to reversing Petri nets tackle backward conflicts by relying on a new kind of tokens, called *bonds* that keep track of the execution history. Bonds are rich enough for allowing other approaches to reversibility, such as *out-of-order* reversibility [12], but they cannot cope with cyclic nets. We propose here a reversible model for P/T nets that can handle cyclic nets by relying on standard notions in Petri net theory. We first observe that a Petri Net can be mapped via the standard unfolding construction to an occurrence net, i.e., an acyclic net that does not have backward conflicts and makes causal dependencies explicit. Then, an occurrence net can be "simply" reversed by reversing each of its transitions. Such construction gives a model that features causally-consistent reversibility.

This is shown by proving that each reachable marking in the reversible version of the occurrence net is a marking that can be reached by just forward computational steps. We observe that the unfolding construction could produce an infinite occurrence net. However, the unfolding can be seen as the definition of a coloured net, where colours account for causal histories. Such interpretation associates a P/T net with an equivalent coloured P/T net, which can be reversed in the "simple" way. The correctness of the construction is shown by exhibiting a one-to-one correspondence of its executions with the ones of the reversible version of the unfolding. Interestingly, the colours used by the construction resemble the memories common in reversible calculi [6,14].

We remark that our proposal deals with reversing (undoing) computation in a Petri net and not with the classical problem of reversibility [3] which requires every computation to be able to reach back the initial state of the system (but not necessary by undoing the previous events). In this sense, the problem of making a net reversible equates to adding a minimal amount of transitions that make a net reversible [2]. Reversibility is a global property while reversing a computation is a local one, as discussed in [2].

2   Background

2.1   Petri Nets

Petri nets are built up from *places* (denoting, e.g., resources and message types), which are repositories for *tokens* (representing instances of resources), and *transitions*, which fetch and produce tokens. We consider the infinite sets $\mathcal{P}$ of places and $\mathcal{T}$ of transitions, and assume that they are disjoint, i.e., $\mathcal{P} \cap \mathcal{T} = \emptyset$. We let $a, a', \ldots$ range over $\mathcal{P}$ and $t, t', \ldots$ over $\mathcal{T}$. We write $x, y, \ldots$ for elements in $\mathcal{P} \cup \mathcal{T}$.

A *multiset* over a set S is a function $m : S \to \mathbb{N}$ (where $\mathbb{N}$ denotes the natural numbers including zero). We write $\mathbb{N}^S$ for the set of multisets over S. For $m \in \mathbb{N}^S$, $supp(m) = \{x \in S \mid m(x) > 0\}$ is the *support* of m, and $|m| = \sum_{x \in S} m(x)$ stands for its *cardinality*. We write $\emptyset$ for the empty multiset, i.e., $supp(\emptyset) = \emptyset$. The union of $m_1, m_2 \in \mathbb{N}^S$, written $(m_1 \oplus m_2)$, is defined such that $(m_1 \oplus m_2)(x) = m_1(x) + m_2(x)$ for all $x \in S$. Note that $\oplus$ is associative and commutative, and has $\emptyset$ as identity. Hence, $\mathbb{N}^S$ is the free commutative monoid $S^\oplus$ over S. We write x for a singleton multiset, i.e., $supp(x) = \{x\}$ and $m(x) = 1$. Moreover, we write $x_1 \ldots x_n$ for $x_1 \oplus \ldots \oplus x_n$. Let $f : S \to S'$, we write f also for its obvious extension to multisets, i.e., $f(x_0 \ldots x_n) = f(x_0) \ldots f(x_n)$. We avoid writing $supp(\_)$ when applying set operators to multisets, e.g., we write $x \in m$ or $m_1 \cap m_2$ instead of $x \in supp(m)$ or $supp(m_1) \cap supp(m_2)$.

Definition 1 (Petri Net). *A net N is a 4-tuple $N = (S_N, T_N, {}^\bullet\_{\_N}, \_{}^\bullet_N)$ where $S_N \subseteq \mathcal{P}$ is the (nonempty) set of places, $T_N \subseteq \mathcal{T}$ is the set of transitions and the functions ${}^\bullet\_{\_N}, \_{}^\bullet_N : T_N \to 2^{S_N}$ assign source and target to each transition such that ${}^\bullet t \neq \emptyset$ and $t^\bullet \neq \emptyset$ for all $t \in T_N$. A marking of a net N is a multiset over S_N, i.e., $m \in \mathbb{N}^S$. A Petri net is a pair (N, m) where N is a net and m is a marking of N.*

We denote $S_N \cup T_N$ by N, and omit the subscript N if no confusion arises. We abbreviate a transition $t \in T$ with $preset\ {}^\bullet t = s_1$ and $postset\ t^\bullet = s_2$ as $s_1 [\rangle s_2$. Hereafter, we only consider nets whose transitions have non-empty presets. The pre and postset of a place $a \in S$ are defined respectively as ${}^\bullet a = \{t \mid a \in t^\bullet\}$ and $a^\bullet = \{t \mid a \in {}^\bullet t\}$. We let ${}^\circ N = \{x \in N \mid {}^\bullet x = \emptyset\}$ and $N^\circ = \{x \in N \mid x^\bullet = \emptyset\}$ denote the sets of *initial* and *final elements* of N respectively. Note that we only consider nets whose initial and final elements are places since transitions have non-empty pre and postsets, i.e., ${}^\bullet t \neq \emptyset$ and $t^\bullet \neq \emptyset$ holds for all t.

Definition 2 (Net morphisms). *Let N, N' be nets. A pair $f = (f_S : S_N \to S_{N'}, f_T : T_N \to T_{N'})$ is a net morphism from N to N' (written $f : N \to N'$) if $f_S({}^\bullet t_N) = {}^\bullet(f_T(t))_{N'}$ and $f_S(t_N^\bullet) = (f_T(t))_{N'}^\bullet$, for any t. Moreover, we say N and N' are* isomorphic *if f is bijective.*

The operational (interleaving) semantics of a Petri net is given by the least relation on Petri nets satisfying the following inference rule:

$$\textsc{(firing)}\quad \frac{t = m \mid\rangle m' \in T_N}{(N, m \oplus m'') \xrightarrow{t} (N, m' \oplus m'')}$$

which describes the evolution of the state of a net (represented by the marking $m \oplus m''$) by the firing of a transition $m [\rangle m'$ that consumes the tokens m in its preset and produces the tokens m' in its postset. We sometimes omit t in $\xrightarrow{t}$ when the fired transition is uninteresting.

According to Definition 1, transitions consume and produce at most one token in each place. On the other hand, P/T nets below fetch and consume multiple tokens by defining the pre- and postsets of transitions as multisets.

Definition 3 (P/T net). *A Place/Transition Petri net (P/T net) is a 4-tuple $N = (S_N, T_N, {}^\bullet\_{\_N}, \_{\_N}^\bullet)$ where $S_N \subseteq \mathcal{P}$ is the (nonempty) set of places, $T_N \subseteq \mathcal{T}$ is the set of transitions and the functions ${}^\bullet\_{\_N}, \_{\_N}^\bullet : T_N \to \mathbb{N}^{S_N}$ assign source and target to each transition. A marking of a net N is multiset over S_N, i.e., $m \in \mathbb{N}^S$. A marked P/T net is a pair (N, m) where N is a P/T net and m is a marking of N.*

The notions of pre- and postset, initial and final elements, morphisms and operational semantics are straightforwardly extended to P/T nets. Note that Petri nets can be regarded as a P/T net whose arcs have unary weights.

Next, we introduce some notation for sequences of transitions. Let ';' denote concatenation of such sequences. For the sequence $s = t_1; t_2; \ldots; t_n$, we write $(N, m_0) \xrightarrow{s} (N, m_n)$ if $(N, m_0) \xrightarrow{t_1} (N, m_1) \xrightarrow{t_2} \ldots \xrightarrow{t_n} (N, m_n)$; we call s a firing sequence. We write $(N, m_0) \to^* (N, m_n)$ if there exists s such that $(N, m_0) \xrightarrow{s} (N, m_n)$, and ϵ_m for the empty sequence.

Definition 4. *Let (N, m) be a P/T net. The set of* reachable *markings $reach(N, m)$ is defined as $\{m' \mid (N, m) \to^* (N, m')\}$.*

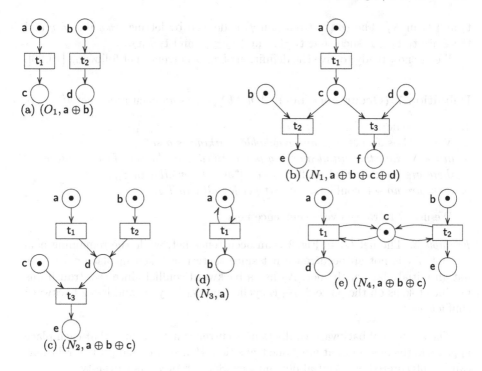

(a) $(O_1, a \oplus b)$

(b) $(N_1, a \oplus b \oplus c \oplus d)$

(c) $(N_2, a \oplus b \oplus c)$

(d) (N_3, a)

(e) $(N_4, a \oplus b \oplus c)$

Fig. 2. P/T nets

We say a marked P/T net (N, m) is *(1-)safe* if every reachable marking is a set, i.e., $m' \in reach(N, m)$ implies $m' \in 2^{S_N}$.

Example 5. Figure 2 shows different P/T nets, which will be used throughout the paper. As usual, places and transitions are represented by circles and boxes, respectively. The nets O_1 and N_4 are Petri nets, and N_1, N_2 and N_3 are P/T nets which, when executing, may produce multiple tokens in some places.

2.2 Unfolding of P/T Nets

Our approach to reversing Petri nets relies on their occurrence net semantics, which explicitly exhibit the causal ordering, concurrency, and conflicts among events. We start by introducing several useful notions and notations. First, we shall describe a flow of causal dependencies in a net with the relation $\prec$:

Definition 6. *Let $\prec$ be $\{(a, t) | a \in S_N \wedge t \in a^{\bullet}\} \cup \{(t, a) | a \in S_N \wedge t \in {}^{\bullet}a\}$. We write $\preceq$ for the reflexive and transitive closure of $\prec$.*

Consider Fig. 2. We have $a \prec t_1$ and $t_1 \prec c$ in O_1 as well as $t_1 \preceq t_2$ in N_1.

Two transitions t_1 and t_2 are in an *immediate conflict*, written $t_1 \#_0 t_2$, when $t_1 \neq t_2$ and ${}^{\bullet}t_1 \cap {}^{\bullet}t_2 \neq \emptyset$. For example, t_1 and t_2 in N_4 in Fig. 2 are in an immediate conflict since they share a token in the place c. Correspondingly, for

t_2 and t_3 in N_1. The *conflict* relation $\#$ is defined by letting $x \# y$ if $x \neq y$ and there are $t_1, t_2 \in T$ such that $t_1 \preceq x$, and $t_2 \preceq y$, and $t_1 \#_0 t_2$.

We are now ready to give the definition of an occurrence net following [10, 20].

Definition 7 (Occurrence net). *A net (N, m) is an occurrence net if*

1. *N is acyclic;*
2. *N is a (1-)safe net, i.e, any reachable marking is a set;*
3. *$m = {}^\circ N$, i.e., the initial marking is identified with the set of initial places;*
4. *there are no backward conflicts, i.e., $|{}^\bullet a| \leq 1$ for all a in S_N;*
5. *there are no self-conflicts, i.e, $\neg(t \# t)$ for all t in T_N.*

We use O to range over occurrence nets.

Example 8. The net O_1 in Fig. 2 is an occurrence net, while the remaining nets are not. N_1 is not an occurrence net since there is a token in place c and c is not an initial place of the net. N_2 has a backward conflict since two transitions produce tokens on the place d. N_3 is cyclic, and N_4 is cyclic and has a backward conflict on c.

The absence of backward conflicts in occurrence nets ensures that each place appears in the postset of at most one transition. Hence, pre- and postset relations can be interpreted as a causal dependency. So, $\preceq$ represents causality.

We say $x, y \in N$ are *concurrent*, written x co y, if $x \neq y$ and $x \not\preceq y$, $y \not\preceq x$, and $\neg x \# y$. A set $X \subseteq N$ is concurrent, written $CO(X)$, if $\forall x, y \in X : x \neq y \Rightarrow x$ co y, and $|\{t \in T_N \mid \exists x \in X, t \preceq x\}|$ is finite. For example, the set $\{t_1, t_2\}$ of firings in O_1 of Fig. 2 is concurrent, so we can write $CO(\{t_1, t_2\})$.

Two transitions are *coinitial* if they start with the same marking, and *cofinal* if they end up in the same marking. We now have a simple version of the Square Lemma [6] for forward concurrent transitions. It will be helpful in proving our Lemma 16 in the next section.

Lemma 9. *Let t and t' be coinitial concurrent transitions. Then, there exist transitions t_1 and t_1' such that $t; t_1'$ and $t'; t_1$ are cofinal.*

The lemma says that if transitions t and t' originate from one corner of a square, and if they represent independent (concurrent) events, then the square completes with two other independent transitions (t_1 and t_1') meeting at the opposite corner of the square. The order in which concurrent transitions are executed in a firing sequence does not matter. Indeed, the order which should be preserved among firings in a sequence is the causal order. We then consider sequences equivalent up to the swapping of concurrent transitions. This corresponds to considering the set of Mazurkiewicz traces induced by co as the independence relation.

Formally, trace equivalence $\equiv$ is the least congruence over firing sequences s such that $\forall t_1, t_2 : t_1$ co $t_2 \implies t_1; t_2 \equiv t_2; t_1$. The equivalence classes of $\equiv$ are the (Mazurkiewicz) *traces*. We use ω to range over such traces. We also will use ϵ for the empty trace, and ; for the concatenation operator.

(INI-MK)
$$\frac{m(\mathsf{a}) = n}{\{\mathsf{a}(\emptyset, i) \mid 1 \le i \le n\} \subseteq S}$$

(PRE)
$$\frac{H = \{\mathsf{a}_j(h_j, i_j) \mid j \in J\} \subseteq S \quad Co(H) \quad \mathsf{t} \in T_N \quad {}^\bullet \mathsf{t}_N = \oplus_{j \in J} \mathsf{a}_j}{\mathsf{t}(H) \in T, \quad {}^\bullet(\mathsf{t}(H)) = H}$$

(POST)
$$\frac{x = \mathsf{t}(H) \in T}{Q = \{\mathsf{a}(\{x\}, i) \mid 1 \le i \le \mathsf{t}_N^\bullet(\mathsf{a})\} \subseteq S, \quad x^\bullet = Q}$$

Fig. 3. Unfolding rules.

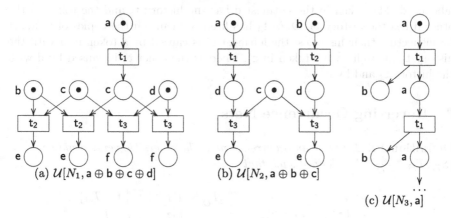

(a) $\mathcal{U}[N_1, \mathsf{a} \oplus \mathsf{b} \oplus \mathsf{c} \oplus \mathsf{d}]$ (b) $\mathcal{U}[N_2, \mathsf{a} \oplus \mathsf{b} \oplus \mathsf{c}]$

(c) $\mathcal{U}[N_3, \mathsf{a}]$

Fig. 4. Unfoldings of P/T nets

For occurrence nets we have this standard property:

$$s_1 \equiv s_2 \ \textit{iff} \ (O, m_0) \xrightarrow{s_1} (O, m_n) \iff (O, m_0) \xrightarrow{s_2} (O, m_n) \tag{1}$$

Two traces are *coinitial* if they start with the same marking, and *cofinal* if they end up in the same marking. Hence, Eq. (1) tells us that two traces that are *coinitial* and *cofinal* are then trace equivalent.

The unfolding of a net N is the least occurrence net that can account for all the possible computations of N and makes explicit causal dependencies, conflicts and concurrency between firings [20].

Definition 10 (Unfolding). *Let (N, m) be a P/T net. The unfolding of N is the occurrence net $\mathcal{U}[N, m] = (S, T, \delta_0, \delta_1)$ generated inductively by the inference rules in Fig. 3 and the folding morphism $(f_S, f_T) : \mathcal{U}[N, m] \to N$ defined such that $f_S(\mathsf{a}, \_, \_) = \mathsf{a}$ and $f_T(\mathsf{t}, \_) = \mathsf{t}$.*

Places are named by triples $\mathsf{a}(H, i)$ where: a is a place of N where tokens reside; H is the set of immediate causes (i.e., the history of tokens); and i is a positive integer used to disambiguate tokens with the same history. Transitions (or events) are encoded as $t(H)$, where H is as above and t is the fired transition.

Example 11. The unfoldings of the nets $(N_1, a \oplus b \oplus c \oplus d)$, $(N_2, a \oplus b \oplus c)$ and (N_3, a) in Fig. 2 are shown in Fig. 4. Note that since O_1 is an occurrence net its unfolding is isomorphic to O_1, thus it is omitted. Consider the occurrence net $\mathcal{U}[N_1, a \oplus b \oplus c \oplus d]$. The leftmost transition t_2 is different from the other transition t_2 since they have different histories: the leftmost t_2 is caused by the tokens in b and c (which are available in the initial marking), whereas the other t_2 is caused only by the token in b and the token that is produced by the firing of t_1. Correspondingly, for the two transitions labelled t_3. Consider $\mathcal{U}[N_2, a \oplus b \oplus c]$. After the transitions t_1 and t_2 have fired, there is a token in each of the places labelled d. The token in the leftmost d has the history t_1 and the token in the other d has the history t_2. Once t_3 has fired, we can tell the copies of t_3 apart by inspecting their histories: the leftmost t_3 is caused by a token in d with the history t_1 (as well as the token in c), whereas the other t_3 is caused by d with the history t_2 and by c.

3   Reversing Occurrence Nets

Definition 12. *Let O be an occurrence net. The reversible version of O is $\overleftarrow{O} = (S_{\overleftarrow{O}}, T_{\overleftarrow{O}}, {}^\bullet{-}_{\overleftarrow{O}}, {-}^\bullet_{\overleftarrow{O}})$ defined such that*

$$S_{\overleftarrow{O}} = S_O \qquad\qquad\qquad T_{\overleftarrow{O}} = T_O \cup \{\overleftarrow{t} \mid t \in T_O\}$$

$$ {}^\bullet t_{\overleftarrow{O}} = \begin{cases} {}^\bullet t_O & \text{if } t \in T_O \\ t^\bullet_O & \text{otherwise} \end{cases} \qquad\qquad t^\bullet_{\overleftarrow{O}} = \begin{cases} t^\bullet_O & \text{if } t \in T_O \\ {}^\bullet t_O & \text{otherwise} \end{cases} $$

Given a transition t we write $\overleftarrow{t}$ for a transition that reverses t. We shall call transitions like $\overleftarrow{t_1}$ and $\overleftarrow{t_2}$ in Fig. 5 *reverse* (or backwards) transitions (or firings), and use t, t_1 and t_2 to denote transitions or reverse transitions.

For $\overleftarrow{O}$, we write $(\overleftarrow{O}, m) \overset{t}{\twoheadrightarrow} (\overleftarrow{O}, m')$ for a forward firing when $t \in T_O$, and $(\overleftarrow{O}, m) \overset{t}{\rightsquigarrow} (\overleftarrow{O}, m')$ for the reverse (or backward) firing when $t \notin T_O$. We also let $\overset{t}{\rightarrow}$ be $\overset{t}{\twoheadrightarrow} \cup \overset{t}{\rightsquigarrow}$. We will often refer to a firing $(\overleftarrow{O}, m) \overset{t}{\rightarrow} (\overleftarrow{O}, m')$ as t. Given a firing t we indicate with $\overleftarrow{t}$ its inverse that is

$$(\overleftarrow{O}, m) \overset{\overleftarrow{t}}{\twoheadrightarrow} (\overleftarrow{O}, m') \quad \text{if} \quad (\overleftarrow{O}, m') \overset{t}{\rightsquigarrow} (\overleftarrow{O}, m)$$

$$(\overleftarrow{O}, m) \overset{\overleftarrow{t}}{\rightsquigarrow} (\overleftarrow{O}, m') \quad \text{if} \quad (\overleftarrow{O}, m') \overset{t}{\twoheadrightarrow} (\overleftarrow{O}, m)$$

Hence, we have $\overleftarrow{\overleftarrow{t}} = t$. We shall work with sequences of transitions and reverse transitions, ranged over by s, s_1 and s_2. We say that a sequence is a *forward* (resp. *backward*) *sequence* when all its firings are forward (resp. backward).

Next, we extend the notions of causality, conflict and concurrency to transitions and reverse transitions in reverse versions of occurrence nets. We extend

$\prec$ in Definition 6 to cover reverse transitions in an obvious way using Definition 12. As a result, we obtain $t \preceq \overleftarrow{t}$ and $\overleftarrow{t} \preceq t$. As for the conflict relation, we define an immediate conflict between different $\overleftarrow{t_1}$ and $\overleftarrow{t_2}$ as ${}^\bullet\overleftarrow{t_1} \cap {}^\bullet\overleftarrow{t_2} \neq \emptyset$. This is $t_1{}^\bullet \cap t_2{}^\bullet \neq \emptyset$, meaning t_1 and t_2 are in backward conflict, which is ruled out in occurrence nets. Hence, the immediate conflict relation is empty between reverse transitions, and so is the conflict relation. The immediate conflict relation between t and $\overleftarrow{t'}$ is defined as ${}^\bullet t \cap {}^\bullet\overleftarrow{t'} \neq \emptyset$. This is equivalent to ${}^\bullet t \cap t'{}^\bullet \neq \emptyset$, which means $t' \preceq t$. Consequently, the conflict relation on transitions in $\overleftarrow{O}$ is given by the conflict relation on the forward transitions, and can be defined using the causality relation for pairs of a transition and reverse transition. This allows us to define concurrent transitions in $\overleftarrow{O}$. We say $t \; co \; t'$ if (a) $t \; co \; t'$ for $t, t' \in T_O$, (b) $t \not\preceq t'$ and $t' \not\preceq t$ if t, t' are reverse transitions, and (c) $t \not\preceq t', t' \not\preceq t$ and $\overleftarrow{t'} \not\preceq t$ if t is a transition and t' is a reverse transition.

Next, we show that $\overleftarrow{O}$ is a conservative extension of O.

Lemma 13. $(O, m) \xrightarrow{t} (O, m')$ iff $(\overleftarrow{O}, m) \xrightarrow{t} (\overleftarrow{O}, m')$.

In general, a reversible occurrence net is not an occurrence net. This is because adding reverse transitions may introduce backward conflict for these transitions. Consider N_1 in Fig. 2. We notice that initially t_1 and t_2 are in conflict. Then, in $\overleftarrow{N}_1$ in Fig. 5, the place c with a token has two reverse transitions in its preset, namely $\overleftarrow{t_2}$ and $\overleftarrow{t_3}$, hence there is a backward conflict.

4 Properties

We now study the properties of the reversible versions of occurrence nets.

An important property of a *fully* reversible system is the Loop Lemma stating that any reduction can be undone. Formally:

Lemma 14 (Loop Lemma). $(\overleftarrow{O}, m) \xrightarrow{t} (\overleftarrow{O}, m')$ iff $(\overleftarrow{O}, m') \xrightarrow{\overleftarrow{t}} (\overleftarrow{O}, m)$.

We can generalise the result of the Loop Lemma to sequences as follows:

Corollary 15. $(\overleftarrow{O}, m) \rightarrow^* (\overleftarrow{O}, m')$ iff $(\overleftarrow{O}, m') \rightarrow^* (\overleftarrow{O}, m)$.

Next, we have a lemma which is instrumental for the proof of causal-consistent reversibility in reversible calculi [6,14]. Note that t and t' can be either forward or reverse transitions.

Lemma 16 (Square Lemma). *Let t and t' be coinitial concurrent transitions. Then, there exist transitions t_1 and t'_1 such that $t; t'_1$ and $t'; t_1$ are cofinal.*

In order to prove causal consistency we first define a notion of equivalence on sequences of transitions and reverse transitions in reversible occurrence nets. By following Lévy's approach [18], we define the notion of *reverse equivalence* on such sequences as the least equivalence relation $\asymp$ which is closed under composition with ; such that the following hold (recall that t, t' are transitions or reverse transitions):

$$t; t' \asymp t'; t \quad \text{if } t \ co \ t' \qquad t; \overleftarrow{t} \asymp \epsilon \qquad \overleftarrow{t}; t \asymp \epsilon$$

Reversible equivalence $\asymp$ allows us to swap the order of t and t' in an execution sequence as long as t, t' are concurrent. Moreover, it allows cancellation of a transition and its inverse. We have that $\equiv \subset \asymp$. The equivalence classes of $\asymp$ are called *traces*; it is clear that they contain the Mazurkiewicz traces. Hence, we shall use ω, ω_1 and ω_2 to range over such traces.

The following lemma says that, up to reverse equivalence, one can always reach for the maximum freedom of choice, going backward, and only then going forwards.

Lemma 17 (Parabolic Lemma). *Let ω be a trace. There exist two forward traces ω_1 and ω_2 such that $\omega \asymp \overleftarrow{\omega_1}; \omega_2$.*

Proof. By lexicographic induction on length of ω and on the distance between the beginning of ω and the earliest pair of opposing firings in ω. The analysis uses both the Loop Lemma (Lemma 14) and the Square Lemma (Lemma 16). $\square$

The following lemma says that, if two traces ω_1 and ω_2 are coinitial and cofinal (e.g. they start from the same marking and end in the same marking) and ω_2 is a forward only trace, then ω_1 has some forward firings and their reverse ones that cancel each other. And this implies that ω_1 is causally equivalent to a forward trace in which all those pairs of fairing are cancelled out.

Lemma 18 (Shortening Lemma). *Let $\omega_1 \asymp \omega_2$ with ω_2 forward. Then, $|\omega_2| \leq |\omega_1|$.*

Proof. The proof is by induction on length of ω_1, using Lemma 16 and Lemma 17. In the proof, the forward trace ω_2 is the main guideline for shortening ω_1 into a forward trace. Indeed, the proof relies crucially on the fact that ω_1 and ω_2 share the same source and target and that ω_2 is a forward trace. $\square$

Theorem 19 (Causal Consistency). *Two traces ω_1 and ω_2 are reversible equivalent iff they are coinitial and cofinal, namely*

$$\omega_1 \asymp \omega_2 \text{ iff } (\overleftarrow{O}, m_0) \xrightarrow{\omega_1} (\overleftarrow{O}, m_n) \iff (\overleftarrow{O}, m_0) \xrightarrow{\omega_2} (\overleftarrow{O}, m_n).$$

Proof. The "if" direction follows by definition of reverse equivalence and trace composition. The "only if" direction exploits the properties the Square, Parabolic and Shortening Lemmas. $\square$

With Theorem 19 we proved that the notion of causal consistency characterises a space for admissible rollbacks which are: (1) consistent (in the sense that they do not lead to previously unreachable configurations) and (2) flexible enough to allow rearranging of undo actions. This implies that starting from an initial marking, all the markings reached by mixed computations are markings that could be reached by performing only forward computations. Hence, we have:

Theorem 20. *Let O be an occurrence net and m_0 an initial marking. Then,*

$$(\overleftarrow{O}, m_0) \to^* (\overleftarrow{O}, m') \iff (\overleftarrow{O}, m_0) \twoheadrightarrow^* (\overleftarrow{O}, m').$$

5 Reversing P/T Nets

This section takes advantage of the classical unfolding construction for P/T nets and the reversible semantics of occurrence nets to add causally-consistent reversibility to P/T nets.

Definition 21. *Let (N, m) be a marked P/T net and $\mathcal{U}[N, m]$ its unfolding. The reversible version of (N, m), written $\overleftarrow{(N, m)}$, is $\overleftarrow{\mathcal{U}[N, m]}$.*

Example 22. The reversible version of the nets in Fig. 2 are shown in Fig. 5. We remark that they are the reversible versions of the nets in Fig. 4, which are the unfoldings of the original nets.

The following result states that a reversible net is a conservative extension of its original version, i.e., reversibility does not change the set of reachable markings. The result is a direct consequence of Lemma 13 and the fact that unfoldings preserve reductions up-to the folding morphism $\mathcal{U}$.

Lemma 23. $(N, m) \to^* (N, m')$ *iff* $\overleftarrow{(N, m)} \twoheadrightarrow^* (\overleftarrow{O}, m'')$ *and* $m' = f_s(m'')$, *where* $(f_s, f_t) : \mathcal{U}[N, m] \to N$, *defined such that* $f_S(\mathsf{a}, \_, \_) = \mathsf{a}$ *and* $f_T(\mathsf{t}, \_) = \mathsf{t}$, *is the folding morphism.*

We remark that the reversible version of a P/T is defined as the reversible version of an occurrence net (i.e., its unfolding). Consequently, all properties shown in the previous section apply to the reversible semantics of P/T nets. In particular, Lemma 23 combined with Theorem 20 ensures that all markings reachable by the reversible semantics are just the reachable markings of the original P/T net.

6 Finite Representation of Reversible P/T Nets

As shown in Fig. 5(c), the reversible version of a finite net may be infinite. In this section we show how to represent reversible nets in a compact, finite way by using coloured Petri nets. We assume infinite sets $\mathcal{X}$ of variables and $\mathcal{C}$ of colours, defined such that $\mathcal{X} \subset \mathcal{C}$. For $c \in \mathcal{C}$, we write $vars(c)$ for the set of variables in c. With abuse of notation we write $vars(m)$ for the set of variables in a multiset $m \in \mathbb{N}^{P \times \mathcal{C}}$. Let $\sigma : \mathcal{X} \to \mathcal{C}$ be a partial function and c a colour (also, $m \in \mathbb{N}^{P \times \mathcal{C}}$), we write $c\sigma$ (resp., $m\sigma$) for the simultaneous substitution of each variable x in c (resp., m) by $\sigma(x)$.

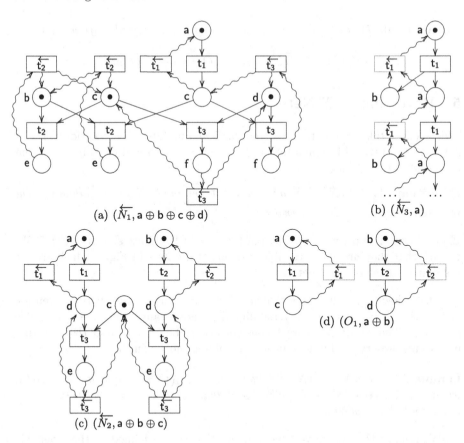

Fig. 5. Reversible P/T and Petri nets

Definition 24 (C-P/T net). *A coloured place/transition net (C-P/T net) is a 4-tuple* $N = (S_N, T_N, {}^\bullet\_N, \_{}^\bullet_N)$ *where* $S_N \subseteq \mathcal{P}$ *is the (nonempty) set of places,* $T_N \subseteq \mathcal{T}$ *is the set of transitions and the functions* ${}^\bullet\_N, \_{}^\bullet_N : T_N \to \mathbb{N}^{S_N \times \mathcal{C}}$ *assign source and target to each transition defined such that* $vars(t^\bullet) \subseteq vars({}^\bullet t)$. *A marking of a C-P/T net* N *is multiset over* $S_N \times \mathcal{C}$ *that does not contain variables, i.e.,* $m \in \mathbb{N}^{S \times \mathcal{C}}$ *and* $vars(m) = \emptyset$. *A marked C-P/T net is a pair* (N, m) *where* N *is a P/T net and* m *is a marking of* N.

C-P/T nets generalise P/T nets by extending markings to multisets of coloured tokens, and transitions to patterns that need to be instantiated with appropriate colours for firing, as formally stated by the firing rule below.

$$(\text{COLOURED-FIRING}) \quad \frac{t = m \,[\rangle\, m' \in T_N}{(N, m\sigma \oplus m'') \xrightarrow{t} (N, m'\sigma \oplus m'')}$$

The firing of a transition $t = m \mathbin{[\rangle} m'$ requires to instantiate m and m' by substituting variables by colours, i.e., the firing of t consumes the instance $m\sigma$ of the preset m and produces the instance $m'\sigma$ of the postset of m'.

We now introduce an encoding that associates each P/T net N with an equivalent C-P/T net $[\![N]\!]$, whose tokens carry their execution history. We rely on the set of colours $\mathcal{C}$ defined as the least set that contains $\mathcal{X}$ and it is closed under the following rules.

$$
\begin{array}{cc}
(\textsc{token}) & (\textsc{elem}) \\[4pt]
\dfrac{h \in 2^{\mathcal{C}} \quad n \in \mathbb{N}}{(h,n) \in \mathcal{C}} & \dfrac{x \in \mathcal{T} \cup \mathcal{P} \quad h \in 2^{\mathcal{C}}}{x(h) \in \mathcal{C}}
\end{array}
$$

Colours resemble the unfolding construction (Fig. 3): the colours for tokens are (h, n), where h denotes its (possible empty) set of causes and n is a natural number used for distinguishing tokens with identical causal history. Causal histories are build from coloured versions of transitions ($\mathsf{t}(h)$) and places ($\mathsf{a}(h)$).

Definition 25 (P/T as C-P/T). *Let $N = (S_N, T_N, {}^{\bullet}\_N, \_^{\bullet}_N)$ be a P/T net. Then, $[\![N]\!]$ is the C-P/T defined such that $[\![N]\!] = (S_N, T_N, {}^{\bullet}\_[\![N]\!], \_^{\bullet}_{[\![N]\!]})$ and*

- ${}^{\bullet}\mathsf{t}_{[\![N]\!]} = \mathsf{a}_1(x_1) \oplus \ldots \oplus \mathsf{a}_n(x_n)$ *where* ${}^{\bullet}\mathsf{t}_N = \mathsf{a}_1 \ldots \mathsf{a}_n$ *and* $\forall 1 \le i \le n.x_i \in \mathcal{X}$.
- $\mathsf{t}^{\bullet}_{[\![N]\!]} = \{\mathsf{a}(\{\mathsf{t}(h)\}, i) \mid \mathsf{a} \in supp(\mathsf{t}^{\bullet}_N) \ \wedge \ 1 \le i \le \mathsf{t}^{\bullet}_N(\mathsf{a}) \ \wedge \ h = {}^{\bullet}\mathsf{t}_{[\![N]\!]}\}$.

A marked net (N, m) is encoded as $[\![(N, m)]\!] = ([\![N]\!], [\![m]\!])$ *where* $[\![m]\!] = \{\mathsf{a}(\emptyset, i) \mid \mathsf{a} \in supp(m) \ \wedge \ 1 \le i \le m(\mathsf{a})\}$.

The encoding does not alter the structure of a net; it only adds colours to its tokens. In fact, an encoded net has the same places and transitions as the original net, and pre- and postsets of each transition have the same support. Added colours do not interfere with firing because the preset of each transition uses different colour variables for different tokens. The colour $\{\mathsf{t}(h)\}$ assigned to each token produced by the firing of t describes the causal history of the token, i.e., it indicates that the token has been produced by t after consuming the tokens in the preset of t, which is denoted by h. The natural number i is used for distinguishing multiple tokens produced by the same firing. Tokens in the initial marking are coloured as $(\emptyset, i)$, i.e., they have empty causal history.

Example 26. The encoding of the nets in Fig. 2 are shown in Fig. 6. We comment on the encoding of N_1. The transition $\mathsf{t}_1 = \mathsf{a}\mathbin{[\rangle}\mathsf{c}$ in N_1 is encoded as $\mathsf{a}(x)\mathbin{[\rangle}\mathsf{c}(\mathsf{t}_1(\mathsf{a}(x)), 1)$, i.e., the firing of t_1 that consumes a token with colour h from place a generates a token in c with colour $(\mathsf{t}_1(\mathsf{a}(h)), 1)$. The transition $\mathsf{t}_2 = \mathsf{b} \oplus \mathsf{c}\mathbin{[\rangle}\mathsf{e}$ has two places in the preset and uses two variables x and y in its encoded form $\mathsf{b}(x) \oplus \mathsf{c}(y)\mathbin{[\rangle}\mathsf{e}(\mathsf{t}_2(\mathsf{b}(x) \oplus \mathsf{c}(y)), 1)$. Note that the colour of the token produced in c carries the information of the tokens consumed from both places b and c. The encoding for t_3 is defined analogously.

We illustrate a sequence of firings of $[\![(N_1, \mathsf{a} \oplus \mathsf{b} \oplus \mathsf{c} \oplus \mathsf{d})]\!]$.

$$([\![N_1]\!], \mathsf{a}(\emptyset, 1) \oplus \mathsf{b}(\emptyset, 1) \oplus \mathsf{c}(\emptyset, 1) \oplus \mathsf{d}(\emptyset, 1))$$
$$\xrightarrow{t_1} ([\![N_1]\!], \mathsf{b}(\emptyset, 1) \oplus \mathsf{c}(t_1(\mathsf{a}(\emptyset, 1)), 1) \oplus \mathsf{c}(\emptyset, 1) \oplus \mathsf{d}(\emptyset, 1))$$
$$\xrightarrow{t_2} ([\![N_1]\!], \mathsf{e}(t_2(\mathsf{b}(\emptyset, 1) \oplus \mathsf{c}(t_1(\mathsf{a}(\emptyset, 1)), 1)), 1) \oplus \mathsf{c}(\emptyset, 1) \oplus \mathsf{d}(\emptyset, 1))$$

The firing of t_1 consumes the token $(\emptyset, 1)$ from a and produces the token $(t_1(\mathsf{a}(\emptyset, 1)), 1)$ in place c. The causal history of the token $t_1(\mathsf{a}(\emptyset, 1)$ indicates that the token has been produced by the firing of t_1 that consumed the token $(\emptyset, 1)$ from a. The second reduction takes place because of the firing of t_2. By inspecting the causal history of the token produced in the place e we can conclude that t_2 has consumed the token previously generated by t_1.

The following result shows that there is a tight correspondence between the semantics of the coloured version of a P/T net and its unfolding.

Lemma 27. *Let (N, m) be a marked* P/T *net and* $\mathcal{U}[N, m] = (O, m')$ *its unfolding. Then,* $[\![N, m]\!] \xrightarrow{s} ([\![N]\!], m'')$ *iff* $(O, m') \xrightarrow{s} (O, m'')$.

Proof. The *if* part follows by induction on the length of the reduction. The base case follows by taking $m'' = m'$ and noting that $[\![N, m]\!] = ([\![N]\!], m')$. The inductive step $s = s'; t$ follows by applying inductive hypothesis on s' to conclude that $[\![N, m]\!] \xrightarrow{s'} ([\![N]\!], m''')$ iff $(O, m) \xrightarrow{s'} (O, m''')$. *If)* $([\![N]\!], m''') \xrightarrow{t} ([\![N]\!], m'')$ implies $m''' = {}^\bullet t_{[\![N]\!]} \oplus m''''$ and $m'' = t^\bullet_{[\![N]\!]} \oplus m''''$. Since $(O, m) \xrightarrow{s'} (O, m''')$, $CO({}^\bullet t)$. Then, by the unfolding construction we conclude $(O, m''') \xrightarrow{t} (O, m'')$. The *only if* follows analogously.

The reversible version of $[\![N]\!]$ is defined as for occurrence nets, by adding transitions that are the swapped versions of the ones in N.

Definition 28 (Reversible P/T net). *Let N be a* P/T *net. The reversible version of N is $\overleftarrow{[\![N]\!]}$. The reversible version of a marked* P/T *net (N, m) is the marked* C-P/T *net $(\overleftarrow{[\![N]\!]}, [\![m]\!])$.*

Example 29. The net $\overleftarrow{[\![N_2]\!]}$, the reversible version of $[\![N_2]\!]$ from Fig. 6, is shown in Fig. 7. We now illustrate the execution of $\overleftarrow{[\![N_2]\!]}$.

$$(\overleftarrow{[\![N_2]\!]}, \mathsf{a}(\emptyset, 1) \oplus \mathsf{b}(\emptyset, 1) \oplus \mathsf{c}(\emptyset, 1) \oplus \mathsf{d}(\emptyset, 1))$$
$$\xrightarrow{t_1}(\overleftarrow{[\![N_2]\!]}, \mathsf{b}(\emptyset, 1) \oplus \mathsf{b}(t_1(\mathsf{a}(\emptyset, 1)), 1) \oplus \mathsf{c}(\emptyset, 1) \oplus \mathsf{d}(\emptyset, 1))$$
$$\xrightarrow{t_2}(\overleftarrow{[\![N_2]\!]}, \mathsf{b}(t_1(\mathsf{a}(\emptyset, 1)), 1) \oplus \mathsf{c}(\emptyset, 1) \oplus \mathsf{e}(\mathsf{b}(\emptyset, 1)\mathsf{c}(\emptyset, 1), 1), \mathsf{d}(\emptyset, 1))$$
$$\xrightarrow{\overleftarrow{t_1}}(\overleftarrow{[\![N_2]\!]}, \mathsf{a}(\emptyset, 1) \oplus \mathsf{e}(\mathsf{b}(\emptyset, 1)\mathsf{c}(\emptyset, 1), 1) \oplus \mathsf{d}(\emptyset, 1))$$
$$\xrightarrow{\overleftarrow{t_2}}(\overleftarrow{[\![N_2]\!]}, \mathsf{a}(\emptyset, 1) \oplus \mathsf{b}(\emptyset, 1) \oplus \mathsf{c}(\emptyset, 1) \oplus \mathsf{d}(\emptyset, 1))$$

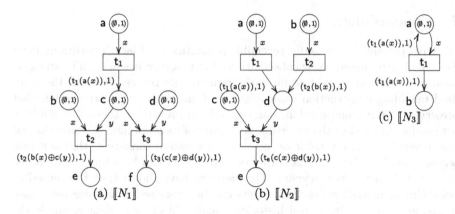

Fig. 6. P/T nets as C-P/T nets

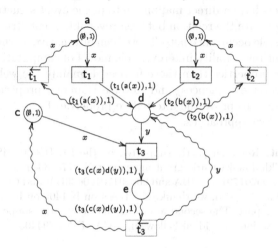

Fig. 7. Reversible coloured net $[\![\overleftarrow{N_2}]\!]$.

In the example above, the firing t_2 can choose to consume either the token $b(\emptyset, 1)$ or the token $b(t_1(a(\emptyset, 1)), 1)$. Since the first one is chosen, then after t_2 it is still possible to undo t_1. If t_2 chose the second token, then in order to undo t_1 we would first undo t_2, since firing $\overleftarrow{t_1}$ is not enabled by the token $a(\emptyset, 1)$.

The following result states that the reductions of the reversible C-P/T of a net are in one-to-one correspondence with the reductions of its reversible unfolding.

Theorem 30 (Correctness). *Let (N, m) be a marked P/T net and $\mathcal{U}[N, m] = (O, m')$ its unfolding. Then, $[\![\overleftarrow{N}, [\![m]\!]]\!] \xrightarrow{s} ([\![N]\!], m'')$ iff $(\overleftarrow{O}, m') \xrightarrow{s} (\overleftarrow{O}, m'')$.*

7   Conclusions

We have presented a causally reversible semantics for Place/Transitions Petri Nets (P/T nets) based on two observations. First, occurrence net can be straight-forwardly reversed by adding for each transition its reverse. Second, the standard unfolding construction associates a P/T net with an occurrence net that preserves all of its computation. Consequently, the reversible semantics of a P/T net can be obtained as the reversible semantics of its unfolding. We have showed that reversibility in reversible occurrence net is causal-consistent, that is it preserves causality. The unfolding of an occurrence net can be infinite (e.g., it the original P/T net is not acyclic). Therefore we have shown that the reversible behaviour of reversible occurrence nets can be expressed as a finite net whose tokens are coloured by causal histories. Colours in our encoding resemble the causal memories that are typical in reversible process calculi [6,14].

Occurrence nets have a direct mapping into prime event structures. We shall investigate in the future the relation between reversible event structures [5,9,24, 28] and our reversible occurrence nets. There is an alternative method for proving causally-consistent reversibility in a reversible model of computation. It is based on showing other properties than those in Sect. 4, mainly the well-foundedness (lack of infinite reverse sequences) and Reverse Diamond properties [22,23]. It would be worthwhile to prove the alternative properties for our reversible nets, and compare the two approaches.

Acknowledgment. Research partly supported by the EU H2020 RISE programme under the Marie Skłodowska Curie grant agreement No 778233. Partly supported by UBACyT projects 20020170100544BA and 20020170100086BA, and CONICET project PIP 11220130100148CO. Also, we thank COST Action IC1405 on Reversible Computation for partial support. The second author acknowledges the support of the Marie Skłodowska Curie Action Individual Fellowship RCADE No 794405.

References

1. Barylska, K., Gogolińska, A., Mikulski, Ł., Philippou, A., Piątkowski, M., Psara, K.: Reversing computations modelled by coloured Petri nets. In: van der Aalst, W.M.P., Bergenthum, R., Carmona, J. (eds.) ATED, vol. 2115, pp. 91–111. CEUR-WS.org (2018)
2. Barylska, K., Koutny, M., Mikulski, Ł., Piątkowski, M.: Reversible computation vs. reversibility in Petri nets. Sci. Comput. Program. **151**, 48–60 (2018). https://doi.org/10.1016/j.scico.2017.10.008
3. Cardoza, E., Lipton, R., Meyer, A.R.: Exponential space complete problems for Petri nets and commutative semigroups (preliminary report). In: Proceedings of STOC, pp. 50–54. ACM (1976). https://doi.org/10.1145/800113.803630
4. Cristescu, I., Krivine, J., Varacca, D.: A compositional semantics for the reversible π-calculus. In: Symposium on Logic in Computer Science, LICS, pp. 388–397. IEEE Computer Society (2013)
5. Cristescu, I.D., Krivine, J., Varacca, D.: Rigid families for CCS and the π-calculus. In: Leucker, M., Rueda, C., Valencia, F.D. (eds.) ICTAC 2015. LNCS, vol. 9399, pp. 223–240. Springer, Cham (2015). https://doi.org/10.1007/978-3-319-25150-9_14

6. Danos, V., Krivine, J.: Reversible communicating systems. In: Gardner, P., Yoshida, N. (eds.) CONCUR 2004. LNCS, vol. 3170, pp. 292–307. Springer, Heidelberg (2004). https://doi.org/10.1007/978-3-540-28644-8_19

7. Danos, V., Krivine, J.: Transactions in RCCS. In: Abadi, M., de Alfaro, L. (eds.) CONCUR 2005. LNCS, vol. 3653, pp. 398–412. Springer, Heidelberg (2005). https://doi.org/10.1007/11539452_31

8. Giachino, E., Lanese, I., Mezzina, C.A.: Causal-consistent reversible debugging. In: Gnesi, S., Rensink, A. (eds.) FASE 2014. LNCS, vol. 8411, pp. 370–384. Springer, Heidelberg (2014). https://doi.org/10.1007/978-3-642-54804-8_26

9. Graversen, E., Phillips, I., Yoshida, N.: Event structure semantics of (controlled) reversible CCS. In: Kari, J., Ulidowski, I. (eds.) RC 2018. LNCS, vol. 11106, pp. 102–122. Springer, Cham (2018). https://doi.org/10.1007/978-3-319-99498-7_7

10. Hayman, J., Winskel, G.: The unfolding of general Petri nets. In: Hariharan, R., Mukund, M., Vinay, V. (eds.) FSTTCS. LIPIcs, vol. 2, pp. 223–234 (2008). https://doi.org/10.4230/LIPIcs.FSTTCS.2008.1755

11. Hoey, J., Ulidowski, I., Yuen, S.: Reversing imperative parallel programs with blocks and procedures. In: Proceedings of EXPRESS/SOS (2018)

12. Kuhn, S., Ulidowski, I.: A calculus for local reversibility. In: Devitt, S., Lanese, I. (eds.) RC 2016. LNCS, vol. 9720, pp. 20–35. Springer, Cham (2016). https://doi.org/10.1007/978-3-319-40578-0_2

13. Lanese, I., Lienhardt, M., Mezzina, C.A., Schmitt, A., Stefani, J.-B.: Concurrent flexible reversibility. In: Felleisen, M., Gardner, P. (eds.) ESOP 2013. LNCS, vol. 7792, pp. 370–390. Springer, Heidelberg (2013). https://doi.org/10.1007/978-3-642-37036-6_21

14. Lanese, I., Mezzina, C.A., Stefani, J.: Reversibility in the higher-order π-calculus. Theor. Comput. Sci. **625**, 25–84 (2016). https://doi.org/10.1016/j.tcs.2016.02.019

15. Lanese, I., Mezzina, C.A., Tiezzi, F.: Causal-consistent reversibility. Bull. EATCS **114** (2014)

16. Lanese, I., Nishida, N., Palacios, A., Vidal, G.: CauDEr: a causal-consistent reversible debugger for Erlang. In: Gallagher, J.P., Sulzmann, M. (eds.) FLOPS 2018. LNCS, vol. 10818, pp. 247–263. Springer, Cham (2018). https://doi.org/10.1007/978-3-319-90686-7_16

17. Leeman Jr., G.B.: A formal approach to undo operations in programming languages. ACM Trans. Program. Lang. Syst. **8**(1), 50–87 (1986). https://doi.org/10.1145/5001.5005

18. Lévy, J.: An algebraic interpretation of the λβK-calculus; and an application of a labelled λ-calculus. Theor. Comput. Sci. **2**(1), 97–114 (1976). https://doi.org/10.1016/0304-3975(76)90009-8

19. Medic, D., Mezzina, C.A., Phillips, I., Yoshida, N.: A parametric framework for reversible π-calculi. In: Pérez, J.A., Tini, S. (eds.) Proceedings of EXPRESS/SOS. EPTCS, vol. 276, pp. 87–103 (2018)

20. Nielsen, M., Plotkin, G.D., Winskel, G.: Petri nets, event structures and domains, part I. Theor. Comput. Sci. **13**, 85–108 (1981). https://doi.org/10.1016/0304-3975(81)90112-2

21. Philippou, A., Psara, K.: Reversible computation in Petri nets. In: Kari, J., Ulidowski, I. (eds.) RC 2018. LNCS, vol. 11106, pp. 84–101. Springer, Cham (2018). https://doi.org/10.1007/978-3-319-99498-7_6

22. Phillips, I., Ulidowski, I.: Reversibility and models for concurrency. In: Proceedings of SOS 2007. ENTCS, vol. 192, pp. 93–108 (2007)

23. Phillips, I., Ulidowski, I.: Reversing algebraic process calculi. J. Log. Algebr. Program. **73**(1–2), 70–96 (2007). https://doi.org/10.1016/j.jlap.2006.11.002

24. Phillips, I., Ulidowski, I.: Reversibility and asymmetric conflict in event structures. J. Log. Algebr. Meth. Program. **84**(6), 781–805 (2015). https://doi.org/10.1016/j.jlamp.2015.07.004

25. Phillips, I., Ulidowski, I., Yuen, S.: A reversible process calculus and the modelling of the ERK signalling pathway. In: Glück, R., Yokoyama, T. (eds.) RC 2012. LNCS, vol. 7581, pp. 218–232. Springer, Heidelberg (2013). https://doi.org/10.1007/978-3-642-36315-3_18

26. Pinna, G.M.: Reversing steps in membrane systems computations. In: Gheorghe, M., Rozenberg, G., Salomaa, A., Zandron, C. (eds.) CMC 2017. LNCS, vol. 10725, pp. 245–261. Springer, Cham (2018). https://doi.org/10.1007/978-3-319-73359-3_16

27. Schordan, M., Oppelstrup, T., Jefferson Jr., D., Barnes, P.D.: Generation of reversible C++ code for optimistic parallel discrete event simulation. New Gener. Comput. **36**(3), 257–280 (2018). https://doi.org/10.1007/s00354-018-0038-2

28. Ulidowski, I., Phillips, I., Yuen, S.: Reversing event structures. New Gener. Comput. **36**(3), 281–306 (2018). https://doi.org/10.1007/s00354-018-0040-8

29. Vassor, M., Stefani, J.-B.: Checkpoint/rollback vs causally-consistent reversibility. In: Kari, J., Ulidowski, I. (eds.) RC 2018. LNCS, vol. 11106, pp. 286–303. Springer, Cham (2018). https://doi.org/10.1007/978-3-319-99498-7_20

30. Vos, A.D., Baerdemacker, S.D., Rentergem, Y.V.: Synthesis of Quantum Circuits vs. Synthesis of Classical Reversible Circuits. Synthesis Lectures on Digital Circuits and Systems, Morgan & Claypool Publishers (2018). https://doi.org/10.2200/S00856ED1V01Y201805DCS054

Towards Races in Linear Logic

Wen Kokke[1]([⊠]), J. Garrett Morris[2], and Philip Wadler[1]

[1] University of Edinburgh, Edinburgh, UK
`wen.kokke@ed.ac.uk`, `wadler@inf.ed.ac.uk`
[2] University of Kansas, Lawrence, KS, USA
`garrett@ittc.ku.edu`

Abstract. Process calculi based in logic, such as πDILL and CP, provide a foundation for deadlock-free concurrent programming, but exclude non-determinism and races. HCP is a reformulation of CP which addresses a fundamental shortcoming: the fundamental operator for parallel composition from the π-calculus does not correspond to any rule of linear logic, and therefore not to any term construct in CP.

We introduce $\text{HCP}_{\text{ND}}^{-}$, which extends HCP with a novel account of non-determinism. Our approach draws on bounded linear logic to provide a strongly-typed account of standard process calculus expressions of non-determinism. We show that our extension is expressive enough to capture many uses of non-determinism in untyped calculi, such as non-deterministic choice, while preserving HCP's meta-theoretic properties, including deadlock freedom.

Keywords: π-calculus · Linear logic · Session types · Non-determinism · Deadlock freedom

1 Introduction

Consider the following scenario:

> Ami and Boé are working from home one morning when they each get a craving for a slice of cake. Being denizens of the web, they quickly find the nearest store which does home deliveries. Unfortunately for them, they both order their cake at the *same* store, which has only one slice left. After that, all it can deliver is disappointment.

This is an example of a *race condition*. We can model this scenario in the π-calculus, where 😀, 🙂 and 🏪 are processes modelling Ami, Boé and the store, and 🍰 and 🙌 are channels giving access to a slice of cake and disappointment, respectively. This process has two possible outcomes: either Ami gets the cake, and Boé gets disappointment, or vice versa.

$$(x[\text{🍰}].x[\text{🙌}].\text{🏪} \mid x(y).\text{😀} \mid x(z).\text{🙂})$$

$$\Downarrow^{*}$$

$$(\text{🏪} \mid \text{😀}\{\text{🍰}/y\} \mid \text{🙂}\{\text{🙌}/z\}) \quad \text{or} \quad (\text{🏪} \mid \text{😀}\{\text{🙌}/y\} \mid \text{🙂}\{\text{🍰}/z\})$$

H. Riis Nielson and E. Tuosto (Eds.): COORDINATION 2019, LNCS 11533, pp. 37–53, 2019.
https://doi.org/10.1007/978-3-030-22397-7_3

While Ami or Boé may not like all of the outcomes, it is the store which is responsible for implementing the online delivery service, and the store is happy with either outcome. Thus, the above is an interaction we would like to be able to model.

Now consider another scenario, which takes place *after* Ami has already bought the cake:

> Boé is *really* disappointed when she finds out the cake has sold out. Ami, always looking to make some money, offers to sell the slice to her for a profit. Boé agrees to engage in a little bit of back-alley cake resale, but sadly there is no trust between the two. Ami demands payment first. Boé would rather get her slice of cake before she gives Ami the money.

This is an example of a *deadlock*. We can also model this scenario in the π-calculus, where ▦ is a channel giving access to some adequate amount of money.

$$(x(z).y[\text{▱}].\text{●} \mid y(w).x[\text{▦}].\text{◉}) \quad \not\Rightarrow {}^{*}$$

The above process does not reduce. As both Ami and Boé would prefer the exchange to be made, this interaction is desired by *neither*. Thus, the above is an interaction we would like to exclude.

Session types [10] statically guarantee that concurrent programs, such as those above, respect communication protocols. Session-typed calculi with logical foundations, such as πDILL [8] and CP [16], obtain deadlock freedom as a result of a close correspondence with logic. These systems, however, also rule out non-determinism and race conditions. In this paper, we demonstrate that logic-inspired type systems need not rule out races.

We present $\text{HCP}^{-}_{\text{ND}}$, an extension of CP with a novel account of non-determinism and races. Inspired by bounded linear logic [9], we introduce a form of shared channels in which the type of a shared channel tracks how many times it is reused. As in the untyped π-calculus, sharing introduces the potential for non-determinism. We show that our approach is sufficient to capture practical examples of races, such as an online store, as well as other formal characterizations of non-determinism, such as non-deterministic choice. However, $\text{HCP}^{-}_{\text{ND}}$ does not lose the meta-theoretical benefits of CP: we show that it enjoys termination and deadlock-freedom.

An important limitation of our work is that types in $\text{HCP}^{-}_{\text{ND}}$ explicitly count the potential races on a channel. It works fine when there are two or three races, but not n for an arbitrary n. The latter case is obviously important, and we see the main value of our work as a stepping stone to this more general case.

$\text{HCP}^{-}_{\text{ND}}$ is based on HCP [11,12]. HCP is a reformulation of CP which addresses a fundamental shortcoming: the fundamental operator for parallel composition from the π-calculus does not correspond to any rule of linear logic, and therefore not to any term construct in CP.

There are two versions of HCP: a version with delayed actions, introduced by Kokke, Montesi, and Peressotti [12]; and a version without delayed actions, introduced by Kokke, Montesi, and Peressotti [11], referred to as HCP^{-}. In this work, we will base ourselves on the latter, as the former does not yet have reduction semantics.

This paper proceeds as follows. In Sect. 2, we discuss recent approaches to non-determinism in logic-inspired session-typed process calculi. In Sect. 3, we introduce a variant of CP and prove progress and preservation. In Sect. 4, we introduce $\mathrm{HCP}_{\mathrm{ND}}^{-}$. In Sect. 5, we discuss cuts with leftovers. Finally, in Sect. 7, we conclude with a discussion of the work done in this paper and potential avenues for future work.

2   Non-determinism, Logic, and Session Types

Recent work extended πDILL and CP with operators for non-deterministic behaviour [1,6,7]. These extensions all implement an operator known as non-deterministic local choice. (This operator is written as $P + Q$, but should not be confused with input-guarded choice from the π-calculus [14].) Non-deterministic local choice can be summarised by the following typing and reduction rules:

$$\frac{P \vdash \Gamma \qquad Q \vdash \Gamma}{P + Q \vdash \Gamma} \qquad\qquad \begin{array}{l} P + Q \Longrightarrow P \\ P + Q \Longrightarrow Q \end{array}$$

Local choice introduces non-determinism explicitly, by listing all possible choices. This is unlike the π-calculus, where non-determinism arises due to multiple processes communicating on shared channels. We can easily implement local choice in the π-calculus, using a nullary communication:

$$(x[].0 \mid x().P \mid x().Q)$$

$$\Downarrow_*$$

$$(P \mid x().Q) \quad \text{or} \quad (x().P \mid Q)$$

In this implementation, the process $x[].0$ will "unlock" either P or Q, leaving the other process deadlocked. Or we could use input-guarded choice:

$$(x[].0 \mid (x().P + x().Q))$$

However, there are many non-deterministic processes in the π-calculus that are awkward to encode using non-deterministic local choice. Let us recall our example:

$$(x[\text{🔑}].x[\text{👣}].\text{📠} \mid x(y).\text{😮} \mid x(z).\text{🐱})$$

$$\Downarrow_*$$

$$(\text{📠} \mid \text{😮}\{\text{🔑}/y\} \mid \text{🐱}\{\text{👣}/z\}) \quad \text{or} \quad (\text{📠} \mid \text{😮}\{\text{👣}/y\} \mid \text{🐱}\{\text{🔑}/z\})$$

This non-deterministic interaction involves communication. If we wanted to write down a process which exhibited the same behaviour using non-deterministic local choice, we would have to write the following process:

$$(x[\text{🍰}].y[\text{💢}].\text{🏪} \mid x(z).\text{😮} \mid y(w).\text{🙍}) + (y[\text{🍰}].x[\text{💢}].\text{🏪} \mid x(z).\text{😮} \mid y(w).\text{🙍})$$

$$\Downarrow_*$$

$$(\text{🏪} \mid \text{😮}\{\text{🍰}/y\} \mid \text{🙍}\{\text{💢}/z\}) \quad \text{or} \quad (\text{🏪} \mid \text{😮}\{\text{💢}/y\} \mid \text{🙍}\{\text{🍰}/z\})$$

In essence, instead of modelling a non-deterministic interaction, we are enumerating the resulting deterministic interactions. This means non-deterministic local choice cannot model non-determinism in the way the π-calculus does. Enumerating all possible outcomes becomes worse the more processes are involved in an interaction. Imagine the following scenario:

> Three customers, Ami, Boé, and Cat, have a craving for cake. Should cake be sold out, however, well... a doughnut will do. They prepare to order their goods via an online store. Unfortunately, they all decide to use the same *shockingly* under-stocked store, which has only one slice of cake, and a single doughnut. After that, all it can deliver is disappointment.

We can model this scenario in the π-calculus, where 😮, 🙍, 🙎, and 🏪 are four processes modelling Ami, Boé, Cat, and the store, and 🍰, 🍩, and 💢 are three channels giving access to a slice of cake, a so-so doughnut, and disappointment, respectively.

$$(x[\text{🍰}].x[\text{🍩}].x[\text{💢}].\text{🏪} \mid x(y).\text{😮} \mid x(z).\text{🙍} \mid x(w).\text{🙎})$$

$$\Downarrow_*$$

$$(\text{🏪} \mid \text{😮}\{\text{🍰}/y\} \mid \text{🙍}\{\text{🍩}/z\} \mid \text{🙎}\{\text{💢}/w\}) \text{ or } (\text{🏪} \mid \text{😮}\{\text{🍰}/y\} \mid \text{🙍}\{\text{💢}/z\} \mid \text{🙎}\{\text{🍩}/w\})$$

$$(\text{🏪} \mid \text{😮}\{\text{🍩}/y\} \mid \text{🙍}\{\text{💢}/z\} \mid \text{🙎}\{\text{🍰}/w\}) \text{ or } (\text{🏪} \mid \text{😮}\{\text{🍩}/y\} \mid \text{🙍}\{\text{🍰}/z\} \mid \text{🙎}\{\text{💢}/w\})$$

$$(\text{🏪} \mid \text{😮}\{\text{💢}/y\} \mid \text{🙍}\{\text{🍰}/z\} \mid \text{🙎}\{\text{🍩}/w\}) \text{ or } (\text{🏪} \mid \text{😮}\{\text{💢}/y\} \mid \text{🙍}\{\text{🍩}/z\} \mid \text{🙎}\{\text{🍰}/w\})$$

With the addition of one process, modelling Cat, we have increased the number of possible outcomes enormously! In general, the number of outcomes for these types of scenarios is $n!$, where n is the number of processes. This means that if we wish to translate any non-deterministic process to one using non-deterministic local choice, we can expect a factorial growth in the size of the term.

3   Hypersequent Classical Processes

In this section, we introduce HCP [11,12], the basis for our calculus HCP_{ND}^-. The term language for HCP^- is a variant of the π-calculus [14].

Definition 1 (Terms).

$$
\begin{array}{lll}
P, Q, R ::= & x \leftrightarrow y & \textit{link} \\
& | \ 0 & \textit{terminated process} \\
& | \ (\nu x)P & \textit{name restriction, "cut"} \\
& | \ (P \mid Q) & \textit{parallel composition, "mix"} \\
& | \ x[y].P & \textit{output} \\
& | \ x(y).P & \textit{input} \\
& | \ x[].P & \textit{halt} \\
& | \ x().P & \textit{wait} \\
& | \ x \triangleleft \texttt{inl}.P & \textit{select left choice} \\
& | \ x \triangleleft \texttt{inr}.P & \textit{select right choice} \\
& | \ x \triangleright \{\texttt{inl}: P; \texttt{inr}: Q\} & \textit{offer binary choice} \\
& | \ x \triangleright \{\} & \textit{offer nullary choice}
\end{array}
$$

The variables x, y, z and w range over channel names. Occasionally, we use a, b, and c to range over *free* channel names. The construct $x \leftrightarrow y$ links two channels [5, 15], forwarding messages received on x to y and vice versa. The construct $(\nu x)P$ creates a new channel x, and the construct $P \mid Q$ and composes two processes. In $x(y).P$ and $x[y].P$, round brackets denote input, square brackets denote output. We use bound output [15], meaning that both input and output bind a new name.

Terms in HCP$^-$ are identified up to structural congruence.

Definition 2 (Structural congruence). *The structural congruence $\equiv$ is the congruence closure over terms which satisfies the following additional axioms:*

$$
\begin{array}{llll}
(\leftrightarrow\textit{-comm}) & x \leftrightarrow y \equiv y \leftrightarrow x & (\nu\textit{-comm}) & (\nu x)(\nu y)P \equiv (\nu y)(\nu x)P \\
(\mid\textit{-comm}) & P \mid Q \equiv Q \mid P & (\mid\textit{-assoc}) & P \mid (Q \mid R) \equiv (P \mid Q) \mid R \\
(\textit{halt}) & P \mid 0 \equiv P & (\textit{scope-ext}) & (\nu x)(P \mid Q) \equiv P \mid (\nu x)Q \ \ \textit{if } x \notin P
\end{array}
$$

Channels in HCP$^-$ are typed using a session type system which is a conservative extension of linear logic.

Definition 3 (Types).

$$
\begin{array}{llll}
A, B, C ::= & A \otimes B \ \textit{independent channels} & | & \mathbf{1} \ \textit{unit for } \otimes \\
& | \ A \ \bindnasrepma \ B \ \textit{interdependent channels} & | & \bot \ \textit{unit for } \bindnasrepma \\
& | \ A \oplus B \ \textit{internal choice} & | & \mathbf{0} \ \textit{unit for } \oplus \\
& | \ A \ \& \ B \ \textit{external choice} & | & \top \ \textit{unit for } \&
\end{array}
$$

Duality plays a crucial role in both linear logic and session types. In HCP$^-$, the two endpoints of a channel are assigned dual types. This ensures that, for instance, whenever a process *sends* across a channel, the process on the other end of that channel is waiting to *receive*. Each type A has a dual, written $A^\perp$. Duality $(\cdot^\perp)$ is an involutive function on types.

Definition 4 (Duality).

$$
\begin{array}{llll}
(A \otimes B)^\perp = A^\perp \ \bindnasrepma \ B^\perp & \mathbf{1}^\perp = \bot & (A \ \bindnasrepma \ B)^\perp = A^\perp \otimes B^\perp & \bot^\perp = \mathbf{1} \\
(A \oplus B)^\perp = A^\perp \ \& \ B^\perp & \mathbf{0}^\perp = \top & (A \ \& \ B)^\perp = A^\perp \oplus B^\perp & \top^\perp = \mathbf{0}
\end{array}
$$

Environments associate channels with types. Names in environments must be unique, and environments Γ and Δ can only be combined (Γ, Δ) if $\mathrm{cn}(\Gamma) \cap \mathrm{cn}(\Delta) = \varnothing$, where $\mathrm{cn}(\Gamma)$ denotes the set of channel names in Γ.

Definition 5 (Environments). $\Gamma, \Delta, \Theta ::= x_1 : A_1 \ldots x_n : A_n$

HCP$^-$ registers parallelism using hyper-environments. A hyper-environment is a multiset of environments. While names within environments must be unique, names may be shared between multiple environments in a hyper-environment. We write $\mathcal{G} \mid \mathcal{H}$ to combine two hyper-environments.

Definition 6 (Hyper-environments). $\mathcal{G}, \mathcal{H} ::= \varnothing \mid \mathcal{G} \mid \Gamma$

Typing judgements associate processes with collections of typed channels.

Definition 7 (Typing judgements). *A typing judgement* $P \vdash \Gamma_1 \mid \ldots \mid \Gamma_n$ *denotes that the process* P *consists of* n *independent, but potentially entangled processes, each of which communicates according to its own protocol* Γ_i. *Typing judgements can be constructed using the inference rules below.*
Structural rules

$$\frac{}{x \leftrightarrow y \vdash x : A, y : A^\perp} \text{Ax} \qquad \frac{P \vdash \mathcal{G} \mid \Gamma, x : A \mid \Delta, x : A^\perp}{(\nu x) P \vdash \mathcal{G} \mid \Gamma, \Delta} \text{Cut}$$

$$\frac{P \vdash \mathcal{G} \qquad Q \vdash \mathcal{H}}{P \mid Q \vdash \mathcal{G} \mid \mathcal{H}} \text{H-Mix} \qquad \frac{}{0 \vdash \varnothing} \text{H-Mix}_0$$

Logical rules

$$\frac{P \vdash \mathcal{G} \mid \Gamma, y : A \mid \Delta, x : B}{x[y].P \vdash \mathcal{G} \mid \Gamma, \Delta, x : A \otimes B} \otimes \qquad \frac{P \vdash \mathcal{G} \mid \Gamma, y : A, x : B}{x(y).P \vdash \mathcal{G} \mid \Gamma, x : A \otimes B} (\otimes)$$

$$\frac{P \vdash \mathcal{G}}{x[].P \vdash \mathcal{G} \mid x : \mathbf{1}} \mathbf{1} \qquad \frac{P \vdash \mathcal{G} \mid \Gamma}{x().P \vdash \mathcal{G} \mid \Gamma, x : \perp} (\perp)$$

$$\frac{P \vdash \mathcal{G} \mid \Gamma, x : A}{x \triangleleft \texttt{inl}.P \vdash \mathcal{G} \mid \Gamma, x : A \oplus B} (\oplus_1) \qquad \frac{P \vdash \mathcal{G} \mid \Gamma, x : B}{x \triangleleft \texttt{inr}.P \vdash \mathcal{G} \mid \Gamma, x : A \oplus B} (\oplus_2)$$

$$\frac{P \vdash \Gamma, x : A \qquad Q \vdash \Gamma, x : B}{x \triangleright \{\texttt{inl} : P; \texttt{inr} : Q\} \vdash \Gamma, x : A \,\&\, B} (\&)$$

$$(\textit{no rule for } \mathbf{0}) \qquad \frac{}{x \triangleright \{\} \vdash \Gamma, x : \top} (\top)$$

Furthermore, each logical rule has the side condition that $x \notin \mathcal{G}$.

Reductions relate processes with their reduced forms.

Definition 8 (Reduction). *Reductions are described by the smallest relation* $\Longrightarrow$ *on process terms closed under the rules below:*

$$\begin{array}{lll}
(\leftrightarrow) & (\nu x)(w \leftrightarrow x \mid P) & \Longrightarrow P\{w/x\} \\
(\beta \otimes \otimes) & (\nu x)(x[y].P \mid x(y).R) & \Longrightarrow (\nu x)(\nu y)(P \mid R) \\
(\beta \mathbf{1} \perp) & (\nu x)(x[].P \mid x().Q) & \Longrightarrow P \mid Q \\
(\beta \oplus \&_1) & (\nu x)(x \triangleleft \texttt{inl}.P \mid x \triangleright \{\texttt{inl} : Q; \texttt{inr} : R\}) & \Longrightarrow (\nu x)(P \mid Q) \\
(\beta \oplus \&_2) & (\nu x)(x \triangleleft \texttt{inr}.P \mid x \triangleright \{\texttt{inl} : Q; \texttt{inr} : R\}) & \Longrightarrow (\nu x)(P \mid R)
\end{array}$$

$$\frac{P \Longrightarrow P'}{(\nu x)P \Longrightarrow (\nu x)P'} \; (\gamma\nu) \qquad \frac{P \Longrightarrow P'}{P \mid Q \Longrightarrow P' \mid Q} \; (\gamma\mid)$$

$$\frac{P \equiv Q \qquad Q \Longrightarrow Q' \qquad Q' \equiv P'}{P \Longrightarrow P'} \; (\gamma\equiv)$$

3.1 Example

HCP$^-$ uses hyper-sequents to structure communication, and it is this structure which rules out deadlocked interactions. Let us go back to our example of a deadlocked interaction from Sect. 1. If we want to type this interaction in HCP$^-$, we run into a problem: to communicate on x, we need to add name restrictions on x and y, e.g.,

$$(\nu x)(\nu y)(x(z).y[\text{⬚}].\text{😀} \mid y(w).x[\text{⬚}].\text{😀}).$$

However, there is no typing derivation for this term. We illustrate this with the partial typing derivation below. In this derivation, there is no way to proceed and type the final name restriction. The CUT rule needs a hypersequent separator to eliminate, so that it only ever links up two independent processes, but the bottom-most sequent has none. Furthermore, the two occurrences of x appearing in the same environment make it ill-formed.

$$\cfrac{\cfrac{\text{😀} \vdash \Gamma, z : \bar{\textstyle\frac{1}{3}}^{\perp}, \text{⬚} : \text{🏰}}{y[\text{⬚}].\text{😀} \vdash \Gamma, z : \bar{\textstyle\frac{1}{3}}^{\perp}, y : \text{🏰}} \otimes}{x(z).y[\text{⬚}].\text{😀} \vdash \Gamma, x : \bar{\textstyle\frac{1}{3}}^{\perp}, y : \text{🏰}} \;\text{⅋}}{\cfrac{\cfrac{\cfrac{\text{😀} \vdash \Delta, \text{⬚} : \bar{\textstyle\frac{1}{3}}, w : \text{🏰}^{\perp}}{x[\text{⬚}].\text{😀} \vdash \Delta, x : \bar{\textstyle\frac{1}{3}}, w : \text{🏰}^{\perp}} \otimes}{y(w).x[\text{⬚}].\text{😀} \vdash \Delta, x : \bar{\textstyle\frac{1}{3}}, y : \text{🏰}^{\perp}} \;\text{⅋}}{}}$$

$$\cfrac{(x(z).y[\text{⬚}].\text{😀} \mid y(w).x[\text{⬚}].\text{😀}) \vdash \Gamma, x : \bar{\textstyle\frac{1}{3}}^{\perp}, y : \text{🏰} \mid \Delta, x : \bar{\textstyle\frac{1}{3}}, y : \text{🏰}^{\perp}}{(\nu y)(x(z).y[\text{⬚}].\text{😀} \mid y(w).x[\text{⬚}].\text{😀}) \vdash \Gamma, \Delta, x : \bar{\textstyle\frac{1}{3}}^{\perp}, x : \bar{\textstyle\frac{1}{3}}} \; \text{H-MIX, CUT}$$

3.2 Metatheory

HCP$^-$ enjoys subject reduction, termination, and progress [11].

Lemma 9 (Preservation for $\equiv$). *If $P \equiv Q$, then $P \vdash \mathcal{G}$ iff $Q \vdash \mathcal{G}$.*

Proof. By induction on the derivation of $P \equiv Q$.

Theorem 10 (Preservation). *If $P \vdash \mathcal{G}$ and $P \Longrightarrow Q$, then $Q \vdash \mathcal{G}$.*

Proof. By induction on the derivation of $P \Longrightarrow Q$.

Definition 11 (Actions). *A process P acts on x whenever x is free in the outermost term constructor of P, e.g., $x[y].P$ acts on x but not on y, and $x \leftrightarrow y$ acts on both x and y. A process P is an action if it acts on some channel x.*

Definition 12 (Canonical forms). *A process P is in canonical form if*

$$P \equiv (\nu x_1)\dots(\nu x_n)(P_1 \mid \cdots \mid P_{n+m+1}),$$

such that: no process P_i is a cut or a mix; no process P_i is a link acting on a bound channel x_i; and no two processes P_i and P_j are acting on the same bound channel x_i.

Lemma 13. *If a well-typed process P is in canonical form, then it is blocked on an external communication, i.e., $P \equiv (\nu x_1) \ldots (\nu x_n)(P_1 \mid \cdots \mid P_{n+m+1})$ such that at least one process P_i acts on a free name.*

Proof. We have $P \equiv (\nu x_1) \ldots (\nu x_n)(P_1 \mid \ldots \mid P_{n+m+1})$, such that no P_i is a cut or a link acting on a bound channel, and no two processes P_i and P_j are acting on the same bound channel. The prefix of cuts and mixes introduces n channels. Each application of cut requires an application of mix, so the prefix introduces $n+m+1$ processes. Therefore, at least $m+1$ of the processes P_i must be acting on a free channel, i.e., blocked on an external communication. □

Theorem 14 (Progress). *If $P \vdash \Gamma$, then either P is in canonical form, or there exists a process Q such that $P \Longrightarrow Q$.*

Proof. We consider the maximum prefix of cuts and mixes of P such that $P \equiv (\nu x_1) \ldots (\nu x_n)(P_1 \mid \ldots \mid P_{n+m+1})$, and no P_i is a cut. If any process P_i is a link, we reduce by ($\leftrightarrow$). If any two processes P_i and P_j are acting on the same channel x_i, we rewrite by $\equiv$ and reduce by the appropriate β-rule. Otherwise, P is in canonical form. □

Theorem 15 (Termination). *If $P \vdash \mathcal{G}$, then there are no infinite $\Longrightarrow$-reduction sequences.*

Proof. Every reduction reduces a single cut to zero, one or two cuts. However, each of these cuts is smaller, measured in the size of the cut formula. Furthermore, each instance of the structural congruence preserves the size of the cut. Therefore, there cannot be an infinite $\Longrightarrow$-reduction sequence. □

4   Shared Channels and Non-determinism

In this section, we will discuss our main contribution: an extension of HCP⁻ which allows for races while still excluding deadlocks. We have seen in Sect. 3.1 how HCP⁻ excludes deadlocks, but how exactly does HCP⁻ exclude races? Let us return to our example from Sect. 1, to the interaction between Ami, Boé and the store.

$$(x[\text{\tiny⬛}].x[\text{\tiny👫}].\text{\tiny▦} \mid x(y).\text{\tiny●} \mid x(z).\text{\tiny◉})$$

$$\Downarrow *$$

$$(\text{\tiny▦} \mid \text{\tiny●}\{\text{\tiny⬛}/y\} \mid \text{\tiny◉}\{\text{\tiny👫}/z\}) \quad \text{or} \quad (\text{\tiny▦} \mid \text{\tiny●}\{\text{\tiny👫}/y\} \mid \text{\tiny◉}\{\text{\tiny⬛}/z\})$$

Races occur when more than two processes attempt to communicate simultaneously over the *same* channel. However, the CUT rule of HCP⁻ requires that *exactly two* processes communicate over each channel:

$$\frac{P \vdash \mathcal{G} \mid \Gamma, x : A \mid \Delta, x : A^{\perp}}{(\nu x)P \vdash \mathcal{G} \mid \Gamma, \Delta} \text{ CUT}$$

We could attempt to write down a protocol for our example, stating that the store has a pair of channels $x, y : 🍰$ with which it communicates with Ami and Boé, taking 🍰 to be the type of interactions in which cake *may* be obtained, i.e. of both 🍰 and 😖, and state that the store communicates with Ami *and* Boé over a channel of type $🍰 ⅋ 🍰$. However, this *only* models interactions such as the following:

$$\cfrac{\cfrac{\cfrac{🏪 \vdash \Gamma, x : 🍰^{\perp} \qquad 👩 \vdash \Delta, y : 🍰^{\perp}}{(🏪 \mid 👩) \vdash \Gamma, x : 🍰^{\perp} \mid \Delta, x : 🍰^{\perp}} \text{H-Mix}}{y[x].(🏪 \mid 👩) \vdash \Gamma, \Delta, y : 🍰^{\perp} \otimes 🍰^{\perp}} \otimes \qquad \cfrac{🏬 \vdash \Theta, x : 🍰, y : 🍰}{y(x).🏬 \vdash \Theta, y : 🍰 ⅋ 🍰} ⅋}{\cfrac{(y[x].(🏪 \mid 👩) \mid y(x).🏬) \vdash \Gamma, \Delta, y : 🍰^{\perp} \otimes 🍰^{\perp} \mid \Theta, y : 🍰 ⅋ 🍰}{(\nu y)(y[x].(🏪 \mid 👩) \mid y(x).🏬) \vdash \Gamma, \Delta, \Theta} \text{Cut}} \text{H-Mix}$$

In this interaction, Ami will get whatever the store decides to send on x, and Boé will get whatever the store decides to send on y. This means that this interactions gives the choice of who receives what *to the store*. This is not an accurate model of our original example, where the choice of who receives the cake is non-deterministic and depends on factors outside of any of the participants' control!

Modelling racy behaviour, such as that in our example, is essential to describing the interactions that take place in realistic concurrent systems. We would like to extend HCP⁻ to allow such races in a way which mirrors the way in which the π-calculus handles non-determinism. Let us return to our example:

$$(x[🍰].x[😖].🏬 \mid x(y).💀 \mid x(z).👩)$$

In this interaction, we see that the channel x is only used as a way to connect the various clients, Ami and Boé, to the store. The *real* communication, sending the slice of cake and disappointment, takes places on the channels 🍰, 😖, y and z. Inspired by this, we add two new constructs to the term language of HCP⁻ for sending and receiving on a *shared* channel. These actions are marked with a $\star$ to distinguish them from ordinary sending and receiving.

Definition 16 (Terms). *We extend Definition 1 as follows:*

$$P, Q, R ::= \ldots$$
$$\mid \star x[y].P \quad \textit{client creation}$$
$$\mid \star x(y).P \quad \textit{server interaction}$$

As before, round brackets denote input, square brackets denote output. Note that $\star x[y].P$, much like $x[y].P$, is a bound output: both client creation and server interaction bind a new name. The structural congruence, which identifies certain terms, is the same as Definition 2.

In any non-deadlock interaction between a server and some clients, there must be *exactly* as many clients as there are server interactions. Therefore, we add two new *dual* types for client pools and servers, which track how many clients or server interactions they represent.

Definition 17 (Types). *We extend Definition 3 as follows:*

$$A, B, C ::= \ldots$$
$$| \ !_n A \ \ pool\ of\ n\ clients$$
$$| \ ?_n A \ \ n\ server\ interactions$$

The types $!_n A$ and $?_n A^\perp$ are dual. Duality remains an involutive function.

We have to add typing rules to associate our new client and server interactions with their types. The definition for environments will remain unchanged, but we will extend the definition for the typing judgement. To determine the new typing rules, we essentially answer the question "What typing constructs do we need to complete the following proof?"

$$ \begin{array}{ccc} \text{😀} \vdash \Gamma, y : \text{👤}^\perp & \text{👩} \vdash \Delta, y' : \text{👤}^\perp & \text{🗄} \vdash \Theta, z : \text{👤}, z' : \text{👤} \\ \vdots & \vdots & \vdots \end{array} $$

$$(\nu x)((\star x[y].\text{😀} \mid \star x[y'].\text{👩}) \mid \star x(z).\star x(z').\text{🗄}) \vdash \Gamma, \Delta, \Theta$$

The constructs $\star x[y].P$ and $\star x(y).P$ introduce a single client or server action, respectively—hence, channels of type $!_1$ and $?_1$. However, when we cut, we want to cut on both interactions simultaneously. We need rules for the *contraction* of shared channel names.

4.1 Clients and Pooling

A client pool represents a number of independent processes, each wanting to interact with the same server. Examples of such a pool include Ami and Boé from our example, customers for online stores in general, and any number of processes which interact with a single, centralised server.

We introduce two new rules: one to construct clients, and one to pool them together. The first rule, $(!_1)$, interacts over a channel as a client. It does this by receiving a channel y over a *shared* channel x. The channel y is the channel across which the actual interaction will eventually take place. The second rule, CONT$_!$, allows us to contract shared channel names with the same type. When used together with H-MIX, this allows us to pool clients together.

$$\frac{P \vdash \mathcal{G} \mid \Gamma, y : A}{\star x[y].P \vdash \mathcal{G} \mid \Gamma, x : !_1 A} \ (!_1) \qquad \frac{P \vdash \mathcal{G} \mid \Gamma, x : !_m A \mid \Delta, y : !_n A}{P\{x/y\} \vdash \mathcal{G} \mid \Gamma, \Delta, x : !_{m+n} A} \ \text{CONT}_!$$

Using these rules, we can derive the left-hand side of our proof by marking Ami and Boé as clients, and pooling them together.

$$\dfrac{\dfrac{😈 \vdash \Gamma, y : 🎂^{\perp}}{\star x[y].😈 \vdash \Gamma, y : !_1 🎂^{\perp}} \, (!_1) \qquad \dfrac{👩 \vdash \Delta, y' : 🎂^{\perp}}{\star x'[y'].👩 \vdash \Delta, x' : !_1 🎂^{\perp}} \, (!_1)}{\dfrac{(\star x[y].😈 \mid \star x'[y'].👩) \vdash \Gamma, x : !_1 🎂^{\perp} \mid \Delta, x' : !_1 🎂^{\perp}} {(\star x[y].😈 \mid \star x[y'].👩) \vdash \Gamma, \Delta, x : !_2 🎂^{\perp}} \text{Cont}_!} \text{H-Mix}}$$

4.2 Servers and Sequencing

Dual to a pool of n clients in parallel is a server with n actions in sequence. Our interpretation of a server is a process which offers some number of interdependent interactions of the same type. Examples include the store from our example, which gives out slices of cake and disappointment, online stores in general, and any central server which interacts with some number of client processes.

We introduce two new rules to construct servers. The first rule, $(?_1)$, marks a interaction over some channel as a server interaction. It does this by sending a channel y over a *shared* channel x. The channel y is the channel across which the actual interaction will take place. The second rule, $\text{Cont}_?$, allows us to merge two (possibly interleaved) sequences of server interactions. This allows us to construct a server which has multiple interactions of the same type, across the same shared channel.

$$\dfrac{P \vdash \mathcal{G} \mid \Gamma, y : A}{\star x(y).P \vdash \mathcal{G} \mid \Gamma, x : ?_1 A} \, (?_1) \qquad \dfrac{P \vdash \mathcal{G} \mid \Gamma, x : ?_m A, y : ?_n A}{P\{x/y\} \vdash \mathcal{G} \mid \Gamma, x : ?_{m+n} A} \text{Cont}_?$$

Using these rules, we can derive the right-hand side of our proof, by marking each of the store's interactions as server interactions, and then contracting them.

$$\dfrac{\dfrac{\dfrac{🏪 \vdash \Theta, z : 🎂, z' : 🎂}{\star x'(z').🏪 \vdash \Theta, z : 🎂, x' : ?_1 🎂} \, (?_1)}{\star x(z).\star x'(z').🏪 \vdash \Theta, x : ?_1 🎂, x' : ?_1 🎂} \, (?_1)}{\star x(z).\star x(z').🏪 \vdash \Theta, x : ?_2 🎂} \text{Cont}_?}$$

Thus, we complete the typing derivation of our example.

Definition 18 (Typing judgements). *We extend Definition 7 as follows:*

$$\dfrac{P \vdash \mathcal{G} \mid \Gamma, y : A}{\star x[y].P \vdash \mathcal{G} \mid \Gamma, x : !_1 A} \, (!_1) \qquad \dfrac{P \vdash \mathcal{G} \mid \Gamma, y : A}{\star x(y).P \vdash \mathcal{G} \mid \Gamma, x : ?_1 A} \, (?_1)$$

$$\dfrac{P \vdash \mathcal{G} \mid \Gamma, x : !_m A \mid \Delta, y : !_n A}{P\{x/y\} \vdash \mathcal{G} \mid \Gamma, \Delta, x : !_{m+n} A} \text{Cont}_! \qquad \dfrac{P \vdash \mathcal{G} \mid \Gamma, x : ?_m A, y : ?_n A}{P\{x/y\} \vdash \mathcal{G} \mid \Gamma, x : ?_{m+n} A} \text{Cont}_?$$

4.3 Running Clients and Servers

Finally, we need to extend the reduction rules to allow for the reduction of client and server processes. The reduction rule we add is a variant of the reduction rule for $\otimes$ and $⅋$, $(\beta_{\otimes⅋})$.

Definition 19 (Reduction). *We extend Definition 8 as follows:*

$$(\beta\star)\ (\nu x)((\star x[y].P \mid \star x(z).Q) \mid R) \implies (\nu x)((\nu y)(P \mid Q\{y/z\}) \mid R)$$

The difference between $(\beta\star)$ and $(\beta\otimes\mathcal{8})$ is that the former allows reduction to happen in the presence of an unrelated process R, which is passed along unchanged. This is necessary, as there may be other clients waiting to interact with the server on the shared channel x, which cannot be moved out of scope of the name restriction (νx). When there is no unrelated process R, *i.e.*, when there is only a single client, we can rewrite by (halt) before and after applying $(\beta\star)$.

So where does the non-determinism in $\mathrm{HCP}^-_{\mathrm{ND}}$ come from? Let us say we have a term of the following form:

$$(\nu x)((\star x[y_1].P_1 \mid \cdots \mid \star x[y_n].P_n) \mid \star x(y_1).\ldots.\star x(y_n).Q)$$

As parallel composition is commutative and associative, we can rewrite this term to pair any client in the pool with the server before applying $(\beta\star)$. Thus, like in the π-calculus, the non-determinism is introduced by the structural congruence.

Does this mean that, for an arbitrary client pool P in $(\nu x)(P \mid \star x(z).Q)$, every client in that pool is competing for the server interaction on x? Not necessarily, as some portion of the clients can be blocked on an external communication. For instance, in the term below, clients $\star x[y_{n+1}].P_{n+1} \ldots \star x[y_m].P_m$ are blocked on a communication on the external channel a:

$$\nu x.(((\star x[y_1].P_1 \mid \cdots \mid \star x[y_n].P_n)$$
$$\mid a().(\star x[y_{n+1}].P_{n+1} \mid \cdots \mid \star x[y_m].P_m))$$
$$\mid \star x(y_1).\ldots.\star x(y_m).Q)$$

If we reduce this term, then only the clients $\star x[y_1].P_1 \ldots \star x[y_n].P_n$ will be assigned server interactions, and we end up with the following canonical form:

$$\nu x.(\ a().(\star x[y_{n+1}].P_{n+1} \mid \cdots \mid \star x[y_m].P_m)$$
$$\mid \star x(y_{n+1}).\ldots.\star x(y_m).Q)$$

This matches our intuition and the behaviour of the π-calculus.

Alternative Syntax. If we choose to reuse the terms $x[y].P$ and $x(y).P$ for shared channels, we could replace $(\beta\otimes\mathcal{8})$ with $(\beta\star)$, using the latter rule for both cases.

4.4 Metatheory

$\mathrm{HCP}^-_{\mathrm{ND}}$ enjoys subject reduction, termination, and progress.

Lemma 20 (Preservation for $\equiv$). *If $P \equiv Q$ and $P \vdash \mathcal{G}$, then $Q \vdash \mathcal{G}$.*

Proof. By induction on the derivation of $P \equiv Q$.

Theorem 21 (Preservation). *If $P \vdash \mathcal{G}$ and $P \implies Q$, then $Q \vdash \mathcal{G}$.*

Proof. By induction on the derivation of $P \implies Q$.

Definition 22 (Actions). *A process P acts on x whenever x is free in the outermost term constructor of P, e.g., $\star x(y).P$ acts on x but not on y, and $x \leftrightarrow y$ acts on both x and y. A process P is an action if it acts on some channel x. Two actions are dual when they introduce dual type constructors, e.g., $x[y].P$ is dual to $x(z).Q$, but $x \leftrightarrow y$ is not dual to any action.*

Definition 23 (Canonical forms). *A process P is in canonical form if*

$$P \equiv (\nu x_1) \ldots (\nu x_n)(P_1 \mid \cdots \mid P_{n+m+1}),$$

such that: no process P_i is a cut or a mix; no process P_i is a link acting on a bound channel x_i; and no two processes P_i and P_j are acting on the same bound channel x_i with dual actions.

The new definition of canonical forms is slightly more precise than Definition 12: we added the phrase "with dual actions". With the addition of shared channels, it has become possible to have a process which cannot reduce, but in which two processes are waiting to act on the same channel, *e.g.*, in $(\star x[y]. \text{☻} \mid \star x[y']. \text{☻})$.

Lemma 24. *If a well-typed process P is in canonical form, then it is blocked on an external communication, i.e., $P \equiv (\nu x_1) \ldots (\nu x_n)(P_1 \mid \cdots \mid P_{n+m+1})$ such that at least one process P_i acts on a free name.*

Proof. We have $P \equiv (\nu x_1) \ldots (\nu x_n)(P_1 \mid \ldots \mid P_{n+m+1})$, such that no P_i is a cut or a link acting on a bound channel, and no two processes P_i and P_j are acting on the same bound channel with dual actions. The prefix of cuts and mixes introduces n channels. Each application of cut requires an application of mix, so the prefix introduces $n + m + 1$ processes. Each application of $\text{CONT}_!$ requires an application of mix, so there are at most m clients acting on the same bound channel. Therefore, at least *one* of the processes P_i must be acting on a free channel, i.e., blocked on an external communication.

Theorem 25 (Progress). *If $P \vdash \Gamma$, then either P is in canonical form, or there exists a process Q such that $P \implies Q$.*

Proof. We consider the maximum prefix of cuts and mixes of P such that $P \equiv (\nu x_1) \ldots (\nu x_n)(P_1 \mid \ldots \mid P_{n+m+1})$, and no P_i is a cut. If any process P_i is a link, we reduce by ($\leftrightarrow$). If any two processes P_i and P_j are acting on the same channel x_i with dual actions, we rewrite by $\equiv$ and reduce by the appropriate β-rule. Otherwise, P is in canonical form.

Theorem 26 (Termination). *If $P \vdash \mathcal{G}$, then there are no infinite $\implies$-reduction sequences.*

Proof. Every reduction reduces a single cut to zero, one or two cuts. However, each of these cuts is smaller, measured in the size of the cut formula. Furthermore, each instance of the structural congruence preserves the size of the cut. Therefore, there cannot be an infinite $\implies$-reduction sequence.

4.5 HCP$_{ND}^-$ and Non-deterministic Local Choice

In Sect. 2, we discussed the non-deterministic local choice operator, which is used in several extensions of πDILL and CP [1,6,7]. This operator is admissible in HCP$_{ND}^-$. We can derive the non-deterministic choice $P + Q$ by constructing the following term:

$$\nu x.((\ \star x[y].y \triangleleft \mathtt{inl}.y[].0$$
$$|\ \star x[z].z \triangleleft \mathtt{inr}.z[].0\ )$$
$$|\ \star x(y).\star x(z).y \triangleright$$
$$\{\mathtt{inl}:\ (\nu w)(z \triangleright \{\mathtt{inl}: z().w[].0; \mathtt{inr}: z().w[].0\}\ |\ w().P)$$
$$;\mathtt{inr}:\ (\nu w)(z \triangleright \{\mathtt{inl}: z().w[].0; \mathtt{inr}: z().w[].0\}\ |\ w().Q)\ \})$$

This term is a cut between two processes.

- On the left-hand side, we have a pool of two processes, $\star x[y].y \triangleleft \mathtt{inl}.y[].0$ and $\star x[z].z \triangleleft \mathtt{inr}.z[].0$. Each makes a choice: the first sends inl, and the second sends inr.
- On the right-hand side, we have a server with both P and Q. This server has two channels on which a choice is offered, y and z. The choice on y selects between P and Q. The choice on z does not affect the outcome of the process at all. Instead, it is discarded.

When these clients and the server are put together, the choices offered by the server will be non-deterministically lined up with the clients which make choices, and either P or Q will run.

While there is a certain amount of overhead involved in this encoding, it scales linearly in terms of the number of processes. The reverse—encoding the non-determinism present in HCP$_{ND}^-$ using non-deterministic local choice—scales exponentially, see, *e.g.*, the examples in Sect. 2.

5 Cuts with Leftovers

So far, our account of a non-determinism in client/server interactions only allows for interactions between equal numbers of clients and server interactions. A natural question is whether or not we can deal with the scenario in which there are more client than server interactions or vice versa, *i.e.*, whether or not the following rules are derivable:

$$\frac{\vdash \Gamma, !_{n+m}A \qquad \vdash \Delta, ?_n A^\perp}{\vdash \Gamma, \Delta, !_m A} \qquad \frac{\vdash \Gamma, !_n A \qquad \vdash \Delta, ?_{n+m}A^\perp}{\vdash \Gamma, \Delta, ?_m A^\perp}$$

These rules are derivable using a link. For instance, we can derive the rule for the case in which there are more clients than servers as follows:

$$\dfrac{P \vdash \Gamma, x\!:\!!_{n+m}A \quad \dfrac{\dfrac{Q \vdash \Delta, x\!:\!?_nA^\perp \quad x \leftrightarrow w \vdash x'\!:\!?_mA^\perp, w\!:\!!_mA}{(Q \mid x \leftrightarrow w) \vdash \Delta, x\!:\!?_nA^\perp \mid x'\!:\!?_mA^\perp, w\!:\!!_mA}\,\text{H-Mix}}{(Q \mid x \leftrightarrow w) \vdash \Delta, x\!:\!?_{n+m}A^\perp, w\!:\!!_mA}\,\text{Cont}_!}{\dfrac{(P \mid (Q \mid x \leftrightarrow w)) \vdash \Gamma, x\!:\!!_{n+m}A \mid \Delta, x\!:\!?_{n+m}A^\perp, w\!:\!!_mA}{(\nu x)(P \mid (Q \mid x \leftrightarrow w)) \vdash \Gamma, \Delta, w\!:\!!_mA}\,\text{Cut}}\,\text{H-Mix}}$$

6   Relation to Manifest Sharing

In Sect. 2, we mentioned related work which extends πDILL and CP with non-deterministic local choice [1,6,7], and contrasted these approaches with ours. In this section, we will contrast our work with the more recent work on manifest sharing [2].

Manifest sharing extends the session-typed language SILL with two connectives, $\uparrow_L^S A$ and $\downarrow_L^S A$, which represent the places in a protocol where a shared resource is acquired and released, respectively. In the resulting language, SILL$_S$, we can define a type for, $e.g.$, shared queues (using the notation for types introduced in this paper):

$$\text{queue } A ::= \uparrow_L^S (\, A^\perp \,\otimes\, \downarrow_L^S (\text{queue } A) \,) \,\&\, (\,(A \oplus \perp) \,\otimes\, \downarrow_L^S (\text{queue } A)\,)$$

The type queue A types a shared channel which, after we acquire exclusive access, gives us the choice between enqueuing a value ($A^\perp$) and releasing the queue, or dequeuing a value if there is any ($A \oplus \perp$) and releasing the queue.

The language SILL$_S$ is much more expressive than HCP$_{\text{ND}}^-$, as it has support for both shared channels and recursion. In fact, Balzer, Pfenning, and Toninho [3] show that SILL$_S$ is expressive enough to embed the untyped asynchronous π-calculus. This expressiveness comes with a cost, as SILL$_S$ processes are not guaranteed to be deadlock free, though recent work addresses this issue [4].

Despite the difference in expressiveness, there are some similarities between HCP$_{\text{ND}}^-$ and SILL$_S$. In the former, shared channels represent (length-indexed) streams of interactions of the same type. In the latter, it is necessary for type preservation that shared channels are always released at the same type at which they were acquired, meaning that shared channels also represent (possibly infinite) streams of interactions of the same type. In fact, in HCP$_{\text{ND}}^-$, the type for queues (with n interactions) can be written as $!_n(A^\perp \,\&\, (A \oplus \perp))$.

One key difference between HCP$_{\text{ND}}^-$ and SILL$_S$ is that in SILL$_S$ a server must finish interacting with one client before interacting with another, whereas in HCP$_{\text{ND}}^-$ the server may interact with multiple clients simultaneously.

7   Discussion and Future Work

We presented HCP$_{\text{ND}}^-$, an extension of HCP$^-$ which permits non-deterministic communication without losing the strong connection to logic. We gave proofs for preservation, progress, and termination for the term reduction system of HCP$_{\text{ND}}^-$. We showed that we can define non-deterministic local choice in HCP$_{\text{ND}}^-$.

Our formalism so far has only captured servers that provide for a fixed number of clients. More realistically, we would want to define servers that provide for arbitrary numbers of clients. This poses two problems: how would we define arbitrarily-interacting stateful processes, and how would we extend the typing discipline of $\mathrm{HCP}^-_{\mathrm{ND}}$ to account for them without losing its static guarantees.

One approach to defining server processes would be to combine $\mathrm{HCP}^-_{\mathrm{ND}}$ with structural recursion and corecursion, following the $\mu\mathrm{CP}$ extension of Lindley and Morris [13]. Their approach can express processes which produce streams of A channels. Such a process would expose a channel with the co-recursive type $\nu X.A \otimes (1 \oplus X)$. Given such a process, it is possible to produce a channel of type $A \otimes A \otimes \cdots \otimes A$ for any number of As, allowing us to satisfy the type $?_n A$ for an arbitrary n.

We would also need to extend the typing discipline to capture arbitrary use of shared channels. One approach would be to introduce resource variables and quantification. Following this approach, in addition to having types $?_n A$ and $!_n A$ for concrete n, we would also have types $?_x A$ and $!_x A$ for resource variables x. These variables would be introduced by quantifiers $\forall x A$ and $\exists x A$. Defining terms corresponding to $\forall x A$, and its relationship with structured recursion, presents an interesting area of further work.

Our account of HCP^- did not include the exponentials $?A$ and $!A$. The type $!A$ denotes arbitrarily many independent instances of A, while the type $?A$ denotes a concrete (if unspecified) number of potentially-dependent instances of A. Existing interpretations of linear logic as session types have taken $!A$ to denote A-servers, while $?A$ denotes A-clients. However, the analogy is imperfect: while we expect servers to provide arbitrarily many instances of their behaviour, we also expect those instances to be interdependent.

With quantification over resource variables, we can give precise accounts of both CP's exponentials and idealised servers and clients. CP exponentials could be embedded into this framework using the definitions $!A ::= \forall n!_n A$ and $?A ::= \exists n?_n A$. We would also have types that precisely matched our intuitions for server and client behavior: an A server is of type $\forall n?_n A$, as it serves an unbounded number of requests with the requests being interdependent, while a collection of A clients is of type $\exists n!_n A$, as we have a specific number of clients with each client being independent.

References

1. Atkey, R., Lindley, S., Morris, J.G.: Conflation confers concurrency. In: Lindley, S., McBride, C., Trinder, P., Sannella, D. (eds.) A List of Successes That Can Change the World. LNCS, vol. 9600, pp. 32–55. Springer, Cham (2016). https://doi.org/10.1007/978-3-319-30936-1_2
2. Balzer, S., Pfenning, F.: Manifest sharing with session types. Proc. ACM Program. Lang. 1(ICFP), 1–29 (2017). https://doi.org/10.1145/3110281

3. Balzer, S., Pfenning, F., Toninho, B.: A universal session type for untyped asynchronous communication. In: Schewe, S., Zhang, L. (eds.) 29th International Conference on Concurrency Theory (CONCUR 2018). Leibniz International Proceedings in Informatics (LIPIcs), vol. 118, pp. 30:1–30:18. Schloss Dagstuhl-Leibniz-Zentrum fuer Informatik, Dagstuhl, Germany (2018). https://doi.org/10.4230/LIPIcs.CONCUR.2018.30

4. Balzer, S., Toninho, B., Pfenning, F.: Manifest deadlock-freedom for shared session types. In: Caires, L. (ed.) ESOP 2019. LNCS, vol. 11423, pp. 611–639. Springer, Cham (2019). https://doi.org/10.1007/978-3-030-17184-1_22

5. Boreale, M.: On the expressiveness of internal mobility in name-passing calculi. Theor. Comput. Sci. **195**(2), 205–226 (1998). https://doi.org/10.1016/s0304-3975(97)00220-x

6. Caires, L.: Types and logic, concurrency and non-determinism. In: Abadi, M., Gardner, P., Gordon, A., Mardare, R. (eds.) Essays for the Luca Cardelli Fest. Microsoft Research (2014)

7. Caires, L., Pérez, J.A.: Linearity, control effects, and behavioral types. In: Yang, H. (ed.) ESOP 2017. LNCS, vol. 10201, pp. 229–259. Springer, Heidelberg (2017). https://doi.org/10.1007/978-3-662-54434-1_9

8. Caires, L., Pfenning, F.: Session types as intuitionistic linear propositions. In: Gastin, P., Laroussinie, F. (eds.) CONCUR 2010. LNCS, vol. 6269, pp. 222–236. Springer, Heidelberg (2010). https://doi.org/10.1007/978-3-642-15375-4_16

9. Girard, J.Y., Scedrov, A., Scott, P.J.: Bounded linear logic: a modular approach to polynomial-time computability. Theor. Comput. Sci. **97**(1), 1–66 (1992). https://doi.org/10.1016/0304-3975(92)90386-T

10. Honda, K.: Types for dyadic interaction. In: Best, E. (ed.) CONCUR 1993. LNCS, vol. 715, pp. 509–523. Springer, Heidelberg (1993). https://doi.org/10.1007/3-540-57208-2_35

11. Kokke, W., Montesi, F., Peressotti, M.: Taking linear logic apart. In: Workshop on Linearity & TLLA at FloC 2018, July 2018

12. Kokke, W., Montesi, F., Peressotti, M.: Better late than never: a fully-abstract semantics for classical processes. PACMPL **3**(POPL), 24 (2019)

13. Lindley, S., Morris, J.G.: Talking bananas: structural recursion for session types. In: Proceedings of the 21st ACM SIGPLAN International Conference on Functional Programming, ICFP 2016, pp. 434–447. ACM, New York (2016). https://doi.org/10.1145/2951913.2951921

14. Milner, R., Parrow, J., Walker, D.: A calculus of mobile processes, II. Inf. Comput. **100**(1), 41–77 (1992). https://doi.org/10.1016/0890-5401(92)90009-5

15. Sangiorgi, D.: π-calculus, internal mobility, and agent-passing calculi. Theor. Comput. Sci. **167**(1–2), 235–274 (1996). https://doi.org/10.1016/0304-3975(96)00075-8

16. Wadler, P.: Propositions as sessions. In: Proceedings of the 17th ACM SIGPLAN International Conference on Functional Programming, ICFP 2012, pp. 273–286. ACM, New York (2012). https://doi.org/10.1145/2364527.2364568

The share Operator for Field-Based Coordination

Giorgio Audrito[1] , Jacob Beal[2] , Ferruccio Damiani[1(✉)] ,
Danilo Pianini[3] , and Mirko Viroli[3]

[1] Dipartimento di Informatica, University of Torino, Turin, Italy
{giorgio.audrito,ferruccio.damiani}@unito.it
[2] Raytheon BBN Technologies, Cambridge, MA, USA
jakebeal@ieee.org
[3] Alma Mater Studiorum–Università di Bologna, Cesena, Italy
{danilo.pianini,mirko.viroli}@unibo.it

Abstract. Recent work in the area of coordination models and collective adaptive systems promotes a view of distributed computations as functions manipulating computational fields (data structures spread over space and evolving over time), and introduces the field calculus as a formal foundation for field computations. With the field calculus, evolution (time) and neighbor interaction (space) are handled by separate functional operators: however, this intrinsically limits the speed of information propagation that can be achieved by their combined use. In this paper, we propose a new field-based coordination operator called **share**, which captures the space-time nature of field computations in a single operator that declaratively achieves: *(i)* observation of neighbors' values; *(ii)* reduction to a single local value; and *(iii)* update and converse sharing to neighbors of a local variable. In addition to conceptual economy, use of the **share** operator also allows many prior field calculus algorithms to be greatly accelerated, which we validate empirically with simulations of a number of frequently used network propagation and collection algorithms.

Keywords: Aggregate programming · Computational field ·
Information propagation speed · Spatial computing

1 Introduction

The number and density of networking computing devices distributed throughout our environment is continuing to increase rapidly. In order to manage and make effective use of such systems, there is likewise an increasing need for software engineering paradigms that simplify the engineering of resilient distributed

This work has been partially supported by Ateneo/CSP project "AP: Aggregate Programming" (http://ap-project.di.unito.it/). This document does not contain technology or technical data controlled under either U.S. International Traffic in Arms Regulation or U.S. Export Administration Regulations.

H. Riis Nielson and E. Tuosto (Eds.): COORDINATION 2019, LNCS 11533, pp. 54–71, 2019.
https://doi.org/10.1007/978-3-030-22397-7_4

systems. Aggregate programming [11,37] is one such promising approach, providing a layered architecture in which programmers can describe computations in terms of resilient operations on "aggregate" data structures with values spread over space and evolving in time.

The foundation of this approach is field computation, formalized by the field calculus [36], a terse mathematical model of distributed computation that simultaneously describes both collective system behavior and the independent, unsynchronized actions of individual devices that will produce that collective behavior [8]. Traditionally, in this approach each construct and reusable component is a pure function from fields to fields—a field is a map from a set of space-time computational events to a set of values—and each primitive construct handles just one key aspect of computation: hence, one construct deals with time (i.e, **rep**, providing field evolution) and one with space (i.e., **nbr**, handling neighbor interaction). However, in recent work on the universality of the field calculus, we have identified that the combination of time evolution and neighbor interaction operators in the original field calculus induces a delay, limiting the speed of information propagation that can be achieved efficiently [2].

In this paper, we address this limitation by extending the field calculus with the **share** construct, combining time evolution and neighbor interaction into a single new atomic coordination operator that simultaneously implements: *(i)* observation of neighbors' values; *(ii)* reduction to a single local value; and *(iii)* update and converse sharing to neighbors of a local variable.

Following a review of the field calculus and its motivating context in Sect. 2, we introduce the **share** construct in Sect. 3, empirically validate the predicted acceleration of speed in frequently used network propagation and collection algorithms in Sect. 4, and conclude with a summary and discussion of future work in Sect. 5.

2   Background, Motivation, and Related Work

Programming collective adaptive systems is a challenge that has been recognized and addressed in a wide variety of different contexts. Despite the wide variety of goals and starting points, however, the commonalities in underlying challenges have tended to shape the resulting aggregate programming approaches into several clusters of common approaches, as enumerated in [10]: *(i)* "device-abstraction" methods that abstract and simplify the programming of individual devices and interactions (e.g., TOTA [29], Hood [39], chemical models [38], "paintable computing" [13], Meld [1]) or entirely abstract away the network (e.g., BSP [35], MapReduce [18], Kairos [22]); *(ii)* spatial patterning languages that focus on geometric or topological constructs (e.g., Growing Point Language [16], Origami Shape Language [31], self-healing geometries [15,26], cellular automata patterning [40]); *(iii)* information summarization languages that focus on collection and routing of information (e.g., TinyDB [28], Cougar [41], TinyLime [17], and Regiment [32]); *(iv)* general purpose space-time computing models (e.g., StarLisp [27], MGS [20,21], Proto [9], aggregate programming [11]).

The field calculus [8, 36] belongs to the last of these classes, the general purpose models. Like other core calculi, such as λ-calculus [14] or π-calculus [30], the field calculus was designed to provide a minimal, mathematically tractable model of computation—in this case with the goal of unifying across a broad class of aggregate programming approaches and providing a principled basis for integration and composition. Indeed, recent analysis [2] has determined that the current formulation of field calculus is space-time universal, meaning that it is able to capture every possible computation over collections of devices sending messages. Field calculus can thus serve as a unifying abstraction for programming collective adaptive systems, and results regarding field calculus have potential implications for all other works in this field.

That same work establishing universality, however, also identified a key limitation of the current formulation of the field calculus, which we are addressing in this paper. In particular, the operators for time evolution and neighbor interaction in field calculus interact such that for most programs either the message size grows with the distance that information must travel or else information must travel significantly slower than the maximum potential speed. The remainder of this section provides a brief review of these key results from [2]: Sect. 2.1 introduces the underlying space-time computational model used by the field calculus, Sect. 2.2 provides a review of the field calculus itself, and Sect. 2.3 explains and illustrates the problematic interaction between time evolution and neighbor interaction operators that will be addressed by the **share** operator in the next section.

2.1   Space-Time Computation

Field calculus considers a computational model in which a program P is periodically and asynchronously executed by each device δ. When an individual device performs a round of execution, that device follows these steps in order: (i) collects information from sensors, local memory, and the most recent messages from neighbors,[1] the latter in the form of a *neighboring value* map $\phi : \delta \to v$ from neighbors to values, (ii) evaluates program P with the information collected as its input, (iii) stores the results of the computation locally, as well as broadcasting it to neighbors and possibly feeding it to actuators, and (iv) sleeps until it is time for the next round of execution. Note that as execution is asynchronous, devices perform executions independently and without reference to the executions of other devices, except insofar as they use state that has arrived in messages. Messages, in turn, are assumed to be collected by some separate thread, independent of execution rounds.

If we take every such execution as an *event* ϵ, then the collection of such executions across space (i.e., across devices) and time (i.e., over multiple rounds) may be considered as the execution of a single aggregate machine with a topology based on information exchanges $\rightsquigarrow$. The causal relationship between events may then be formalized as defined in [2]:

---

[1] Stale messages may expire after some timeout.

Definition 1 (Event Structure). *An* event structure $\mathbf{E} = \langle E, \leadsto, < \rangle$ *is a countable set of events E together with a neighboring relation $\leadsto \subseteq E \times E$ and a causality relation $< \subseteq E \times E$, such that the transitive closure of $\leadsto$ forms the irreflexive partial order $<$ and the set $\{\epsilon' \in E | \epsilon' < \epsilon\}$ is finite for all ϵ (i.e., $<$ is locally finite).*

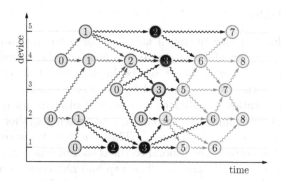

Fig. 1. Example of a space-time event structure, comprising events (circles) and neighbor relations (arrows). Colors indicate causal structure with respect to the doubly-circled event (magenta), splitting events into causal past (red), causal future (cyan) and concurrent (non-ordered, in black). The numbers written within events represent a sample space-time value (cf. Definition 2) associated with that event structure. Figure adapted from [2]. (Color figure online)

Figure 1 shows an example of such an event structure, showing how these relations partition events into "causal past", "causal future", and non-ordered "concurrent" subspaces with respect to any given event. Interpreting this in terms of physical devices and message passing, a physical device is instantiated as a chain of events connected by $\leadsto$ relations (representing evolution of state over time with the device carrying state from one event to the next), and any $\leadsto$ relation between devices represents information exchange from the tail neighbor to the head neighbor. Notice that this is a very flexible and permissive model: there are no assumptions about synchronization, shared identifiers or clocks, or even regularity of events (though of course these things are not prohibited either).

In principle, an execution at ϵ can depend on information from any event in its past and its results can influence any event in its future. As we will see in Sect. 2.3, however, this is problematic for the field calculus as it has been previously defined.

Our aggregate constructs manipulate then space-time data values (see Fig. 1) that map events to values for each event in an event structure:

Definition 2 (Space-Time Value). *Let V be any domain of computational values and $\mathbf{E}$ be a given event structure. A space-time value $\Phi = \langle \mathbf{E}, f \rangle$ is a pair* *comprising the space and a function* $f : E \to V$ *that maps the events* E *of* **E** *to values.*

We can then understand an aggregate computer as a "collective" device manipulating such space-time values, and the field calculus as a definition of operations defined both on individual events and simultaneously on aggregate computers.

2.2   Field Calculus

The field calculus is a tiny universal language for computation of space-time values. Figure 2 gives an abstract syntax for field calculus based on the presentation in [36] (covering a subset of the higher-order field calculus in [8], but including all of the issues addressed by the **share** construct). In this syntax, the overbar notation $\bar{e}$ indicates a sequences of elements (e.g., $\bar{e}$ stands for $e_1, e_2, \ldots, e_n$), and multiple overbars are expanded together (e.g., $\bar{\delta} \mapsto \bar{\ell}$ stands for $\delta_1 \mapsto \ell_1, \delta_2 \mapsto \ell_2, \ldots, \delta_n \mapsto \ell_n$). There are four keywords in this syntax: **def** and **if** respectively correspond to the standard function definition and the branching expression constructs, while **rep** and **nbr** correspond to the two peculiar field calculus constructs that are the focus of this paper, respectively responsible for evolution of state over time and for sharing information between neighbors.

P ::= $\bar{F}$ e	program
F ::= def d($\bar{x}$) {e}	function declaration
e ::= x │ v │ f($\bar{e}$) │ if(e){e}{e} │ nbr{e} │ rep(e){(x) => e}	expression
f ::= d │ b	function name
v ::= ℓ │ ϕ	value
ℓ ::= c($\bar{\ell}$)	local value
ϕ ::= $\bar{\delta} \mapsto \bar{\ell}$	neighboring field value

Fig. 2. Abstract syntax of the field calculus, adapted from [36]

A field calculus program P is a set of function declarations $\bar{F}$ and the main expression e. This main expression e simultaneously defines both the aggregate computation executed on the overall event structure of an aggregate computer and the local computation executed at each of the individual events therein. An expression e can be:

- A *variable* x, e.g. a function parameter.
- A *value* v, which can be of the following two kinds:
  - a *local value* ℓ, defined via data constructor c and arguments $\bar{\ell}$, such as a Boolean, number, string, pair, tuple, etc;
  - A *neighboring (field) value* ϕ that associates neighbor devices δ to local values ℓ, e.g., a map of neighbors to the distances to those neighbors.

- A function call f($\bar{e}$) to either a *user-declared function* d (declared with the def keyword) or a *built-in function* b, such as a mathematical or logical operator, a data structure operation, or a function returning the value of a sensor.
- A *branching expression* if(e_1){e_2} else {e_3}, used to split a computation into operations on two isolated event structures, where/when e_1 evaluates to true or false: the result is computation of e_2 in the former area, and e_3 in the latter.
- The nbr{e} construct creates a neighboring field value mapping neighbors to their latest available result of evaluating e. In particular, each device δ:
    1. shares its value of e with its neighbors, and
    2. evaluates the expression into a neighboring field value ϕ mapping each neighbor δ' of δ to the latest value that δ' has shared for e.

    Note that within an if branch, sharing is restricted to being between device events within the subspace of the branch.
- The rep(e_1){(x) => e_2} construct models state evolution over time: the value of x is initialized to e_1, then evolved at each execution by evaluating e_2.

Thus, for example, distance to the closest member of a set of "source" devices can be computed with the following simple function:

```
def mux(b, x, y) { if (b) {x} {y} }
def distanceTo(source) {
  rep (infinity) { (d) =>
    mux( source, 0, minHood(nbr{d}+nbrRange()) )
} }
```

Here, we use the def construct to define a distanceTo function that takes a Boolean source variable as input. The rep construct defines a distance estimate d that starts at infinity, then decreases in one of two ways. If the source variable is true, then the device is currently a source, and its distance to itself is zero. Otherwise, distance is estimated via the triangle inequality, taking the minimum of a neighbor field value (built-in function minHood) of the distance to each neighbor (built-in function nbrRange) plus that neighbor's distance estimate nbr{d} . Function mux ensures that all its arguments are evaluated before being selected.

Additional illustrative examples and full mathematical details of these constructs and the formal semantics of their evaluation can be found in [36].

2.3 Problematic Interaction Between rep and nbr Constructs

Unfortunately, the apparently straight-forward combination of state evolution with nbr and state sharing with rep turns out to contain a hidden delay, which was identified and explained in [2]. This problem may be illustrated by attempting to construct a simple function that spreads information from an event as quickly as possible. Let us say there is a Boolean space-time value condition, and we wish to compute a space-time function ever that returns true precisely at events where condition is true and in the causal future of those events—i.e., spreading out at the maximum theoretical speed throughout the network of devices. One might expect this could be implemented as follows in field calculus:

```
def ever1(condition) {
  rep (false) { (old) => anyHoodPlusSelf(nbr{old}) || condition }
}
```

where **anyHoodPlusSelf** is a built-in function that returns true if any value is true in its neighboring field input (including the value **old** held for the current device). Walking through the evaluation of this function, however, reveals that there is a hidden delay. In each round, the **old** variable is updated, and will become true if either **condition** is true now for the current device or if **old** was true in the previous round for the current device or for any of its neighbors. Once **old** becomes true, it stays true for the rest of the computation. Notice, however, that a neighboring device does not actually learn that **condition** is true, but that **old** is true. In an event where **condition** first becomes true, the value of **old** that is shared is still false, since the **rep** does not update its value until after the **nbr** has already been evaluated. Only in the next round do neighbors see an updated value of **old**, meaning that **ever1** is not spreading information fast enough to be a correct implementation of **ever**.

We might try to improve this routine by directly sharing the value of **condition**:

```
def ever2(condition) {
  rep (false) { (old) => anyHoodPlusSelf(nbr{old || condition}) }
}
```

This solves the problem for immediate neighbors, but does not solve the problem for neighbors of neighbors, which still have to wait an additional round before **old** is updated.

In fact, it appears that the only way to avoid delays at some depth of neighbor relations is by using unbounded recursion, as previously outlined in [2]:

```
def ever3(condition) {
  rep (false) { (old) =>
    if (countHood() == 0) { old || condition } {
      ever3(anyHoodPlusSelf(nbr{old || condition}))
} } }
```

where **countHood** counts the number of neighbors, i.e., determining whether any neighbor has reached the same depth of recursion in the branch. Thus, in **ever3**, neighbors' values of **cond** are fed to a nested call to **ever3** (if there are any); and this process is iterated until no more values to be considered are present. This function therefore has a recursion depth equal to the longest sequence of events $\epsilon_0 \rightsquigarrow \ldots \rightsquigarrow \epsilon$ ending in the current event ϵ, inducing a linearly increasing computational time and message size and making the routine effectively infeasible for long-running systems.

This case study illustrates the more general problem of delays induced by the interaction of **rep** and **nbr** constructs in field calculus, as identified in [2]. With these constructs, it is never possible to build computations involving long-range communication that are as fast as possible and also lightweight in the amount of communication required.

3   The Share Construct

In order to overcome the problematic interaction between **rep** and **nbr**, we propose a new construct that combines aspects of both:

$$\text{share}(e_1)\{(x) \Rightarrow e_2\}$$

While the syntax of this new **share** construct is identical to that of **rep**, the two constructs differ in the way the construct variable x is interpreted each round:

- in **rep**, the value of x is the value produced by evaluating the construct in the previous round, or the result of evaluating e_1 if there is no prior-round value;
- in **share**, on the other hand, x is a *neighboring field* comprising that same value for the current device plus any values of the construct produced by neighbors in their most recent evaluation.

Notice that since x is a neighboring field rather than a local value, e_2 is responsible for processing it into a local value that can be shared with neighbors at the end of the evaluation. Furthermore, notice that the value for δ in the field x corresponds exactly to the value that would be substituted in x for a corresponding **rep** construct. Thus, a **rep** construct may as well be equivalently rewritten as a **share** construct as follows:

$$\text{rep}(e_1)\{(x) \Rightarrow e_2\} \longrightarrow \text{share}(e_1)\{(x) \Rightarrow e_2[x := \text{localHood}(x)]\}$$

where localHood is a built-in operator that given a neighboring field ϕ returns the value $\phi(\delta)$ for the current device.

   Whenever a field calculus program used x only as nbr$\{x\}$ inside the e_2 expression of a **rep**, however, the **share** construct can improve over **rep**. In this case, the following *non-equivalent* rewriting improves the communication speed of an algorithm, while preserving its computational efficiency and overall meaning:

$$\text{rep}(e_1)\{(x) \Rightarrow e_2[\text{nbr}\{x\}]\} \longrightarrow \text{share}(e_1)\{(x) \Rightarrow e_2[x]\}$$

In other words, **share** can be used to *automatically* improve communication speeds of algorithms. Many algorithms with more varied uses of x (e.g., using both x and nbr$\{x\}$ in e_2) can be similarly transformed into improved versions.

3.1   Typing and Operational Semantics

Formal typing and operational semantics for the **share** construct is presented in Fig. 3 (bottom frame), as an extension to the type system and semantics given in [36, Electronic Appendix]. The typing judgement $\mathcal{A} \vdash e : T$ is to be read "expression e has type T under the set of assumptions $\mathcal{A}$", where $\mathcal{A}$ is a set of assumptions of the form x : T giving type T to variable x. The typing rule [T-SHARE] requires e_1 and e_2 to have the same local (i.e. non-field) type L, assuming x to have the corresponding field type field(L), and assigns the same type L to the whole construct.

Value-trees and value-tree environments:

$$\theta ::= \mathtt{v}\langle \overline{\theta} \rangle \qquad\qquad\qquad\qquad\qquad\qquad\qquad\qquad \text{value-tree}$$

$$\Theta ::= \overline{\delta} \mapsto \overline{\theta} \qquad\qquad\qquad\qquad\qquad\qquad\qquad \text{value-tree environment}$$

Auxiliary functions:

$$\phi_0[\phi_1] = \phi_2 \quad \text{where} \quad \phi_2(\delta) = \begin{cases} \phi_1(\delta) \text{ if } \delta \in \mathbf{dom}(\phi_1) \\ \phi_0(\delta) \text{ otherwise} \end{cases}$$

$$\rho(\mathtt{v}\langle \overline{\theta} \rangle) = \mathtt{v}$$

$$\pi_i(\mathtt{v}\langle \theta_1, \ldots, \theta_n \rangle) = \theta_i \quad \text{if } 1 \le i \le n \qquad\qquad \pi_i(\theta) = \bullet \quad \text{otherwise}$$

$$\text{For } aux \in \rho, \pi_i : \begin{cases} aux(\delta \mapsto \theta) = \delta \mapsto aux(\theta) & \text{if } aux(\theta) \ne \bullet \\ aux(\delta \mapsto \theta) = \bullet & \text{if } aux(\theta) = \bullet \\ aux(\Theta, \Theta') = aux(\Theta), aux(\Theta') \end{cases}$$

Rules for typing and expression evaluation:

$$[\text{T-SHARE}] \quad \frac{\mathcal{A} \vdash \mathtt{e}_1 : L \qquad \mathcal{A}, \mathtt{x} : \mathtt{field}(L) \vdash \mathtt{e}_2 : L}{\mathcal{A} \vdash \mathtt{share}(\mathtt{e}_1)\{(\mathtt{x}) \Rightarrow \mathtt{e}_2\} : L}$$

$$[\text{E-SHARE}] \quad \frac{\delta; \pi_1(\Theta); \sigma \vdash \mathtt{e}_1 \Downarrow \theta_1 \qquad\qquad \phi' = \rho(\pi_2(\Theta))}{\delta; \pi_2(\Theta); \sigma \vdash \mathtt{e}_2[\mathtt{x} := \phi] \Downarrow \theta_2 \qquad \phi = (\delta \mapsto \rho(\theta_1))[\phi']}{\delta; \Theta; \sigma \vdash \mathtt{share}(\mathtt{e}_1)\{(\mathtt{x}) \Rightarrow \mathtt{e}_2\} \Downarrow \rho(\theta_2)\langle \theta_1, \theta_2 \rangle}$$

Fig. 3. Typing and operational semantics for the `share` construct.

Example 1 (Typing). Consider the body e of function `ever` as a paradigmatic example (with assumptions $\mathcal{A} = \mathtt{condition} : \mathtt{bool}$):

```
share (false) { (old) => anyHoodPlusSelf(old) || condition }
```

Clearly, $\mathcal{A} \vdash \mathtt{false} : \mathtt{bool}$. Assuming that `anyHoodPlusSelf` is a built-in of type $\mathtt{field}(\mathtt{bool}) \rightarrow \mathtt{bool}$, we can also conclude that:

$$\mathcal{A}, \mathtt{old} : \mathtt{field}(\mathtt{bool}) \vdash \mathtt{anyHoodPlusSelf(old)}||\mathtt{condition} : \mathtt{bool}.$$

It follows that $\mathcal{A} \vdash \mathtt{e} : \mathtt{bool}$.

The evaluation rule is based on the auxiliary functions given in Fig. 3 (middle frame). Function $\rho(\theta)$ extracts the root from a given value-tree, while function $\pi_i(\theta)$ selects the i-th sub-tree of the given value-tree. Both of them can be applied to value-tree environments Θ as well, obtaining a neighboring field (for ρ) or another value-tree environment (for π_i). Furthermore, we use the notation $\phi_0[\phi_1]$ to represent "field update", so that its result ϕ_2 has $\mathbf{dom}(\phi_2) = \mathbf{dom}(\phi_0) \cup \mathbf{dom}(\phi_1)$ and coincides with ϕ_1 on its domain, or with ϕ_0 otherwise.

The evaluation rule [E-SHARE] produces a value-tree with two branches (for $\mathtt{e}_1$ and $\mathtt{e}_2$ respectively). First, it evaluates $\mathtt{e}_1$ with respect to the corresponding branches of neighbors $\pi_1(\Theta)$ obtaining θ_1. Then, it collects the results for the construct from neighbors into the neighboring field $\phi' = \rho(\pi_2(\Theta))$. In case ϕ' does not have an entry for δ, $\rho(\theta_1)$ is used obtaining $\phi = (\delta \mapsto \rho(\theta_1))[\phi']$. Finally, ϕ is substituted for $\mathtt{x}$ in the evaluation of $\mathtt{e}_2$ (with respect to the corresponding branches of neighbors $\pi_2(\Theta)$) obtaining θ_2, setting $\rho(\theta_2)$ to be the overall value.

Example 2 (Operational Semantics). Consider the body of function `ever`:

```
share (false) { (old) => anyHoodPlusSelf(old) || condition }
```

Suppose that device $\delta = 0$ first executes a round of computation without neighbors (i.e. Θ is empty), and with `condition` equal to `false`. The evaluation of the `share` construct proceeds by evaluating `false` into $\theta_1 = $ `false`$\langle\rangle$, gathering neighbor values into $\phi' = \bullet$ (no values are present), and adding the value for the current device obtaining $\phi = (0 \mapsto $ `false`$)[\bullet] = 0 \mapsto $ `false`. Finally, the evaluation completes by storing in θ_2 the result of `anyHoodPlusSelf`$(0 \mapsto$ `false`$)||$`false` (which is `false`$\langle\ldots\rangle^2$). At the end of the round, device 0 sends a broadcast message containing the result of its overall evaluation, and thus including $\theta^0 = $ `false`$\langle$`false`, `false`$\langle\ldots\rangle\rangle$.

Suppose now that device $\delta = 1$ receives the broadcast message and then executes a round of computation where `condition` is `true`. The evaluation of the `share` constructs starts similarly as before with $\theta_1 = $ `false`$\langle\rangle$, $\phi' = 0 \mapsto$ `false`, $\phi = 0 \mapsto $ `false`, $1 \mapsto $ `false`. Then the body of the `share` is evaluated as `anyHoodPlusSelf`$(0 \mapsto$ `false`, $1 \mapsto$ `false`$)||$`true` into θ_2, which is `true`$\langle\ldots\rangle$. At the end of the round, device 1 broadcasts the result of its overall evaluation, including $\theta^1 = $ `true`$\langle$`false`, `true`$\langle\ldots\rangle\rangle$.

Then, suppose that device $\delta = 0$ receives the broadcast from device 1 and then performs another round of computation with `condition` equal to `false`. As before, $\theta_1 = $ `false`$\langle\rangle$, $\phi = \phi' = 0 \mapsto $ `false`, $1 \mapsto $ `true` and the body is evaluated as `anyHoodPlusSelf`$(0 \mapsto$ `false`, $1 \mapsto$ `true`$)||$`false` which produces `true`$\langle\ldots\rangle$ for an overall result of $\theta^2 = $ `true`$\langle$`false`, `true`$\langle\ldots\rangle\rangle$.

Finally, suppose that device $\delta = 1$ does not receive that broadcast and discards 0 from its list of neighbor before performing another round of computation with `condition` equal to `false`. Then, $\theta_1 = $ `false`$\langle\rangle$, $\phi' = 1 \mapsto $ `true`, $\phi = (1 \mapsto $ `false`$)[1 \mapsto $ `true`$] = 1 \mapsto $ `true`, and the body is evaluated as `anyHoodPlusSelf`$(1 \mapsto $ `true`$)||$`false` which produces `true`$\langle\ldots\rangle$.

3.2   The share Construct Improves Communication Speed

To illustrate how `share` solves the problem illustrated in Sect. 2.3, let us once again consider the `ever` function discussed in that section, for propagating when a `condition` Boolean has ever become true. With the `share` construct, we can finally write a fully functional implementation of `ever` as follows:

```
def ever(condition) {
   share (false) { (old) => anyHoodPlusSelf(old) || condition }
}
```

Function `ever` is simultaneously *(i)* compact and readable, even more so than `ever1` and `ever2` (note that we no longer need to include the `nbr` construct); *(ii)* lightweight, as it involves the communication of a single Boolean value each

---

[2] We omit the part of the value tree that are produced by semantic rules not included in this paper, and refer to [36, Electronic Appendix] for the missing parts.

round and few operations; and *(iii)* optimally efficient in communication speed, since it is true for any event ϵ with a causal predecessor $\epsilon' \leq \epsilon$ where `condition` was true. In particular

- in such an event ϵ' the overall `share` construct is true, since it does so `anyHoodPlusSelf(old) || true` regardless of the values in `old` ;
- in any subsequent event ϵ'' (i.e. $\epsilon' \rightsquigarrow \epsilon''$) the `share` construct is true since `old` contains a true value (the one coming from ϵ'), and
- the same holds for further following events ϵ by inductive arguments.

In field calculus alone, such optimal communication speed can be achieved only through unbounded recursion, as argued in [2] and reviewed above in Sect. 2.3.

The average improvement in communication speed of a routine being converted from the usage of `rep` + `nbr` to `share` according to the rewriting proposed at the beginning of this section can also be statistically estimated, depending on the communication pattern used by the routine.

An algorithm follows a *single-path* communication pattern if its outcome in an event depends essentially on the value of a single selected neighbor: prototypical examples of such algorithms are distance estimations [4–6], which are computed out of the value of the single neighbor on the optimal path to the source. In this case, letting T be the average interval between subsequent rounds, the communication delay of an hop is $T/2$ with `share` (since it can randomly vary from 0 to T) and $T/2 + T = 3/2T$ with `rep` + `nbr` (since a full additional round T is wasted in this case). Thus, the usage of `share` allows for an expected three-fold improvement in communication speed for these algorithms.

An algorithm follows a *multi-path* communication pattern if its outcome in an event is obtained from the values of all neighbors: prototypical examples of such algorithms are data collections [3], especially when they are idempotent (e.g. minimums or maximums). In this case, the existence of a single communication path $\epsilon_0 \rightsquigarrow \ldots \rightsquigarrow \epsilon$ is sufficient for the value in ϵ_0 to be taken into account in ϵ. Even though the delay of any one of such paths follows the same distribution as for single-path algorithms (0 to T per step with `share`, T to $2T$ per step with `rep` + `nbr`), the overall delay is *minimized* among each existing path. It follows that for sufficiently large numbers of paths, the delay is closer to the minimum of a single hop (0 with `share`, T with `rep` + `nbr`) resulting in an even larger improvement.

4   Application and Empirical Validation

Having developed the `share` construct and shown that it should be able to significantly improve the performance of field calculus programs, we have also applied this development by extending the Protelis [34] implementation of field calculus to support `share` (the implementation is a simple addition of another keyword and accompanying implementation code following the semantics expressed above). We have further upgraded every function in the `protelis-lang` library [19] with an applicable `rep/nbr` combination to use the

share construct instead, thereby also improving every program that makes use of these libraries of resilient functions. To validate the efficacy of both our analysis and its applied implementation, we empirically validate the improvements in performance for a number of these upgraded functions in simulation.

4.1 Evaluation Setup

We experimentally validate the improvements of the **share** construct through two simulation examples. In both, we deploy a number of mobile devices, computing rounds asynchronously at a frequency of 1 ± 0.1 Hz, and communicating within a range of 75 m. All aggregate programs have been written in Protelis [34] and simulations performed in the Alchemist environment [33]. All the results reported in this paper are the average of 200 simulations with different seeds, which lead to different initial device locations, different waypoint generation, and different round frequency. Data generated by the simulator has been processed with Xarray [24] and matplotlib [25]. For the sake of brevity, we do not report the actual code in this paper; however, to guarantee the complete reproducibility of the experiments, the execution of the experiment has been entirely automated, and all the resources have been made publicly available along with instructions.[3]

In the first scenario, we position 2000 mobile devices into a corridor room with sides of, respectively, 200 m and 2000 m. All but two of the devices are free to move within the corridor randomly, while the remaining two are "sources" that are fixed and located at opposite ends of the corridor. At every point of time, only one of the two sources is active, switching at 80 s and 200 s (i.e., the active one gets disabled, the disabled one is re-enabled). Devices are programmed to compute a field yielding everywhere the farthest distance from any device to the current active source. In order to do so, they execute the following commonly used coordination algorithms:

1. they compute a potential field measuring the distance from the active source through BIS [6] (`bisGradient` routine in `protelis:coord:spreading`);
2. they accumulate the maximum distance value descending the potential towards the source, through Parametric Weighted Multi-Path C [3] (an optimized version of C in `protelis:coord:accumulation`);
3. they broadcast the information along the potential, from the source to every other device in the system (an optimized version of the `broadcast` algorithm found in `protelis:coord:spreading`, which tags values from the source with a timestamp and propagates them by selecting more recent values).

The choice of the algorithms to be used in validation revealed to be critical. The usage of **share** is able to directly improve the performance of algorithms with solid theoretical guarantees; however, it may also exacerbate errors and instabilities for more ad-hoc algorithms, by allowing them to propagate quicker and more freely, preventing (or slowing down) the stabilization of the algorithm result whenever the network configuration and input is not constant. Of the

---

[3] https://bitbucket.org/danysk/experiment-2019-coordination-aggregate-share/.

set of available algorithms for spreading and collecting data, we thus selected variants with smoother recovery from perturbation: optimal single-path distance estimation (BIS gradient [6]), optimal multi-path broadcast [36], and the latest version of data collection (parametric weighted multi-path [3], fine-tuning the weight function).

We are interested in measuring the error of each step (namely, in distance vs. the true values), together with the lag through which these values were generated (namely, by propagating a time-stamp together with values, and computing the difference with the current time). Moreover, we want to inspect how the improvements introduced by share accumulate across the composition of algorithms. To do so, we measure the error in two conditions: (i) composite behavior, in which each step is fed the result computed by the previous step, and (ii) individual behavior, in which each step is fed an ideal result for the previous step, as provided by an oracle.

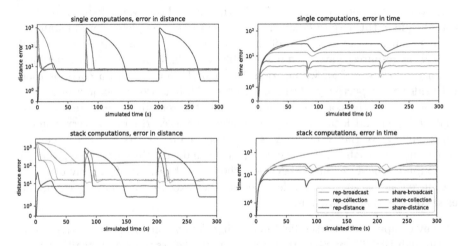

Fig. 4. Performance in the corridor scenario, for both individual algorithms (top) and the composite computation (bottom). Vertical axis is linear in $[0, 1]$ and logarithmic above. Charts on the left column show distance error, while the right column shows time error. The versions of the algorithms implemented with share (warm colors) produce significantly less error and converge significantly faster in case of large disruptions than with rep (cold colors). (Color figure online)

Figure 4 shows the results from this scenario. Observing the behavior of the individual computations, it is immediately clear how the share-based version of the algorithm provides faster recovery from network input discontinuities and lower errors at the limit. These effects are exacerbated when multiple algorithms are composed to build aggregate applications. The only counterexample is the limit of distance estimations, for which rep is marginally better, with a relative error less than 1% lower than that of share.

Moreover, notice that the collection algorithm with `rep` was not able to recover from changes at all, as shown by the linearly increasing delay in time (and the absence of spikes in distance error). The known weakness of multi-path collection strategies, that is, failing to react to changes due to the creation of information loops, proved to be much more relevant and invalidating with `rep` than with **share**.

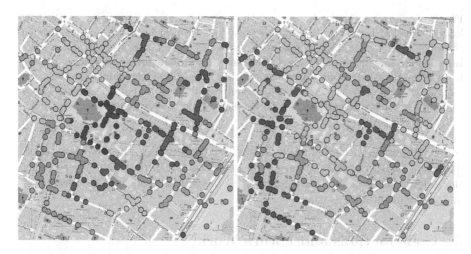

Fig. 5. Snapshots of the Voronoi partitioning scenario using **share** (left) or `rep` (right). Colored dots are simulated devices, with each region having a different color. Faster communication with **share** leads to a higher accuracy in distance estimation, allowing the **share** implementation to perform a better division into regions and preventing regions from expanding beyond their limits. (Color figure online)

In the second example, we deploy 500 devices in a city center, and let them move as though being carried by pedestrians, moving at walking speed $(1.4\frac{m}{s})$ towards random waypoints along roads open to pedestrian traffic (using map data from OpenStreetMaps [23]). In this scenario, devices must self-organize service management regions with a radius of at most 200 m, creating a Voronoi partition as shown in Fig. 5 (functions `S` and `voronoiPatitioningWithMetric` from `protelis:coord:sparsechoice`). We evaluate performance by measuring the number of partitions generated by the algorithm, and the average and maximum node distance error, where the error for a node n measures how far a node is beyond of the maximum boundary for its cluster. This is computed as $\epsilon_n = \max(0, d(n, l_n) - r)$, where d computes the distance between two devices, l_n is the leader for the cluster n belongs to, and r is the maximum allowed radius of the cluster.

Figure 6 shows the results from this scenario, which also confirm the benefits of faster communication with **share**. The algorithm implemented with **share** has much lower error, mainly due to faster convergence of the distance estimates, and

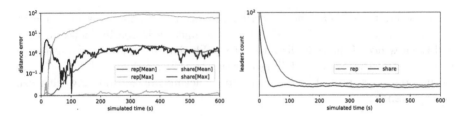

Fig. 6. Performance in the Voronoi partition scenario: error in distance on the left, leaders count with time on the right. Vertical axis is linear in $[0, 0.1]$ and logarithmic elsewhere. The version implemented with `share` has much lower error: the mean error is negligible, and the most incorrect value, after an initial convergence phase, is close to two orders of magnitude lower than with `rep`, as faster communication leads to more accurate distance estimates. The leader count shows that the systems create a comparable number of partitions, with the `share`-based featuring faster convergence.

consequent higher accuracy in measuring the distance from the partition leader. Simultaneously, it creates a marginally lower number of partitions, by reducing the amount of occasional single-device regions which arise during convergence and re-organization.

5   Contributions and Future Work

We have introduced a novel `share` construct whose introduction allows a significant acceleration of field calculus programs. We have also made this construct available for use in applications though an extension of the Protelis field calculus implementation and its accompanying libraries, and have empirically validated the expected improvements in performance through experiments in simulation.

In future work, we plan to study for which algorithms the usage of `share` may lead to increased instability, thus fine-tuning the choice of `rep` and `nbr` over `share` in the Protelis library. Furthermore, we intend to fully analyze the consequences of `share` for improvement of space-time universality [2], self-adaption [12], and variants of the semantics [7] of the field calculus. It also appears likely that the field calculus can be simplified by the elimination of both `rep` and `nbr` by finding a mapping by which `share` can also be used to implement any usage of `nbr`. Finally, we believe that the improvements in performance will also have positive consequences for nearly all current and future applications that are making use of the field calculus and its implementations and derivatives.

Acknowledgements. We thank the anonymous COORDINATION referees for their comments and suggestions on improving the presentation.

References

1. Ashley-Rollman, M.P., Goldstein, S.C., Lee, P., Mowry, T.C., Pillai, P.: Meld: a declarative approach to programming ensembles. In: IEEE International Conference on Intelligent Robots and Systems (IROS 2007), pp. 2794–2800 (2007). https://doi.org/10.1109/IROS.2007.4399480
2. Audrito, G., Beal, J., Damiani, F., Viroli, M.: Space-time universality of field calculus. In: Di Marzo Serugendo, G., Loreti, M. (eds.) COORDINATION 2018. LNCS, vol. 10852, pp. 1–20. Springer, Cham (2018). https://doi.org/10.1007/978-3-319-92408-3_1
3. Audrito, G., Bergamini, S., Damiani, F., Viroli, M.: Effective collective summarisation of distributed data in mobile multi-agent systems. In: International Conference on Autonomous Agents and Multiagent Systems (AAMAS), pp. 1618–1626. ACM (2019). https://dl.acm.org/citation.cfm?id=3331882
4. Audrito, G., Casadei, R., Damiani, F., Viroli, M.: Compositional blocks for optimal self-healing gradients. In: 11th International Conference on Self-Adaptive and Self-Organizing Systems (SASO 2017), pp. 91–100. IEEE (2017). https://doi.org/10.1109/SASO.2017.18
5. Audrito, G., Damiani, F., Viroli, M.: Optimally-self-healing distributed gradient structures through bounded information speed. In: Jacquet, J.-M., Massink, M. (eds.) COORDINATION 2017. LNCS, vol. 10319, pp. 59–77. Springer, Cham (2017). https://doi.org/10.1007/978-3-319-59746-1_4
6. Audrito, G., Damiani, F., Viroli, M.: Optimal single-path information propagation in gradient-based algorithms. Sci. Comput. Program. **166**, 146–166 (2018). https://doi.org/10.1016/j.scico.2018.06.002
7. Audrito, G., Damiani, F., Viroli, M., Casadei, R.: Run-time management of computation domains in field calculus. In: 1st International Workshops on Foundations and Applications of Self* Systems (FAS*W), pp. 192–197. IEEE (2016). https://doi.org/10.1109/FAS-W.2016.50
8. Audrito, G., Viroli, M., Damiani, F., Pianini, D., Beal, J.: A higher-order calculus of computational fields. ACM Trans. Comput. Logic (TOCL) **20**(1), 5:1–5:55 (2019). https://doi.org/10.1145/3285956
9. Beal, J., Bachrach, J.: Infrastructure for engineered emergence in sensor/actuator networks. IEEE Intell. Syst. **21**, 10–19 (2006). https://doi.org/10.1109/MIS.2006.29
10. Beal, J., Dulman, S., Usbeck, K., Viroli, M., Correll, N.: Organizing the aggregate: languages for spatial computing. In: Formal and Practical Aspects of Domain-Specific Languages: Recent Developments, chap. 16, pp. 436–501. IGI Global (2013). https://doi.org/10.4018/978-1-4666-2092-6.ch01
11. Beal, J., Pianini, D., Viroli, M.: Aggregate programming for the internet of things. IEEE Comput. **48**(9), 22–30 (2015). https://doi.org/10.1109/MC.2015.261
12. Beal, J., Viroli, M., Pianini, D., Damiani, F.: Self-adaptation to device distribution in the internet of things. ACM Trans. Auton. Adapt. Syst. (TAAS) **12**(3), 12:1–12:29 (2017). https://doi.org/10.1145/3105758
13. Butera, W.: Programming a paintable computer. Ph.D. thesis, MIT, Cambridge, USA (2002)
14. Church, A.: A set of postulates for the foundation of logic. Ann. Math. **33**(2), 346–366 (1932). https://doi.org/10.2307/1968337
15. Clement, L., Nagpal, R.: Self-assembly and self-repairing topologies. In: Workshop on Adaptability in Multi-Agent Systems, RoboCup Australian Open (2003)

16. Coore, D.: Botanical computing: a developmental approach to generating inter connect topologies on an amorphous computer. Ph.D. thesis, MIT, Cambridge, MA, USA (1999)
17. Curino, C., Giani, M., Giorgetta, M., Giusti, A., Murphy, A.L., Picco, G.P.: Mobile data collection in sensor networks: the tinylime middleware. Elsevier Pervasive Mob. Comput. J. **4**, 446–469 (2005). https://doi.org/10.1016/j.pmcj.2005.08.003
18. Dean, J., Ghemawat, S.: MapReduce: simplified data processing on large clusters. Commun. ACM **51**(1), 107–113 (2008). https://doi.org/10.1145/1327452.1327492
19. Francia, M., Pianini, D., Beal, J., Viroli, M.: Towards a foundational API for resilient distributed systems design. In: 2017 IEEE 2nd International Workshops on Foundations and Applications of Self* Systems (FAS* W), pp. 27–32. IEEE (2017). https://doi.org/10.1109/FAS-W.2017.116
20. Giavitto, J.L., Godin, C., Michel, O., Prusinkiewicz, P.: Computational models for integrative and developmental biology. Technical report, 72–2002, U. d'Evry, LaMI (2002)
21. Giavitto, J.-L., Michel, O., Cohen, J., Spicher, A.: Computations in space and space in computations. In: Banâtre, J.-P., Fradet, P., Giavitto, J.-L., Michel, O. (eds.) UPP 2004. LNCS, vol. 3566, pp. 137–152. Springer, Heidelberg (2005). https://doi.org/10.1007/11527800_11
22. Gummadi, R., Gnawali, O., Govindan, R.: Macro-programming wireless sensor networks using *Kairos*. In: Prasanna, V.K., Iyengar, S.S., Spirakis, P.G., Welsh, M. (eds.) DCOSS 2005. LNCS, vol. 3560, pp. 126–140. Springer, Heidelberg (2005). https://doi.org/10.1007/11502593_12
23. Haklay, M., Weber, P.: OpenStreetMap: user-generated street maps. IEEE Pervasive Comput. **7**(4), 12–18 (2008). https://doi.org/10.1109/MPRV.2008.80
24. Hoyer, S., Hamman, J.: xarray: N-D labeled arrays and datasets in Python. J. Open Res. Softw. **5**(1), 10 (2017). https://doi.org/10.5334/jors.148
25. Hunter, J.D.: Matplotlib: a 2D graphics environment. Comput. Sci. Eng. **9**(3), 90–95 (2007). https://doi.org/10.1109/MCSE.2007.55
26. Kondacs, A.: Biologically-inspired self-assembly of 2D shapes, using global-to-local compilation. In: International Joint Conference on Artificial Intelligence (IJCAI), pp. 633–638. Morgan Kaufmann Publishers Inc. (2003)
27. Lasser, C., Massar, J., Miney, J., Dayton, L.: Starlisp Reference Manual. Thinking Machines Corporation (1988)
28. Madden, S., Franklin, M.J., Hellerstein, J.M., Hong, W.: TAG: a tiny AGgregation service for ad-hoc sensor networks. SIGOPS Oper. Syst. Rev. **36**, 131–146 (2002). https://doi.org/10.1145/844128.844142
29. Mamei, M., Zambonelli, F.: Programming pervasive and mobile computing applications: the tota approach. ACM Trans. Softw. Eng. Methodol. (TOSEM) **18**(4), 1–56 (2009). https://doi.org/10.1145/1538942.1538945
30. Milner, R., Parrow, J., Walker, D.: A calculus of mobile processes, part I. Inf. Comput. **100**(1), 1–40 (1992). https://doi.org/10.1016/0890-5401(92)90008-4
31. Nagpal, R.: Programmable self-assembly: constructing global shape using biologically-inspired local interactions and origami mathematics. Ph.D. thesis, MIT, Cambridge, MA, USA (2001)
32. Newton, R., Welsh, M.: Region streams: functional macroprogramming for sensor networks. In: Workshop on Data Management for Sensor Networks, DMSN 2004, pp. 78–87. ACM (2004). https://doi.org/10.1145/1052199.1052213
33. Pianini, D., Montagna, S., Viroli, M.: Chemical-oriented simulation of computational systems with ALCHEMIST. J. Simul. **7**(3), 202–215 (2013). https://doi.org/10.1057/jos.2012.27

34. Pianini, D., Viroli, M., Beal, J.: Protelis: practical aggregate programming. In: ACM Symposium on Applied Computing 2015, pp. 1846–1853 (2015). https://doi.org/10.1145/2695664.2695913

35. Valiant, L.G.: A bridging model for parallel computation. Commun. ACM **33**(8), 103–111 (1990). https://doi.org/10.1145/79173.79181

36. Viroli, M., Audrito, G., Beal, J., Damiani, F., Pianini, D.: Engineering resilient collective adaptive systems by self-stabilisation. ACM Trans. Model. Comput. Simul. (TOMACS) **28**(2), 16:1–16:28 (2018). https://doi.org/10.1145/3177774

37. Viroli, M., Beal, J., Damiani, F., Audrito, G., Casadei, R., Pianini, D.: From field-based coordination to aggregate computing. In: Di Marzo Serugendo, G., Loreti, M. (eds.) COORDINATION 2018. LNCS, vol. 10852, pp. 252–279. Springer, Cham (2018). https://doi.org/10.1007/978-3-319-92408-3_12

38. Viroli, M., Pianini, D., Montagna, S., Stevenson, G., Zambonelli, F.: A coordination model of pervasive service ecosystems. Sci. Comput. Program. **110**, 3–22 (2015). https://doi.org/10.1016/j.scico.2015.06.003

39. Whitehouse, K., Sharp, C., Brewer, E., Culler, D.: Hood: a neighborhood abstraction for sensor networks. In: Proceedings of the 2nd International Conference on Mobile Systems, Applications, and Services. ACM Press (2004). https://doi.org/10.1145/990064.990079

40. Yamins, D.: A theory of local-to-global algorithms for one-dimensional spatial multi-agent systems. Ph.D. thesis, Harvard, Cambridge, MA, USA (2007). https://doi.org/10.1145/601858.601861

41. Yao, Y., Gehrke, J.: The cougar approach to in-network query processing in sensor networks. SIGMOD Rec. **31**, 9–18 (2002)

Tools (1)

Scan: A Simple Coordination Workbench

Jean-Marie Jacquet$^{(\boxtimes)}$ ⓘ and Manel Barkallah ⓘ

Nadi Research Institute, Faculty of Computer Science,
University of Namur, Rue Grandgagnage 21, 5000 Namur, Belgium
{jean-marie.jacquet,manel.barkallah}@unamur.be

Abstract. Although many research efforts have been spent on the theory and implementation of data-based coordination languages, not much effort has been devoted to constructing programming environments to analyze and reason on programs written in these languages. This paper proposes a simple workbench for describing concurrent systems using a Linda-like language, for animating them and for reasoning on them using a fragment of linear temporal logic. In contrast to some tools developed for traditional process algebras like CCS, a key feature of our workbench is that it maintains a direct relation between what is written by the user and its internal representation in the workbench. Another feature, particularly useful for didactic purposes, is the production of trace examples, replayable, when LTL formulae are satisfied.

Keywords: Coordination · Bach · Animation · Verification

1 Introduction

In the aim of building interactive distributed systems, a clear separation between the interactional and the computational aspects of software components has been advocated by Gelernter and Carriero in [14]. Their claim has been supported by the design of a model, Linda [4], originally presented as a set of inter-agent communication primitives which may be added to almost any programming language. Besides process creation, this set includes primitives for adding, deleting, and testing the presence/absence of data in a shared dataspace.

A number of other models, now referred to as coordination models, have been proposed afterwards. The authors have themselves contributed to that trend of research, as exemplified for instance in [1,2,7–10,15,17,21–23]. However, although many pieces of work (including ours) have been devoted to the proposal of new languages, semantics and implementations, few articles have addressed the concerns of practically constructing programs in coordination languages, in particular in checking that what is described by programs actually corresponds to what has to be modeled.

Based on previous work by the first author on a Linda-like dialect, named Bach, this paper aims at introducing a workbench to reason on programs written in Bach extended with several facilities. More specifically, our goal is threefold:

© IFIP International Federation for Information Processing 2019
Published by Springer Nature Switzerland AG 2019
H. Riis Nielson and E. Tuosto (Eds.): COORDINATION 2019, LNCS 11533, pp. 75–91, 2019.
https://doi.org/10.1007/978-3-030-22397-7_5

 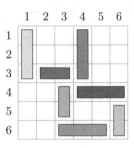

Fig. 1. Rush Hour Problem. On the left part, the game as illustrated at https://www.michaelfogleman.com/rush. On the right part, the game modeled as a grid of 6×6, with cars and trucks depicted as rectangles of different colors. (Color figure online)

– to allow the user to understand the meaning of instructions written in Bach, by showing how they can be executed step by step and how the contents of the shared space, central to coordination languages, can be modified so as to release suspended processes;
– to allow the user to better grasp the modeling of real-life systems in Bach, by connecting agents in Bach to animations, representing the evolution of the modeled system;
– to allow the user to check properties by model checking temporal logic formulae and by producing traces that can be replayed as evidences of the establishment of the formulae.

In building the workbench, we also aim at two main properties:

– the tool should be simple to deploy and to use. As a result, we shall build it as a standalone executable file launched by a simple command line. We shall also propose a simple process algebra that allows the user to concentrate on the key coordination and animation features and consequently avoid him the burden of handling extra features typically required by sophisticated commercial systems;
– the tool should maintain a direct relation between what is written by the user and its internal representation. This property allows the user to better grasp what is actually computed as well as to produce meaningful traces.

To make our developments more concrete, we shall use the rush hour puzzle as a running example. This game, illustrated in Fig. 1, consists in moving cars and trucks on a 6×6 grid, according to their direction, such that the red car can exit. It can be formulated as a coordination problem by considering cars and trucks as autonomous agents which have to coordinate on the basis of free places.

The rest of this paper is organized as follows. Section 2 describes the functionalities of Scan and, in doing so, provides an overview of the tool. Section 3 specifies the coordination language and temporal logic to be used in the tool. Section 4 sketches how Scan is implemented. Section 5 compares our work with

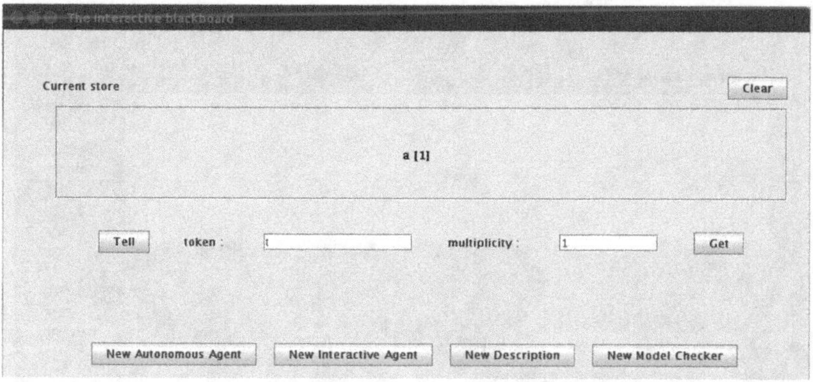

Fig. 2. The interactive blackboard window

related work. Finally, Sect. 6 draws our conclusion and suggests future work. For illustration purposes, a video demonstrating the use of Scan is available at https://staff.info.unamur.be/jmj/Scan/. A link is also proposed there to download the workbench.

2   Scan Design and Overview

Following Linda, the Bach language relies on a shared space to coordinate processes. It is this space that provides the decoupling of time and space of processes which is central to so-called data-based coordination languages [26]. As a natural consequence, following the blackboard metaphor [13], according to which a group of specialists iteratively updates knowledge on a blackboard starting from a problem specification, Scan is articulated around a so-called interactive blackboard. As depicted in Fig. 2, it starts by displaying the current contents of the shared space and allows to interact directly through the tell, get and clear buttons. Moreover, it offers to create four types of processes.

The first two processes, named respectively *Autonomous Agent* and *Interactive Agent*, allow the user to enter instructions in Bach and to execute them. As depicted in part (a) of Fig. 3, windows of the first kind, perform computations step-by-step by letting the user choose which primitives to execute. In contrast, as shown in part (b) of Fig. 3, windows of the second type execute computations in one run if the run button is activated or step by step if the next button is selected but in both cases with the Scan workbench deciding (in a random manner) the primitives to be executed. It is worth noting that the execution in the windows are made in a parallel fashion, hence the name *agent* to indicate entities capable of concurrent activities.

The facilities offered by the interactive and autonomous agents are nice to debug, at a low level, concurrent executions executed around the shared space, possibly deadlocking on data not being available. However, they do not provide much insights on whether what is described in Bach really reflects what

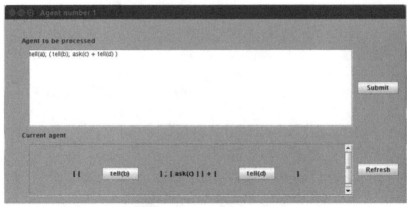

(a) The interactive agent window

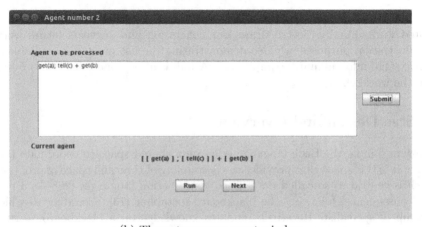

(b) The autonomous agent window

Fig. 3. Interacting with the blackboard

the programmer intends to model. Moreover, they provide too many details on the main execution steps leading to a solution of the problem under consideration. To that end, Scan provides animations through a third kind of processes launched by the new description button (see Fig. 2). As shown in part (a) of Fig. 4, such animations are obtained by describing a so-called scene from a set of pictures which are handled by means of primitives for inserting them on the scene at specific places, making them visible or invisible, and making them move to specific places. In doing so, these primitives allow to draw and animate, at a high-level, pictures such as the one of part (b) of Fig. 4. Note that, as these primitives may be inserted inside instructions of autonomous agents, the concurrent execution of these agents provides dynamic simulations of the problem under consideration.

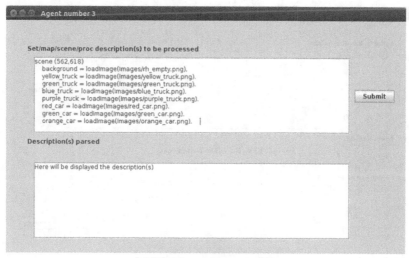

(a) The description window

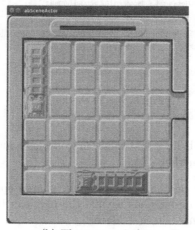

(b) The scene window

Fig. 4. Animation

Although nice, simulating graphically systems does not necessarily provide a solution to the problem under consideration. The rush hour problem is a clear example of that. To that end, the Scan workbench offers a fourth type of processes, materialized by the **new model checker** button of Fig. 2 which generates windows of the type depicted in Fig. 5. As illustrated in this figure, Scan allows to verify formulae written in a fragment of linear temporal logic, to determine traces of execution that establish the formulae and to replay these traces, including the primitives that generate animations.

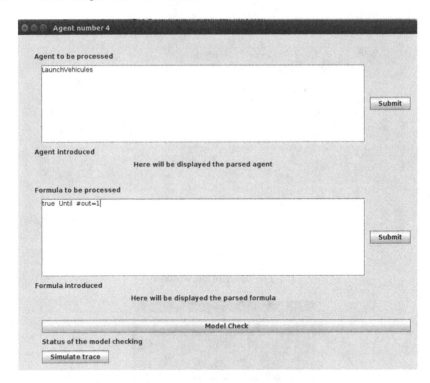

Fig. 5. Model-checking

Although simple we believe that the Scan workbench meets the threefold goal expressed in the introduction:

- by providing a view on the contents of the shared space and by means of the interactive and autonomous agents, the user can better understand the execution of programs written in Bach;
- the animation facilities provide a high-level view on what is actually computed as well as an intuitive perception of the modeling of the problem under consideration;
- the model checker facilities allow to check properties and, by using animation facilities, to replay executions graphically as a form of visual proofs.

3   The Anim-Bach Language and Its Temporal Logic

The facilities offered by Scan being described, let us turn to the process algebra to be used in the workbench. This algebra is subsequently referred to as Anim-Bach.

3.1   Definition of Data

Following Linda, the Bach language [10, 16] uses four primitives for manipulating pieces of information: *tell* to put a piece of information on a shared space, *ask* to check its presence, *nask* to check its absence and *get* to check its presence and remove one occurrence. In its simplest version, named BachT, pieces of information consist of atomic tokens and the shared space, called the store, amounts to a multiset of tokens. Although in principle sufficient to code many applications, this is however too elementary in practice to code them easily. To that end, we introduce more structured pieces of information which may employ sets defined by the user. Concretely, such sets are defined by associating an identifier with an enumeration of elements, such as in

```
set  Cols = { 1,  2,  3,  4,  5,  6}.
     Rows = { 1,  2,  3,  4,  5,  6}.
```

As the reader will have easily noticed, these two sets allow to identify an element of the grid of the rush hour example by using the row and column coordinates. We shall subsequently take the convention that the upper leftmost element of the grid is on the first row and on the first column.

The fact that sets are written as enumerations reflects the fact that the elements are naturally ordered by their order of appearance, which then allows to compare them. Moreover, they implicitly define the **pred** and **succ** functions, providing respectively the predecessors and successors of elements (if any).

In addition to sets, maps can be defined between them as functions that take zero or more arguments. In practice, Scan uses mapping equations as rewriting rules, from left to right in the aim of progressively reducing a complex map expression into a set element.

As an example of a map, assuming that trucks take three cells and are identified by the upper and left-most cell they occupy, the operation down_truck determines the cell to be taken by a truck moving down:

```
map down_truck  :  Rows -> Rows.
eqn down_truck(1) = 4. down_truck(2) = 5. down_truck(3) = 6.
```

Note from this example that mappings may be partially defined, with the responsibility put on the programmer to use them only when defined.

Structured pieces of information to be placed on the store consist of flat tokens as well as expressions of the form $f(a_1, \cdots, a_n)$ where f is a functor and $a_1, \ldots, a_n$ are set elements. As an example, in the rush hour example, it is convenient to represent the free places of the game as pieces of information of the form free(i,j) with i a row and j a column.

In summary of this subsection, we may assume subsequently to be defined a series of sets, a series of mappings, and a set of structured pieces of information, say $\mathcal{I}$. Thanks to the mapping definitions, we additionally assume a rewriting relation $\rightsquigarrow$ that rewrites any mapping expression into a set element. With this defined, we can proceed with the definition of agents in Anim-Bach.

3.2   Agents

The primitives of Anim-Bach consist of the `tell`, `ask`, `nask` and `get` primitives already mentioned for Bach, which take as arguments elements of $\mathcal{I}$. They can be composed to form more complex agents by using traditional composition operators from concurrency theory: sequential composition, parallel composition and non-deterministic choice. We add another mechanism: conditional statements of the form $c \rightarrow s_1 \diamond s_2$, which computes s_1 if c evaluates to true or s_2 otherwise. Conditions of type c are obtained from elementary ones, thanks to the classical and, or and negation operators, denoted respectively by &, | and !. Elementary conditions are obtained by relating set elements or mappings on them by equalities (denoted =) or inequalities (denoted =, <, <=, >, >=).

This being given, the statements of the Anim-Bach language, also called agents by abuse of language, consist of the statements A generated by the following grammar:

$$A ::= Prim \mid Proc \mid A \; ; \; A \mid A \parallel A \mid A + A \mid C \rightarrow A \diamond A$$

where $Prim$ represents a primitive, $Proc$ a procedure call and C a condition.

Procedures are defined similarly to mappings through the `proc` keyword by associating an agent with a procedure name. As in classical concurrency theory, we assume that the defining agents are guarded, in the sense that any call to a procedure is preceded by the execution of a primitive or can be rewritten in such a form.

As an example, the behavior of a vertical truck can be described as follows:

```
proc VerticalTruck(r: Rows, c: Cols) =
 ( (r>1 & r<5) -> ( get(free(pred(r),c)); tell(free(succ(r),c);
                    VerticalTruck(pred(r),c) )
 +
 ( (r<5) -> ( get(free(down_truck(r),c)); tell(free(r,c));
              VerticalTruck(succ(r),c)) ).
```

The operational semantics of primitives and complex agents are respectively defined through the transition rules of Figs. 6 and 7. Configurations consist of agents (summarizing the current state of the agents running on the store) and a multi-set of structured pieces of information (denoting the current state of the store). In order to express the termination of the computation of an agent, the set of agents is extended by a special terminating symbol E that can be seen as a completely computed agent. For uniformity purposes, we abuse the language by qualifying E as an agent. To meet the intuition, we shall always rewrite agents of the form $(E; A)$, $(E \parallel A)$ and $(A \parallel E)$ as A.

The rules of Fig. 6 follow the intuitive description of the primitives. Note however that before being processed, a structured piece of information t is rewritten in u by means of the rewriting relation $\leadsto$.

The rules of Fig. 7 are quite classical. Rules (S), (P) and (C) provide the usual semantics for sequential, parallel and choice compositions. As expected, rule (Co) specifies that the conditional instruction $C \rightarrow A \diamond B$ behaves as A if

$$(\mathbf{T}) \quad \frac{t \rightsquigarrow u}{\langle \, tell(t) \mid \sigma \, \rangle \longrightarrow \langle \, E \mid \sigma \cup \{u\} \, \rangle}$$

$$(\mathbf{A}) \quad \frac{t \rightsquigarrow u}{\langle \, ask(t) \mid \sigma \cup \{u\} \, \rangle \longrightarrow \langle \, E \mid \sigma \cup \{u\} \, \rangle}$$

$$(\mathbf{G}) \quad \frac{t \rightsquigarrow u}{\langle \, get(t) \mid \sigma \cup \{u\} \, \rangle \longrightarrow \langle \, E \mid \sigma \, \rangle}$$

$$(\mathbf{N}) \quad \frac{t \rightsquigarrow u, u \notin \sigma}{\langle \, nask(t) \mid \sigma \, \rangle \longrightarrow \langle \, E \mid \sigma \, \rangle}$$

Fig. 6. Transition rules for the primitives

condition C can be evaluated to true and as B otherwise. Note that the notation $\models C$ is used to denote the fact that C evaluates to true. Finally, rule (Pc) makes procedure call $P(\overline{u})$ behave as the agent A defining procedure P with the formal arguments $\overline{x}$ replaced by the actual ones $\overline{u}$.

3.3   Animations

Animations are obtained in a twofold manner: on the one hand, by describing the scene to be painted and, on the other hand, by primitives to place images, to make them appear or disappear and to move them.

The description of a scene is obtained by defining the size of the canvas to be used by the animation, the background image of the animation and a series of images to be used. Such a definition takes the following form:

```
scene (640,640)
    background = loadImage(Images/the_background_img.png).
    red_car = loadImage(Images/rcar.jpg).
    yellow_truck = loadImage(Images/ytruck.gif).
```

where the file names are given with respect to the path in which Scan is executed.

Images are manipulated by means of the following primitives where coordinates are expressed in pixels with respect to the canvas, with $(0,0)$ being the upper-left corner of the canvas:

- `place_at(i,x,y)`: to place image identified by i at the coordinates (x, y)
- `move_to(i,x,y)`: to move image identified by i from its current position to the new coordinates (x, y)
- `hide(i)`: to hide image identified by i
- `show(i)`: to make appear image identified by i

Such primitives are added to the tell, get, nask and ask primitives in the definition of Anim-Bach.

$$(\textbf{S}) \quad \frac{\langle A \mid \sigma \rangle \longrightarrow \langle A' \mid \sigma' \rangle}{\langle A \,;\, B \mid \sigma \rangle \longrightarrow \langle A' \,;\, B \mid \sigma' \rangle}$$

$$(\textbf{P}) \quad \frac{\langle A \mid \sigma \rangle \longrightarrow \langle A' \mid \sigma' \rangle}{\begin{array}{c}\langle A \parallel B \mid \sigma \rangle \longrightarrow \langle A' \parallel B \mid \sigma' \rangle \\ \langle B \parallel A \mid \sigma \rangle \longrightarrow \langle B \parallel A' \mid \sigma' \rangle\end{array}}$$

$$(\textbf{C}) \quad \frac{\langle A \mid \sigma \rangle \longrightarrow \langle A' \mid \sigma' \rangle}{\begin{array}{c}\langle A + B \mid \sigma \rangle \longrightarrow \langle A' \mid \sigma' \rangle \\ \langle B + A \mid \sigma \rangle \longrightarrow \langle A' \mid \sigma' \rangle\end{array}}$$

$$(\textbf{Co}) \quad \frac{\models C,\ \langle A \mid \sigma \rangle \longrightarrow \langle A' \mid \sigma' \rangle}{\begin{array}{c}\langle C \to A \diamond B \mid \sigma \rangle \longrightarrow \langle A' \mid \sigma' \rangle \\ \langle !C \to B \diamond A \mid \sigma \rangle \longrightarrow \langle A' \mid \sigma' \rangle\end{array}}$$

$$(\textbf{Pc}) \quad \frac{P(\bar{x}) = A,\ \langle A[\bar{x}/\bar{u} \mid \sigma \rangle \longrightarrow \langle A' \mid \sigma' \rangle}{\langle P(\bar{u}) \mid \sigma \rangle \longrightarrow \langle A' \mid \sigma' \rangle}$$

Fig. 7. Transition rules for the operators

It is worth observing that the map constructs (introduced before) allow to declare coordinates in a symbolic manner making it easy to specify the position of images.

3.4 A Fragment of Temporal Logic

Linear temporal logic is a logic widely used to reason on dynamic systems. The Scan workbench uses a fragment of PLTL [12] with, as main goal, to check the reachability of states.

As usual, the logic employed relies on propositional state formulae. In our coordination context, these formulae are to be verified on the current contents of the store. Consequently, given a structured piece of information t, we introduce $\#t$ to denote the number of occurrences of t on the store and define as basic propositional formulae, equalities or inequalities combining algebraic expressions involving integers and number of occurrences of structured pieces of information. An example of such a basic formulae is $\#free(1,1) = 1$ which states that the cell of coordinates $(1,1)$ is free.

Propositional state formulae are built from these basic formulae by using the classical propositional connectors. As particular cases, we use *true* and *false* to denote propositional formulae that are respectively always true and false. Such formulae are in fact shorthands to denote respectively $p \vee \neg p$ and $p \wedge \neg p$, for some basic propositional formula p.

The fragment of temporal logic used in Scan is then defined by the following grammar:

$$TF ::= PF \mid Next\ TF \mid PF\ Until\ TF$$

where PF is a propositional formula. As will be explained in the next section, it has been designed so as to allow for an efficient implementation.

As an example, if the red car indicates that it leaves the grid by placing *out* on the store, a solution to the rush problem is obtained by verifying the formula

$$true\ Until\ (\#out = 1)$$

4 Implementation

The Scan workbench has been implemented in Scala [24] on top of the Processing library [27]. Scala is a programming language which combines the object-oriented and functional paradigms and benefits from strong static type systems. Scala source code is compiled to Java bytecode, which eases its interface with Java libraries. Moreover, Scala includes powerful parsing facilities. All these properties make it well-suited to interpret the Anim-Bach language, which as can be appreciated by the previous sections, can be easily described by recursive definitions.

Processing is a graphical library built to teach programming to artists in a visual context. Although it is generally used through a specific IDE, Processing can be employed as a Java library, which is the case for Scan. Processing is based on a key method, named `draw`, that is invoked several times per second (typically 60 times per second), which accordingly creates animations by modifying parameters such as the coordinates of images.

The page limit does not allow to enter deeply in the code of the implementation. However, the following subsections should allow the reader to understand the key elements of our implementation.

4.1 Internal Representation of Data

Scala case classes offer an elegant mechanism to represent data in an internal manner while keeping a close link to the textual representation in Anim-Bach. For instance, an abstract class AB_AG has been introduced to represent agents of Anim-Bach. Case classes have then been defined to represent particular agents, such as AB_AST_Empty_Agent() to represent the empty agent, AB_AST_Primitive(primitive: String, stinfo: AB_SI_ELM) to represent a primitive or AB_AST_Agent(op: String, agi: AB_AG, agii: AB_AG) to represent a composed agent using the operator op – for instance, || for the parallel composition – and two subagents agi and agii.

Other structures are used similarly to code sets, structured pieces of information, map equations, and temporal logic formulae.

As might be appreciated by this brief description, a close link is indeed made between the internal representation and the textual description in Anim-Bach. As a result, in contrast to tools such as mCRL2 [5], it is quite easy to provide the user with messages directly connected to what he has written.

4.2   Parsing Anim-Bach Constructs

As exposed in Chap. 33 of [24], Scala offers facilities to parse languages. The main ingredients to do so are, on the one hand, a library to define parsers, which basically allows to define the class AnimBachParsers as inherited from the class RegexParsers, parsing regular expressions, and the possibility of applying functions to the result of strings having been parsed.

4.3   The Store

The store is implemented as a mutable map in Scala. Initially empty, it is enriched for each told structured piece of information by an association of it to a number representing the number of its occurrences on the store. The implementation of the primitives follows directly from this intuition. For instance, the execution of a tell primitive, say tell(t), consists in checking whether t is already in the map. If it is then the number of occurrences associated with it is simply incremented by one. Otherwise a new association (t,1) is added to the map. Dually, the execution of get(t) consists in checking whether t is in the map and, in this case, in decrementing by one the number of occurrences. In case one of these two conditions is not met then the get primitive cannot be executed.

The declaration of sets, map equations and procedure definitions are memorized similarly through maps or lists for equations.

4.4   The Simulator

The simulator consists in repeatedly executing transition steps. In our implementation, this boils down to the definition of function run_one, which assumes given an agent in a parsed form and which returns a pair composed of a boolean and an agent in parsed form. The boolean aims at specifying whether a transition step has taken place. In this case, the associated agent consists of the agent obtained by the transition step. Otherwise, failure is reported with the given agent as associated agent.

The function is defined inductively on the structure of its argument, say ag. If ag is a primitive, then the run_one function simply consists in executing the primitive on the store. If ag is a sequentially composed agent ag_i ; ag_{ii}, then the transition step proceeds by trying to execute the first subagent ag_i. Assume this succeeds and delivers ag' as resulting agent. Then the agent returned is ag' ; ag_{ii} in case ag' is not empty or more simply ag_{ii} in case ag' is empty. Of course, the whole computation fails in case ag_i cannot perform a transition step, namely in case run_one applied to ag_i fails.

The case of an agent composed by a parallel or choice operator is more subtle. Indeed for both cases one should not always favor the first or second subagent. To avoid that behavior, we use a boolean variable, randomly assigned to 0 or 1, and depending upon this value we start by evaluating the first or second subagent. In case of failure, we then evaluate the other one and if both fails we report a failure. In case of success for the parallel composition we determine the resulting agent in a similar way to what we did for the sequentially composed agent. For a composition by the choice operator the tried alternative is simply selected.

The computation of a procedure call and of a conditional statement are performed similarly as one may expect.

4.5 The Scene

The scene and its animation are implemented by means of Processing. The declaration of a scene induces dedicated declarations in the `setup` method used by Processing. Moving an image is obtained by an update in the `draw` method employed by Processing using a linear interpolation of the initial and final coordinates. Placing images and hiding or showing them is achieved by modifications of the corresponding variables and attributes.

4.6 Temporal Formulae

Scan temporal formulae are verified by means of a home-made program inspired by the techniques proposed in [28]. It essentially uses a limited depth-first search algorithm based on the simulator described in Subsect. 4.4 with a recursive reasoning on the temporal formulae. More concretely, the key function `check_lts` takes as arguments an integer I, a temporal formula F, an agent A and a trace T. The first argument is the length of the remaining search allowed. The second and third arguments are the temporal formula to be checked against the agent. The path consists of the trace prefix already computed. The function returns a boolean, stating whether the formula has been checked, together with a path, describing the last path explored. It provides an execution witness of the truth of the formula in case the return boolean is true.

The `check_lts` function is coded by using a recursive reasoning on the formula F:

- if F is a propositional formula, then the current contents of the store should verify it. If this is the case, `true` is returned together with the path P. Otherwise, `false` is returned together with P.
- if F is of the form *Next TF* and if I is strictly positive, then `check_lts` is successively called on the list of next possible agents returned by `run_one` with $I-1$ as integer, the agent produced by `run_one` as agent, TF as formula and P augmented with a reference to the computation step as path. In case one of these calls succeed, namely returns `true` with the associated path, then this result is returned. Otherwise or in case $I = 0$, then `false` is returned together with the path P.
- the case where F is of the form *PF Until TF* is treated similarly. Either TF holds on the current store, in which case `true` is returned together with P, or PF holds in the current store and there is one successor agent (explored as for the above case) for which TF holds. In this latter case, `true` is returned together with the discovered path. In case none of the two situations holds, then `false` is returned with the path P.

It is worth noting that the algorithm is not complete. If it returns `true` then the considered formula has been established and the returned path provides a witness execution that can be replayed. Otherwise, because of the limited depth-first search, `false` may be returned wrongly because the formula could have been proven by using a more exhaustive search. Nevertheless such a simple algorithm is in practice already useful to establish formulae.

Note also that, in case of success, the algorithm is sound because of the limited form of the temporal formulae considered in Scan, which in particular, does not involve negations.

5 Related Work

Although many pieces of work in the coordination community have been devoted to the proposal of new languages, semantics and implementations, few articles have addressed the concerns of practically constructing programs in coordination languages, in particular in checking that what is described by programs actually corresponds to what has to be modeled. Notable exceptions include the Extensible Coordination Tools [18], ReoLive [6], and TAPAs [3].

The Extensible Coordination Tools (ECT) has been developed for the control-based coordination language Reo, a language quite different from Anim-Bach. ECT consists of a set of plug-ins for the Eclipse platform that provide graphical editing facilities of Reo connectors, the animation of these connectors as well as model checking based on constraint automata or a translation to the process algebra mCRL2 [5]. Although it is certainly less elaborated, our work differs in several respects. First, it deals with tuple spaces instead of connectors. Second, it allows to grasp the modeling of real-life systems by connecting agents of Bach to animations at the application level. Consequently, although one may animate connectors in ECT, one cannot animate the modeling of the rush hour problem for instance, as we did with Anim-Bach. Finally, in contrast to our work, model checking in ECT does not preserve a one-to-one link with textual representations, in particular when mCRL2 is used.

ReoLive is also dedicated to Reo. It proposes similar tools but by means of a set of web-based tools using ScalaJS. As a consequence, the above comparison with ECT also applies to ReoLive.

TAPAs [3] is a tool developed essentially for CCSP with a plug-in for an extension of the Klaim coordination language. It allows to graphically specify systems and to verify their equivalence by means of bisimulations based equivalences (strong, weak and branching) or decorated trace equivalences (weak and strong variants of trace completed trace, divergence sensitive trace, must, testing). It also allows to model check systems by using formulae of the μ-calculus. The two main differences of our work with TAPAs are, on the one hand, our concern for tuple-based coordination languages, and, on the other hand, the facilities offered by Anim-Bach for animations. In contrast, as written above, model checking in Anim-Bach is quite simple and is much less elaborated than that of TAPAs. Future work will aim at improving this aspect.

Declarative invariant assertions are proposed in [20] to detect inconsistencies in models expressed in the Peer model, a coordination model based on shared tuple spaces, messages and Petri nets. In addition to the fact that the Peer Model is quite different from Anim-Bach, our work differs in two main respects. On the one hand, assertions in [20] are verified at runtime whereas our temporal formulae are checked statically. On the other hand, in contrast to our work, no animation facilities are provided.

Although it includes facilities to view the evolution of the shared space, TUCSON [25] does not provide facilities to animate computations nor to model-check them.

Finally, a Linda workbench is presented in [11] with the goal of providing a simple tool that allows users to experiment with a Linda-inspired language. It is integrated with Netbeans and uses the JavaSpaces language, an extension of Java supporting Linda primitives. It is hence named JavaSpaces Netbeans. This workbench provides a tuple browser and a distributed debugger, including record facilities to replay a sequence of tuple space operations. Although our work provides facilities to explore and modify the tuple space, we do not provide debugging facilities. In contrast however we provide animation facilities as well as model checking facilities which are not included in JavaSpaces Netbeans.

6   Conclusion

The paper has introduced a workbench for reasoning on a Linda-like coordination language at three levels: (i) by executing in a step by step or automatic manner instructions while showing their impact on the shared space, (ii) by illustrating computations by animations and (iii) by model checking properties by means of temporal formulae.

The current version has been designed to be as simple as possible yet incorporating key ideas. As a result, it can be improved in many aspects, in particular, by refining the interfaces, by integrating it in IDE's, by improving the specification of animations and by handling more sophisticated temporal logics, like the μ−calculus [19].

References

1. Brogi, A., Jacquet, J.M.: On the expressiveness of Linda-like concurrent languages. Electron. Notes Theoret. Comput. Sci. **16**(2), 61–82 (1998)
2. Brogi, A., Jacquet, J.M.: On the expressiveness of coordination via shared datas-paces. Sci. Comput. Program. **46**(1–2), 71–98 (2003)
3. Calzolai, F., De Nicola, R., Loreti, M., Tiezzi, F.: TAPAs: a tool for the analysis of process algebras. In: Jensen, K., van der Aalst, W.M.P., Billington, J. (eds.) Transactions on Petri Nets and Other Models of Concurrency I. LNCS, vol. 5100, pp. 54–70. Springer, Heidelberg (2008). https://doi.org/10.1007/978-3-540-89287-8_4
4. Carriero, N., Gelernter, D.: Linda in context. Commun. ACM **32**(4), 444–458 (1989)

5. Cranen, S., et al.: An overview of the mCRL2 toolset and its recent advances. In: Piterman, N., Smolka, S.A. (eds.) TACAS 2013. LNCS, vol. 7795, pp. 199–213. Springer, Heidelberg (2013). https://doi.org/10.1007/978-3-642-36742-7_15

6. Cruz, R., Proença, J.: ReoLive: analysing connectors in your browser. In: Mazzara, M., Ober, I., Salaün, G. (eds.) STAF 2018. LNCS, vol. 11176, pp. 336–350. Springer, Cham (2018). https://doi.org/10.1007/978-3-030-04771-9_25

7. Jacquet, J.-M., Linden, I., Darquennes, D.: On density in coordination languages. In: Canal, C., Villari, M. (eds.) ESOCC 2013. CCIS, vol. 393, pp. 189–203. Springer, Heidelberg (2013). https://doi.org/10.1007/978-3-642-45364-9_16

8. Darquennes, D., Jacquet, J.M., Linden, I.: On the introduction of density in tuple-space coordination languages. Sci. Comput. Program. **115**, 149–176 (2013)

9. Darquennes, D., Jacquet, J.M., Linden, I.: On distributed density in tuple-based coordination languages. In: Cámara, J., Proença, J. (eds.) Foundations of Coordination Languages and Self-Adaptive Systems. EPTCS, vol. 175, pp. 36–53. Springer, Rome (2015)

10. Darquennes, D., Jacquet, J.M., Linden, I.: On multiplicities in tuple-based coordination languages: the bach family of languages and its expressiveness study. In: Serugendo, G.D.M., Loreti, M. (eds.) Coordination 2018. LNCS, vol. 10852, pp. 81–109. Springer, Cham (2018). https://doi.org/10.1007/978-3-319-92408-3_4

11. Dukielska, M., Sroka, J.: JavaSpaces NetBeans: a linda workbench for distributed programming course. In: Ayfer, R., Impagliazzo, J., Laxer, C. (eds.) Proceedings of the 15th Annual SIGCSE Conference on Innovation and Technology in Computer Science Education, pp. 23–27. ACM (2010)

12. Emerson, E.A.: Temporal and modal logic. In: Handbook of Theoretical Computer Science, Volume B: Formal Models and Semantics (B), pp. 995–1072. Elsevier (1990)

13. Erman, L., Hayes-Roth, F., Lesser, V., Reddy, D.: The Hearsay-II speech-understanding system: integrating knowledge to resolve uncertainty. ACM Comput. Surv. **12**(2), 213 (1980)

14. Gelernter, D., Carriero, N.: Coordination languages and their significance. Commun. ACM **35**(2), 97–107 (1992)

15. Jacquet, J.-M., De Bosschere, K., Brogi, A.: On timed coordination languages. In: Porto, A., Roman, G.-C. (eds.) COORDINATION 2000. LNCS, vol. 1906, pp. 81–98. Springer, Heidelberg (2000). https://doi.org/10.1007/3-540-45263-X_6

16. Jacquet, J.M., Linden, I.: Coordinating context-aware applications in mobile ad-hoc networks. In: Braun, T., Konstantas, D., Mascolo, S., Wulff, M. (eds.) Proceedings of the First ERCIM Workshop on eMobility, pp. 107–118. The University of Bern (2007)

17. Jacquet, J.M., Linden, I.: Fully abstract models and refinements as tools to compare agents in timed coordination languages. Theor. Comput. Sci. **410**(2–3), 221–253 (2009)

18. Kokash, N., Arbab, F.: Formal design and verification of long-running transactions with extensible coordination tools. IEEE Trans. Serv. Comput. **6**(2), 186–200 (2013)

19. Kozen, D.: Results on the propositional μ-calculus. Theor. Comput. Sci. **27**, 333–354 (1983)

20. Kühn, E., Radschek, S., Elaraby, N.: Distributed coordination runtime assertions for the peer model. In: Di Marzo Serugendo, G., Loreti, M. (eds.) COORDINATION 2018. LNCS, vol. 10852, pp. 200–219. Springer, Cham (2018). https://doi.org/10.1007/978-3-319-92408-3_9

21. Linden, I., Jacquet, J.-M.: On the expressiveness of absolute-time coordination languages. In: De Nicola, R., Ferrari, G.-L., Meredith, G. (eds.) COORDINATION 2004. LNCS, vol. 2949, pp. 232–247. Springer, Heidelberg (2004). https://doi.org/10.1007/978-3-540-24634-3_18

22. Linden, I., Jacquet, J.M.: On the expressiveness of timed coordination via shared dataspaces. Electron. Notes Theor. Comput. Sci. **180**(2), 71–89 (2007)

23. Linden, I., Jacquet, J.M., Bosschere, K.D., Brogi, A.: On the expressiveness of relative-timed coordination models. Electron. Notes Theor. Comput. Sci. **97**, 125–153 (2004)

24. Odersky, M., Spoon, L., Venners, B.: Programming in Scala, A comprehensive step-by-step guide. Artemis (2016)

25. Omicini, A., Ricci, A., Rimassa, G., Viroli, M.: Integrating objective & subjective coordination in FIPA: a roadmap to TuCSoN. In: Armano, G., Paoli, F.D., Omicini, A., Vargiu, E. (eds.) Proceedings of the 4th AI*IA/TABOO Joint Workshop "From Objects to Agents": Intelligent Systems and Pervasive Computing, pp. 85–91. Pitagora Editrice Bologna (2003)

26. Papadopoulos, G., Arbab, F.: Coordination models and languages. Technical report SEN-R9834. Centrum voor Wiskunde en Informatica (CWI), ISSN 1386-369X (1998)

27. Reas, C., Fry, B.: Processing: A Programming Handbook for Visual Designers. The MIT Press, Cambridge (2014)

28. Reynolds, M.: A Traditional Tree-style Tableau for LTL. CoRR arXiv:1604.03962 (2016)

CHOReVOLUTION: Automating the Realization of Highly–Collaborative Distributed Applications

Marco Autili, Amleto Di Salle$^{(\boxtimes)}$, Francesco Gallo, Claudio Pompilio, and Massimo Tivoli

University of L'Aquila, Via Vetoio snc, 67100 L'Aquila, Italy
{marco.autili,amleto.disalle,francesco.gallo,
claudio.pompilio,massimo.tivoli}@univaq.it
http://www.disim.univaq.it

Abstract. CHOReVOLUTION is a platform for the tool-assisted development and execution of scalable applications that leverage the distributed collaboration of services specified through service choreographies. It offers an Integrated Development and Runtime Environment (IDRE) comprising a wizard-aided development environment, a system monitoring console, and a back-end for managing the deployment and execution of the system on the cloud. We describe the platform by using a simple example and evaluate it against two industrial use cases in the domain of Smart Mobility & Tourism and Urban Traffic Coordination.

Keywords: Service choreographies · Distributed computing · Automated synthesis

1 Introduction

The Future Internet [20] reflects the changing scale of the Internet and its trend toward the integration and cooperation of different domains supported by an expanding network infrastructure. It relies on large-scale computing environments that will increasingly be connected to a virtually infinite number of services.

This vision is embodied by reuse-based service-oriented systems, in which services play a central role as effective means to achieve interoperability among parties of a business process, and new systems can be built by reusing and composing existing services.

Service choreographies are a form of decentralized composition that model the external interaction of the participant services by specifying peer-to-peer message exchanges from a global perspective. When third-party (possibly black-box) services are to be composed, obtaining the distributed coordination logic required to enforce the realizability of the specified choreography is a non-trivial and error prone task. Automatic support is then needed. The need for

© IFIP International Federation for Information Processing 2019
Published by Springer Nature Switzerland AG 2019
H. Riis Nielson and E. Tuosto (Eds.): COORDINATION 2019, LNCS 11533, pp. 92–108, 2019.
https://doi.org/10.1007/978-3-030-22397-7_6

choreographies was recognized in the Business Process Modeling Notation 2.0 (BPMN2) [24], which introduced *Choreography Diagrams* to offer choreography modeling constructs. Choreography diagrams specify the message exchanges among the choreography participants from a global point of view.

The CHOReVOLUTION H2020 EU project[1] develops a platform for the generation and execution of scalable distributed applications that leverage the distributed collaboration of services and things by means of service choreographies. In particular, it realizes an Integrated Development and Runtime Environment (IDRE) that comprises a wizard-aided development environment, a system monitoring console, and a back-end for managing the deployment and execution of the system on the cloud.

The CHOReVOLUTION IDRE makes the realization of choreography-based smart applications easier by sparing developers from writing code that goes beyond the realization of the internal business logic. For "internal business logic" we mean the one related to the provisioning of the single system functionalities, as taken in isolation. That is, the distributed coordination logic, which is needed to realize the global collaboration prescribed by the choreography specification, is automatically synthesized by the IDRE. Thus, while coding, developers can avoid to care about coordination aspects. Furthermore, developers can also more easily reuse existing consumers/providers services. These aspects have been appreciated by the industrial partners in that the approach permits to develop distributed applications according to their daily development practices.

The IDRE is an open-source and free software, available under Apache license. It is available as a ready-to-use bundle by the OW2 consortium from https://l.ow2.org/idrevm, and all the documentation can be found at http://www.chorevolution.eu/bin/view/Documentation/WebHome. The source code is also available at https://gitlab.ow2.org/chorevolution.

The remainder of the paper is organized as follows. Section 2 describes the development approach supported by CHOReVOLUTION. Section 3 describes the components constituting the CHOReVOLUTION IDRE. Section 4 highlights the use of the IDRE through a running example. Section 5 briefly evaluates the two CHOReVOLUTION use cases, and Sect. 6 concludes the paper.

2 CHOReVOLUTION Approach

The CHOReVOLUTION synthesis process consists of a set of core *code generation phases* (see Fig. 1) that takes as input a choreography specification together with a set of existing concrete services as possible candidates to play the choreography roles and automatically generates a set of additional software entities. When interposed among the services, these software entities "proxify" the participant services to externally coordinate and adapt their business-level interaction, as well as to bridge the gap of their middleware-level communication paradigms and enforce security constraints.

---

[1] http://www.chorevolution.eu.

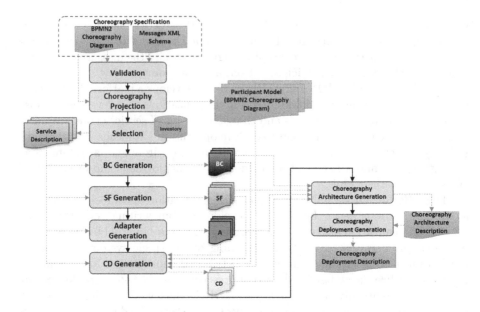

Fig. 1. CHOReVOLUTION development process

Validation – This activity validates the correctness of the choreography specification against the constraints imposed by the BPMN2 standard specification. The goal is to check practical constraints concerning both choreography realizability and its enforceability (see [4,13–15,21–23,26]).

Choreography Projection – Taking as input the BPMN2 Choreography Diagram and the related Messages XML schema, this activity automatically extracts all the choreography participants and applies a model-to-model (M2M) transformation to derive the related Participant Models, one for each participant. A participant model is itself a BPMN2 Choreography Diagram. It contains only the choreography flows that involve the considered participant. The generated participant models will be then taken as input by the Coordination Delegate (CD) Generation activity.

Selection – This activity is about querying the Service Inventory in order to select concrete services that can play the roles of the choreography participants. Once the right services have been selected, the related description models will be used to generate the Binding Components (BCs), Security Filters (SFs), Adapters (As), and Coordination Delegates (CDs).

BC Generation – BCs are generated when the middleware-level interaction paradigm of a selected service is different from SOAP [28], which is used by the CDs as the middleware-level interaction paradigm [16].

SF Generation – SFs are generated for those (selected) services having security policies associated. SFs filter the services interactions according to the specified security requirements.

Adapter Generation – When needed, adapters allow to bridge the gap among the interfaces and interaction protocols of the selected services and the ones of the (respective) participant roles they have to play, as obtained via projection. In other words, adapters solve possible interoperability issues due to operation names mismatches and I/O data mapping mismatches (see [9,10,27]).

CD Generation – CDs are in charge of coordinating the interactions among the selected services so as to fulfill the global collaboration prescribed by the choreography specification, in a fully distributed way (see [5–8,11,12]).

Choreography Architecture Generation – Considering the selected services and the generated BCs, SFs, As, and CDs, an architectural description is automatically generated, and a graphic representation of the choreographed system is provided, where all the system's architectural elements and their interdependencies are represented.

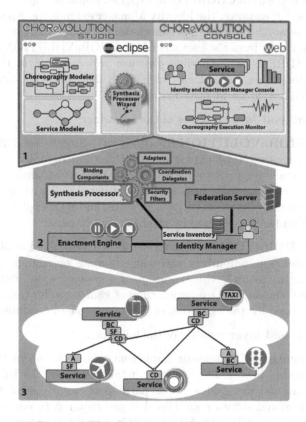

Fig. 2. CHOReVOLUTION IDRE overview

Choreography Deployment Generation – The last activity of the development process concerns the generation of the Choreography Deployment Description (called `ChorSpec`) out of the Choreography Architecture model. The deployment description will be used for deploying and enacting the realized choreography.

3   CHOReVOLUTION IDRE

CHOReVOLUTION IDRE includes software tools for choreography modeling, synthesis, security, identity management and cloud (with monitoring and overall management at run-time).

As depicted in Fig. 2, the CHOReVOLUTION IDRE is layered into: (1) a front–end layer; (2) a back–end layer; and (3) a cloud layer. The red boxes in the figure contain the IDRE components developed within CHOReVOLUTION from scratch. In particular, they are: the CHOReVOLUTION Studio, the CHOReVOLUTION Console, and the Synthesis Processor together with the artifacts it generates. As detailed below, the components outside the boxes are the ones developed within CHOReVOLUTION and built on top of existing open-source projects. For instance, the Identity Manager extends the Apache Syncope project [3]. It is worth noticing that the choice about the existing projects the IDRE relies on comes from the partners of the CHOReVOLUTION consortium. However, the IDRE is an extensible platform and, as such, in the future, it may also support other technologies such as: Kubernetes for deployment and enactment, IBM's AIM for identity management.

(1) The Front–end layer consists of the following:

(1.1) – The **CHOReVOLUTION Studio** is an Eclipse-based IDE that allows to (i) design a choreography exploiting BPMN2 Choreography Diagrams; (ii) define all the details required to instrument the interaction among the services involved in the choreography (e.g. service signatures, identity attributes and roles); (iii) drive the generation of BCs, SFs, As, and CDs exploiting the automated generation facilities offered by the back–end layer.

(1.2) – The **CHOReVOLUTION Console** is a web-based application that allows to (i) configure, administer and trigger actions on running services and choreographies; (ii) monitor the execution of a choreography with respect to relevant parameters, such as execution time of choreography tasks, number of messages exchanged for the execution of tasks, end-to-end deadlines, etc.

(2) The Back–end layer consists of the following:

(2.1) – The **Synthesis Processor** implements the activities of the synthesis process described in Sect. 2. In particular, it takes as input the BPMN2 choreography diagram and the models of the participant services, and generates all the needed additional software entities that are required to concretely realize the choreography, i.e., CDs, As, SFs, and BCs. Finally, it generates a concrete description of the choreography (`ChorSpec`) that is passed to the Enactment Engine (via the Identity Manager) for deployment and enactment purposes.

(2.2) – The **Enactment Engine (EE)** is a REST API that extends the Apache Brooklyn project [2]. It automatically deploys the choreography based on the choreography deployment description by using the Cloud Layer. The EE also interacts with the Identity Manager to include into the deployment description the actual deployment and runtime details. Then, once a choreography is deployed and running, the EE listens for command requests from the Identity Manager for runtime choreography control. It is worth noticing that, although choreography monitoring and control is performed by centralized IDRE components (e.g., EE and IdM), the realization and running of the choreography still remain fully distributed into the various artifacts generated by the Synthesis Processor.

(2.3) – The **Federation Server** handles the runtime authentication and authorization for services that uses different security mechanism at the protocol level by storing various credentials on behalf of the caller.

(2.4) – The **Identity Manager (IdM)** is based on Apache Syncope project [3] and it is responsible for managing users and services. In particular, the IdM is able to query the services for supported application contexts and played roles; force a specific application context for a certain service (put in "maintenance" or disable/enable). The Service Inventory is a sub-component of the IdM. It acts as a central repository for the description models of the services and things that can be used during the synthesis process.

(3) The Cloud layer executes concrete service choreography instances on a cloud infrastructure and adapts their execution based on the actual application context. At execution time, for each choreography, in the CHOReVOLUTION cloud, there are (i) a set of choreography instances at different execution states; (ii) a set of virtual machines executing a custom-tailored mix of services and middleware components to serve different parts of the choreography. VMs are installed and configured with services according to selectable policies. Due to the fact that EE is based on Apache Brooklyn, the CHOReVOLUTION IDRE is not constrained to a specific Infrastructure as a Service (IaaS) platform (e.g., Open Stack [25], Amazon EC2 [1]).

The IDRE mainly targets three types of users described as follows.

Service providers interact with the CHOReVOLUTION Studio to define the description models (i.e., interface and security models) of existing services and then publish them into the Service Inventory. The benefit they obtain is to foster and ease the reuse of their services by developers, hence increasing the opportunities to be involved in new businesses.

Choreography developers interact with the CHOReVOLUTION Studio to (i) model a choreography by using the Choreography Modeler. (ii) Realize the modeled choreography through the automatic synthesis of BCs (for solving heterogeneity issues), CDs (for solving coordination issues), As (for solving interface mismatches), and SFs (to make the choreography secure). This is done by exploiting the Synthesis Processor.

Choreography operators interact with the CHOReVOLUTION console to (i) deploy and enact the generated choreography-based application through a structured process that involves the back-end layer; (ii) monitor the status of the execution cloud environment; (iii) monitor the execution of the choreography instances and managing their lifecycle.

4   Running Example

This section describes a simple example, called **Chor-eCOM**, that is used as a guide-through to explain the CHOReVOLUTION IDRE. The simple case study falls within the e–commerce domain. It concerns the purchasing of one or more products of different nature.

In our example, the customer is connected to the Internet through a web client or a mobile app. The customer can select a list of items and, once the payment has been performed, the order can be processed, and the invoice can be sent back to her. Then, according to the delivery schedule, the items are packaged and sent to the customer, who will in turn receive shipping information.

Figure 3 shows the Chor-eCOM example choreography specification by means of a BPMN2 Choreography Diagram. A choreography diagram specifies the way the choreography participants exchange information (messages) from a global point of view. The main element of a choreography diagram is the choreography task (e.g., `Order Products` task on left of Fig. 3). Graphically, BPMN2 diagrams uses rounded-corner boxes to denote choreography tasks. Each of them is labeled with the roles of the two participants involved in the task. The white box denotes the initiating participant that decides when the interaction takes place. A task is an atomic activity that represents an interaction by means of one or two (request and optionally response) message exchanges (`orderRequest`) between two participants (`Order Processor` and `Scheduler`).

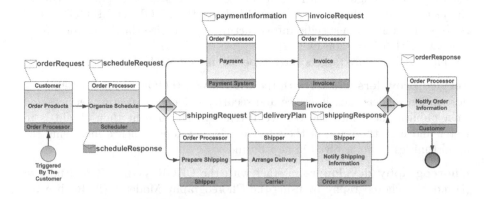

Fig. 3. Chor-eCOM choreography diagram

The use case starts with the mobile application `Customer` sending her information together with the ordering data. From this information, `Order Processor` sends the message `scheduleRequest` to the `Scheduler` participant for scheduling the order. Then, it initiates two parallel flows in order to retrieve the information for delivering and paying the order (see the parallel branch represented as a rhombus marked with a "+", with two outgoing arrows, namely a Diverging Parallel Gateway, just after the choreography task `Organize Schedule`). In particular, the top-most branch retrieves payment and invoice information, while the bottom-most branch gathers delivery information. Finally, the two parallel flows are joined together in order to notify order information to the user by means of `Notify Order Information` choreography task.

We used the choreography specification in Fig. 3 to realize a simple e–commerce choreography–based system where a number of publicly available services can be reused. They have been reused – as black-box third-party software – to instantiate the roles of the participants `Scheduler`, `Payment System`, `Invoicer`, and `Carrier`. The other participants (`Order Processor` and `Shipper`) had to be developed from scratch, and here our synthesis method comes into play. These participants represent the missing logic to be composed and coordinated with the logic offered by the reused services. Note that, the `Customer` participant represents the mobile app used by the user.

In the remainder of this section the Chor-eCOM example is used to show the realization of a choreography-based system by highlighting the roles played by the three types of users of the CHOReVOLUTION IDRE described in Sect. 3.

Service Provider – A service provider uses the IDRE in order to publish the description models of the services into the Service Inventory. The IDRE allows to deal with the heterogeneity of the services involved in a choreography. To this

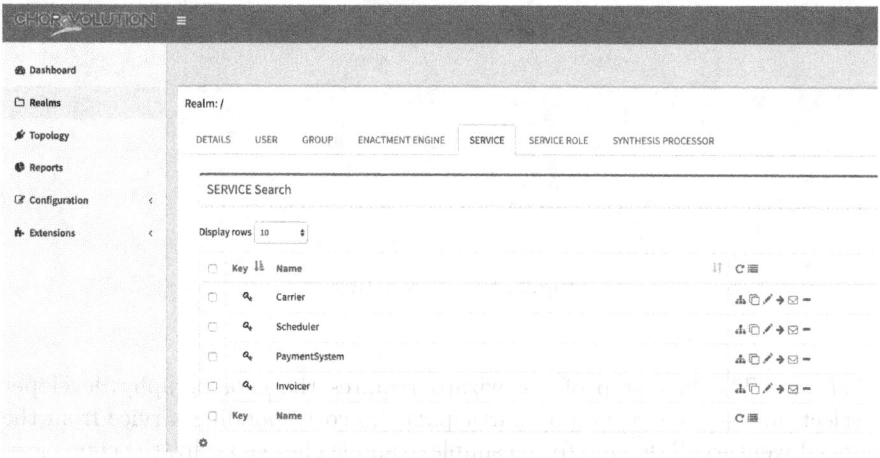

Fig. 4. Service inventory

extent, it provides a uniform description for any service or thing, given by means of the Generic Interface Description Language (GIDL) [16] or the WSDL [29] in case of SOAP services. GIDL supports interface description for any kind of possible services (e.g., REST services) and thing. As already said in Sect. 2, the published services are selected in order to play the participants roles of a choreography. Then, the next phases will use the services models to synthesize the additional software artefacts (i.e., BCs, SFs, CDs, As) of the choreography.

Referring to the Chor-eCOM example, the service provider has to create a Service/Thing project inside the CHOReVOLUTION Studio by using a GIDL description for the following services: **Scheduler**, **Payment System**, **Invoicer**, and **Carrier**. Due to lack of space, we do not provide the steps to create and publish services within the Service Inventory. At the end of this process, the Service Inventory contains the following published services (see Fig. 4).

Choreography Developer – A choreography developer exploits the CHOReV-OLUTION Studio to model a choreography and to realize it. For this purpose the developer has to create a CHOReVOLUTION Synthesis project. Then, he or she models the BPMN2 choreography diagram together with the XML messages by using the Eclipse BPMN2 choreography modeler [18]. As already discussed in Sect. 2, after the modeling phase, the choreography developer starts the synthesis process. The first two activities of the process (i.e., Validation and Choreography Projection) do not require any user interaction. Then, the choreography developer starts a wizard interface that through several steps realizes the other activities of the synthesis process.

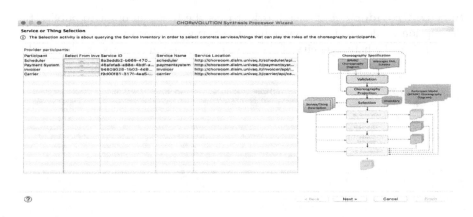

Fig. 5. Selection activity

Selection – The first step of the wizard requires the choreography developer to select, for each choreography participant, its corresponding service from the Service Inventory. Referring to the simple example choreography, the choreography developer has to select all the services published into the Service Inventory as described previously, see Fig. 5.

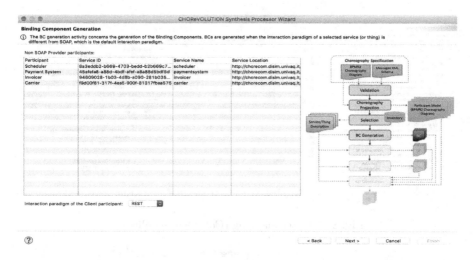

Fig. 6. BC generation activity

BC Generation – Figure 6 shows the step of the wizard used by the choreography developer to configure the Binding Components generator for those selected concrete services that do not use the SOAP [28] protocol. Moreover, the choreography developer has to specify the interaction paradigm used by the client participant of the choreography, by choosing either REST or SOAP.

Considering the Chor-eCOM example, since all the services selected in the previous step are REST services, they are listed in the wizard together with their GIDL description. Moreover, the example provides the purchase information through a mobile application, so the choreography developer has to choose REST as the interaction paradigm of the client participant (`Customer`).

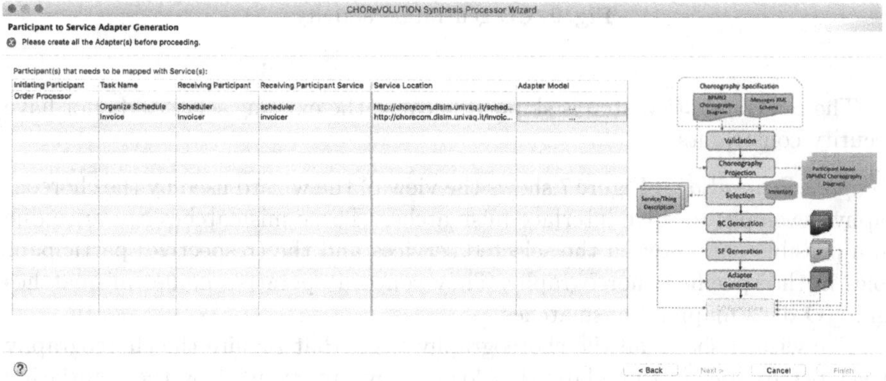

Fig. 7. Adapter generation activity

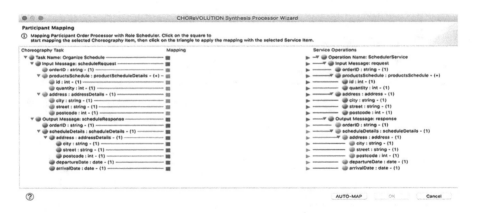

Fig. 8. Adapter mapping (Color figure online)

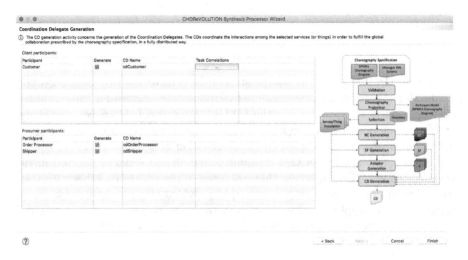

Fig. 9. CD generation activity

The *SF Generation* step is skipped because the existing services do not have security constraints.

Adapter Generation – Figure 7 shows the view of the wizard used by the choreography developer to solve interface mismatches. These mismatches can arise due to a possible gap between the selected services and the (respective) participant roles in the specified choreography. They concern operation names mismatches and I/O data mapping mismatches.

The wizard shows all the choreography tasks that require the choreography developer to specify the adaptation logic, they are grouped by their initiating participant, see the left-most column in Fig. 7. By clicking on the button labeled with "..." a new window is opened, as shown in Fig. 8.

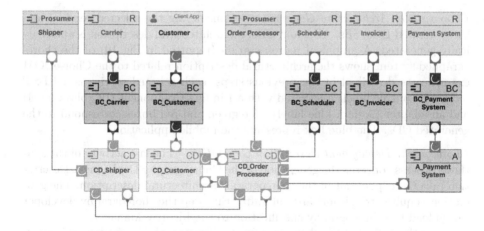

Fig. 10. Choreography architecture (Color figure online)

By interacting with this new dialog window, the choreography developer specifies the mapping between the choreography task messages, reported on the left-most column, and the service operations messages, reported on the right-most column. The elements identified with the red shapes are mandatory to be mapped, whereas those in orange are optional. First, the choreography developer has to map the choreography task with a service operation, and then the related Input and Output messages are auto-mapped. Furthermore, the items forming the message(s) associated to the choreography task under study have to be mapped with the related items forming the specific service message.

CD Generation – It concerns the generation of the Coordination Delegates. The choreography developer has to specify the Correlations Tasks, i.e., a correlation between two choreography tasks. The first task involves a client participant as the initiating participant and a service as the receiving participant. The second task of the correlation involves the same service as the initiating participant and the same client as the receiving participant. In other words, a Correlation Task serves to specify that, in the specified choreography, there are two different tasks that are correlated. Note that these tasks are not necessarily consecutive in the defined choreography flow. This means that the two interactions represented by the two correlated tasks, between the considered client and service, will be indeed realized by a single request-response operation (synchronous interaction) on the service side. The first task corresponds to the invocation by the client of the service' operation and the second task corresponds to the reply by the service to the invocation previously performed by the client.

Considering the Chor-eCOM example, the mobile application starts the choreography by sending the ordering information and then it gets back all the information related to the order. Thus, the choreography developer has to specify a correlation between the task Order Products and the task Notify Order Information (see Fig. 9).

Choreography Architecture Generation – Considering the selected services and the generated BCs, SFs, ADs, and CDs, an architectural description is automatically generated. A graphical representation (reported in Fig. 10) of the choreographed system shows the architectural description related to the Chor-eCOM example. As described in the previous steps, each selected service is a REST service (R purple label) associated with a Binding Component (BC black label) and an adapter (A dark blue label). The green and red boxes correspond to the generated CDs. The blue box represents the mobile application.

Choreography Deployment Description Generation – The last activity of the synthesis process concerns the generation of the Choreography Deployment Description (aka **ChorSpec**) out of the choreography architectural description. The generation is quite straightforward, and after this step the choreography developer can upload the choreography specification to the Identity Manager.

After the upload of the choreography specification, the choreography is available in the CHOReVOLUTION console (see Fig. 11).

Choreography Operator – At the end of the synthesis phase, the choreography is in the **CREATED** status on the CHOReVOLUTION Console (see Fig. 12). At this point, the Operator can use the "gear" icon to deploy the choreography into the Cloud by passing the **ChorSpec** to the Enactment Engine. After few minutes the status changes to **STARTED**.

Once correctly enacted, the choreography operator can check the health of the virtual machines running the choreography by clicking on the magnifying glass icon. The choreography details page reports monitoring data collected from each virtual machine, and these data can be used by the choreography operator to take action to adapt the virtual machine pool to the expected load, see Fig. 12.

5   CHOReVOLUTION Case Studies Evaluation

CHOReVOLUTION has been evaluated through two use cases: Smart Mobility and Tourism (SMT) and Urban Traffic Coordination (UTC).

The SMT use case has been implemented in cooperation with Softeco, the industrial partner from the Genoa city (Italy). The main scope of the SMT use case is to realize a Collaborative Travel Agent System (CTAS) through the

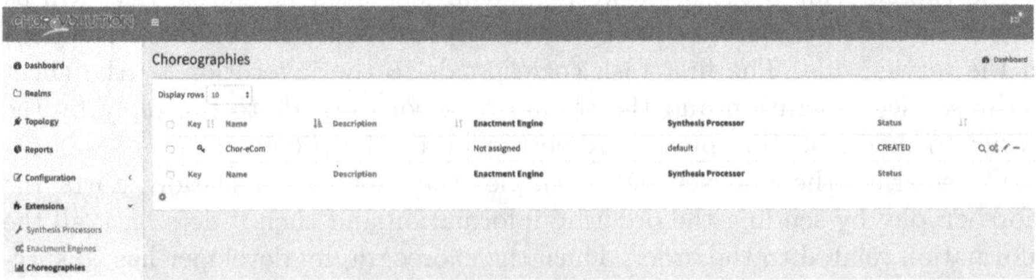

Fig. 11. Uploaded choreography

Fig. 12. Monitoring a choreography

cooperation of several content and service providers, organizations and authorities publicly available in Genoa. The SMT use case involves a mobile application as an "Electronic Touristic Guide" that exploits CTAS in order to provide both smart mobility and touristic information.

The Urban Traffic Coordination (UTC) use case has been implemented in cooperation with RISE Viktoria, the industrial partner from the Götheborg city (Sweden). As described in detail in [17], the main scope of the UTC use case is to realize a Cooperative intelligent transport systems (C-ITS) that allows vehicles and transport infrastructure to interconnect, share information and use it to coordinate their actions. The C-ITS provides traffic coordination services exploited through a mobile app for assisting drivers in an eco-friendly and comfortable driving experience.

We evaluated the CHOReVOLUTION IDRE by conducting an experiment for each use case. The goal of the two experiments was to measure the time saving for realizing, maintaining and evolving the two use cases with the CHOReVOLUTION approach when compared to the development approaches the partners daily use. The considered development phases are: **implementation, maintenance** and **evolution**. The implementation phase consists of the development of a choreography-based system from scratch. The maintenance phase concerns the implementation of updates through service substitution. The evolution phase concerns the development effort required to tackle business goal changes through the modification of the choreography specification. According to the considered phases, the experiment aims to test the following hypotheses. The CHOReVOLUTION approach allows developers to implement (**Hypothesis 1**), maintain (**Hypothesis 2**), and evolve (**Hypothesis 3**) a choreography-based system more quickly.

Table 1. Overall calculation of time savings

EUs	Implementation	Maintenance	Evolution	Time saving
SMT use case				
1	7	0,7	1	–
2	113 **106 saved**	10 **9,3 saved**	27 **26 saved**	**141,3**
3	58,5 **51,5 saved**	8,5 **7,8 saved**	14 **13 saved**	**72,3**
UTC use case				
1	11	0,7	1,5	–
2	152 **141 saved**	12,5 **11,8 saved**	26,5 **25 saved**	**177,8**

The time saving is measured in terms of person-hour (ph). In particular, regarding the SMT use case, we employed the following experimental units:

SMT Experimental unit 1 (SMT-EU1): *CHOReVOLUTION approach –* full usage of the CHOReVOLUTION IDRE except for the development of the mobile application, which is out of the scope.

SMT Experimental unit 2 (SMT-EU2): *General-purpose enterprise-oriented technology –* full usage of the technologies daily adopted by the Softeco partner, i.e., Microsoft .Net, C#, and Visual Studio.

SMT Experimental unit 3 (SMT-EU3): *Domain-specific system integration platform –* full usage of the proprietary platform developed by the Softeco partner, i.e., emixer [19]. It is a content and system integrator that is specific for the travel and mobility information domain.

With respect to the UTC use case, we defined two experimental units. The UTC-EU1 is the same as the SMT-EU1. The second one is defined as follows

UTC Experimental unit 2 (UTC-EU2): *General-purpose enterprise-oriented technology –* full usage of the development technology daily adopted by the RISE partner, i.e., NodeJS and ExpressJS, and Microsoft Visual Studio.

The technologies of SMT-EU2, UTC-EU2, and SMT-EU3 were selected considering that the industrial partners were already skilled with them.

Table 1 summarizes the results of the experiment on the two use cases by distinguishing the implementation, maintenance, and evolution phases. In particular, the EU2 and EU3 highlight in bold the ph saved by using our approach.

The industrial partners experienced a significant time decrease with respect to the their daily development approaches.

6   Conclusions

This paper has presented the CHOReVOLUTION IDRE, an integrated platform for developing, deploying, executing and monitoring choreography-based distributed applications. A simple explanatory example, has been used to show the CHOReVOLUTION IDRE at work. We evaluated the IDRE against two industrial use cases. During the evaluation, the industrial partners experienced a significant time decrease with respect to their daily development approaches. The results of the experiments indicate that CHOReVOLUTION has a great potential in developing choreography-based applications and the two use cases got a full benefit from it. More pilots and development cases will allow to consolidate the technical maturity of the product and pose the basis for a commercial validation.

Acknowledgments. Supported by: (i) EU H2020 Programme under grant no. 644178 (CHOReVOLUTION - Automated Synthesis of Dynamic and Secured Choreographies for the Future Internet), (ii) the Ministry of Economy and Finance, Cipe resolution n. 135/2012 (INCIPICT), and (iii) the GAUSS national PRIN project (Contract no. 2015KWREMX).

References

1. Amazon: Amazon Elastic Compute Cloud (Amazon EC2). https://aws.amazon.com/ec2/?nc2=h_m1
2. Apache: Apache Brooklyn. https://brooklyn.apache.org/
3. Apache: Apache Syncope. https://syncope.apache.org/
4. Autili, M., Inverardi, P., Tivoli, M.: Automated synthesis of service choreographies. IEEE Softw. **32**(1), 50–57 (2015)
5. Autili, M., Inverardi, P., Perucci, A., Tivoli, M.: Synthesis of distributed and adaptable coordinators to enable choreography evolution. In: de Lemos, R., Garlan, D., Ghezzi, C., Giese, H. (eds.) Software Engineering for Self-Adaptive Systems III. Assurances. LNCS, vol. 9640, pp. 282–306. Springer, Cham (2017). https://doi.org/10.1007/978-3-319-74183-3_10
6. Autili, M., Inverardi, P., Tivoli, M.: Choreography realizability enforcement through the automatic synthesis of distributed coordination delegates. Sci. Comput. Program. **160**, 3–29 (2018)
7. Autili, M., Di Ruscio, D., Di Salle, A., Inverardi, P., Tivoli, M.: A model-based synthesis process for choreography realizability enforcement. In: Cortellessa, V., Varró, D. (eds.) FASE 2013. LNCS, vol. 7793, pp. 37–52. Springer, Heidelberg (2013). https://doi.org/10.1007/978-3-642-37057-1_4
8. Autili, M., Ruscio, D.D., Salle, A.D., Perucci, A.: CHOReOSynt: enforcing choreography realizability in the future internet. In: Proceedings of the 22nd ACM SIGSOFT International Symposium on Foundations of Software Engineering, (FSE-22), Hong Kong, China, 16–22 November 2014, pp. 723–726 (2014)
9. Autili, M., Salle, A.D., Gallo, F., Pompilio, C., Tivoli, M.: Model-driven adaptation of service choreographies. In: Proceedings of the 33rd Annual ACM Symposium on Applied Computing, SAC 2018, pp. 1441–1450 (2018)
10. Autili, M., Salle, A.D., Gallo, F., Pompilio, C., Tivoli, M.: On the model-driven synthesis of adaptable choreographies. In: Proceedings of MODELS 2018 Workshops: ModComp, Copenhagen, Denmark, 14 October 2018, pp. 12–17 (2018)
11. Autili, M., Salle, A.D., Gallo, F., Pompilio, C., Tivoli, M.: On the model-driven synthesis of evolvable service choreographies. In: 12th European Conference on Software Architecture: Companion Proceedings, ECSA, pp. 20:1–20:6 (2018)

12. Autili, M., Salle, A.D., Gallo, F., Pompilio, C., Tivoli, M.: Aiding the realization of service-oriented distributed systems. In: Proceedings of the 34th Annual ACM Symposium on Applied Computing, SAC 2019, Limassol, Cyprus, 8–12 April 2019, pp. 1701–1710 (2019)
13. Autili, M., Tivoli, M.: Distributed enforcement of service choreographies. In: Proceedings 13th International Workshop on Foundations of Coordination Languages and Self-Adaptive Systems, FOCLASA 2014, pp. 18–35 (2014)
14. Basu, S., Bultan, T.: Choreography conformance via synchronizability. In: Proceedings of the 20th International Conference on World Wide Web, WWW 2011 (2011)
15. Basu, S., Bultan, T., Ouederni, M.: Deciding choreography realizability. In: Proceedings of the 39th ACM SIGPLAN-SIGACT Symposium on Principles of Programming Languages, POPL 2012. ACM (2012)
16. Bouloukakis, G.: Enabling emergent mobile systems in the IoT: from middleware-layer communication interoperability to associated QoS analysis. (Systèmes Mobiles Émergents dans l'IoT: de l'Interopérabilité au niveau Middleware de Communication à l'Analyse de la Qualité de Service Associée). Ph.D. thesis, Inria, Paris, France (2017)
17. Chen, L., Englund, C.: Choreographing services for smart cities: smart traffic demonstration. In: 85th IEEE Vehicular Technology Conference, VTC Spring 2017, Sydney, Australia, 4–7 June 2017, pp. 1–5 (2017)
18. Eclipse: Eclipse BPMN2 Modeler, April 2018. https://www.eclipse.org/bpmn2-modeler/
19. EMixer: EMixer. http://www.e-mixer.com
20. European Commission: Digital Agenda for Europe - Future Internet Research and Experimentation (FIRE) initiative (2017). https://ec.europa.eu/digital-single-market/en/future-internet-research-and-experimentation
21. Güdemann, M., Poizat, P., Salaün, G., Ye, L.: VerChor: a framework for the design and verification of choreographies. IEEE Trans. Serv. Comput. **9**(4), 647–660 (2016)
22. Hallé, S., Bultan, T.: Realizability analysis for message-based interactions using shared-state projections. In: Proceedings of the 18th ACM SIGSOFT International Symposium on Foundations of Software Engineering, 2010, Santa Fe, NM, USA, pp. 27–36 (2010)
23. Kazhamiakin, R., Pistore, M.: Analysis of realizability conditions for web service choreographies. In: Najm, E., Pradat-Peyre, J.-F., Donzeau-Gouge, V.V. (eds.) FORTE 2006. LNCS, vol. 4229, pp. 61–76. Springer, Heidelberg (2006). https://doi.org/10.1007/11888116_5
24. OMG: Business Process Model And Notation vol 2.0.2, January 2014. http://www.omg.org/spec/BPMN/2.0.2/
25. OpenStack: Open Stack. https://www.openstack.org/
26. Salaün, G., Bultan, T., Roohi, N.: Realizability of choreographies using process algebra encodings. IEEE Trans. Serv. Comput. **5**(3), 290–304 (2012)
27. Di Salle, A., Gallo, F., Perucci, A.: Towards adapting choreography-based service compositions through enterprise integration patterns. In: Bianculli, D., Calinescu, R., Rumpe, B. (eds.) SEFM 2015. LNCS, vol. 9509, pp. 240–252. Springer, Heidelberg (2015). https://doi.org/10.1007/978-3-662-49224-6_20
28. W3C: SOAP Version 1.2, April 2007. http://www.w3.org/TR/soap/
29. W3C: Web Services Description Language (WSDL) Version 2.0, June 2007. https://www.w3.org/TR/wsdl20-primer/

Exploring New Frontiers

ABEL - A Domain Specific Framework for Programming with Attribute-Based Communication

Rocco De Nicola[1(✉)], Tan Duong[2(✉)], and Michele Loreti[3(✉)]

[1] IMT - School for Advanced Studies, Lucca, Italy
rocco.denicola@imtlucca.it
[2] Gran Sasso Science Institute, L'Aquila, Italy
tan.duong@gssi.it
[3] University of Camerino, Camerino, Italy
michele.loreti@unicam.it

Abstract. Attribute-based communication is a promising paradigm for modelling and programming complex interactions in open distributed systems such as collective adaptive systems (CAS). This new paradigm has been formalized in AbC, a kernel calculus with a minimal set of primitives that can be used to model formally verifiable CAS. The calculus assumes an underlying coordination infrastructure that has to guarantee the wanted communication and leaves open the actual implementation of the way communication partners are selected. The proposed implementations of messages exchange for AbC are either not in full agreement with the original semantics or do miss detailed performance evaluations. In this paper, we continue the search for efficient implementations of AbC and present $ABEL$ - a domain specific framework that offers programming constructs with a direct correspondence to those of AbC. We use *Erlang* to implement $ABEL$ inter- and intra-components interaction that together faithfully model AbC semantics and enable us to verify properties of $ABEL$ program. We also consider a number of case studies and, by experimenting with them, show that it is possible to preserve AbC semantics while guaranteeing good performance. We also argue that even better performances can be achieved if the "strong" AbC requirement on the total order of message delivery is relaxed.

Keywords: Attribute-based communication · Process calculi · Distributed programming · Erlang

1 Introduction

Attribute-based communication, originally proposed in [12] is a novel paradigm that allows the dynamic selection of communication groups while taking into account run-time properties and status of interacting entities. At its core, the paradigm relies on a pair of communication primitives. The command $send(v)@\pi$

© IFIP International Federation for Information Processing 2019
Published by Springer Nature Switzerland AG 2019
H. Riis Nielson and E. Tuosto (Eds.): COORDINATION 2019, LNCS 11533, pp. 111–128, 2019.
https://doi.org/10.1007/978-3-030-22397-7_7

is used to send a tuple of values v to all components satisfying the predicate π. The command $receive(x)@\pi'$ is used to receive a tuple of values on x with contents satisfying the predicate π'. The interaction predicates are also parametrised with local attributes and when their values change, the interaction groups do implicitly change, allowing opportunistic interactions.

This paradigm was formalized in the AbC kernel calculus [3,5] to study the impact of attribute-based communication in the realm of CAS [7]. In AbC, components are equipped with a set of attributes describing their features, which can change at runtime. Component interactions is driven by conditions over their states to enable anonymity, adaptivity and open-endedness. The expressive power of AbC in terms of representing different communication paradigms, such as point-to-point, group based, channel-based, and broadcast-based models has been demonstrated in [5]. AbC communication model follows broadcast in the style of [16]; output action can take place even without the presence of any receivers while input action instead waits to synchronize with available messages.

The original semantics of AbC has been formulated in a way that when a component sends a message, that message is delivered to all components in the system in a single move and each individual receiver decides whether to use the message or to discard it. This semantics implies a restriction on the ordering of message delivery because only one component can send its message at a time. That is, message delivery in AbC is performed according to a *total order* [8].

Some proposals have already been put forward to efficiently implement message exchange for AbC. It has been implemented in Java [4], Google Go [1] and Erlang [11]. However, these implementations are either not in full agreement with the original semantics or do miss detailed performance evaluations. This may give rise to doubts about efficiency and correctness and thus prevent the adoption of attribute-based communication.

Indeed, there are a number of challenges to face when providing an implementation fully respecting the exact semantics of AbC. The first is posed by the fact that its message passing model requires guaranteeing a total order on message delivery. While various protocols for total order broadcast have been proposed in the literature, see, e.g., [9,15], the anonymity and open-endedness features of AbC makes then unsuitable in this context because components cannot contribute to establishing an order. A closely related work in building total order for AbC has recently been presented in [2] where a sequencer-based protocol is formalized and proved correct on different topologies of networks. However, there is still the possibility for the proposed protocol to give rise to unexpected behaviours due to the complex behaviour of AbC components. Moreover, since AbC components contain parallel processes operating independently on a shared, dynamic changing attribute environment, to simulate the right interleaving semantics among processes, any implementation should carefully coordinate processes, otherwise situations may arise where processes interfere without exhibiting the wanted behaviour.

In this paper, we continue the search for efficient implementations of AbC and present $ABEL$ - a programming framework for systems whose elements interact according to the AbC style. Our framework provides an execution environment for AbC specifications, that supports AbC programming abstractions for writing and running programs, and, at the same time, fully preserves the original semantics of AbC. More concretely:

1. We provide a set of attribute-based programming constructs, implemented as an *Erlang* library that allows easily defining component programs.
2. We implement coordination mechanisms for intra- and inter-components interactions in *Erlang*, each dealing with one of the parallel operators of AbC and together guaranteeing the original semantics.
3. We demonstrate with experiments that better performances can be achieved if the "strong" AbC requirement on the total order of message delivery is relaxed.

We show that by starting from a given AbC specification, it is straightforward to derive a corresponding *Erlang* program containing API calls. We also show that the close correspondence between AbC and $ABEL$ enables us to reason about the execution code by using verification tools developed for AbC [10]. Moreover, by experimenting with a number of case studies, we show that it is possible to preserve AbC semantics while guaranteeing good performance and that by, slightly relaxing the ordering requirements, better ones can be obtained.

The rest of the paper is organized as follows. In Sect. 2 we briefly review the AbC calculus, and provide examples illustrating its programming paradigm. In Sect. 3, we present the API support for AbC. In Sect. 4, we describe the coordination mechanisms used to handle intra- and inter-components interactions. Section 5 reports our experiments on case studies, taking into account different message ordering strategies. Section 6 concludes the paper by discussing the difference between our work and previous proposals, together with some conclusions and hints to future works.

2 Programming with AbC

The AbC calculus provides concrete primitives that permit the construction of formally verifiable models of CASs according to the attribute-based communication paradigm. A system is rendered as a collection of interacting components. A component C is either a process P associated with an attribute environment Γ and an interface I, or the parallel composition of two components.

$$\text{(Components)} \qquad C ::= \Gamma :_I P \mid C_1 \parallel C_2$$

The environment Γ is a partial mapping from attribute names to values, representing the component state. The interface $I \subseteq Dom(\Gamma)$ contains a set of names, exposed for interaction purpose. The process P can be either an inactive process 0, a prefixing process $\alpha.P$, an update process U, an awareness process $\langle \Pi \rangle P$, a choice process $P_1 + P_2$, a parallel process $P_1 | P_2$, or a process call K (with a unique definition $K \triangleq P$).

(Processes)	$P ::= 0 \mid (\tilde{E})@\Pi.U \mid \Pi(\tilde{x}).U \mid \langle\Pi\rangle P \mid P_1 + P_2 \mid P_1|P_2 \mid K$
(Update)	$U ::= [a := E]U \mid P$
(Expressions)	$E ::= v \mid x \mid a \mid this.a \mid f(\tilde{E})$
(Predicates)	$\Pi ::= \text{tt} \mid p(\tilde{E}) \mid \Pi_1 \wedge \Pi_2 \mid \neg\Pi$

AbC prefixing actions exploit run-time attributes and predicates over them to determine the internal behaviour of components and the communication partners.

$(\tilde{E})@\Pi$ is an output action that evaluates expressions $\tilde{E}$ under the local environment and sends the result to those components whose attributes satisfy predicate Π;

$\Pi(\tilde{x})$ is an input action that binds to the variables $\tilde{x}$ the message received from any component whose attributes and the communicated values satisfy the receiving predicate Π;

$[a := E]$ is an update operation that assigns to attribute a the evaluation of expression E under the local environment;

$\langle\Pi\rangle$ blocks the following process until Π is satisfied under the local environment.

Attribute updates and awareness predicates are local to components and their executions are atomic with the associated communication action.

An expression E may be a constant value v, a variable x, an attribute name a, or a reference *this.a* to attribute a in the local environment. Predicate Π can be either tt, or can be built using comparison operators $\bowtie$ between two expressions and logical connectives $\wedge, \neg, \ldots$. Both expressions and predicates can take more complex forms, of which we deliberately omit the precise syntax; we just refer to them as n-ary operators on subexpressions, i.e., $f(\tilde{E})$ and $p(\tilde{E})$.

The original semantics of *AbC* has been formulated in a way that when a component sends a message, this is delivered in a single move to all components in the system. Atomically, each individual receiver decides whether to keep the message or to discard it. This semantics imposes a restriction on the ordering of message delivery because only one component at a time can send a message. That is, message delivery in the original *AbC* is performed according to a total order [8].

Even if this approach is useful to describe in an abstract way the *AbC* one-to-many interactions, it may be considered too strong when large scaled distributed systems are considered. To relax the *total ordering* formulation of the original *AbC* semantics, we have extended *AbC* syntax to explicitly model the *infrastructure* responsible of message dispatching already used in [2].

To this goal we introduce the new category of *servers*. *AbC* systems are now built by using *servers* of the form $\{\cdot\}^{\iota,\omega}$ that are responsible for managing a set of *components*. Each server is equipped with an *input queue* ι and an *output queue* ω. The former is the queue of messages, coming from the environment, that the server must deliver to the managed components. The latter is the queue of messages that have been generated locally and that the server must forward to other components. Each message m is a triple of the form $(\Gamma, \pi, \tilde{v})$ where Γ

is the environment of the sending component, π is the target predicate used to select the receivers, and $\tilde{v}$ is the tuple of sent values. In what follows we will use q to denote a queue of messages, and $[]$ to denote the empty queue. Moreover, we will use $m :: q$ (resp. $q :: m$) to represent an extended queue obtained by adding message m at the beginning (resp. at the end) of q.

The syntax of AbC servers is the following:

$$\text{(Servers)} \quad S ::= \{M\}^{\iota,\omega}$$
$$\text{(Managed Elements)} \quad M ::= C \mid S \parallel S$$

A server thus equips its managed element (which in turn can be either single AbC component or recursively other servers) with input and output queues. Servers communicate with one another by adding and withdrawing messages from their queues, thereby relaxing the original synchronous semantics.

The operational semantics of AbC systems is defined via the transition relation $\rightarrow \subseteq \text{Sys} \times \text{Lab} \times \text{Sys}$, where Lab is the set of transition labels λ defined by the following syntax:

$$\lambda ::= \Gamma \triangleright \overline{\Pi}(\tilde{v}) \mid \Gamma \triangleright \Pi(\tilde{v}) \mid \tau$$

The transition label $\Gamma \triangleright \overline{\Pi}(\tilde{v})$ represents an output of $\tilde{v}$ executed by a component with environment Γ that is sent to receivers satisfying Π. Input actions are represented by label $\Gamma \triangleright \Pi(\tilde{v})$ that represents the capability of a system to receive message $\tilde{v}$ sent by a component with environment Γ to receivers satisfying Π. Finally, τ represents internal/silent actions.

We have fully formalized the new semantics that relies on the two queues of the servers. Due to lack of space, in Table 1 we only report some the rules of the operational semantics that we consider more relevant.

The rules for parallel composition ($\parallel$) are the expected ones: SYNC states that S_1 and S_2, when in parallel, can both receive the same message; COML and

Table 1. Operational semantics: relevant rules

$$\frac{S_1 \xrightarrow{\Gamma \triangleright \Pi(\tilde{v})} S_1' \quad S_2 \xrightarrow{\Gamma \triangleright \Pi(\tilde{v})} S_2'}{S_1 \parallel S_2 \xrightarrow{\Gamma \triangleright \Pi(\tilde{v})} S_1' \parallel S_2'} \; \text{SYNC}$$

$$\frac{S_1 \xrightarrow{\Gamma \triangleright \overline{\Pi}(\tilde{v})} S_1' \quad S_2 \xrightarrow{\Gamma \triangleright \Pi(\tilde{v})} S_2'}{S_1 \parallel S_2 \xrightarrow{\Gamma \triangleright \overline{\Pi}(\tilde{v})} S_1' \parallel S_2'} \; \text{COML} \qquad \frac{S_1 \xrightarrow{\Gamma \triangleright \Pi(\tilde{v})} S_1' \quad S_2 \xrightarrow{\Gamma \triangleright \overline{\Pi}(\tilde{v})} S_2'}{S_1 \parallel S_2 \xrightarrow{\Gamma \triangleright \overline{\Pi}(\tilde{v})} S_1' \parallel S_2'} \; \text{COMR}$$

$$\frac{m = (\Gamma, \tilde{v}, \Pi) \quad M_1 \xrightarrow{\Gamma \triangleright \Pi(\tilde{v})} M_2}{\{M_1\}^{m::\iota,\omega} \xrightarrow{\tau} \{M_2\}^{\iota,\omega}} \; \text{SERDIN} \qquad \frac{M_1 \xrightarrow{\Gamma \triangleright \overline{\Pi}(\tilde{v}) M_2}}{\{M_1\}^{\iota,\omega} \xrightarrow{\tau} \{M_2\}^{\iota,\omega::(\Gamma,\tilde{v},\Pi)}} \; \text{SERDOUT}$$

$$\frac{}{\{M_1\}^{\iota,\omega} \xrightarrow{\Gamma \triangleright \Pi(\tilde{v})} \{M_2\}^{\iota::(\Gamma,\tilde{v},\Pi),\omega}} \; \text{SERIN} \qquad \frac{}{\{M_1\}^{\iota,(\Gamma,\tilde{v},\Pi)::\omega} \xrightarrow{\Gamma \triangleright \overline{\Pi}(\tilde{v})} \{M_2\}^{\iota,\omega}} \; \text{SEROUT}$$

COMR state that messages sent by S_1 (resp. S_2) are received by S_2 (resp. S_1) and the result of the synchronisation is an *output label* to allow other components in parallel to receive the same message.

The rules describing behaviour of a *server* are SERDIN, SERDOUT, SERIN and SEROUT. The first two rules model the interaction of the server with the enclosed element, while the last two describe the interaction of the server with the enclosing environment. Rule SERDIN states that the first message is consumed from the input queue when the managed element M_1 receives it. Rule SERDOUT states that a message is added at the end of the output queue whenever the managed element M_1 executes an output action. A message is added at the end of the input queue whenever a new message is received from the enclosing environment (rule SERIN). Conversely, a server sends a message by removing it from the front of output queue (rule SEROUT).

2.1 *AbC* at Work

In order to illustrate *AbC* primitives and assess our implementation we now provide a couple of simple case studies that we will later use also for assessing performances of our implementations.

Stable Matching. We consider a variant of the well-known stable matching problem (SMP) [13] that can be naturally expressed in terms of partners' attributes [10]. Solving an SMP problem amounts to finding a stable matching between two equally-sized sets of elements, after each element has specified an ordering of preferences over all members of the opposite set. The original algorithm [13] goes through a sequence of proposals initiated by members of one group, say M, according to their preference lists. Members of the other group, say W, after receiving a proposal, do choose the best candidate between their current partner and the one making advances. The algorithm guarantees the existence of a unique set of pairs, which is stable, i.e. there is no pair of unmatched elements, that prefer each other to their current partners. An *AbC* specification for this algorithm can be found in [4].

Our variant allows participating agents to express their interests in potential partners by relying on partner's attributes rather than on their identities. In this scenario, M components start by proposing to those W components that satisfy their highest requirements, i.e., a predicate that specifies all wanted attributes. If an M agent cannot find any partner for a given demand, it retries after weakening the predicate by dropping one of the wanted attributes. W components are reactive to proposals and perform "select and swap" partners as before. However, since a proposal may target multiple partners, the protocol needs extra acknowledgement messages between agents of two types to select the partner. And, an agent of type M relaxes a predicate Π only if all potential partners, addressed by Π, rejected it.

In *AbC* the two types of components M and W are modelled as follows:

$$M_i \triangleq \Gamma_{mi} :_{\{id,a_1,a_2,...\}} P_M \quad \text{and} \quad W_j \triangleq \Gamma_{wj} :_{\{id,b_1,b_2,...\}} P_W$$

where the interfaces expose the names of attributes that represent the features of the components and P_M and P_W their actual behaviour.

Below, we specify part of the system concerned components of type M, whose behaviour combines 4 processes

$$P_M \triangleq Q \mid P \mid A \mid R$$

An agent m that is looking for partners satisfying predicate Π[1] has first to learn about the number of potential partners, say c, satisfying this predicate. This is taken care by process Q that first broadcasts a query message and then collects interested replies (not detailed here). For each attempt, m keeps track of the set bl of partners which have rejected it. As long as there are available partners $(c > |bl|)$, process P sends a 'propose' message containing the agent's characteristics (denoted by the sequence $\widetilde{msg}$) to predicate Π, excluding those in bl.

$$P \triangleq \langle partner = 0 \wedge c > |bl| \wedge send = 1 \rangle$$
$$(`propose', this.id, \widetilde{msg})@(\Pi \wedge \text{id} \notin \text{this.bl}).[send := 0]P + \dots$$

Other branches of P have a similar structure and will be used for proposing with other requirements. Process A, reported below, handles multiple 'yes' messages which may arrive in parallel. The continuation H chooses the sender (bound to y) of the first message to match, confirms to y that it has been selected and updates new **partner**. A 'toolate' message is sent to senders of subsequent 'yes' messages:

$$A \triangleq (x = `yes')(x, y).(H \mid A)$$
$$H \triangleq (\langle partner = 0 \rangle(`confirm')@(id = y).[partner := y]0$$
$$+ \langle partner > 0 \rangle(`toolate')@(id = y).0$$

The sent proposal may also be rejected. Process R collects messages of this type. The arrivals of 'no' and 'split' requests cause the addition of the senders to the set bl and enabling **send**. A 'split' message which originates from some matched partner resets the current **partner** and opens the possibility for process P to become active and retry.

$$R \triangleq (x = `split')(x, y).[bl := bl \cup \{y\}, send := 1, partner := 0]R$$
$$+ (x = `no')(x, y).[bl := bl \cup \{y\}, send := 1]R$$

Graph Colouring. We now consider a distributed graph colouring problem where vertices exchange messages with their neighbours to collaborate on deciding a colour (in our case a positive number) for each of them in such a way that

---

[1] As an example, consider a user interested in finding a server that has some specific resources. A possible communication predicate would be $\Pi = (cores = this.pcores \wedge mem = this.pmem)$ where *cores* and *mem* are two attributes of servers, and *pcores* and *pmem* are two attributes of users.

adjacent vertices do not get the same colour. The following AbC specification is adapted from [6]. A graph is modelled naturally as a set of components $V_i \triangleq \Gamma_i :_{\{id,nbr\}} P_V$, one for each vertex, with attribute **id** representing a unique identifier, and **nbr** representing a set of neighbours ids. Vertices operate in rounds and in each round they use a predicate $(this.id \in nbr)$ to send messages to neighbours. Vertices concurrently execute the four processes F, T, D, A until they get assigned a 'definitive' colour.

Every non **assigned** vertex selects the first available colour which has not been used by his neighbours, that is $min\{i \notin this.\mathsf{used}\}$. A try message of the form $('try', c, r)$ is sent to inform others that the sending vertex wants to attain colour c at round r.

$$F \triangleq ('try', min\{i \notin this.\mathsf{used}\}, this.r)@(this.id \in nbr).$$
$$[\mathrm{colour} := min\{i \notin \mathrm{used}\}, \mathrm{counter} := \mathrm{counter} + 1]0$$

Each vertex counts the number of 'try' messages (including its own) using the attribute **counter**. Process T collects 'try' messages from neighbours where it records colours proposed from neighbours with greater ids in a set **constraints** to avoid conflict. Other branches of T (not shown here) deal with 'try' messages from neighbours operating in one round ahead, i.e., $(this.r < z)$ for which the relevant information are kept in attributes **counter1, constraints1**.

$$T \triangleq (x = 'try' \wedge this.\mathrm{id} < \mathrm{id} \wedge this.r = z)(x, y, z).$$
$$[\mathrm{counter} := \mathrm{counter} + 1, \mathrm{constraints} := \mathrm{constraints} \cup \{y\}]T$$
$$+ (x = 'try' \wedge this.\mathrm{id} > \mathrm{id} \wedge this.r = z)(x, y, z).$$
$$[\mathrm{counter} := \mathrm{counter} + 1]T + \dots$$

After collecting all 'try' messages, i.e., $(counter = |nbr| + 1)$, each vertex checks whether the colour it proposed among neighbours is valid, encoded in process A below. If this is the case[2], the vertex sends a 'done' message of the form $('done', c, r)$ to indicate that c has been taken at round r, setting **assigned** to true and terminates. If the proposed colour leads to conflict, the vertex starts a new round by sending a new 'try' message. At this point, the vertex has learnt about neighbours and thus tries to take the best decision by selecting a new colour excluding also **constraints**, i.e., $min\{i \notin this.\mathsf{used} \cup this.\mathsf{constraints}\}$. During this new round, $r + 1$, the vertex does not count messages from those vertices who might have sent a 'try' message (collected by process T above via **counter1**) and from 'done' neighbours (collected by process D presented next).

---

[2] It happens for those vertices whose ids are greatest among the unassigned neighbors.

$A \triangleq \langle(\text{counter} = |\text{nbr}| + 1) \wedge \text{colour} \notin \text{constraints} \cup \text{used}\rangle$
    $(\text{`done'}, \text{this.colour}, \text{this.r})@(\text{this.id} \in \text{nbr}).[\text{assigned} := tt]0$
$+ \ \langle(\text{counter} = |\text{nbr}| + 1) \wedge \text{colour} \in \text{constraints} \cup \text{used}\rangle$
    $(\text{`try'}, min\{i \notin this.used \cup this.constraints\}, this.r + 1)@(\text{this.id} \in \text{nbr}).$
    $[\text{r} := \text{r} + 1, \text{counter} := \text{done} + \text{counter1} + 1, \text{constraints} := \text{constraints1}, \ldots]A$

Each vertex collects 'done' messages to update the set of **used** colours, and counts 'done' neighbours in **done**. In addition, if the messages come from the previous round, i.e., $(this.r > z)$, the vertex treats them as 'try' messages in the current round, and thus increments the **counter**.

$D \triangleq (x = \text{`done'} \wedge \text{this.r} = z)(x, y, z).$
    $[\text{done} := \text{done} + 1, \text{used} := \text{used} \cup \{y\}]D$
$+ \ (x = \text{`done'} \wedge \text{this.r} > z)(x, y, z).$
    $[\text{done} := \text{done} + 1, \text{used} := \text{used} \cup \{\text{y}\}, \text{counter} := \text{counter} + 1]D$

3   Programming Support for AbC

Our framework aims at providing a direct mapping from *AbC* specifications to executable programs in *Erlang*, allowing experimentations with attribute-based communication with little of efforts. An *ABEL* program is based on a sequence of behaviour definitions for processes, and top-level commands for starting all components. The running program is a set of concurrently executing components.

Creating Components. A component is set up in two steps: it is first created and then assigned an initial behaviour. To create a new component, an attribute environment *Env* and an interface *I* are provided to **new_component**(*Env,I*), which returns a unique address C. The command **start_beh**(C, [*BRef*]) starts the execution of a component C with an initial behaviour specified as a list of behaviour references, whose actual definitions have been previously declared. The term [**elem**] is used to indicate a list of type **elem**.

$$\text{C} = \textbf{new\_component}(Env, I),$$
$$\textbf{start\_beh}(\text{C}, [BRef])$$

In the above commands, environment *Env* is represented as a map whose keys are atoms denoting attribute names. Interface *I* is a tuple of atoms denoting public attributes, to which other components may want to use their values. In particular, when sending a message, any component attaches also the portion of the environment *Env'* corresponding to *Env* but limited by the interface.

Behaviour Definition. The syntax for behaviour definition is given in Fig. 1. Elements wrapped by $\langle\rangle$ are optional. A definition *BDef* is a function that has as first parameter a component address C. The body of a definition is a sequence of commands, which also require C as their first parameters.

$$BDef ::= beh\_name(\mathsf{C}, \langle param\ list \rangle) \to Com.$$
$$BRef ::= \mathbf{fun}(\langle param\ list \rangle) \to Beh(\mathsf{C}, \langle param\ list \rangle)\ \mathbf{end}$$

$Act ::= \{\langle g \rangle, m, s, \langle u \rangle\}$		Output
$\{\langle g \rangle, r, \langle u \rangle\}$		Input
$Com ::= \mathbf{prefix}(\mathsf{C}, \{Act, BRef\})$		**Prefix**
$\mathbf{choice}(\mathsf{C}, [\{Act, BRef\}])$		**Choice**
$\mathbf{parallel}(\mathsf{C}, [BRef])$		**Parallel**
$Beh(\mathsf{C}, \langle param\ list \rangle)$		**Call**

Fig. 1. ABEL API for process definitions.

Action Act gives the descriptions for AbC input and output actions. There we use m to denote message, u to denote update and g, s, r to denote awareness, sending and receiving predicates respectively. We now briefly explain the different commands.

Prefix - takes as a parameter a pair containing a prefixing action Act and a continuation $BRef$. The command executes Act and continues with $BRef$. If Act is an output description, the command evaluates m into $\tilde{v}$, the sending predicate s into s' and broadcast the triple $(Env', s', \tilde{v})$ to all components and possibly performs an attribute update u, whenever guard g (if specified) is satisfied. If Act is an input description; the command returns a message and optionally performs an attribute update u, whenever guard g (if specified) is satisfied and the sender's attributes and the communicated message satisfy the receiving predicate r.

Choice - takes as parameter a list of pairs, each providing a description of the prefixing action Act and a continuation in form of $BRef$. This command executes one of the actions and continues with the behaviour associated to that action.

Parallel - This command dynamically creates parallel processes, each of which executes a behaviour indicated by a reference in the parameter list.

Process Call - executes the behaviour Beh.

The basic elements m, g, r, s, u are represented as follows.

Message. A message m to be sent is represented as a tuple. A message element can be a function parameterized with the sender environment, i.e., $fun(S) \to \ldots end$, for making it possible to refer to attribute values in S.

Predicates. An awareness predicate g is a unary function parameterized with the environment of the executing component, i.e., $fun(E) \to \ldots end$. A sending predicate s is a binary function parameterized with the sender and receiver environments in that order, i.e., $fun(S, R) \to \ldots end$. A receiving predicate r is a ternary function parameterized with the environments of the receiver and the sender, and a communicated message in that order, i.e., $fun(R, S, M) \to \ldots end$.

Attribute Update. An update is represented as a list of pairs; in each pair, the first element is an attribute name and the second is an expression to be used for the update. The expression can be a function parameterized with the local environment (to use also attribute values), and with the communicated message, when in case the update is associated with a receive action.

As an example of using the presented API for deriving execution code from *AbC* specifications, Fig. 2 presents the definitions in *ABEL* for processes F and D in the graph coloring scenario (Example 2). Bold-faces are used to highlight the structural correspondence between the *ABEL* code and the *AbC* one. The rest of the code is used to specify predicates, messages and updates, which can be addressed by automatic translation. Indeed, we have developed the translator from *AbC* to *ABEL* and made it available with the *ABEL* implementation.

```
f(C) →
    M = {'try', fun(S) → min_colour(att(used,S)) end, fun(S) → att(round,S) end},
    P = fun(S,R) → sets:is_element(att(id,S),att(nbr, R)) end,
    U = [{counter, fun(S) → att(counter,S) + 1 end},
         {colour, fun(S) → min_colour(att(used,S)) end}],
    Act = {M,P,U},
    prefix(C,{Act,nil}).

d(C) →
    P1 = fun(R,S,M) → size(M) == 3 andalso element(1,M) == 'done'
                  andalso att(round,S) == element(3,M)
            end,
    U1 = [{done, fun(R,M) → att(done,R) + 1 end},
          {used, fun(R,M) → sets:add_element(element(2,M),att(used,R)) end}],
    Act1 = {P1, U1},
    P2 = fun(R,S,M) → size(M) == 3 andalso element(1,M) == 'done'
                  andalso att(round,S) > element(3,M)
            end,
    U2 = [{done, fun(R,M) → att(done,R) + 1 end},
          {used, fun(R,M) → sets:add_element(element(2,M),att(used,R)) end},
          {counter,fun(R,M) → att(counter,R) + 1 end}],
    Act2 = {P2, U2},
    DRef = fun() → d(C) end,
    choice(C,[{Act1,DRef},{Act2,DRef}]).
```

Fig. 2. Example code derived from the *AbC* processes F and D in graph colouring

4 Coordinating Components

In this section, we consider two alternative implementations for coordinating *AbC* components. The first implementation is obtained by using an infrastructure similar to the one proposed in [2]; minor modifications have been introduced to make the total ordering protocol more robust. The second one is obtained from the former by relaxing some requirements on ordering preservation. For both implementations we have a corresponding formal semantics. The first one exactly captures the original total ordering *AbC* semantics first presented in [3] while the second one is that briefly explained in Sect. 2.

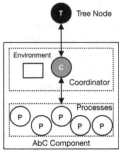

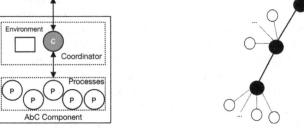

Fig. 3. An *AbC* component in ABEL   **Fig. 4.** A tree-based infrastructure

An *AbC* system in *ABEL* consists of a set of components and an infrastructure with a set of nodes that collaborate on mediating message exchanges. Components join the system via a globally named registration node which assigns them to a node of the infrastructure. Figure 4 shows an example of a tree-structure where each node (black) is responsible for a group of components (white). The model assumes that a node only communicates with those connected to it; likewise a component only communicates with the node they are assigned to. In what follows, we describe the implementations with respect to the behaviour of components and infrastructure nodes.

Coordinating Processes. An *AbC* component is an autonomous entity with multiple processes operating on a shared environment. The behaviour of a component is that of its processes. We have that (i) If more than one process offers an output action, then *only one* of them will be allowed (ii) If more than one process can actually input a message, again *only one* of them will succeed. (iii) A component discards a message only if *all* of its processes discard that message. (iv) Processes and environment influence each other, e.g., a change in the environment caused by one process may enable or disable other processes.

This semantics suggests us considering the attribute environment as a reactive process, rather than a static store. Figure 3 pictures the internal structure of an *AbC* component. Processes *P* represent *AbC* processes that communicate with a coordinator *C* by message passing via the API presented in Sect. 3. Each process submits one action at a time, and continues only after receiving an acknowledgment message. The coordinator keeps track of component environment and decides the actual actions to be executed. The execution of an action may require updating the environment if the action has an associated update request. Actions that cannot be executed because of guards are stored and retried when the environment is updated.

To model interleaving, a coordinator dynamically keeps track of the number of processes, of the set of submitted actions, and uses an input queue for storing messages forwarded from infrastructure. Events that are handled by a coordinator includes commands from processes, messages forwarded from the infrastructure and other implicit information. We briefly explain the operations performed for each event as below.

Parallel events The coordinator creates new processes, and updates the total number of processes.

Sending events When the guard (if specified) is satisfied, the message is forwarded to the infrastructure and the sending process is acknowledged, otherwise, the sending action is added to the set of submitted ones.

Receiving events The action is added to the set of submitted actions.

Choice events The coordinator handles them like normal sending and receiving events, the acknowledgement message to the choice process is a continuation behaviour.

Delivery events These events are internally generated when the input queue is not empty and the number of submitted actions is equal to the number of processes. Predicates of input actions are checked against messages extracted from the queue, one by one until there is a match or the queue is empty. In case of matching, the message is delivered to the receiving process.

Retry events These events are internally triggered when the environment changes. Output actions and choices among output actions in the submitted set are retried.

Coordination Strategies. As mentioned above we have implemented two different strategies for message exchange that may lead to different ordering of message delivery, we call them synchronous and asynchronous.

Synchronous. Encapsulated in the infrastructure presented in [2] there is a sequencer-based protocol that guarantees a total order of message delivery for AbC components. The infrastructure, apart from broadcasting messages for components, plays the role of a sequencer that allocates unique ids for components messages. When a component is willing to send a message, it requests a fresh id for the message. A component can deliver a message labeled with an id only if it has delivered all messages with $id' < id$. This means that messages are delivered in the order of consecutive messages' ids, which is total.

This protocol is used to coordinate $ABEL$ components by relying on a tree-based infrastructure as follows. Every component coordinator keeps a counter c, initially set to 1.

To handle sending events, the coordinator, after checking the guard, requests a fresh id if his previous one has already been used. The output action can take place only if the fresh id matches the counter, otherwise it is postponed. If the action is executed, c is incremented by 1.

To handle delivery events, the coordinator sends a message extracted from the input queue if its id is equals to c, and increases the counter. If the message is not consumed by any input action, the procedure repeats until the queue is empty or there is no message with the expected id.

To handle retry events, the coordinator may send an empty message if there is an unused fresh id which is equal to the local counter and if all components processes can not send a message.

When a non-root tree node receives an id request, it forwards the request to its parent. The root replies its counter value for each request and increments the counter. This fresh id is forwarded along the same path of the original request, but in a reverse order. Eventually, the node which initiated the request receives the fresh id and sends it to the requesting component. When a tree node receives a data message, it forwards the messages to the other connected nodes and to connected AbC components, except the sender. In addition, to guarantee that the number of messages exchanged is bound, each node has an input queue for storing incoming data messages and only forwards a message if its id equals to the node's counter.

Asynchronous. In this implementation, components can send the actual messages simultaneously via the infrastructure without asking and checking for fresh ids. We rely on the tree structure as for the synchronous case but we do not take advantage of it and could have used another structure. A component delivers messages from its input queue in any order to its processes, while trying to filter out as many 'uninteresting' messages as possible. In this case, tree nodes forward messages as soon as they receive them and the root has no special role; which makes the implementation simpler.

5 Experiments

In this section, we report on the performance evaluation of our *Erlang* prototype[3] of *ABEL* by considering the two case studies, stable marriage and graph colouring, whose AbC specifications have been sketched in Sect. 2. These AbC specifications were model checked by following the approach presented in [10].

In particular, we have verified the termination and soundness properties for the graph colouring problem, and the completeness, symmetry of matchings and orchestration properties for stable matching problem.

The explicit-state model checker [14] helped us to verify early designs of these case studies and to come up with correct specifications. From the verified specifications we have then derived the *ABEL* programs introduced in Sect. 3.

For our experiments, we used a workstation with a dual Intel Xeon processor E5-2687W (16 cores in total) and 128 GB of memory. The OS version is Linux 4.9.95-gentoo and the Erlang/OTP version is 21.2. In addition, the coordination infrastructure is the tree-based one with a varying number of nodes and the the previously outlined communication strategies. The tree-based infrastructure was chosen as the default topology after considering the result in [2] showing that it guarantees better performance over others.

5.1 Stable Marriage with Attribute

The input to this case study is randomly generated assuming some predefined probabilities of attributes and preferences. First, we define their ranges, then

---

[3] https://github.com/ArBITRAL/ABEL.

we associate a probability to each value in the range so that the sum of the probabilities is 1. In this way, an attribute (or preference) can take a concrete value v with a probability $p(v)$. In the experiment, we consider 2 attributes and 2 preferences with ranges of 2 values. We select 10 different combinations of probabilities, consider problem sizes of 100 and 200 pairs of elements, and generate 100 instances for each problem size.

We ran the *ABEL* program to solve problem instances and took the average of the execution times. We have also checked the completeness and stability conditions on the outcomes of the program. Table 2 presents the numbers under two different ordering strategies. These numbers are the average over 500 runs with a tree of 7 nodes. The result shows that the interaction protocol for this case study performs faster when using asynchronous messaging.

Table 2. Results of stable matching

Odering	Execution times (in sec.)	
	Size = 100	Size = 200
Total order	5.65	54.63
No order	3.39	35.56

5.2 Graph Colouring

We conducted some experiments with several DIMACS graphs collected from various public sources: flat300_28_0.col (300 vertices and 21695 edges), dsjc500.1.col (500 vertices and 12458 edges), will199GPIA.col (701 vertices and 7065 edges) and dsjc1000.1.col (1000 vertices and 49629 edges). The datasets chosen provides an increasing number of vertices which are considered as AbC components.

The following metrics are considered: the running time in seconds, the total number of messages exchanged between components and the infrastructure and the total size of messages in MB. When measuring, vertices do not wait for each other to report the completion of their colouring: as soon as a vertex decides on a colour, it reports that colour, the number of messages exchanged (and message size) to an external process. Tables 3 and 4 show the results of graph colouring with total ordering and relaxed ordering, respectively. S is the number of nodes used by the tree structure. The other columns show the numbers for colour, round, messages and the total size in that order. The execution times are computed as the average of 50 runs, the other numbers report the average over the results of different number of nodes.

Overall, the *ABEL* code can perform colouring for experiment graphs without any conflicts, and resulted in small speedups when increasing the number of nodes. This is however more obvious with the larger graph. On the other hand, its performance varies on different graphs. This might have to do with their specific topologies. In general, in graphs with more edges, components are more likely

Table 3. Results of graph colouring using total order

Graph	Execution times (in sec.)				#C	#R	#Msg (in milli.)	Size (in MB)
	S = 3	S = 7	S = 15	S = 31				
flat300_28_0	4.57	4.22	4.19	4.4	46	44	1.5	7,141
dsjc500.1	4.22	3.65	3.34	3.39	20	19	2.15	4,008
will199GPIA	7.46	5.95	5.56	5.53	11	25	4.62	4,255
dsjc1000.1.col	32.02	27.19	25.94	24.97	32	30	12.5	42,324

Table 4. Results of graph colouring using relaxed order

Graph	Execution times (in sec.)				#C	#R	#Msg (in milli.)	Size (in MB)
	S = 3	S = 7	S = 15	S = 31				
flat300_28_0	3.76	4.69	4.44	4.53	46	45	1.5	7,095
dsjc500.1	3.17	3.32	2.22	2.94	20	19	2.12	3,905
will199GPIA	6.53	4.03	3.02	2.81	11	25	4.5	4,070
dsjc1000.1.col	49.62	33.58	28.69	21.04	32	30	12.4	41,524

to face colour conflicts among neighbours and thus to require more interactions. This leads to an increased number of rounds and message exchanges.

It can be seen from the results that both ordering strategies return similar outcomes for the same input graphs. Although, in most cases, relaxed ordering guarantees slightly better performance.

6 Concluding Remarks and Related Works

We have presented *ABEL*, an implementation of *AbC* in *Erlang* that builds on an API that mimics *AbC* constructs. Our purpose is to develop and experiment with systems featuring complex interactions according to the *AbC* paradigm. The API is integrated seamlessly with underneath coordination mechanisms that together simulate the original synchronous semantics of *AbC* and a less demanding one. Because of the direct correspondence between the two formal semantics and our actual implementations, we can perform formal verification of *ABEL* programs by considering their *AbC* abstractions. Indeed, from *AbC* specifications we can obtain verifiable models that can be provided as input to model checkers.

There have been other attempts at providing implementations of *AbC*. *AErlang* [11] extends *Erlang* processes to allow attribute-based communication beside the point-to-point one. However, the programming style is based on the host language and it might not be immediate to derive *AErlang* programs from *AbC* specifications. Furthermore, the lack of a corresponding formal semantics of *AErlang* calls for alternative directions, not based on translations, when it comes to reasoning on programs. Other *AbC* implementations such as [1,4] exhibit a gap between *AbC* primitives and their programming constructs. More efforts are needed to derive *AbC* code and automatic translations are not immediate.

We refer the readers to [11] for a more detailed account of related works on concurrent languages and communication models.

In near future, we want to establish a formal relationship between *ABEL* and *AbC* and prove the correctness of the API implementation, as well as the correctness of the developed translation. This would require studying the operational semantics of the inter- and intra- components coordinators, and formalizing the translation rules. We also plan to integrate the model checking part within our framework. Moreover, it might be useful to equip *ABEL* with other communication and synchronization abstractions; we have experienced that programming complex distributed systems using only *AbC* send and receive may be difficult.

References

1. Abd Alrahman, Y., De Nicola, R., Garbi, G.: *GoAt*: attribute-based interaction in Google Go. In: Margaria, T., Steffen, B. (eds.) ISoLA 2018. LNCS, vol. 11246, pp. 288–303. Springer, Cham (2018). https://doi.org/10.1007/978-3-030-03424-5_19
2. Alrahman, Y.A., De Nicola, R., Garbi, G., Loreti, M.: A distributed coordination infrastructure for attribute-based interaction. In: Baier, C., Caires, L. (eds.) FORTE 2018. LNCS, vol. 10854, pp. 1–20. Springer, Cham (2018). https://doi.org/10.1007/978-3-319-92612-4_1
3. Abd Alrahman, Y., De Nicola, R., Loreti, M.: On the power of attribute-based communication. In: Albert, E., Lanese, I. (eds.) FORTE 2016. LNCS, vol. 9688, pp. 1–18. Springer, Cham (2016). https://doi.org/10.1007/978-3-319-39570-8_1
4. Abd Alrahman, Y., De Nicola, R., Loreti, M.: Programming of CAS systems by relying on attribute-based communication. In: Margaria, T., Steffen, B. (eds.) ISoLA 2016. LNCS, vol. 9952, pp. 539–553. Springer, Cham (2016). https://doi.org/10.1007/978-3-319-47166-2_38
5. Alrahman, Y.A., De Nicola, R., Loreti, M.: A behavioural theory for interactions in collective-adaptive systems. CoRR abs/1711.09762 (2017). arXiv:1711.09762
6. Alrahman, Y.A., De Nicola, R., Loreti, M.: Programming the interactions of collective adaptive systems by relying on attribute-based communication. CoRR abs/1711.06092 (2017). arXiv:1711.06092
7. Anderson, S., Bredeche, N., Eiben, A., Kampis, G., van Steen, M.: Adaptive collective systems: herding black sheep. Book Sprints for ICT Research (2013)
8. Baldoni, R., Cimmino, S., Marchetti, C.: Total order communications: a practical analysis. In: Dal Cin, M., Kaâniche, M., Pataricza, A. (eds.) EDCC 2005. LNCS, vol. 3463, pp. 38–54. Springer, Heidelberg (2005). https://doi.org/10.1007/11408901_4
9. Birman, K., Schiper, A., Stephenson, P.: Lightweight causal and atomic group multicast. ACM Trans. Comput. Syst. **9**(3), 272–314 (1991). https://doi.org/10.1145/128738.128742
10. De Nicola, R., Duong, T., Inverso, O., Mazzanti, F.: Verifying properties of systems relying on attribute-based communication. In: Katoen, J.-P., Langerak, R., Rensink, A. (eds.) ModelEd, TestEd, TrustEd. LNCS, vol. 10500, pp. 169–190. Springer, Cham (2017). https://doi.org/10.1007/978-3-319-68270-9_9
11. De Nicola, R., Duong, T., Inverso, O., Trubiani, C.: AErlang: empowering Erlang with attribute-based communication. Sci. Comput. Program. **168**, 71–93 (2018)

12. De Nicola, R., Loreti, M., Pugliese, R., Tiezzi, F.: A formal approach to autonomic systems programming: the SCEL language. ACM Trans. Auton. Adapt. Syst. (TAAS) **9**(2), 7:1–7:29 (2014)
13. Gale, D., Shapley, L.S.: College admissions and the stability of marriage. Am. Math. Mon. **69**(1), 9–15 (1962)
14. Ter Beek, M.H., Fantechi, A., Gnesi, S., Mazzanti, F.: A state/event-based model-checking approach for the analysis of abstract system properties. Sci. Comput. Program. **76**(2), 119–135 (2011)
15. Lamport, L.: Time, clocks, and the ordering of events in a distributed system. Commun. ACM **21**(7), 558–565 (1978)
16. Prasad, K.V.: A calculus of broadcasting systems. Sci. Comput. Program. **25**(2–3), 285–327 (1995)

Bridging the Gap Between Supervisory Control and Coordination of Services: Synthesis of Orchestrations and Choreographies

Davide Basile[1]([✉]) [iD], Maurice H. ter Beek[2] [iD], and Rosario Pugliese[1] [iD]

[1] University of Florence, Florence, Italy
{davide.basile,rosario.pugliese}@unifi.it
[2] ISTI–CNR, Pisa, Italy
maurice.terbeek@isti.cnr.it

Abstract. We explore the frontiers between coordination and control systems by discussing a number of contributions to bridging the gap between supervisory control theory and coordination of services. In particular, we illustrate how the classical synthesis algorithm from supervisory control theory to obtain the so-called most permissive controller can be modified to synthesise orchestrations and choreographies of service contracts formalised as contract automata. The key ingredient to make this possible is a novel notion of controllability. Finally, we present an abstract parametric synthesis algorithm and show that it generalises the classical synthesis as well as the orchestration and choreography syntheses.

Keywords: Service contracts · Contract automata ·
Controller synthesis · Orchestration · Choreography

1 Introduction

Coordination of services describes how control and data exchanges are coordinated in distributed service-based applications and systems. Their principled design is identified as one of the primary research challenges for the next 10 years, and the recent Service Computing Manifesto [22] points out that "Service systems have so far been built without an adequate rigorous foundation that would enable reasoning about them" and, moreover, that "The design of service systems should build upon a formal model of services".

Two widely adopted approaches to the coordination of services are *orchestration* and *choreography*. Intuitively, an orchestration yields the description of a distributed workflow from "one party's perspective" [45], whereas a choreography describes the behaviour of the involved parties from a "global viewpoint" [38].

© IFIP International Federation for Information Processing 2019
Published by Springer Nature Switzerland AG 2019
H. Riis Nielson and E. Tuosto (Eds.): COORDINATION 2019, LNCS 11533, pp. 129–147, 2019.
https://doi.org/10.1007/978-3-030-22397-7_8

In an orchestrated model, the service components are coordinated by a special component, the *orchestrator*, which, by interacting with them, dictates the workflow at runtime. In a choreographed model, instead, the service components autonomously execute and interact with each other on the basis of a local control flow expected to comply with their role as specified by the global viewpoint. Ideally, a choreographed model is more efficient due to the absence of the overhead of communications with the orchestrator. Any choreography can be trivially transformed into an orchestration of services, by adding an idle orchestrator. Similarly, by explicitly adding an orchestrator and its interactions with the service components, and hence the relative overhead, it is possible to transform an orchestration of services into a choreography.

In [13], two orchestrated and choreographed automata-based models of services, called *contract automata*[1] and *communicating finite state machines*, respectively, were studied and related. The goal is to compose the automata so that each service is capable of reaching an accepting (final) state by synchronous/asynchronous one-to-one interactions with the other services in the composition. The main difference relies on the fact that communicating machines name the recipient service of each interaction upfront and use FIFO buffers to interact with each other, whereas contract automata are oblivious of their partners and an orchestration is synthesised to drive their interactions. In particular, the model of contract automata was further developed in, e.g., [11,12,14].

The orchestration synthesis was borrowed from the synthesis of the most permissive controller (mpc) from Supervisory Control Theory [24,47] (SCT), whose aim is to coordinate an ensemble of (local) components into a (global) system that functions correctly. In the context of contract automata, this amounts to refine the composition of service contracts into its largest sub-portion whose behaviour is non-blocking and safe (a notion of service compliance). The adaptation of the mpc synthesis for synthesising an orchestration of services required the introduction of a novel notion of semi-controllability. Basically, the assumption of the presence of an unpredictable environment was dropped in favour of a milder notion of predictable necessary service requests to be fulfilled.

In this paper, we report on the efforts to relate the mpc synthesis and the orchestration synthesis of contract automata through a homogeneous formalisation. The need for semi-controllability is showcased with intuitive examples and its expressiveness is evaluated with respect to standard SCT notions of controllable and uncontrollable actions. Moreover, a novel choreography synthesis algorithm is introduced as a refined version of the orchestration synthesis. Finally, we show that all synthesis algorithms presented in this paper are generalised into a single abstract synthesis algorithm from which each can be obtained through a different instantiation.

The paper is organised as follows. Section 2 contains background notions and results concerning contract automata and SCT. Sections 3 and 4 introduce the synthesis of orchestrations and the novel synthesis of choreographies in the

---

[1] Not to be confused with the contract automata of [7] meant to formalise legal contracts among two parties expressed in natural language.

setting of (modal service) contract automata. Section 5 demonstrates that all the previously introduced syntheses algorithms are instantiations of a more abstract, parametric synthesis algorithm. Section 6 discusses related work, while Sect. 7 concludes the paper and provides some hints for future work.

2   Background

In this section, we provide the background needed to appreciate our contributions on the crossroads of supervisory control theory and coordination of services formalised as modal service contract automata.

2.1   Contract Automata

A Contract Automaton (CA) represents either a single service (in which case it is called a *principal*) or a multi-party composition of services performing actions. The number of principals of a CA is called its *rank*. The states of a CA are vectors of states of principals. In the following, notation $\vec{v}$ stands for a vector and $\vec{v}_{(i)}$ is the ith element. The transitions of CA are labelled with *actions*, which are vectors of elements in the set of *basic actions* $\mathsf{L} = \mathsf{R} \cup \mathsf{O} \cup \{\bullet\}$, with $\mathsf{R} \cap \mathsf{O} = \emptyset$ and $\bullet \notin \mathsf{R} \cup \mathsf{O}$. Intuitively, R is the set of *requests* (depicted as non-overlined labels on arcs, e.g. *ins*), O is the set of *offers* (depicted as overlined labels on arcs, e.g. $\overline{ins}$), and $\bullet$ is a distinguished symbol representing the *idle* action. An *action* is then a vector $\vec{a}$ of basic actions where there is either a single offer, or a single request, or a single pair of request-offer that match, i.e. there exist i and j such that $\vec{a}_{(i)}$ is an offer and $\vec{a}_{(j)}$ is the complementary request; all other elements of the vector are the symbol $\bullet$. Such action is called *request*, *offer*, or *match*, respectively. A transition is also deemed request/offer/match according to its labelling action. The goal of each principal is to reach an accepting (*final*) state such that all its requests and offers are matched. In [14], CA were equipped with *modalities*, i.e. *necessary* ($\square$) and *permitted* ($\diamond$) requests, respectively, and the formalism was called Modal Service Contract Automata (MSCA), formally defined below.

Definition 1 (MSCA [14]). *Given a finite set of states* $Q = \{q_1, q_2, \ldots\}$, *a* Modal Service Contract Automata (MSCA) $\mathcal{A}$ *of rank* n *is a septuple* $\langle Q, \vec{q_0}, A^{\diamond}, A^{\square}, A^o, T, F \rangle$, *with set of states* $Q = Q_1 \times \ldots \times Q_n \subseteq Q^n$, *initial state* $\vec{q_0} \in Q$, $A^{\diamond}, A^{\square} \subseteq \mathsf{R}$ *(pairwise disjoint) finite sets of permitted and necessary requests, respectively, with set of requests* $A^r = A^{\diamond} \cup A^{\square}$, *set of offers* $A^o \subseteq \mathsf{O}$, *set of final states* $F \subseteq Q$, *set of transitions* $T \subseteq Q \times A \times Q$, *where* $A \subseteq (A^r \cup A^o \cup \{\bullet\})^n$, *partitioned into* permitted *transitions* $T^{\diamond}$ *and* necessary *transitions* $T^{\square}$, *s.t.: (i) given* $t = (\vec{q}, \vec{a}, \vec{q}') \in T$, $\vec{a}$ *is either a request or an offer or a match; (ii)* $\forall i \in 1 \ldots n$, $\vec{a}_{(i)} = \bullet$ *implies* $\vec{q}_{(i)} = \vec{q}'_{(i)}$; *(iii)* $t \in T^{\diamond}$ *iff* $\vec{a}$ *is either a request or a match on* $a \in A^{\diamond}$ *or an offer on* $\overline{a} \in A^o$; *otherwise* $t \in T^{\square}$.

A *principal* is an MSCA of rank 1 such that $A^r \cap co(A^o) = \emptyset$, where the involution $co : \mathsf{L} \to \mathsf{L}$ establishing matching among requests and offers is such that (abusing notation) $co(\mathsf{R}) = \mathsf{O}$, $co(\mathsf{O}) = \mathsf{R}$, and $co(\bullet) = \bullet$. A *step* $(w, \vec{q}) \xrightarrow{\vec{a}} (w', \vec{q}')$ occurs iff $w = \vec{a}w'$, $w' \in A^*$, and $(\vec{q}, \vec{a}, \vec{q}') \in T$. Let $\rightarrow^*$ be the reflexive and transitive closure of $\rightarrow$. The *language* of $\mathcal{A}$ is $L(\mathcal{A}) = \{ w \mid (w, \vec{q_0}) \xrightarrow{w}^* (\varepsilon, \vec{q}),\ \vec{q} \in F \}$. A step may be denoted $\vec{q} \xrightarrow{\vec{a}}$ if w, w', and $\vec{q}'$ are irrelevant, and $(w, \vec{q}) \rightarrow (w', \vec{q}')$ if $\vec{a}$ is. Unless stated differently, the MSCA $\mathcal{A} = \langle Q_{\mathcal{A}}, \vec{q_{0\,\mathcal{A}}}, A_{\mathcal{A}}^{\Diamond}, A_{\mathcal{A}}^{\Box}, A_{\mathcal{A}}^{o}, T_{\mathcal{A}}, F_{\mathcal{A}} \rangle$ of rank n is assumed to be given. Subscript $\mathcal{A}$ may be omitted if no confusion may arise.

Composition of services is rendered through the composition of their MSCA models by means of the *composition operator* $\otimes$. This operator basically interleaves or matches the transitions of the component MSCA, but, whenever two component MSCA are ready on their respective request/offer action, then the match is forced to happen. Moreover, a match involving a necessary request is itself necessary. In the resulting MSCA, states and actions are vectors of states and actions of the component MSCA, respectively. The composition is non-associative, i.e. pre-existing matches are not rearranged if a new MSCA joins the composition afterwards.

In a composition of MSCA, typically various properties are analysed. We are especially interested in *agreement* and *strong agreement* (a.k.a. in the literature as progress of interactions, deadlock freedom, compliance or conformance of contracts). In an MSCA in strong agreement, all requests and offers must be matched. Instead, the property of agreement only requires to match all requests. An MSCA admits (strong) agreement if it has a trace satisfying the corresponding property, and it is *safe* if all its traces are such.

2.2 Supervisory Control Theory

The aim of Supervisory Control Theory [24,47] (SCT) is to provide an algorithm to synthesise a finite state automaton model of a *supervisory controller* from given (component) finite state automata models of the uncontrolled system and its requirements. The synthesised supervisory controller, if successfully generated, is such that the controlled system, which is the composition (i.e. synchronous product) of the uncontrolled system and the supervisory controller, satisfies the requirements and is additionally *non-blocking*, *controllable*, and *maximally permissive*.

An automaton is *non-blocking* if from each state at least one of the so-called *marked states* (distinguished stable states representing completed 'tasks' [47]) can be reached without passing through so-called *forbidden states*, meaning that the system always has the possibility to return to an accepted stable state (e.g. a final state). The algorithm assumes that marked states and forbidden states are indicated for each component model. SCT distinguishes between *observable* and *unobservable*, *controllable* and *uncontrollable* actions, where unobservable actions are also uncontrollable. The supervisory controller is not permitted to directly block uncontrollable actions from occurring; the controller is only allowed to disable them by preventing controllable actions from occurring. Intuitively, controllable actions correspond to stimulating the system, while uncontrollable actions correspond to messages provided by the environment, like sensors, which may be neglected but cannot be denied from existing. Finally, the fact that the resulting supervisory controller is *maximally permissive* (or least restrictive) means that as much behaviour of the uncontrolled system as possible is still present in the controlled system without violating neither the requirements, nor controllability, nor the non-blocking condition.

From the seminal work of Ramadge and Wonham [47], we know that a unique maximally permissive supervisory controller exists, provided that all actions are observable. This is called the *most permissive controller* (*mpc*); it coordinates an ensemble of (local) components into a (global) system that works correctly. The synthesis algorithm suffers from the same state space explosion problem as model checking [35].

Intuitively, the synthesis algorithm for computing the mpc of a finite state automaton $\mathcal{A}$ works as follows. The mpc is computed through an iterative procedure that at each step i updates incrementally a set of states R_i containing the *bad* states, i.e. those states that cannot prevent a forbidden state to be eventually reached, and refines an automaton $\mathcal{K}_i$. The algorithm starts with an automaton $\mathcal{K}_0$ equal to $\mathcal{A}$ and a set R_0 containing all *dangling* states, where a state is dangling if it cannot be reached from the initial state or cannot reach a final state. At each step i the algorithm prunes in a backwards fashion transitions with target state in R_i or forbidden source state. The set R_i is updated by possibly adding source states of uncontrollable transitions of $\mathcal{A}$ with a bad target state and dangling states. When no more updates are possible, the algorithm terminates. Since $\mathcal{A}$ is finite state and the set R_i can only increase at each step, termination is ensured. Now, suppose that at its termination the algorithm returns the pair $(\mathcal{K}_s, R_s)$. We have that the mpc is empty, if the initial state of $\mathcal{A}$ is in R_s; otherwise, the mpc is $\mathcal{K}_s$. We report below the standard synthesis algorithm, but we homogenise the notation and simplify the formulation, to align the algorithm with those presented in the next sections. For this purpose, we assume the standard mpc synthesis to operate on MSCA where necessary transitions ($T^\square$) are uncontrollable whilst permitted transitions ($T^\diamond$) are controllable. We use $\langle\ \rangle$ to denote the empty automaton. A state $q \in Q$ is *dangling* iff $\nexists w$ s.t. $q_0 \xrightarrow{w}{}^* q$ or $q \xrightarrow{w}{}^* q_f \in F$. $Dangling(\mathcal{A})$ denotes the set of dangling states of $\mathcal{A}$. Given two MSCA $\mathcal{A}$ and $\mathcal{A}'$, we say that $\mathcal{A}'$ is a *sub-automaton* of $\mathcal{A}$, written $\mathcal{A}' \subseteq \mathcal{A}$, whenever the components of $\mathcal{A}'$ are included in the corresponding ones of $\mathcal{A}$. Moreover, given two sets of states R and R', we let $(\mathcal{A}, R) \leq (\mathcal{A}', R')$ if $\mathcal{A}' \subseteq \mathcal{A}$ and $R \subseteq R'$. It is straightforward to show that $(MSCA \times 2^Q, \leq)$ is a complete partial order (cpo).

The algorithm to compute the mpc is then defined in terms of the *least fixed point* of a monotone function on the cpo $(MSCA \times 2^Q, \leq)$.

Definition 2 (Standard synthesis, adapted from [47]). *Let $\mathcal{A}$ be an MSCA, and let $\mathcal{K}_0 = \mathcal{A}$ and $R_0 = Dangling(\mathcal{K}_0)$. We let the synthesis function $f : MSCA \times 2^Q \to MSCA \times 2^Q$ be defined as follows:*

$$f(\mathcal{K}_{i-1}, R_{i-1}) = (\mathcal{K}_i, R_i), \text{ with}$$
$$T_{\mathcal{K}_i} = T_{\mathcal{K}_{i-1}} \setminus \{ (\vec{q}, \vec{a}, \vec{q}') \in T_{\mathcal{K}_{i-1}} \mid \vec{q}' \in R_{i-1} \lor \vec{q} \text{ is forbidden} \}$$
$$R_i = R_{i-1} \cup \{ \vec{q} \mid (\vec{q}, \vec{a}, \vec{q}') \in T_{\mathcal{A}}^\square, \ \vec{q}' \in R_{i-1} \} \cup Dangling(\mathcal{K}_i)$$

Theorem 1 (Standard mpc, adapted from [47]). *The synthesis function f is monotone on the cpo* $(MSCA \times 2^Q, \leq)$ *and its* least *fixed point is:*

$$(\mathcal{K}_s, R_s) = sup(\{ f^n(\mathcal{K}_0, R_0) \mid n \in \mathbb{N} \})$$

The mpc of $\mathcal{A}$*, denoted by* $\mathcal{K}_\mathcal{A}$*, is:*

$$\mathcal{K}_\mathcal{A} = \begin{cases} \langle \, \rangle & \text{if } \vec{q}_0 \in R_s \\ \langle Q \setminus Dangling(\mathcal{K}_s), \vec{q}_0, A^\diamond, A^\square, A^\circ, T_{\mathcal{K}_s}, F \setminus Dangling(\mathcal{K}_s) \rangle & \text{otherwise} \end{cases}$$

3   Synthesis of Orchestrations

In this section, we discuss how we revised the classical synthesis algorithm from SCT (cf. Theorem 1) to obtain the mpc and synthesise orchestrations of MSCA.

Differently from standard SCT, all transitions of MSCA are *observable*, since MSCA model the execution of services in terms of their requests and offers. Originally, MSCA were capable of expressing only permitted requirements, corresponding to actions that are controllable by the orchestrator. Hence, in the synthesis of the orchestration, all transitions labelled by actions violating the property to be enforced were pruned, and all dangling states were removed (cf. [11]).

While permitted requests of MSCA are in one-to-one correspondence with controllable actions, interestingly this is not the case for necessary requests and uncontrollable actions. A necessary (request) action is indeed a weaker constraint than an uncontrollable one. This stems from the fact that traditionally uncontrollable actions relate to an unpredictable environment. However, the interpretation of such actions as *necessary* service requests to be fulfilled in a service contract, as is the case in the setting of MSCA, implies that it suffices that in the synthesised orchestration at least one such synchronisation (i.e. match) actually occurs. This is precisely what is modelled by the notion of *semi-controllable* actions, anticipated in [14] and introduced in [9,10], discussed next.

The importance of this novel notion in the synthesis algorithm is showcased by an intuitive example. Consider the two MSCA interacting on the necessary service request a depicted in Fig. 1 (left and middle), and their possible composition $\mathcal{A}$ depicted in Fig. 1 (right). Note that $\mathcal{A}$ models two possibilities of fulfilling request a from the leftmost automaton by matching it with a service offer $\overline{a}$ of the middle one. Note that a similar composition can be obtained in other automata-based formalisms (such as, e.g., (timed) I/O automata [3,31,43]). Now assume that a must be matched with $\overline{a}$ to obtain an agreement (i.e. it is *necessary*), and that for some reason the *bad* state ✗ is to be avoided in favour of the *successful* state ✓, i.e. in some sense we would like to express that a must be matched at some point, rather than always. In most automata-based formalisms this is not allowed and the resulting mpc is empty. In the MSCA formalism, it is possible to orchestrate the composition of the two automata on the left in such a way that the result is the automaton $\mathcal{A}$ on the right, but *without the state* ✗ *and its* incident transition.

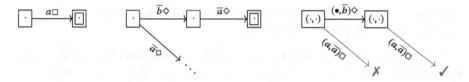

Fig. 1. Two MSCA (left and middle) and a possible composition $\mathcal{A}$ of them (right)

In fact, in the MSCA formalism, $\mathcal{A}$ depicts a composition in which the automata on the left can synchronise on a so-called semi-controllable action $a\square$ either in their initial state or after the middle automaton has performed some other action $\bar{b}\diamond$, ignoring in this case whether a bad or a successful state is reached in the end. Indeed, the notion of semi-controllability is independent from both the specific formalism being used and the requirement (e.g. agreement in case of MSCA) to be enforced.

As far as we know, we were the first to define a synthesis algorithm, in [10], that is capable of producing a controller that guarantees that *at least* one of these two synchronisations actually occurs. Indeed, in the standard synthesis algorithm (cf. Theorem 1), a can either be *controllable* and hence not necessary as we want, or *uncontrollable* thus requiring that a must *always* be matched, a stronger requirement than the one posed by declaring a as necessary.

To formalize the intuitions above[2], a semi-controllable transition t becomes controllable if in a given portion of $\mathcal{A}$ there exists a semi-controllable match transition t', with source and target states not dangling, such that in both t and t' the *same* principal, in the *same* local state, does the *same* request. Otherwise, t is uncontrollable.

Definition 3 (Controllability). *Let $\mathcal{A}$ be an MSCA and let $t = (\vec{q}_1, \vec{a}_1, \vec{q}_1') \in T_{\mathcal{A}}$. Then:*

- *if $\vec{a}_1$ is an action on $a \in A^\diamond \cup A^\circ$, then t is* controllable *(in $\mathcal{A}$) and part of $T^\diamond$;*
- *if $\vec{a}_1$ is a request or match on $a \in A^\square$, then t is* semi-controllable *(in $\mathcal{A}$) and part of $T^\square$.*

Moreover, given $\mathcal{A}' \subseteq \mathcal{A}$, if t is semi-controllable and $\exists\, t' = (\vec{q}_2 \xrightarrow{\vec{a}_2} \vec{q}_2'') \in T_{\mathcal{A}'}^\square$ in $\mathcal{A}'$ s.t. $\vec{a}_2$ is a match, $\vec{q}_2, \vec{q}_2' \notin Dangling(\mathcal{A}')$, $\vec{q}_{1(i)} = \vec{q}_{2(i)}$, and $\vec{a}_{1(i)} = \vec{a}_{2(i)} = a$, then t is controllable *in $\mathcal{A}'$ (via t'); otherwise, t is* uncontrollable *in $\mathcal{A}'$.*

The algorithm for synthesising an orchestration enforcing agreement of MSCA follows. The main adaptation of the mpc synthesis of Theorem 1 is that transitions are no longer declared uncontrollable, but instead they can be either controllable or semi-controllable. More importantly, a semi-controllable transition switches from controllable to uncontrollable only after it has been pruned in a previous iteration, in which case its source state becomes bad. Finally, in this

---

[2] We refer the interested reader to [9,10] for a full account.

case there are no forbidden states but rather forbidden transitions (i.e. requests, according to the property of agreement).

Definition 4 (MSCA orchestration synthesis, adapted from [14]). *Let $\mathcal{A}$ be an MSCA, and let $\mathcal{K}_0 = \mathcal{A}$ and $R_0 = Dangling(\mathcal{K}_0)$. We let the orchestration synthesis function $f_o : MSCA \times 2^Q \rightarrow MSCA \times 2^Q$ be defined as follows:*

$$f_o(\mathcal{K}_{i-1}, R_{i-1}) = (\mathcal{K}_i, R_i), \; with$$
$$T_{\mathcal{K}_i} = T_{\mathcal{K}_{i-1}} \setminus \{ (\vec{q} \rightarrow \vec{q}') = t \in T_{\mathcal{K}_{i-1}} \mid (\vec{q}' \in R_{i-1} \vee t \text{ is a request}) \}$$
$$R_i = R_{i-1} \cup \{ \vec{q} \mid (\vec{q} \rightarrow) \in T_{\mathcal{A}}^{\square} \text{ is uncontrollable in } \mathcal{K}_i \} \cup Dangling(\mathcal{K}_i)$$

Theorem 2 (MSCA orchestration mpc, adapted from [14]). *The orchestration synthesis function f_o is monotone on the cpo $(MSCA \times 2^Q, \leq)$ and its least fixed point is:*

$$(\mathcal{K}_s, R_s) = sup(\{ f_o^n(\mathcal{K}_0, R_0) \mid n \in \mathbb{N} \})$$

The (orchestration) mpc $\mathcal{K}_{\mathcal{A}}$ of $\mathcal{A}$ is:

$$\mathcal{K}_{\mathcal{A}} = \begin{cases} \langle \, \rangle & \text{if } \vec{q}_0 \in R_s \\ \langle Q \setminus R_s, \vec{q}_0, A^\diamond, A^\square, A^\circ, T_{\mathcal{K}_s} \setminus T', F \setminus R_s \rangle & \text{otherwise} \end{cases}$$

where $T' = \{ t = \vec{q} \rightarrow \in \mathcal{K}_s \mid t \text{ is controllable in } \mathcal{K}_s, \; \vec{q} \in R_s \}$.

Semi-controllability. We now show, by means of an example, that the encoding of an automaton $\mathcal{A}$ with semi-controllable actions into an automaton $\mathcal{A}'$ without, such that the same synthesised controllers are obtained, results in an exponential blow-up of the state space. More precisely, the encoding is intended to preserve safety: the mpc of $\mathcal{A}$ equals that of $\mathcal{A}'$. The encoding is sketched in Fig. 2: the automaton $\mathcal{A}'$ is obtained by turning all semi-controllable transitions of the automaton $\mathcal{A}$ from Fig. 1 (right) into uncontrollable transitions in $\mathcal{A}'$. The intuition for this construction is as follows. If the synchronisation on a specific semi-controllable action a occurs in n different transitions in $\mathcal{A}$ (two in our example), then the encoding creates an automaton that is the union of $2^n - 1$ automata (three in our example), which are obtained by all possible combinations of pruning a subset of the n semi-controllable transitions of $\mathcal{A}$, minus the one in which all n semi-controllable transitions are pruned. In fact, without knowing a priori the set of forbidden and successful states, it is impossible to provide a more efficient encoding.

We explain why this is the case. Assume, by contradiction, that there exists an encoding that results in a 'smaller' automaton $\mathcal{A}''$, in which one of the $2^n - 1$ combinations of pruned transitions (say, P) is discarded. It then suffices to specify as a counterexample a property in $\mathcal{A}$ such that all source states of transitions in P are forbidden and all target states of the remaining semi-controllable transitions are successful. The synthesis of $\mathcal{A}$ against such a property would prune exactly the semi-controllable transitions in P. Thus, in the synthesis of $\mathcal{A}''$ such an mpc would not be present, a contradiction.

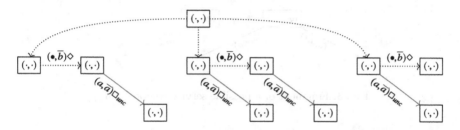

Fig. 2. Automaton $\mathcal{A}'$ uses uncontrollable transitions to encode automaton $\mathcal{A}$ from Fig. 1 (right)

4   Synthesis of Choreographies

In the previous section we have seen that the orchestration of MSCA is rendered as a particular mpc. The orchestrator is however implicit, in the sense that its interactions with the principals are hidden. Basically, one could assume that before interacting, each principal expects a message from the orchestrator and answers with an acknowledgement after the interaction terminates. The main intuition behind switching from an orchestrated to a choreographic coordination of contracts is that there is no longer the need for such 'hidden' interactions. Ideally, the principals moving autonomously are able to accomplish the behaviour foreseen by the synthesis, which in this case acts as a global type. Differently from the traditional choreographic approach, where the starting point is a global type, in MSCA the global type is synthesised automatically.

The requirements for ensuring that the synthesised mpc is a (form of) choreography were studied in [13,41]. Roughly, they amount to the so-called *branching condition* requiring that principals perform their offers/outputs independently of the other principals in the composition. To formalise it, we let $snd(\vec{a}) = i$ when $\vec{a}$ is a match action or an offer action and $\vec{a}_{(i)} \in \mathsf{O}$.

Definition 5 (Branching condition [13]). *An MSCA $\mathcal{A}$ satisfies the* branching condition *iff the following holds for each pair of states $\vec{q}_1$, $\vec{q}_2$ reachable in $\mathcal{A}$:*

$$\forall \vec{a} \ match \ action \ . \ (\vec{q}_1 \xrightarrow{\vec{a}} \land snd(\vec{a}) = i \land \vec{q}_{1\,(i)} = \vec{q}_{2\,(i)}) \ implies \ \vec{q}_2 \xrightarrow{\vec{a}}.$$

The branching condition is related to a phenomenon known as 'state sharing' in other coordination models (cf., e.g., [18]) according to which system components can influence potential synchronisations through their local (component) states even if they are not involved in the actual global (system) transition.

In [13] it is proved that the mpc corresponds to a well-behaving choreography if and only if it satisfies the branching condition and is strongly safe. Notably, in case the two conditions are not satisfied, that paper does not provide any algorithm for automatically synthesising a choreography, rather the contracts have to be manually amended. Instead, in the remainder of this section, we introduce an algorithm for automatically synthesising a well-behaving choreography.

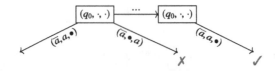

Fig. 3. Fragment of a possible service composition

The property to be enforced during the synthesis is strong agreement: all offers and requests have to be matched, because all messages have to be read (i.e. offers matched). Moreover, in the case of choreography, service contract requests are always permitted whereas service contract offers can be necessary. That is, their roles are swapped with respect to the case of orchestration.

In principle, the synthesis could trivially introduce a coordinator component and its interactions to coordinate the principals. However, this would reduce the choreography to a centralised coordination of contracts. To prevent this, the synthesis can only remove and never add behaviour. Hence, a choreography can only be synthesised if all principals are capable of interacting on their own without resorting to a central coordinator.

Similarly to orchestration synthesis, indicating transitions as either controllable or uncontrollable does not suffice for synthesising a choreography. Moreover, the notion of semi-controllability introduced for the orchestration case does not suffice for expressing necessary offers. Indeed, orchestration synthesis does not ensure the branching condition to be satisfied by the synthesised automaton, as the following example shows.

In Fig. 3, a fragment of a service composition is shown. Two global states are depicted, and in both the first service, say *Alice*, is in its initial local state (say, q_0). *Alice* performs an output (i.e. offer) $\overline{a}$ that can be directed to either *Bob* (second service) or *Carol* (third service), from the initial global state, or only to *Bob* from the other state. It is possible to reach either a successful (✓) or a bad (✗) state, left unspecified for the moment. Notably, the output of *Alice* is neither controllable nor uncontrollable nor semi-controllable by the synthesis.

Now assume that the $\overline{a}$ is controllable and from the initial global state both interactions eventually lead to a bad state (✗). In this case, those transitions are pruned by the synthesis, and the resulting automaton is wrongly approved. Indeed, *Alice* has no mean to understand when her output $\overline{a}$ is enabled, because she has not changed state. The branching condition, which is necessary for obtaining a well-behaving choreography, would be violated. Note that this would happen also if $\overline{a}$ were semi-controllable. In fact, to satisfy the branching condition, the synthesis should remove all outputs $\overline{a}$.

Conversely, assume that the $\overline{a}$ is uncontrollable and that it is possible from the initial global state to reach a successful state (✓) if the message $\overline{a}$ is received by *Bob*. In this case, it would not be possible to prune the transition from the initial state leading to ✗, because it is also uncontrollable. The synthesis would thus be empty, a wrong rejection, because a choreography exists in which *Alice* autonomously interacts with *Bob*.

In conclusion, a necessary action is rendered neither as uncontrollable nor semi-controllable and permitted actions require extra pruning operations during the synthesis. A novel notion of semi-controllability for a necessary action is required that is weaker than uncontrollable but stronger than the semi-controllable notion used in the synthesis of orchestration. Basically, for the choreography synthesis, a (semi-controllable) necessary transition $t = (\vec{q} \xrightarrow{\vec{a}_1}) \in T^{\square}$ is detected to be uncontrollable iff no necessary transition $t' = (\vec{q} \xrightarrow{\vec{a}_2}) \in T^{\square}$ exists from the same source state such that in both t and t' the same offer is provided by the same principal, but possibly with different receivers. Formally:

Definition 6. *Let $\mathcal{A}$ be an MSCA and let $t = (\vec{q}, \vec{a}_1, \vec{q}_1') \in T_{\mathcal{A}}$. Then:*

- *if $\vec{a}_1$ is an action on $a \in A^{\diamond}$, then t is* controllable *(in $\mathcal{A}$);*
- *if $\vec{a}_1$ is an offer or a match on $a \in A^{\square}$, then t is* semi-controllable *(in $\mathcal{A}$).*

Moreover, given $\mathcal{A}' \subseteq \mathcal{A}$, if t is semi-controllable and $\exists\, t' = (\vec{q}, \vec{a}_2, \vec{q}_2') \in T_{\mathcal{A}'}^{\square}$ s.t. $\vec{a}_2$ is a match, $\vec{q}, \vec{q}_2' \notin Dangling(\mathcal{A}')$, and $snd(\vec{a}) = i$ and $\vec{a}_{1\,(i)} = \vec{a}_{2\,(i)} = \overline{a}$, then t is controllable *in $\mathcal{A}'$ (via t'); otherwise, t is* uncontrollable *in $\mathcal{A}'$.*

Hence, again a necessary transition is a particular type of transition that switches from being controllable to uncontrollable in case a condition on the global automaton is not met. Note that this condition is stronger than the one required for the case of orchestration (semi-controllability), because for the case of choreography transitions t and t' in Definition 6 share the source state. Moreover, also in this case it can be shown that the encoding of this type of semi-controllable transition into an uncontrollable one would result in an exponential growth of the state space of the model.

Similarly to the orchestration synthesis in Definition 4, when a semi-controllable transition previously removed by the synthesis switches from controllable to uncontrollable, its source state is detected to be bad. Apart from the different notion of semi-controllability, another difference with respect to the orchestration synthesis is that each time a controllable transition is pruned, all other transitions violating the branching condition must also be removed. Finally, according to the property of strong agreement, both request and offer transitions are forbidden. The formalisation is provided below.

Definition 7 (MSCA choreography synthesis). *Let $\mathcal{A}$ be an MSCA, and let $\mathcal{K}_0 = \mathcal{A}$ and $R_0 = Dangling(\mathcal{K}_0)$. We let the* choreography synthesis function $f_c : MSCA \times 2^Q \to MSCA \times 2^Q$ *be defined as follows:*

$$f_c(\mathcal{K}_{i-1}, R_{i-1}) = (\mathcal{K}_i, R_i), \text{ with}$$
$$T_{\mathcal{K}_i} = T_{\mathcal{K}_{i-1}} \setminus (\{(\vec{q} \to \vec{q}') = t \in T_{\mathcal{K}_{i-1}} \mid \vec{q}' \in R_{i-1} \vee t \text{ is a request or an offer}\}$$
$$\cup \{(\vec{q}_1 \xrightarrow{\vec{a}}) = t \in T_{\mathcal{K}_{i-1}} \mid \exists\, \vec{q}_2 : (snd(\vec{a}) = i \wedge \vec{q}_{1\,(i)} = \vec{q}_{2\,(i)})$$
$$\wedge (\vec{q}_2 \xrightarrow{\vec{a}}) \notin T_{\mathcal{K}_{i-1}} \})$$
$$R_i = R_{i-1} \cup \{\vec{q} \mid (\vec{q} \to) \in T_{\mathcal{A}} \text{ is uncontrollable in } \mathcal{K}_i \} \cup Dangling(\mathcal{K}_i)$$

Theorem 3 (MSCA choreography mpc). *The choreography synthesis function* f_c *is monotone on the cpo* $(MSCA \times 2^Q, \leq)$ *and its least fixed point is:*

$$(\mathcal{K}_s, R_s) = sup(\{ f_c^n(\mathcal{K}_0, R_0) \mid n \in \mathbb{N} \})$$

The (choreography) mpc $\mathcal{K}_\mathcal{A}$ *of* $\mathcal{A}$ *is:*

$$\mathcal{K}_\mathcal{A} = \begin{cases} \langle \, \rangle & \text{if } \vec{q}_0 \in R_s \\ \langle Q \setminus R_s, \vec{q}_0, A^\diamond, A^\square, A^\circ, T_{\mathcal{K}_s} \setminus T', F \setminus R_s \rangle & \text{otherwise} \end{cases}$$

where $T' = \{ t = \vec{q} \rightarrow \, \in \mathcal{K}_s \mid t$ *is controllable in* $\mathcal{K}_s$, $\vec{q} \in R_s \}$.
Moreover, $\mathcal{K}_\mathcal{A}$ *satisfies the branching condition.*

Returning to the example in Fig. 3, the wrongly accepted case is removed because, during the synthesis, the operation of pruning the transitions leading to bad states causes the removal of the remaining transition. Thus, the obtained choreography is empty. Similarly, the wrongly rejected case is not possible because, assuming that the output from the initial state is necessary, this necessary action is not rendered as uncontrollable as long as the output is matched by some other principal from the same initial state.

5   Abstract Synthesis

We have presented in the previous three sections three slightly different synthesis algorithms. As previously stated, in order to bridge the gap between standard synthesis and orchestration and choreography syntheses, the controllable and uncontrollable actions from SCT are related to permitted and necessary modalities, respectively, of MSCA.

The main intuition is that the SCT assumption of an unpredictable environment responsible for the uncontrollable transitions is not realistic in the case of coordination of services whose behaviour is known and observable. As a result, necessary actions are not in correspondence with uncontrollable actions, but rather require the introduction of a milder notion of controllability. The condition under which a controllable transition becomes uncontrollable varies depending on the particular synthesis algorithm (orchestration or choreography). Conversely, in the standard mpc synthesis such information is local, i.e. a transition is declared to be uncontrollable.

In this section, we discuss an abstract synthesis algorithm that generalises the previous algorithms by abstracting away the conditions under which a transition is pruned or a state is deemed bad. These two conditions, called *pruning predicate* (ϕ_p) and *forbidden predicate* (ϕ_f) are parameters to be instantiated by the corresponding instance of the synthesis algorithm (e.g. orchestration or choreography). Predicate ϕ_p is used for selecting the transitions to be pruned. Depending on the specific instance, non-local information about the automaton or the set of bad states is needed by ϕ_p. Therefore, ϕ_p takes as input the current transition to be checked, the automaton, and the set of bad states. If ϕ_p evaluates to true, then the corresponding transition will be pruned. Predicate ϕ_f is used for deciding whether a state becomes bad. The input parameters are the same as ϕ_p. However, ϕ_f only inspects necessary transitions ($T^{\square}$). If ϕ_f evaluates to true, then the source state is deemed bad and added to the set R_i. The abstract synthesis algorithm is formally defined below.

Definition 8 (Abstract synthesis). *Let $\mathcal{A}$ be an MSCA, and let $\mathcal{K}_0 = \mathcal{A}$ and $R_0 = Dangling(\mathcal{K}_0)$. Given two predicates $\phi_p, \phi_f : T \times MSCA \times Q \to Bool$, we let the abstract synthesis function $f_{(\phi_p, \phi_f)} : MSCA \times 2^Q \to MSCA \times 2^Q$ be defined as follows:*

$$f_{(\phi_p,\phi_f)}(\mathcal{K}_{i-1}, R_{i-1}) = (\mathcal{K}_i, R_i), with$$
$$T_{\mathcal{K}_i} = T_{\mathcal{K}_{i-1}} \setminus \{ (\vec{q} \xrightarrow{\vec{a}}) = t \in T_{\mathcal{K}_{i-1}} \mid \phi_p(t, \mathcal{K}_{i-1}, R_{i-1}) = true \}$$
$$R_i = R_{i-1} \cup \{ \vec{q} \mid (\vec{q} \to) = t \in T_{\mathcal{A}}^{\square},\ \phi_f(t, \mathcal{K}_{i-1}, R_{i-1}) = true \} \cup Dangling(\mathcal{K}_i)$$

As in the previous cases, the mpc relative to the pair (ϕ_p, ϕ_f) is obtained by computing the least fixed point $(\mathcal{K}_s, R_s)$ of $f_{(\phi_p,\phi_f)}$ and removing the states R_s from $\mathcal{K}_s$.

In the following, we show how to instantiate the abstract synthesis function to the standard synthesis function, to the orchestration synthesis function, or to the choreography synthesis function, and prove their correspondences.

Theorem 4 (Abstract mpc synthesis). *The standard synthesis function of Definition 2 coincides with the instantiation of the abstract synthesis function of Definition 8 where, for a generic transition $t = (\vec{q}, \vec{a}, \vec{q}')$, predicates ϕ_p and ϕ_f are defined as follows:*

$$\phi_p^{mpc}(t, \mathcal{K}, R) = (\vec{q}' \in R) \vee (\vec{q} \text{ is forbidden})$$
$$\phi_f^{mpc}(t, \mathcal{K}, R) = (\vec{q}' \in R)$$

Note that in Theorem 4 the predicates do not use any non-local information related to the parameter $\mathcal{K}$. For both orchestration and choreography two different semi-controllability conditions are used to decide whether a state has become forbidden. These conditions are translated into the corresponding forbidden predicates.

Theorem 5 (Abstract orchestration synthesis). *The orchestration synthesis function of Definition 4 coincides with the instantiation of the abstract synthesis function of Definition 8 where, for a generic transition $t = (\vec{q}, \vec{a}, \vec{q}')$, predicates ϕ_p and ϕ_f are defined as follows:*

$$\phi_p^{orc}(t, \mathcal{K}, R) = (t \text{ is a request }) \vee (\vec{q}' \in R)$$

$$\phi_f^{orc}(t, \mathcal{K}, R) = \nexists (\vec{q_2} \xrightarrow{\vec{a_2}} \vec{q_2}') \in T_{\mathcal{K}}^{\square} : (\vec{a_2} \text{ is a match}) \wedge (\vec{q_2}, \vec{q_2}' \notin Dangling(\mathcal{K}))$$
$$\wedge (\vec{q}_{(i)} = \vec{q_2}_{(i)}) \wedge (\vec{a}_{(i)} = \vec{a_2}_{(i)} = a)$$

The pruning predicate of Theorem 5 does not use any information coming from the global automaton $\mathcal{K}$, whereas this is no longer the case for the forbidden predicate that indeed specifies the semi-controllability condition for the necessary transitions of an orchestration (cf. Definition 3).

Theorem 6 (Abstract choreography synthesis). *The choreography synthesis function of Definition 7 coincides with the instantiation of the abstract synthesis function of Definition 8 where, for a generic transition $t = (\vec{q}, \vec{a}, \vec{q}')$, predicates ϕ_p and ϕ_f are defined as follows:*

$$\phi_p^{cor}(t, \mathcal{K}, R) = (t \text{ is a request or an offer }) \vee (\vec{q}' \in R)$$
$$\vee (\exists \vec{q_2} \in Q_{\mathcal{K}} : (snd(\vec{a}) = i) \wedge (\vec{q}_{(i)} = \vec{q_2}_{(i)}) \wedge (\vec{q_2} \xrightarrow{\vec{a}} \notin T_{\mathcal{K}}))$$

$$\phi_f^{cor}(t, \mathcal{K}, R) = \nexists (\vec{q} \xrightarrow{\vec{a_2}} \vec{q_2}') \in T_{\mathcal{K}}^{\square} \; : (\vec{a_2} \text{ is a match}) \wedge (\vec{q}, \vec{q_2}' \notin Dangling(\mathcal{K}))$$
$$\wedge (\vec{a}_{(i)} = \vec{a_2}_{(i)} = \overline{a})$$

Notably, in Theorem 6 both predicates require global information on the whole automaton. Similarly to Theorem 5, the forbidden predicate codifies the semi-controllability condition of Definition 6. Moreover, the pruning predicate removes all transitions violating the branching condition (cf. Definition 5).

We believe that the synthesis algorithms are related. In particular, we conjecture that via a partial order of predicates, appropriately defined as $(\phi_{p_1}, \phi_{f_1}) \leq (\phi_{p_2}, \phi_{f_2})$ iff $(\phi_{p_1} \to \phi_{p_2}) \wedge (\phi_{f_1} \to \phi_{f_2})$, it can be proved that $(\phi_p^{orc}, \phi_f^{orc}) \leq (\phi_p^{mpc}, \phi_f^{mpc})$ and therefore $\mathcal{K}_{\mathcal{A}}^{mpc} \subseteq \mathcal{K}_{\mathcal{A}}^{orc}$. More generally, the cpo of predicates permits to perform abstraction of syntheses, in the sense that the lesser the pair of predicates the greater the corresponding synthesised automaton. This can be useful to perform partial syntheses and skip unnecessary checks or even potentially undecidable computations. For instance, given an MSCA $\mathcal{A}$, from $\mathcal{K}_{\mathcal{A}}^{orc} = \langle \, \rangle$, we can conclude $\mathcal{K}_{\mathcal{A}}^{mpc} = \langle \, \rangle$ without actually computing it, which could potentially require more computational effort.

6 Related Work

Our contributions to bridging the gap between SCT and coordination of services concern adaptations of the classical synthesis algorithm from SCT in order to synthesise orchestrations and choreographies of service contracts formalised as MSCA. In the literature, there exist many formalisms for modelling and analysing (service) contracts, ranging from behavioural type systems, including behavioural contracts [1,27,40] and session types [23,26,32,36,44], to automata-based formalisms, including interface automata [2] and (timed) (I/O) automata [3,31,43]. Foundational models for service contracts and session types are surveyed in [8,17,37].

The MSCA formalism used in this paper differs fundamentally from these models, which typically study notions of contract compliance involving only two parties, since MSCA primitively support *multi-party* compliance of contracts that *compete* on offering or requesting the same service. Furthermore, the above models do not consider modalities of services whereas MSCA provide primitive support for *permitted* and *necessary* service actions, resulting in the introduction of a novel notion of *semi-controllability* in the context of SCT. Modal Transition Systems (MTS) and their extensions [39], as adopted for instance in Software Product Line Engineering (SPLE [4,46]), like modal I/O automata [42] and MTS with variability constraints [19], do natively distinguish may and must modalities, but the other differences remain. In particular, they cannot explicitly handle dynamic composition by allowing new services that join composite services to intercept already matched actions.

We are only aware of two other applications of SCT to MTS. In [30], there is no direct relation between may/must and controllable/uncontrollable, and the modal automaton (i.e. MTS with final states) is seen as a predicate that is satisfied if the plant automaton (i.e. the system to be refined against the predicate) is a sort of alternate refinement of the predicate. Similarly, in [33], the control objectives (i.e. the predicate) is a modal automaton, non-blockingness is not considered, and another modal automaton describes which actions are controllable and which are uncontrollable in the plant automaton. In this paper, the predicate is an invariant (i.e. forbidden states and forbidden transitions are given), the modal automaton (i.e. MSCA) is the plant, and a necessary transition induces different notions of controllability according to the adopted coordination paradigm.

SCT was first applied to SPLE in [20] by showing how the CIF 3 toolset [16] can automatically synthesise a single (global, family) model representing an automaton for each of the valid products of a product line from (i) a feature constraint with attributes (e.g. cost), (ii) behavioural component models associated with the features, and (iii) additional behavioural requirements like state invariants, action orderings, and guards on actions (reminiscent of the Featured Transition Systems of [28]). The resulting CIF 3 model satisfies all feature-related constraints as well as all given behavioural requirements. Since CIF 3 allows the export of such models in a format accepted by the mCRL2 model checker [29], the latter can be used to verify arbitrary behavioural properties expressed in the modal μ-calculus with data or its feature-oriented variant of [21]. An important advantage is that both CIF 3 and mCRL2 can be used off-the-shelf, meaning that no additional tools are required. Differently from our approach, all actions are controllable and orchestration is not considered, whilst a prototype tool supporting orchestration synthesis for contract automata is presented in [12].

The only approach by others to bridge the gap between SCT and coordination of services that we are aware of is that of [6], where services are formalised as so-called Service Labelled Transition Systems (SLTS), which are a kind of guarded automata with data. To this aim, SCT is adapted to deal with conditions and variables as well as with a means to enforce services based on runtime information. However, service composition through SLTS is based on the standard synchronous product, whilst the contract composition expresses competing contracts.

More importantly, in [6], input actions are considered uncontrollable whilst output actions are controllable, in the standard view of a service interacting with the environment. Our contribution induces novel notions of controllability to express necessary requirements that are semi-controllable. The standard controller synthesis algorithm is used in [34] to synthesise adapters between services. These adapters act like proxies and are used to enforce properties such as deadlock-freedom. Compared to our work, the interactions between services are driven by their contracts rather than by adapters. The standard controller synthesis algorithm cannot be applied for synthesising a correct composition of contracts.

We conclude this section by describing two further extensions of MSCA, developed for different purposes, and for which we also defined adapted synthesis algorithms. In [9], we present Featured Modal Contract Automata (FMCA). Technically, we extend MSCA with a variability mechanism concerning structural constraints that operate on the service contract, used to define different configurations. This reflects the fact that services are typically reused in configurations that vary over time and need to dynamically adapt to changing environments [48]. Configurations are characterised by which service actions are mandatory and which forbidden. The valid configurations are those respecting all structural constraints. We follow the well-established paradigm of SPLE, which aims at efficiently managing a product line (family) of highly (re)configurable systems to allow for mass customisation [4,46]. To compactly represent a product line, i.e. the set of valid product configurations, we use a so-called feature constraint, a propositional formula φ whose atoms are features [15], and we identify features as service actions (offers as well as requests). A valid product then distinguishes a set of mandatory and a set of forbidden actions. Consequently, we define an algorithm to compute the FMCA $\mathcal{K}_{\mathcal{A}_p}$ as the mpc for a valid product p of an FMCA $\mathcal{A}$. The main adaptation of the synthesis algorithm for MSCA is to consider as bad states also those that cannot prevent a forbidden action to be eventually executed and to discard the transitions labelled with actions forbidden by p. Moreover, if some action that is mandatory in p is unavailable in the automaton that results from the fixed point iteration, then the mpc is empty. In [10], we introduced Timed Service Contract Automata (TSCA) as an extension of the FMCA from [9] with real-time constraints. Formally, a configuration of a TSCA is a triple consisting of a recognised trace, a state, and a valuation of clocks. The (finite) behaviour recognised by a TSCA are traces of alternating time and discrete transitions, i.e. in a given configuration either time progresses (a silent action in the languages recognised by TSCA) or a discrete step to a new configuration is performed. Consequently, we define an algorithm to compute the orchestration synthesis of TSCA. To respect the timing constraints, we use the notion of zones from timed games [5,25]. The resulting synthesis algorithm resembles a timed game, but it differs from classical timed game algorithms [5,25,31] by combining two separate games, viz. *reachability* games (to ensure that marked states must be reachable) and *safety* games (to ensure that forbidden states are never traversed). A TSCA might be such that all bad configurations are unreachable (i.e. it is safe), while at the same time no final configuration is reachable (i.e. the resulting orchestration is empty).

7   Conclusion

In this paper, we have presented recent efforts in bridging the gap between the most permissive controller synthesis from Supervisory Control Theory with synthesis algorithms of orchestrations and choreographies of a formal model of service contracts called modal service contract automata. We have introduced a new algorithm capable of synthesising a safe non-blocking composition of service contracts that is directly translatable into a choreographed formalism. We have also introduced an abstract synthesis algorithm that generalises the synthesis of the choreography, as well as that of the orchestration and that of the most permissive controller.

The properties to be enforced in the algorithms that we have presented are all invariants specified through either forbidden states or forbidden transitions. Future work is needed to investigate the abstract syntheses under other non-invariant properties. Finally, further work is necessary to formally demonstrate that the different synthesis algorithms are related, as conjectured at the end of Sect. 5.

References

1. Acciai, L., Boreale, M., Zavattaro, G.: Behavioural contracts with request-response operations. Sci. Comp. Program. **78**(2), 248–267 (2013)
2. de Alfaro, L., Henzinger, T.: Interface automata. In: ESEC/FSE, pp. 109–120. ACM (2001)
3. Alur, R., Dill, D.: A theory of timed automata. Theoret. Comp. Sci. **126**(2), 183–235 (1994)
4. Apel, S., Batory, D.S., Kästner, C., Saake, G.: Feature-Oriented Software Product Lines: Concepts and Implementation. Springer, Heidelberg (2013). https://doi.org/10.1007/978-3-642-37521-7
5. Asarin, E., Maler, O., Pnueli, A., Sifakis, J.: Controller synthesis for timed automata. IFAC Proc. **31**(18), 447–452 (1998)
6. Atampore, F., Dingel, J., Rudie, K.: Automated service composition via supervisory control theory. In: WODES, pp. 28–35. IEEE (2016)
7. Azzopardi, S., Pace, G.J., Schapachnik, F., Schneider, G.: Contract automata: an operational view of contracts between interactive parties. Artif. Intell. Law **24**(3), 203–243 (2016)
8. Bartoletti, M., Cimoli, T., Zunino, R.: Compliance in behavioural contracts: a brief survey. In: Bodei, C., Ferrari, G.-L., Priami, C. (eds.) Programming Languages with Applications to Biology and Security. LNCS, vol. 9465, pp. 103–121. Springer, Cham (2015). https://doi.org/10.1007/978-3-319-25527-9_9
9. Basile, D., et al.: Controller synthesis of service contracts with variability. Sci. Comput. Program. (2019, under revision)
10. Basile, D., ter Beek, M.H., Legay, A., Traonouez, L.-M.: Orchestration synthesis for real-time service contracts. In: Atig, M.F., Bensalem, S., Bliudze, S., Monsuez, B. (eds.) VECoS 2018. LNCS, vol. 11181, pp. 31–47. Springer, Cham (2018). https://doi.org/10.1007/978-3-030-00359-3_3
11. Basile, D., Degano, P., Ferrari, G.L.: Automata for specifying and orchestrating service contracts. Log. Meth. Comp. Sci. **12**(4:6), 1–51 (2016)

12. Basile, D., Degano, P., Ferrari, G.-L., Tuosto, E.: Playing with our CAT and communication-centric applications. In: Albert, E., Lanese, I. (eds.) FORTE 2016. LNCS, vol. 9688, pp. 62–73. Springer, Cham (2016). https://doi.org/10.1007/978-3-319-39570-8_5

13. Basile, D., Degano, P., Ferrari, G.L., Tuosto, E.: Relating two automata-based models of orchestration and choreography. J. Log. Algebr. Meth. Program. **85**(3), 425–446 (2016)

14. Basile, D., Di Giandomenico, F., Gnesi, S., Degano, P., Ferrari, G.L.: Specifying variability in service contracts. In: VaMoS, pp. 20–27. ACM (2017)

15. Batory, D.: Feature models, grammars, and propositional formulas. In: Obbink, H., Pohl, K. (eds.) SPLC 2005. LNCS, vol. 3714, pp. 7–20. Springer, Heidelberg (2005). https://doi.org/10.1007/11554844_3

16. van Beek, D.A., et al.: CIF 3: model-based engineering of supervisory controllers. In: Ábrahám, E., Havelund, K. (eds.) TACAS 2014. LNCS, vol. 8413, pp. 575–580. Springer, Heidelberg (2014). https://doi.org/10.1007/978-3-642-54862-8_48

17. ter Beek, M.H., Bucchiarone, A., Gnesi, S.: Web service composition approaches: from industrial standards to formal methods. In: ICIW. IEEE (2007)

18. ter Beek, M.H., Carmona, J., Hennicker, R., Kleijn, J.: Communication requirements for team automata. In: Jacquet, J.-M., Massink, M. (eds.) COORDINATION 2017. LNCS, vol. 10319, pp. 256–277. Springer, Cham (2017). https://doi.org/10.1007/978-3-319-59746-1_14

19. ter Beek, M.H., Fantechi, A., Gnesi, S., Mazzanti, F.: Modelling and analysing variability in product families: model checking of modal transition systems with variability constraints. J. Log. Algebr. Meth. Program. **85**(2), 287–315 (2016)

20. ter Beek, M.H., Reniers, M.A., de Vink, E.P.: Supervisory controller synthesis for product lines using CIF 3. In: Margaria, T., Steffen, B. (eds.) ISoLA 2016. LNCS, vol. 9952, pp. 856–873. Springer, Cham (2016). https://doi.org/10.1007/978-3-319-47166-2_59

21. ter Beek, M.H., de Vink, E.P., Willemse, T.A.C.: Family-based model checking with mCRL2. In: Huisman, M., Rubin, J. (eds.) FASE 2017. LNCS, vol. 10202, pp. 387–405. Springer, Heidelberg (2017). https://doi.org/10.1007/978-3-662-54494-5_23

22. Bouguettaya, A., et al.: A service computing manifesto: the next 10 years. Commun. ACM **60**(4), 64–72 (2017)

23. Bruni, R., Lanese, I., Melgratti, H., Tuosto, E.: Multiparty sessions in SOC. In: Lea, D., Zavattaro, G. (eds.) COORDINATION 2008. LNCS, vol. 5052, pp. 67–82. Springer, Heidelberg (2008). https://doi.org/10.1007/978-3-540-68265-3_5

24. Cassandras, C.G., Lafortune, S.: Introduction to Discrete Event Systems. Springer, Heidelberg (2006). https://doi.org/10.1007/978-0-387-68612-7

25. Cassez, F., David, A., Fleury, E., Larsen, K.G., Lime, D.: Efficient on-the-fly algorithms for the analysis of timed games. In: Abadi, M., de Alfaro, L. (eds.) CONCUR 2005. LNCS, vol. 3653, pp. 66–80. Springer, Heidelberg (2005). https://doi.org/10.1007/11539452_9

26. Castagna, G., Dezani-Ciancaglini, M., Padovani, L.: On global types and multiparty sessions. Log. Meth. Comp. Sci. **8**(1:24), 1–45 (2012)

27. Castagna, G., Gesbert, N., Padovani, L.: A theory of contracts for web services. ACM Trans. Program. Lang. Syst. **31**(5), 19:1–19:61 (2009)

28. Classen, A., Cordy, M., Schobbens, P.Y., Heymans, P., Legay, A., Raskin, J.F.: Featured transition systems: foundations for verifying variability-intensive systems and their application to LTL model checking. IEEE Trans. Softw. Eng. **39**(8), 1069–1089 (2013)

29. Cranen, S., et al.: An overview of the mCRL2 toolset and its recent advances. In: Piterman, N., Smolka, S.A. (eds.) TACAS 2013. LNCS, vol. 7795, pp. 199–213. Springer, Heidelberg (2013). https://doi.org/10.1007/978-3-642-36742-7_15

30. Darondeau, P., Dubreil, J., Marchand, H.: Supervisory control for modal specifications of services. IFAC Proc. **43**(12), 418–425 (2010)

31. David, A., Larsen, K.G., Legay, A., Nyman, U., Wąsowski, A.: Timed I/O automata: a complete specification theory for real-time systems. In: HSCC, pp. 91–100. ACM (2010)

32. Dezani-Ciancaglini, M., de'Liguoro, U.: Sessions and session types: an overview. In: Laneve, C., Su, J. (eds.) WS-FM 2009. LNCS, vol. 6194, pp. 1–28. Springer, Heidelberg (2010). https://doi.org/10.1007/978-3-642-14458-5_1

33. Feuillade, G., Pinchinat, S.: Modal specifications for the control theory of discrete event systems. Discrete Event Dyn. Syst. **17**(2), 211–232 (2007)

34. Gierds, C., Mooij, A.J., Wolf, K.: Reducing adapter synthesis to controller synthesis. IEEE Trans. Serv. Comput. **5**(1), 72–85 (2012)

35. Gohari, P., Wonham, W.M.: On the complexity of supervisory control design in the RW framework. IEEE Trans. Syst. Man Cybern. B Cybern. **30**(5), 643–652 (2000)

36. Honda, K., Yoshida, N., Carbone, M.: Multiparty asynchronous session types. In: POPL, pp. 273–284. ACM (2008)

37. Hüttel, H., et al.: Foundations of session types and behavioural contracts. ACM Comput. Surv. **49**(1), 3:1–3:36 (2016)

38. Kavantzas, N., Burdett, D., Ritzinger, G., Fletcher, T., Lafon, Y., Barreto, C.: Web Services Choreography Description Language v1.0 (2005). https://www.w3.org/TR/ws-cdl-10/

39. Křetínský, J.: 30 years of modal transition systems: survey of extensions and analysis. In: Aceto, L., Bacci, G., Bacci, G., Ingólfsdóttir, A., Legay, A., Mardare, R. (eds.) Models, Algorithms, Logics and Tools. LNCS, vol. 10460, pp. 36–74. Springer, Cham (2017). https://doi.org/10.1007/978-3-319-63121-9_3

40. Laneve, C., Padovani, L.: An algebraic theory for web service contracts. Form. Asp. Comput. **27**(4), 613–640 (2015)

41. Lange, J., Tuosto, E., Yoshida, N.: From communicating machines to graphical choreographies. In: POPL, pp. 221–232. ACM (2015)

42. Larsen, K.G., Nyman, U., Wąsowski, A.: Modal I/O automata for interface and product line theories. In: De Nicola, R. (ed.) ESOP 2007. LNCS, vol. 4421, pp. 64–79. Springer, Heidelberg (2007). https://doi.org/10.1007/978-3-540-71316-6_6

43. Lynch, N., Tuttle, M.: An introduction to input/output automata. CWI Q. **2**, 219–246 (1989)

44. Michaux, J., Najm, E., Fantechi, A.: Session types for safe web service orchestration. J. Log. Algebr. Program. **82**(8), 282–310 (2013)

45. Peltz, C.: Web services orchestration and choreography. IEEE Comp. **36**(10), 46–52 (2003)

46. Pohl, K., Böckle, G., van der Linden, F.J.: Software Product Line Engineering: Foundations, Principles, and Techniques. Springer, Heidelberg (2005). https://doi.org/10.1007/3-540-28901-1

47. Ramadge, P.J., Wonham, W.M.: Supervisory control of a class of discrete event processes. SIAM J. Control Optim. **25**(1), 206–230 (1987)

48. Yi, Q., Liu, X., Bouguettaya, A., Medjahed, B.: Deploying and managing Web services: issues, solutions, and directions. VLDB J. **17**(3), 735–572 (2008)

No More, No Less

A Formal Model for Serverless Computing

Maurizio Gabbrielli[1,2], Saverio Giallorenzo[3(✉)], Ivan Lanese[1,2],
Fabrizio Montesi[3], Marco Peressotti[3], and Stefano Pio Zingaro[1,2]

[1] Inria, Sophia Antipolis Cedex, France
[2] Università di Bologna, Bologna, Italy
{maurizio.gabbrielli,ivan.lanese,stefanopio.zingaro}@unibo.it
[3] University of Southern Denmark, Odense, Denmark
{saverio,fmontesi,peressotti}@imada.sdu.dk

Abstract. Serverless computing, also known as Functions-as-a-Service, is a recent paradigm aimed at simplifying the programming of cloud applications. The idea is that developers design applications in terms of functions, which are then deployed on a cloud infrastructure. The infrastructure takes care of executing the functions whenever requested by remote clients, dealing automatically with distribution and scaling with respect to inbound traffic.

While vendors already support a variety of programming languages for serverless computing (e.g. Go, Java, Javascript, Python), as far as we know there is no reference model yet to formally reason on this paradigm. In this paper, we propose the first core formal programming model for serverless computing, which combines ideas from both the λ-calculus (for functions) and the π-calculus (for communication). To illustrate our proposal, we model a real-world serverless system. Thanks to our model, we capture limitations of current vendors and formalise possible amendments.

1 Introduction

Serverless computing [24], also known as Functions-as-a-Service, narrows the development of Cloud applications to the definition and composition of stateless functions, while the provider handles the deployment, scaling, and balancing of the host infrastructure. Hence, although a bit of a misnomer—as servers are of course involved—the "less" in serverless refers to the removal of some server-related concerns, namely, their *maintenance*, *scaling*, and expenses related to a sub-optimal management (e.g. idle servers). Essentially, serverless pushes to the extreme the per-usage model of Cloud Computing: in serverless, users pay only for the computing resources used at each function invocation. This is why recent reports [18,24] address serverless computing as the actual realisation of the long-standing promise of the Cloud to deliver *computation as a commodity*. AWS Lambda [4], launched in 2014, is the first and most widely-used serverless

© IFIP International Federation for Information Processing 2019
Published by Springer Nature Switzerland AG 2019
H. Riis Nielson and E. Tuosto (Eds.): COORDINATION 2019, LNCS 11533, pp. 148–157, 2019.
https://doi.org/10.1007/978-3-030-22397-7_9

implementation, however many players like Google, Microsoft, Apache, IBM, and also open-source communities recently joined the serverless market [3, 16, 19, 21, 22, 29]. Current serverless proposals support the definition of functions—written in mainstream languages such as Go, Java, Javascript or Python—activated by specific events in the system, like a user request to a web gateway, the delivery of content from a message broker or a notification from a database. The serverless infrastructure transparently handles the instantiation of functions, as well as monitoring, logging, and fault tolerance.

Serverless offerings have become more and more common, yet the technology is still in its infancy and presents limitations [6, 18, 24] which hinder its wide adoption. For example, current serverless implementations favour operational flexibility (asynchrony and scalability) over developer control (function composition). Concretely, they do not support the direct composition of functions, which must call some stateful service in the infrastructure (e.g. a message broker) which will take care of triggering an event bound to the callee. On the one hand, that limitation is beneficial, since programmers must develop their functions as highly fine-grained, re-usable components (reminiscent of service-oriented architectures and microservices [12]). On the other hand, such openness and fine granularity increases the complexity of the system: programmers cannot assume sequential consistency or serialisability among their functions, which complicates reasoning on the semantics of the transformations applied to the global state of their architecture. This holds true also when estimating resource usage/costs, due to the complexity of unfolding all possible concurrent computations.

The above criticisms pushed us to investigate a core calculus for serverless computing, to reason on the paradigm, to model desirable features of future implementations, and to formalise guarantees over programs. In Sect. 2 we introduce the Serverless Kernel Calculus (SKC); as far as we know, the first core formal model for serverless computing. SKC combines ideas from both the λ-calculus (for functions) and the π-calculus (for communication). In Sect. 2, we also extend SKC to capture limitations of current serverless implementations. In Sect. 3 we use our extension to model a real-world serverless architecture [1], implemented on AWS Lambda. Finally, in Sect. 4 we discuss future developments of SKC.

2   A Serverless Kernel Calculus

Our kernel calculus defines a serverless architecture as a pair $\langle S, \mathcal{D} \rangle$, where S is the system of *running functions* and $\mathcal{D}$ is a *definition repository*, containing function definitions. The repository $\mathcal{D}$ is a partial function from function names f to function bodies M. M includes function application ($M\ M'$), asynchronous execution of new functions (**async** M), function names f, and values V. Values include variables x, λ-abstractions λx. M, named *futures* [5, 17, 32] c, and the unit value (). A system S contains *running functions* $c \blacktriangleleft M$, where c will contain the result of the computation of the function M. Systems can be composed in parallel | and include the empty system **0**. Futures can be restricted in systems via $\nu c\, S$.

$$\frac{}{\langle \mathcal{E}[(\lambda x.M)\ V], \mathcal{D}\rangle \longrightarrow \langle \mathcal{E}[M\{V/x\}], \mathcal{D}\rangle}\ \lfloor\beta\rfloor \qquad \frac{\mathcal{D}(f) = M}{\langle \mathcal{E}[f], \mathcal{D}\rangle \longrightarrow \langle \mathcal{E}[M], \mathcal{D}\rangle}\ \lfloor\text{RET}\rfloor$$

$$\frac{c \notin \text{fn}(M)}{\langle \mathcal{E}[\textbf{async}\ M], \mathcal{D}\rangle \longrightarrow \langle \nu c(\mathcal{E}[c]\mid c \blacktriangleleft M), \mathcal{D}\rangle}\ \lfloor\text{ASYNC}\rfloor \qquad \frac{}{\langle \nu c(S\mid c \blacktriangleleft V), \mathcal{D}\rangle \longrightarrow \langle S\{V/c\}, \mathcal{D}\rangle}\ \lfloor\text{PUSH}\rfloor$$

$$\frac{S_0 \equiv S_0' \quad \langle S_0', \mathcal{D}\rangle \longrightarrow \langle S_1', \mathcal{D}'\rangle \quad S_1' \equiv S_1}{\langle S_0, \mathcal{D}\rangle \longrightarrow \langle S_1, \mathcal{D}'\rangle}\ \lfloor\text{STR}\rfloor$$

$$\frac{\langle S, \mathcal{D}\rangle \longrightarrow \langle S', \mathcal{D}'\rangle}{\langle \nu c\, S, \mathcal{D}\rangle \longrightarrow \langle \nu c\, S', \mathcal{D}'\rangle}\ \lfloor\text{RES}\rfloor \qquad \frac{\langle S_1, \mathcal{D}\rangle \longrightarrow \langle S_1', \mathcal{D}'\rangle}{\langle S_1 \mid S_2, \mathcal{D}\rangle \longrightarrow \langle S_1' \mid S_2, \mathcal{D}'\rangle}\ \lfloor\text{LPAR}\rfloor$$

Fig. 1. SKC reduction semantics.

$$S, S' ::= c \blacktriangleleft M \mid S \mid S' \mid \nu c\, S \mid \mathbf{0} \qquad\qquad \text{(Systems)}$$

$$M, M' ::= M\ M' \mid \textbf{async}\ M \mid f \mid V \qquad\qquad \text{(Functions)}$$

$$V, V' ::= x \mid \lambda x.M \mid c \mid () \qquad\qquad\qquad \text{(Values)}$$

We assume futures to appear only at runtime and not in initial systems. Moreover, we consider a standard structural congruence $\equiv$ that supports changing the scope of restrictions to avoid name capture, and where parallel composition is associative, commutative, and has $\mathbf{0}$ as neutral element.

$$\nu c\, \nu c'\, S \equiv \nu c'\, \nu c\, S \qquad \nu c(S \mid S') \equiv \nu c\, S \mid S' \qquad \text{if } c \notin \text{fn}(S')$$

$$S \equiv S \mid \mathbf{0} \qquad S \mid S' \equiv S' \mid S \qquad (S \mid S') \mid S'' \equiv S \mid (S' \mid S'')$$

We define the semantics of our calculus using evaluation contexts $\mathcal{E}$ and $\mathcal{E}_\lambda$, to evaluate, respectively, systems and functions.

$$\mathcal{E} ::= c \blacktriangleleft \mathcal{E}_\lambda \qquad\qquad \mathcal{E}_\lambda ::= [-] \mid (\lambda x.M)\mathcal{E}_\lambda \mid \mathcal{E}_\lambda M$$

We report in Fig. 1 the semantics of serverless architectures $\langle S, \mathcal{D}\rangle$, expressed as reduction rules. Rule $\lfloor\beta\rfloor$ is the traditional function application of λ-calculus. Rule $\lfloor\text{RET}\rfloor$ retrieves the body of function f from the definition repository $\mathcal{D}$. Rule $\lfloor\text{ASYNC}\rfloor$ models the execution of new functions: it creates a fresh future c and, in parallel, it executes function M so that c will store the evaluation of M. When the evaluation of a function reduces to a value, rule $\lfloor\text{PUSH}\rfloor$ returns the value to the associated future and removes both the terminated function and its restriction. Rules $\lfloor\text{STR}\rfloor$, $\lfloor\text{RES}\rfloor$, and $\lfloor\text{LPAR}\rfloor$ perform the closure under, respectively, structural congruence, restriction, and parallel composition. We include in SKC standard components (conditionals, etc.) and extend evaluation contexts ($\mathcal{E}$) accordingly:

$$M ::= \cdots \mid \textbf{if}\ M\ \textbf{then}\ M'\ \textbf{else}\ M'' \mid \textbf{fst}\ M \mid \textbf{snd}\ M$$

$$V ::= \cdots \mid \textsf{True} \mid \textsf{False} \mid (V, V')$$

We define standard macros for **fix**point, **let** and **let rec** declarations, and pairs.

$$\textbf{fix} \triangleq \lambda f.(\lambda x.f(xx))(\lambda x.f(xx)) \qquad \textbf{let}\ x = M\ \textbf{in}\ M' \triangleq (\lambda x.M')\ M$$

$$\texttt{let rec } x = M \texttt{ in } M' \triangleq \texttt{let } x = \texttt{fix } \lambda x.M \texttt{ in } M'$$

$$\lambda(x,y).M \triangleq \lambda z.(\lambda x.\lambda y.M) \texttt{ (fst z) (snd z)}$$

2.1 SKC$_\sigma$ - A Stateful Extension of SKC

SKC considers static definition repositories, i.e. no rules mutate the state of $\mathcal{D}$. We now present SKC$_\sigma$, an extension of SKC which includes two primitives to define transformations on definition repositories. As shown in Sect. 3, SKC$_\sigma$ is powerful enough to encode stateful services, like databases and message queues.

$$M, M' ::= \cdots \mid \texttt{set f } M \mid \texttt{take f}$$

The first primitive included in SKC$_\sigma$ is **set f** M, which updates the definition repository $\mathcal{D}$ to map f to M: users can use the **set** primitive to deploy new function definitions or update/override existing ones. The second primitive is **take f**, which removes the definition of f from $\mathcal{D}$, returning it to the caller. We report below the semantics of the new primitives.

$$\frac{\mathsf{futures}(M) = \emptyset}{\langle \mathcal{E}[\texttt{set f } M], \mathcal{D} \rangle \longrightarrow \langle \mathcal{E}[\texttt{f}], \mathcal{D}[\texttt{f} \mapsto \texttt{M}] \rangle} \; [\text{SET}]$$

$$\frac{\mathcal{D}(\texttt{f}) = M}{\langle \mathcal{E}[\texttt{take f}], \mathcal{D} \rangle \longrightarrow \langle \mathcal{E}[\texttt{let rec f=}M \texttt{ in } M], \mathsf{undef}(\mathcal{D}, \texttt{f}) \rangle} \; [\text{TAKE}]$$

The only restriction on the application of rule [SET] is that the body M of the newly deployed function f does not contain futures ($\mathsf{futures}(M)$ is the set of futures occurring in M). This preserves the semantics of restriction of futures in function evaluations (cf. rules [ASYNC] and [PUSH]). In the reductum, the rule returns the name of the deployed function, useful to invoke it in the continuation. Rule [TAKE] removes the definition M of a deployed function f. For simplicity, we define [TAKE] applicable only if f is defined. In the reductum, the caller of the **take** obtains the **recursive let** declaration of the function (useful for internal application) while the association for f is removed from $\mathcal{D}$ by function undef.

2.2 SKC$_e$ - Event-Based Function Composition in SKC

We present an idiom of SKC, called SKC$_e$, which models event-based function composition. SKC$_e$ captures one of the main limitations of current serverless vendors: the lack of support for direct function invocation, replaced by an event-handling/event-triggering invocation model. Indeed, current serverless implementations, such as AWS Lambda, work as follows: they include infrastructural stateful services, such as API gateways, that we can model using our stateful extension SKC$_\sigma$, and these services throw events. User-defined functions are invoked as handlers of these events. User-defined functions can then invoke the infrastructural services above. Notably, a user-defined function cannot directly invoke another user-defined function. We will see an instance of the event-based pattern in Sect. 3, while we describe below event handling mechanisms.

We model events (e and variations thereof) inside SKC as function names associated with peculiar function bodies in the repository $\mathcal{D}$ that asynchronously evaluate the corresponding event handler and discard the handler result. For convenience, (*i*) we package the asynchronous call of an event handler in the helper function callHandler below (hereafter, we assume that $\mathcal{D}$ contains callHandler) and (*ii*) we write _ for unused variable symbols in binding constructs.

$$\text{callHandler} \mapsto \lambda h. \lambda x. \textbf{let } \_ = \textbf{async } (h \ () \ x) \textbf{ in } ()$$

Event e is defined in $\mathcal{D}$ as e $\mapsto$ callHandler $\lambda\_.h_e$ and its event handler as $h_e \mapsto M_e$; we wrap the name h_e in a lambda abstraction to avoid expansion (via $\lfloor\text{RET}\rfloor$) since function names are not values. Raising an event e with some parameter v results in asynchronously executing the corresponding handler, as shown by the derivation below (we abbreviate $\langle S, \mathcal{D}\rangle \longrightarrow \langle S', \mathcal{D}\rangle$ as $S \longrightarrow_{\mathcal{D}} S'$ and label reductions with the names of the most relevant applied rules).

$$\text{e v} \xrightarrow{\lfloor\text{RET}\rfloor}_{\mathcal{D}} \text{callHandler } \lambda\_.h_e \text{ v} \xrightarrow{\lfloor\text{RET}\rfloor}_{\mathcal{D}} (\lambda h.\lambda x.\textbf{let } \_=\textbf{async } (h \ () \ x) \textbf{ in } ()) \ \lambda\_.h_e \text{ v}$$
$$\xrightarrow{\lfloor\beta\rfloor,\lfloor\beta\rfloor}_{\mathcal{D}} \textbf{let } \_=\textbf{async } (\lambda\_.h_e \ () \ v) \textbf{ in } () \xrightarrow{\lfloor\text{ASYNC}\rfloor}_{\mathcal{D}} \nu c (\textbf{let } \_=c \textbf{ in } () \mid c \blacktriangleleft \lambda\_.h_e \ () \ v)$$
$$\xrightarrow{\lfloor\beta\rfloor,\lfloor\beta\rfloor}_{\mathcal{D}} \nu c(() \mid c \blacktriangleleft h_e \ v) \xrightarrow{\lfloor\text{RET}\rfloor}_{\mathcal{D}} () \mid \nu c(c \blacktriangleleft M_e \ v)$$

3   An Illustrative Example

Let $\text{SKC}_{\sigma e}$ be the compound of SKC_σ and SKC_e presented in Sect. 2. Here, we illustrate how $\text{SKC}_{\sigma e}$ can capture real-world serverless systems by encoding a relevant portion (depicted in Fig. 2) of Tailor [1], an architecture for user registration, developed by Autodesk over AWS Lambda. Tailor mixes serverless functions with vendor-specific services: *API Gateways*, key-value databases (*DynamoDB*), and queue-based notification services (*SNS*). In the architecture, each function defines a fragment of the logic of a user-registration procedure, like the initiation of registration requests (talr-receptionist), request validation (talr-validator), etc. To model Fig. 2 in $\text{SKC}_{\sigma e}$, first, we install in $\mathcal{D}$ the event handlers for the *API Gateway*, the *DynamoDB*, and *SNS* services[1]:

$$e_{\text{API}} \mapsto \text{callHandler}(\text{talr-receptionist}) \qquad e_{\text{SNS}} \mapsto \text{callHandler}([\ldots])$$
$$e_{\text{DDB}} \mapsto \text{callHandler}(\text{talr-validator})$$

Then, we define the functions called by the handlers installed above, using the same names of the *AWS Lambda* functions in Fig. 2. Handler e_{API} calls function talr-receptionist, which validates the request and inserts the information of the user in the key/value database. For brevity, we omit the behaviour

---

[1] We omit the name of the function called by e_{SNS}, excluded in the excerpt of Fig. 2.

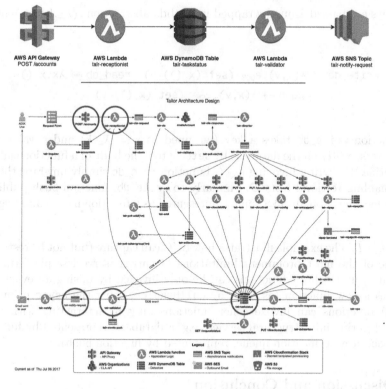

Fig. 2. Scheme of the Autodesk Tailor system. Top, excerpt considered in the example. Bottom, full architecture (circled elements belong to the excerpt).

of `talr-receptionist` in case of invalid requests and the definition of auxiliary functions `validate_request`, `get_key`, `get_value` in $\mathcal{D}$:

$$\text{talr-receptionist} \mapsto \lambda x. \textbf{if } \text{validate\_request } x \textbf{ then}$$
$$\text{write\_db } (\text{get\_key } x, \text{get\_value } x) \textbf{ else } [\ldots]$$

Handler e_{DDB} invokes function `talr-validator`, which retrieves from the database the `status` of task x, checks if it is complete, and sends a notification on *SNS*. We omit the definitions of functions `check` and `compose_msg` and of the **else** branch.

$$\text{talr-validator} \mapsto \lambda x. \textbf{let } \text{status} = \text{read\_db } x \textbf{ in}$$
$$\textbf{if } \text{check status } \textbf{then } \text{push } (\text{compose\_msg } x) \textbf{ else } [\ldots]$$

We conclude illustrating the definitions of functions `write_db`, `read_db`, and `push` in $\mathcal{D}$, which exemplify how $SKC_{\sigma e}$ can encode stateful, event-triggering services. Keys are represented as function names and values are stored in $\mathcal{D}$;

thus keys are passed around wrapped in lambda abstractions ($\lambda\_.k$) as done for events.

$$\text{write\_db} \mapsto \lambda(x,v).e_{DDB} \ (\textbf{set} \ (x \ ()) \ v) \quad \text{read\_db} \mapsto \lambda x.x \ ()$$
$$\text{push} \mapsto \lambda(x,v).e_{SNS} \ (\textbf{set} \ (x \ ()) \ v)$$

Function write_db takes a key (wrapped as $x = \lambda\_.k$) and a value v as parameters, writes on the database by **set**ting to v the body of a function called k, and notifies the write, invoking e_{DDB}[2]. Function read_db simply unwraps the key thus enabling retrieval from $\mathcal{D}$. Similarly to write_db, function push publishes (**set**) a message v on an *SNS* topic (represented as a function name) and triggers e_{SNS}.

Remark 3.1. The example illustrates how SKC can capture (but not be restricted by) one of the most prominent limitations of current serverless platform [18], i.e. that *i*) user-defined functions can be only invoked by raising an event that executes a new function (as done by callHandler, using the **async** primitive) and *ii*) functions can invoke other functions only by interacting with some event-triggering infrastructural service (e.g. a database, represented by function write_db, or a notification queue, represented by function push).

4   Discussion and Conclusion

We propose SKC, the first core formal model to reason on serverless computing. While the design of SKC strives for minimality, it captures the main ingredients [18,24] of serverless architectures: (*i*) the deployment and instantiation of event-triggered, stateless functions and (*ii*) the desiderata of direct function-to-function invocation based on futures—in Sect. 3 we show how this mechanism is powerful enough to cover also the current setting of serverless vendors, where function invocation must rely on third-party services that handle event triggering.

Futures [5,17], which are the main communication mechanism in SKC, are becoming one of the de-facto standards in asynchronous systems [13,15,35,37]. We considered using named channels (as in CCS/π-calculus [30,34]) instead of futures, but we found them too general for the needs of the serverless model (they are bi-directional and re-usable). Besides, futures can encode channels [32].

The work closest to ours is [23], appeared during the submission of this work, in the form of a technical report. It presents a detailed operational semantics that captures the low-level details of current serverless implementations (e.g. cold/warm components, storage, and transactions are primitive features of their

---

[2]   More involved variants of the database are possible. E.g. to avoid clashes among services using the same key for different elements, we can either use scoping or prefix key names with service names—e.g. Tailor uses service-specific tables in *DynamoDB*.

model) whereas SKC identifies a kernel model of serverless computing. Another work close to SKC is [32], where the authors introduce a λ-calculus with futures. Since the aim of [32] is to formalise and reason on a concurrent extension of Standard ML, their calculus is more involved than SKC, as it contains primitive operators (handlers and cells) to encode safe non-deterministic concurrent operations, which can be encoded as macros in SKC. An interesting research direction is to investigate which results from [23,32] can be adapted to SKC.

Being the first core framework to reason on serverless architectures, SKC opens multiple avenues of future research. For example, current serverless technologies offer little guarantee on sequential execution across functions, which compels the investigation of new tools to enforce sequential consistency [28] or serialisability [33] of the transformations of the global state [18]. That challenge can be tackled developing static analysis techniques and type disciplines [2,20] for SKC. Another direction concerns programming models, which should give to programmers an overview over the overall logic of the distributed functions and capture the loosely-consistent execution model of serverless [18]. Choreographic Programming [10,31] is a promising candidate for that task, as choreographies are designed to capture the global interactions in distributed systems [26], and recent results [9,11,14] confirmed their applicability to microservices [12], a neighbouring domain to that of serverless architectures. Other possible research directions, that we do not discuss for space constraints, include monitoring, various kinds of security analysis including "self-DDoS attacks" [25,27,36] and performance analysis. This last one is particularly relevant in the per-usage model of serverless architectures, yet requires to extend SKC with an explicit notion of time in order to support quantitative behavioural reasoning for timed systems [7,8].

Acknowledgements. This work was partially supported by the Independent Research Fund Denmark, grant no. DFF-7014-00041.

References

1. Williams, A.: Tailor - the AWS Account Provisioning Service. https://github.com/alanwill/aws-tailor. Accessed Feb 2019
2. Ancona, D., et al.: Behavioral types in programming languages. Found. Trends Program. Lang. **3**(2–3), 95–230 (2016)
3. Apache: OpenWhisk. https://github.com/apache/incubator-openwhisk. Accessed Feb 2019
4. AWS: Lambda. https://aws.amazon.com/lambda/. Accessed Feb 2019
5. Baker Jr., H.C., Hewitt, C.: The incremental garbage collection of processes. ACM Sigplan Not. **12**(8), 55–59 (1977)
6. Baldini, I., et al.: Serverless computing: current trends and open problems. In: Chaudhary, S., Somani, G., Buyya, R. (eds.) Research Advances in Cloud Computing, pp. 1–20. Springer, Singapore (2017). https://doi.org/10.1007/978-981-10-5026-8_1
7. Brengos, T., Peressotti, M.: A uniform framework for timed automata. In: CONCUR. LIPIcs, vol. 59, pp. 26:1–26:15. Schloss Dagstuhl - Leibniz-Zentrum fuer Informatik (2016)

8. Brengos, T., Peressotti, M.: Behavioural equivalences for timed systems. Log. Methods Comput. Sci. **15**(1), 17:1–17:41 (2019)
9. Carbone, M., Montesi, F.: Deadlock-freedom-by-design: multiparty asynchronous global programming. In: POPL, pp. 263–274. ACM (2013)
10. Cruz-Filipe, L., Montesi, F.: A core model for choreographic programming. In: Kouchnarenko, O., Khosravi, R. (eds.) FACS 2016. LNCS, vol. 10231, pp. 17–35. Springer, Cham (2017). https://doi.org/10.1007/978-3-319-57666-4_3
11. Dalla Preda, M., et al.: Dynamic choreographies: theory and implementation. Log. Methods Comput. Sci. **13**(2), 1–57 (2017)
12. Dragoni, N., et al.: Microservices: yesterday, today, and tomorrow. Present and Ulterior Software Engineering, pp. 195–216. Springer, Cham (2017). https://doi.org/10.1007/978-3-319-67425-4_12
13. Ecmascript 2018 language specification. http://ecma-international.org/ecma-262/9.0/index.html. Accessed Feb 2019
14. Giallorenzo, S., Montesi, F., Gabbrielli, M.: Applied choreographies. In: Baier, C., Caires, L. (eds.) FORTE 2018. LNCS, vol. 10854, pp. 21–40. Springer, Cham (2018). https://doi.org/10.1007/978-3-319-92612-4_2
15. Goetz, B., et al.: Java Concurrency in Practice. Pearson Education, London (2006)
16. Google: Cloud Functions. https://cloud.google.com/functions. Accessed Feb 2019
17. Halstead Jr., R.H.: Multilisp: a language for concurrent symbolic computation. ACM Trans. Program. Languages Syst. (TOPLAS) **7**(4), 501–538 (1985)
18. Hellerstein, J.M., et al.: Serverless computing: one step forward, two steps back. In: CIDR (2019). www.cidrdb.org
19. Hendrickson, S., et al.: Serverless computation with OpenLambda. In: USENIX. USENIX Association (2016)
20. Hüttel, H., et al.: Foundations of session types and behavioural contracts. ACM Comput. Surv. **49**(1), 3:1–3:36 (2016)
21. IBM: Cloud Functions. https://www.ibm.com/cloud/functions. Accessed Feb 2019
22. Iron.io: IronFunctions. https://open.iron.io. Accessed Feb 2019
23. Jangda, A., et al.: Formal foundations of serverless computing. CoRR abs/1902.05870 (2019). arXiv:1902.05870
24. Jonas, E., et al.: Cloud programming simplified: a berkeley view on serverless computing. Technical report, EECS Department, University of California, Berkeley, Feburary 2019
25. K-Optional Software: serverless out of Control. https://koptional.com/2019/01/22/serverless-out-of-control/. Accessed Feb 2019
26. Kavantzas, N., Burdett, D., Ritzinger, G., Lafon, Y.: Web services choreography description language version 1.0, W3C candidate recommendation. Technical report, W3C (2005). http://www.w3.org/TR/ws-cdl-10
27. Kevin Vandenborne: serverless: a lesson learned. The hard way. https://sourcebox.be/blog/2017/08/07/serverless-a-lesson-learned-the-hard-way/. Accessed Feb 2019
28. Lamport, L.: How to make a multiprocessor computer that correctly executes multiprocess programs. IEEE Trans. Comput. **28**(9), 690–691 (1979)
29. Microsoft: Azure Functions. https://azure.microsoft.com/services/functions. Accessed Feb 2019
30. Milner, R. (ed.): A Calculus of Communicating Systems. LNCS, vol. 92. Springer, Heidelberg (1980). https://doi.org/10.1007/3-540-10235-3
31. Montesi, F.: Kickstarting choreographic programming. In: Hildebrandt, T., Ravara, A., van der Werf, J.M., Weidlich, M. (eds.) WS-FM 2014-2015. LNCS, vol. 9421, pp. 3–10. Springer, Cham (2016). https://doi.org/10.1007/978-3-319-33612-1_1

32. Niehren, J., Schwinghammer, J., Smolka, G.: A concurrent lambda calculus with futures. Theor. Comput. Sci. **364**(3), 338–356 (2006)
33. Papadimitriou, C.H.: The serializability of concurrent database updates. J. ACM **26**(4), 631–653 (1979)
34. Sangiorgi, D., Walker, D.: The Pi-Calculus - A Theory of Mobile Processes. Cambridge University Press, Cambridge (2001)
35. Summerfield, M.: Python in Practice: Create Better Programs Using Concurrency, Libraries, and Patterns. Addison-Wesley, Reading (2013)
36. Wright, T.: Beware "RunOnStartup" in Azure Functions – a serverless horror story. http://blog.tdwright.co.uk/2018/09/06/beware-runonstartup-in-azure-functions-a-serverless-horror-story/. Accessed Feb 2019
37. Williams, A.: C++ Concurrency in Action. Manning, New York (2017)

Coordination Patterns

Verification of Concurrent Design Patterns with Data

Simon Bliudze[1], Ludovic Henrio[2], and Eric Madelaine[3(✉)]

[1] Inria Lille – Nord Europe, Villeneuve d'Ascq, France
`simon.bliudze@inria.fr`
[2] Univ Lyon, EnsL, UCBL, CNRS, Inria, LIP, 69342 Lyon Cedex 07, France
`ludovic.henrio@ens-lyon.fr`
[3] Université Côte d'Azur, Inria, CNRS, I3S, 06902 Sophia-Antipolis, France
`eric.madelaine@inria.fr`

Abstract. We provide a solution for the design of safe concurrent systems by compositional application of verified design patterns—called *architectures*—to a small set of functional components. To this end, we extend the theory of architectures developed previously for the BIP framework with the elements necessary for handling data: definition and operations on data domains, syntax and semantics of composition operators involving data transfer. We provide a set of conditions under which composition of architectures preserves their characteristic safety properties. To verify that individual architectures do enforce their associated properties, we provide an encoding into open pNets, an intermediate model that supports SMT-based verification. The approach is illustrated by a case study based on a previously developed BIP model of a nanosatellite on-board software.

Keywords: Symbolic verification · Composition · Safety · Interaction models

1 Introduction

BIP (Behaviour-Interaction-Priority) [7] is a framework for the component-based design of concurrent software and systems. In particular, the BIP tool-set comprises compilers for generating C/C++ code, executable by linking with one of the dedicated engines, which implement the BIP operational semantics [14]. BIP ensures that any property that holds on a BIP model will also hold on the generated code. The notion of BIP *architecture* was proposed in [5] as a mechanism for ensuring correctness by construction during the design of BIP models. Architectures can be viewed as operators transforming BIP models. They formalise design patterns, which enforce global properties characterising the coordination among the components of the system. The architecture-based design process in BIP takes as input a set of components providing basic functionality of the system and a set of temporal properties that must be enforced in the final system.

© IFIP International Federation for Information Processing 2019
Published by Springer Nature Switzerland AG 2019
H. Riis Nielson and E. Tuosto (Eds.): COORDINATION 2019, LNCS 11533, pp. 161–181, 2019.
https://doi.org/10.1007/978-3-030-22397-7_10

For each property, a corresponding architecture is identified and applied to the model, adding coordinator components and modifying the synchronisation patterns between components. In [5], it was shown that application of architectures is compositional w.r.t. safety properties, i.e. if two architectures guarantee two properties, their composition ensures the conjunction of the properties but [5] did not consider properties depending on data.

This article goes one step further in the proof of properties and in the compositionality of architectures, but this step is a significant one: the compositional verification. To prove properties of BIP architectures it is necessary to have a representation of the BIP architecture in a verifiable format. The verification problem has two unbounded parameters: (1) By nature, architectures have holes and are meant to interact with the interfaces of the component that will fill the hole; the properties must hold for all (well-typed) components that can be put inside the hole; (2) BIP interactions can transmit data, and properties might be dependent of the data, the domain of the data is generally huge or unbounded and the values of transmitted data might have a significant impact on the properties. We propose to rely on a translation of BIP architectures into *open pNets*.

Parameterised Networks of synchronised automata (pNets) is a formalism for defining behavioural specification of distributed systems based on a parameterised and hierarchical model. It inherited from the work of Arnold on synchronisation vectors [3]. It has been shown in previous work [27] that pNets can represent the behavioural semantics of a system including value-passing and many kinds of synchronisation methods, including various constructs and languages for distributed objects. The VerCors platform uses pNets to design and verify distributed software components [19,28]. There is no bound on the number of elements inside a pNets or the valuation of parameters. When restricted to finite instantiations, it becomes possible to us pNets for finite model-checking approaches. Closed pNets were used to encode fully defined programs or systems, while open pNets have "holes", playing the role of process parameters. Such open systems can represent composition operators or structuring architectures. It is possible to reason, in an SMT engine, on the symbolic automaton that represents the behaviour of a pNets with holes and that communicates values [36]. The encoding of open pNets into Z3 that is under development is the starting point of this article. We benefit from the possibility to reason on a pNet in an SMT engine in order to prove properties on BIP architectures.

The main contributions of this paper are: (1) The addition of data to the theory of BIP architectures, including a theorem about preservation of data dependent properties by compositions. (2) An encoding of architectures with data into open pNets, allowing for analysis of their temporal properties using pNet's software tools. The paper is illustrated by a running example based on the failure monitor architecture from the CubETH nanosatellite on-board software [34]. This running example also relies on the *maximal progress* assumption, whereby larger interactions are preferred to smaller ones. Due to space limitations, we only discuss this informally. However, proofs of the results provided in the appendix formally account for maximal progress.

The rest of the paper is structured as follows. In Sect. 2, we present notations and background material on pNets. The theory of architectures with data is presented in Sect. 3. In Sect. 4, we present the encoding into open pNets and discuss verification of the running example. Section 5 discusses related work. Section 6 concludes the paper.

2   General Notations and pNets Previous Results

Notations. We extensively use indexed structures over some countable indexed sets, which are equivalent to mappings over the countable set. Thus, $a_i^{i \in I}$ denotes a family of elements a_i indexed over the set I. This notation defines both I the set over which the family is indexed (called *range*), and a_i the elements of the family. E.g., $a^{i \in \{3\}}$ is the mapping with a single entry a at index 3; also abbreviated $(3 \mapsto a)$. When this is not ambiguous, we shall use notations for sets, and typically write "indexed set over I", even though formally we should speak of maps; and write $x \in a_i^{i \in I}$ to mean $\exists i \in I . x = a_i$. An empty family is denoted $\emptyset$.

We assume the existence of a term algebra $\mathcal{T}_{\Sigma, \mathcal{V}}$, where Σ is the signature of the data and action constructors, and $\mathcal{V}$ a set of *variables*. Within $\mathcal{T}_{\Sigma, \mathcal{V}}$, we distinguish a set of *data expressions* $\mathbb{E}_{\mathcal{V}}$, e ranges over expressions; and a set of *Boolean expressions* $\mathbb{B}_{\mathcal{V}} \subseteq \mathbb{E}_{\mathcal{V}}$, g (guards) ranges over Boolean expressions. On top of $\mathbb{E}_{\mathcal{V}}$ we build the *action algebra* $Act_{\mathcal{V}}$, with $Act_{\mathcal{V}} \subseteq \mathcal{T}_{\Sigma, \mathcal{V}}$. We define $\mathbb{A}_{\mathcal{V}}$ as the set of variable assignments of the form: $(x_i := e_i)^{i \in I}$ and let u range over sets of assignments. The function $vars(t)$ identifies the set of variables in a term.

We assume the existence of a universal data domain given as a partially-ordered set $(\mathbb{D}, \leqslant)$, potentially encompassing several copies of any given data type with different orders. We assume that $(\mathbb{D}, \leqslant)$ comprises both the unordered set of Booleans $\mathbb{B} = (\{\mathbf{tt}, \mathbf{ff}\}, \emptyset)$ and the naturally ordered one $\mathbb{B}^{\leqslant} = (\{\mathbf{tt}, \mathbf{ff}\}, \{\mathbf{ff} \leqslant \mathbf{tt}\})$, and similarly for integer and real numbers; as well as the set of intervals ordered by inclusion. When speaking of an ordered sort, e.g. $\mathbb{B}^{\leqslant}$, we will assume that it forms a meet-semilattice and denote by $\wedge$ the meet operator.

For a set of variables $V \subseteq \mathcal{V}$, we denote $\mathbb{D}^V \stackrel{def}{=} \{\sigma : V \to \mathbb{D}\}$ the set of *valuations* of the variables in V and let σ range over valuations. Valuations extend canonically to expressions, denoted $\sigma(e)$. We define:

$$\sigma\big[(x_i := e_i)^{i \in I}\big](x) \stackrel{def}{=} \begin{cases} \sigma(x), & \text{if } x \notin x_i^{i \in I}, \\ \sigma(e_i), & \text{if } x = x_i, \text{for some } i \in I. \end{cases}$$

For two valuations $\sigma^1, \sigma^2 : V \to \mathbb{D}$, we denote $\sigma^1 \triangle \sigma^2 \stackrel{def}{=} \{x \in V \mid \sigma^1(x) \neq \sigma^2(x)\}$ the set of variables that are assigned different values by the two valuations. As usual, we write $\sigma^1 \leqslant \sigma^2$ iff $\sigma^1(x) \leqslant \sigma^2(x)$, for all $x \in V$. An expression e is *monotonic* if, for any two valuations σ^1, σ^2, $\sigma^1 \leqslant \sigma^2$ implies $\sigma^1(e) \leqslant \sigma^2(e)$. Similarly, an assignment $(x_i := e_i)^{i \in I}$ is monotonic if all expressions $e_i^{i \in I}$ are monotonic. We denote $\mathbb{B}_V^{\leqslant} \subset \mathbb{B}_V$, $\mathbb{E}_V^{\leqslant} \subset \mathbb{E}_V$ and $\mathbb{A}_V^{\leqslant} \subset \mathbb{A}_V$ the sets of monotonic Boolean and generic expressions and assignments, respectively.

Open pNets. This section briefly describes pNets, see [29] for more complete description. pNets are tree-like structures, where the leaves are either *parameterised labelled transition systems (pLTSs)*, expressing the behaviour of basic processes, or *holes*, used as placeholders for unknown processes. Nodes of the tree are synchronising artefacts using a set of *synchronisation vectors* that express the possible synchronisation between parameterised actions of some components.

A pLTS is a labelled transition system with variables occurring inside states, actions, guards, and assignments. Variables of each state are pairwise disjoint. Each transition label of a pLTS consists of a parameterised action, a guard and an update assignment. The parameters of actions are either input variables or expressions. Input variables are bound when the action occurs; they accept any value (of the correct type), thus providing a to input data from the environment. Expressions are computed from the values of other variables. They allow providing aggregated values to the environment, without exposing all the underlying variables. We define the set of parameterised actions a pLTS can use (a ranges over action labels): $\alpha = a(?x_i^{i \in I}, e_j^{j \in J})$, where $?x_i^{i \in I}$ are input variables, $e_j^{j \in J}$ are expressions.

Definition 1 (pLTS). *A pLTS is a tuple pLTS $\triangleq \langle\!\langle S, s_0, \rightarrow \rangle\!\rangle$ where: S is a set of states; $s_0 \in S$ is the initial state; $\rightarrow \subseteq S \times L \times S$ is the transition relation and L is the set of labels of the form $\langle \alpha, g, u \rangle$, where α is a parameterised action, $\alpha \in Act_\mathcal{V}$; $g \in \mathbb{B}_\mathcal{V}$ is a guard over variables of the source state and the action, and $u \in \mathbb{A}_\mathcal{V}$ assigns updated value for variables in the destination state.*

A pNet composes several pNets, pLTSs, and holes. A pNet exposes global actions resulting from the synchronisation of internal actions in some sub-pNets, and some actions of the holes. As holes are process parameters, synchronisation with a hole has an obvious concrete meaning when a process is put inside the hole and emits the action. We also define a semantics for open pNets with holes where open transitions express the fact that a pNet can performs a transition provided one or several holes emit some actions. This synchronisation is specified by *synchronisation vectors* expressing the synchronous interaction between actions inside sub-pNets and holes, data transmission is expressed classically using action parameters. Actions involved in the synchronisation vectors do not need to distinguish input variables, i.e. they have the form $a(Expr_j^{j \in J})$.

Definition 2 (pNets). *A pNet is a hierarchical structure where leaves are pLTSs and holes: $Q \triangleq pLTS \mid \langle\!\langle Q_i^{i \in I}, J, SV_k^{k \in K} \rangle\!\rangle$ where*

- *$Q_i^{i \in I}$ is the family of sub-pNets;*
- *J is a set of indexes, called holes. I and J are disjoint: $I \cap J = \emptyset$, $I \cup J \neq \emptyset$*
- *$SV_k^{k \in K}$ is a set of synchronisation vectors. $\forall k \in K, SV_k = \alpha_l^{l \in I_k \uplus J_k} \rightarrow \alpha'_k[g_k]$, where $\alpha'_k \in Act_\mathcal{V}$, $I_k \subseteq I$, $J_k \subseteq J$, and $vars(\alpha'_k) \subseteq \bigcup_{l \in I_k \uplus J_k} vars(\alpha_l)$. The global action is α'_k, g_k is a guard associated to the vector.*

The set of holes Holes(Q) of a pNet is the indexes of the holes of the pNet itself plus the indexes of all the holes of its subnets (we suppose those indexes disjoints). A pNet Q is closed if it has no hole: Holes(Q) = $\emptyset$; else it is said to be open. *The set of* leaves *of a pNet is the set of all pLTSs occurring in the structure, as an indexed family of the form* Leaves$(Q) = \langle\!\langle pLTS_i \rangle\!\rangle^{i \in L}$.

The semantics of an open pNet is expressed as an automaton where each transition coordinates the actions of several holes, the transition occurs if some predicates hold, and can involve state modifications.

Definition 3 (Open transition). *An* open transition *over a set of holes J and a set of states S is a structure of the form:*

$$\frac{\beta_j^{j \in J}, g, u}{s \xrightarrow{\alpha} s'}$$

Where $s, s' \in S$ and $\beta_j \in Act_V$ is an action of the hole j; α is the resulting global action; g is a predicate over the different variables of the terms, labels, and states β_j, s, α. $u \in \mathbb{A}_V$ is a set of assignments that are the effects of the transition. Open transitions are identified modulo logical equivalence on their predicate.

The red dotted rule expresses the implication stating that if the holes perform the designated actions and the condition g is verified, then the variables are modified and the state changes. This implication however uses a simple logic with the expressive power given by the predicate algebra (it must include logical propositions and equality). Proposition and inference rules of the paper use a standard logic, while predicates inside the open transitions should use a more restricted logic, typically a logic that could be handled mechanically and expressed by terms that can be encoded in a simple syntax. Open transitions express in a symbolic way, transitions that are not only parameterised with variables but also actions of not yet known processes.

Definition 4 (Open automaton). *An* open automaton *is a tuple (J, S, s_0, T) where: J is a set of indices, S is a set of states and s_0 an initial state among S, T is a set of open transitions and for each $t \in T$ there exist J' with $J' \subseteq J$, such that t is an open transition over J', and S.*

The semantics of an open pNet is an open automaton where the states are tuples of states of the pLTSs at the leaves, denoted $\triangleleft \ldots \triangleright$. Each open transition between two states contains (1) the actions of the holes involved in the transition, (2) a guard built from the synchronisation vectors coordinating the holes and the transitions involved; (3) assignments and global state change defined by the pLTSs transitions involved; (4) a global action defined by the synchronisation vector.

Example 1 (An open transition). The open transition

$$\frac{\{E \mapsto ask\}, t \in z, \{t := t + 1\}}{\triangleleft 11 \triangleright \xrightarrow{ask} \triangleleft 11 \triangleright}$$

emits a global action ask defined by the synchronisation vector $\langle timeout_T,$ $timeout_C, -, ask \rangle \rightarrow ask$. It requires the hole at label E to fire an ask action, with the condition $t \in z$. In this case, the global pNet loops on the state ⊲11⊳ that has internal variables t and z local to the pLTS T (hence not appearing in the synchronisation vector). The variable t is updated to the new value $t+1$. Figure 2 shows the complete pNet, whereas Fig. 3 shows a complete open automaton.

We used pNets to define a behavioural semantics for distributed components [2] that allows the verification of correctness properties by model-checking. More recently, a bisimulation theory has been formalised for open pNets [29].

3   The Theory of Architectures with Data

This section presents the extension of the theory of architectures [5] with data and briefly discusses a special case of priority models, called *maximal progress*. These extensions require us to define the framework in a manner that would allow formulating and proving the property preservation result (Theorem 1 below). In [5], this result is obtained by requiring, in the definition of architecture composition, that an interaction among coordinated components be only possible if both architectures "agree" that it should be enabled. With respect to data, the main difficulty lies in ensuring that this "agreement" extends to the transferred data values. A trivial extension would allow an interaction only if the data values proposed by both architectures coincide. As this requirement is too restrictive, we go beyond by assuming the data domains to be ordered and taking the *meet* of the proposed values. The property preservation result then holds independently of the proposed values, provided that guards and update assignments are monotonic.

An important insight is that, although the requirement that guards and update assignments be monotonic appears to be a limitation, it is, in fact, a generalisation of the usual setting. Indeed, the usual settings, where data domains are not ordered, can be recovered here by considering trivial partial orders with no two distinct elements being comparable. In such case, *all expressions* are trivially monotonic.

The intuition behind the proof of the preservation of safety properties in [5] is simple. The composition of two architectures combines the "constraints" that they impose on the possible executions of the system: as stated above, an interaction is only enabled if both architectures "agree". In [6], it is shown that this intuition extends well to priorities in the *offer semantics* of BIP. However, this is not the case in the classical semantics. In this section, we informally discuss the special case of the maximal progress priority models, where property preservation does hold in the classical semantics of BIP.

Components and Composition

Definition 5 (Component). *A component is a tuple* $(Q, q^0, V, \sigma^0, P, \varepsilon, \rightarrow)$, *where*

- *Q is a set of states, with $q^0 \in Q$ the initial state,*

- V *is a set of* component variables,
- $\sigma^0 : V \to \mathbb{D}$ *is an* initial valuation *of the component variables,*
- P *is a set of* ports; $\varepsilon : P \to 2^V$ *is the* set of variables exported by each port,
- $\to \subseteq Q \times (2^P \setminus \{\emptyset\}) \times \mathbb{B}_V^{\leq} \times \mathbb{A}_V^{\leq} \times Q$ *is a transition relation, with transitions labelled by* interactions, *i.e. triples consisting of a non-empty set of ports, a monotonic Boolean guard and a monotonic update assignment.*

We call the triple (V, P, ε) *the* interface of the component. [1] *Notations* $q \xrightarrow{a,g,u} q'$ *and* $q \xrightarrow{a,g,u}$ *are as usual; for a component* B, *we denote* Q_B, q_B^0, V_B, σ_B^0, P_B, *and* ε_B *the corresponding constituents of* B. *We will skip the index on the transition relations* $\to$, *since it is always clear from the context.*

In this paper, we use a refined version of the Failure Monitor architecture from [34] as a running example. Although Fig. 1 shows the full definition of this architecture, we will explain its various elements progressively. Figure 1 shows components T(imer) and C(ontrol), with interfaces $(\{t, z\}, \{\text{tick}, \text{cancel}, \text{timeout}_T\}, \{\text{tick} \mapsto \{t, z\}\})$, and $(\{zone\}, \{\text{reset}, \text{fail}, \text{resume}, \text{timeout}_C\}, \{\text{fail} \mapsto \{zone\}\})$ respectively. Variable t is implicitly assumed to be of type Integer (with trivial ordering). Variables $z \stackrel{def}{=} [z.l, z.u]$ and $zone \stackrel{def}{=} [zone.l, zone.u]$ are of type Integer Interval ordered by interval inclusion.

Component *behaviour* is defined by states and transitions. The initial states t_1 and s_1, and valuations $\sigma_T^0 = \{t \mapsto 0, z \mapsto \top\}$, $\sigma_C^0 = \{zone \mapsto [\text{Min}, \text{Max}]\}$ are shown by the incoming arrows $\xrightarrow{t:=0, z:=\top} t_1$ and $\xrightarrow{zone:=[\text{Min},\text{Max}]} s_1$ where $\top = (-\infty, +\infty)$. The constants Min and Max are the parameters of the architecture.

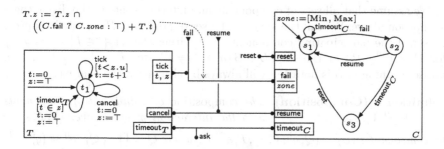

Fig. 1. The BIP specification of the failure monitor architecture

Transitions are labelled with ports of the corresponding components, Boolean guards and update assignments on local variables. E.g., the loop transition $t_1 \xrightarrow{\text{tick}, [t<z.u], t:=t+1} t_1$. The guards and update assignments of the transitions

---

[1] Only exported variables, belonging to a $\varepsilon(p)$, appear in the component interface (see Definition 7). We omit here this separation between internal and exported variables.

of C are omitted. By default, an omitted guard is $\mathtt{tt}$ and an omitted assignment is empty $\emptyset$. Clearly, all guards and update assignments are monotonic.

Definition 6 (Component semantics). *The open semantics of a component* $B = (Q, q^0, V, \sigma^0, P, \varepsilon, \rightarrow)$ *is the LTS denoted* $[B] = (S, s^0, \rightarrow)$, *where* $S = Q \times \mathbb{D}^V$, $s^0 = (q^0, \sigma^0)$ *and* $\rightarrow$ *is the minimal transition relation satisfying the rule*

$$\frac{q \xrightarrow{a,g,u} q' \qquad \sigma \models g \qquad \sigma' = \tilde{\sigma}[u] \qquad \sigma \triangle \tilde{\sigma} \subseteq \varepsilon(a)}{(q, \sigma) \xrightarrow{a,\tilde{\sigma}} (q', \sigma')} . \tag{1}$$

The closed semantics of B *is given by the LTS denoted* $[\![B]\!]$, *comprising only those transitions of* $[B]$, *where* $\tilde{\sigma} = \sigma$.

The use of the intermediate valuation $\tilde{\sigma}$ in the conclusion and the third premise of (1) allows some variables to get new values before the transition is fired. Thus the component is *open* to the exchange of data with its environment. However, the fourth premise states that only the variables exported through the ports participating in the interaction can be affected by the data transfer. The closed semantics excludes this possibility of data exchange.

Definition 7 (Interaction model). *For a finite set of component interfaces* $(V_i, P_i, \varepsilon_i)^{i \in I}$, *such that all* P_i *and all* V_i *are pairwise disjoint, let* $P = \bigcup_{i \in I} P_i$, $V = \bigcup_{i \in I} V_i$ *and* $\varepsilon : P \rightarrow 2^V$ *such that, for any* $p \in P_i$, $\varepsilon(p) = \varepsilon_i(p)$.
  An interaction model over (V, P, ε) *is a set* $\Gamma \subseteq 2^P \times \mathbb{B}_V^{\leqslant} \times \mathbb{A}_V^{\leqslant}$, *such that, for any interaction* $(a, g, u) \in \Gamma$, *we have* $g \in \mathbb{B}_{\varepsilon(a)}^{\leqslant}$ *and* $u \in \mathbb{A}_{\varepsilon(a)}^{\leqslant}$.[2]

We assume that all sets of components and interfaces satisfy the disjointness assumption above. We call the *support* of a set of ports $a \subseteq P$, denoted $\mathrm{supp}(a)$, the set of the participating components. It is either the set $\{i \in I \mid a \cap P_i \neq \emptyset\}$ (for $P = \bigcup_{i=1}^n P_i$) or the set $\{B \in \mathcal{B} \mid a \cap P_B \neq \emptyset\}$ (for $P = \bigcup_{B \in \mathcal{B}} P_B$). The precise meaning of this notation will always be clear from the context.

Definition 8 (Composition). *The* composition *of a finite set of components* $\mathcal{B} = (Q_i, q_i^0, V_i, \sigma_i^0, P_i, \varepsilon_i, \rightarrow_i)^{i \in I}$ *with the interaction model* Γ *over* (V, P, ε) *is the component* $\Gamma(\mathcal{B}) = (Q, q^0, V, \sigma^0, P, \varepsilon, \rightarrow)$, *where* $Q = \prod_{i \in I} Q_i$; $q^0 = (q_i^0)^{i \in I}$; $\sigma^0 : V \rightarrow \mathbb{D}$ *is such that, for any* $v \in V_i$, $\sigma^0(v) = \sigma_i^0(v)$; *and* $\rightarrow$ *is the minimal transition relation satisfying the rule*

$$\frac{\forall i \in \mathrm{supp}(a), q_i \xrightarrow{a \cap P_i, g_i, u_i} q_i' \quad \forall i \notin \mathrm{supp}(a), q_i = q_i' \qquad g' = g \wedge \bigwedge_{i \in \mathrm{supp}(a)} g_i \qquad u' = u; u_i^{i \in \mathrm{supp}(a)} \qquad (a, g, u) \in \Gamma \qquad a \neq \emptyset}{(q_i)^{i \in I} \xrightarrow{a, g', u'} (q_i')^{i \in I}} .$$

---

[2] Notice that this definition allows $(\emptyset, \mathtt{tt}, \emptyset)$ and $(\emptyset, \mathtt{ff}, \emptyset)$ to be included in Γ.

Intuitively, an interaction can be fired if all the involved components are ready to fire their corresponding transitions. The other components do not change their states. Both the interaction guard and those of the participating transitions must be satisfied. The update assignment of the interaction is executed first, followed by those of the components.

Specifying interaction models as sets of sets of ports is not practical due to their potentially exponential size. An algebra of connectors was introduced in [14] in order to structure interactions in BIP models. Connectors are hierarchical, tree-like structures with component ports at the leaves. They define sets of interactions, based on the attributes of the nodes, which may be either *trigger* (triangles in Fig. 1) or *synchron* (bullets in Fig. 1). If all sub-connectors of a connector are synchrons, then an interaction is allowed by the connector only if each subconnector can contribute. If at least one of the sub-connectors is a trigger, then any interaction consisting of contributions of any set of sub-connectors *involving at least one of the triggers* is allowed. The interaction model is defined as the set of all interactions allowed by at least one of the connectors.

For instance, the connector $T.\text{tick}\blacktriangleright\!\!\!-\!\!\bullet(\text{fail}\blacktriangleright\!\!\!-\!\!\bullet C.\text{fail})$ of Fig. 1 is a two-level hierarchical connector. In the subconnector $\text{fail}\blacktriangleright\!\!\!-\!\!\bullet C.\text{fail}$, the port fail is a trigger, whereas $C.\text{fail}$ is a synchron. This subconnector allows two interactions: $\{\text{fail}\}$ and $\{C.\text{fail}, \text{fail}\}$. Similarly, at the top level, $T.\text{tick}$ is a trigger, and the subconnector is a synchron. The entire connector defines the following three interactions (observe that $\top + T.t = \top$ and $T.z \cap \top = T.z$): $(\{T.\text{tick}\}, \text{tt}, \emptyset)$, $(\{\text{fail}, T.\text{tick}\}, \text{tt}, \emptyset)$, $(\{C.\text{fail}, \text{fail}, T.\text{tick}\}, \text{tt}, T.z := T.z \cap (C.\text{zone} + T.t))$

In addition to interaction models, BIP relies on *priority models* that impose a strict partial order on interactions. Intuitively, an interaction can be fired only if all the higher-priority interactions available in the current state are disabled by their respective guards. In the next sections, we will implicitly assume application of the *maximal progress* priority μ, where $(a, g, u) \prec_\mu (b, h, w)$ iff $a \subset b$ and $a \neq b$. For instance, the port $T.\text{tick}$ will never fire alone if the port fail is also enabled.

Architectures. Architectures are partial BIP models, with *dangling* ports that serve as placeholders for the eventual connection with *operand* components.

Definition 9 (Architecture). *An architecture is a tuple $A = (C, V_A, P_A, \varepsilon_A, \Gamma)$, where*

- P_A *and* V_A *are sets of ports and variables, respectively;*
- C *is a finite set of components (called* coordinators*), such that* $\bigcup_{C \in \mathcal{C}} P_C \subseteq P_A$ *and* $\bigcup_{C \in \mathcal{C}} V_C \subseteq V_A$; *ports in* $P_A \setminus \bigcup_{C \in \mathcal{C}} P_C$, *which do not belong to any of the coordinators are called* dangling*;*
- $\varepsilon_A : P_A \to 2^{V_A}$ *is an export function, such that* $\varepsilon_A(p) = \varepsilon_C(p)$, *for any* $C \in \mathcal{C}$ *and* $p \in P_C$ *and* $\varepsilon_A(p) \subseteq V_A \setminus \bigcup_{C \in \mathcal{C}} V_C$ *for any dangling port* p; *and*
- $\Gamma \subseteq 2^{P_A} \times \mathbb{B}_{V_A}^{\leqslant} \times \mathbb{A}_{V_A}^{\leqslant}$ *is an interaction model over* $(V_A, P_A, \varepsilon_A)$.

Definition 10 (Application of an architecture). *Let $A = (C, V_A, P_A, \varepsilon_A, \Gamma)$ be an architecture and let B be a set of components, such that $V_A \subseteq$*

$V \overset{def}{=} \bigcup_{B \in \mathcal{B} \cup \mathcal{C}} V_B$, $P_A \subseteq P \overset{def}{=} \bigcup_{B \in \mathcal{B} \cup \mathcal{C}} P_B$ and $\varepsilon_A(p) = V_A \cap \varepsilon_B(p)$, for any $B \in \mathcal{B}$ and $p \in P_A \cap P_B$. The application of the architecture A to the set of components $\mathcal{B}$ is the component $A(\mathcal{B}) \overset{def}{=} \mu((\Gamma \ltimes P)(\mathcal{C} \cup \mathcal{B}))$, where $\Gamma \ltimes P \overset{def}{=} \{(a, g, u) \mid a \subseteq P, (a \cap P_A, g, u) \in \Gamma\}$ is the interaction model over $(V, P, \varepsilon_A \cup \bigcup_{B \in \mathcal{B}} \varepsilon_B)$ and $\mu(\dots)$ denotes the application of maximal progress.

An architecture A enforces coordination constraints on the components in $\mathcal{B}$. The interface $(V_A, P_A, \varepsilon_A)$ of an architecture A contains all ports of the coordinators $\mathcal{C}$ and the dangling ports, which must belong to the components in $\mathcal{B}$. In the application $A(\mathcal{B})$, the ports belonging to P_A can only participate in the interactions defined by the interaction model Γ of A. Ports which do not belong to P_A are not restricted and can participate in any interaction. The definition of $\Gamma \ltimes P$ requires that an interaction from Γ be involved in every interaction belonging to $\Gamma \ltimes P$. To allow the ports from $P \setminus P_A$ to be fired independently in $A(\mathcal{B})$, one must have $(\emptyset, \mathtt{tt}, \emptyset) \in \Gamma$.

In our running example, there are four dangling ports. Intuitively, the architecture monitors the activation of the dangling port fail, then waits for a period comprised between Min and Max and, unless resume is activated, asks for a system reset through an invocation of the dangling port ask.

Definition 11 (Composition of architectures). *Let* $A_i = (\mathcal{C}_i, V_{A_i}, P_{A_i}, \varepsilon_{A_i}, \Gamma_i)$, *for* $i = 1, 2$, *be two architectures. The* composition *of* A_1 *and* A_2 *is the architecture* $A_1 \oplus A_2 = (\mathcal{C}_1 \cup \mathcal{C}_2, V_{A_1} \cup V_{A_2}, P_{A_1} \cup P_{A_2}, \varepsilon_{A_1} \cup \varepsilon_{A_2}, \Gamma)$, *where*

$$\Gamma = \{(a, g^1 \wedge g^2, u^1 \wedge u^2) \mid (a \cap P_{A_i}, g^i, u^i) \in \Gamma_i, \text{ for } i = 1, 2\}. \qquad (2)$$

$\oplus$ *is associative and commutative.*

It is well known that, since violations of safety properties are characterised by finite executions, they can also be represented as state predicates: intuitively, a safety property corresponds to the predicate characterising the set of states, where this property is not violated.

For a component B, we denote $S_{[\![B]\!]}$ and $s^0_{[\![B]\!]}$ the corresponding constituents of $[\![B]\!]$ (see Definition 6).

Definition 12 (Properties). *Let* B *be a component. A* (safety) property *of* B *is a predicate* Φ *on* $S_{[\![B]\!]}$, *such that* $((q, \sigma) \models \Phi) \wedge (\sigma' \leqslant \sigma)$ *implies* $(q, \sigma') \models \Phi$. *A property* Φ *is* initial *if* $s^0_{[\![B]\!]} \models \Phi$.

Although we define properties as state predicates, any appropriate logic can be used to specify them. For instance, the property *"There is always a possibility to reset the system after a single failure"* (i.e. without additional failures having to occur in the meantime) enforced by the Failure Monitor architecture comprises the safety component that can be specified using CTL as $\mathsf{AG}\left(\mathsf{fail} \rightarrow \mathsf{EX}\,\mathsf{E}\,[\neg\mathsf{fail}\,\mathsf{W}\,\mathsf{reset}]\right)$. An architecture enforces its characteristic property on its operand components. From this point of view, the set of coordinators is not relevant, neither are their states. Thus, properties enforced by architectures only involve the unrestricted composition of the operands:

Definition 13 (Enforcing properties). *Let $A = (\mathcal{C}, P_A, V_A, \varepsilon_A, \Gamma)$ be an architecture; let $\mathcal{B}$ be a set of components and Φ an initial property of their parallel composition $\Gamma_\|(\mathcal{B})$, with $\Gamma_\| = \{(a, \mathtt{tt}, \emptyset) \mid a \subseteq \bigcup_{B \in \mathcal{B}} P_B\}$. We say that A enforces Φ on $\mathcal{B}$ iff, for every state $s = (s_c, s_b)$ reachable in $[\![A(\mathcal{B})]\!]$, with $s_c \in \prod_{C \in \mathcal{C}} S_{[\![C]\!]}$ and $s_b \in \prod_{B \in \mathcal{B}} S_{[\![B]\!]}$, we have $s_b \models \Phi$.*

In the following, when we say that an architecture enforces some property Φ, Φ is supposed to be initial for the coordinated components. In [12], we formally define *upwards compatibility* that ensures property preservation when composing architectures. Informally, two architectures A_1 and A_2 are upwards compatible iff, whenever their composition involves the fusion of two interactions $a_1 = a \cap P_{A_1}$ and $a_2 = a \cap P_{A_2}$ (see (2)) and one, say a_1, is inhibited in a given state by a larger interaction $b_1 \supset a_1$, there exists an interaction $b_2 \supseteq a_2$ that can be fused with b_1 to form an interaction enabled in the same state.

Theorem 1 (Preserving enforced properties). *Let $\mathcal{B}$ be a set of components; let $A_i = (\mathcal{C}_i, V_{A_i}, P_{A_i}, \varepsilon_{A_i}, \Gamma_i)$, for $i = 1, 2$, be two upwards compatible architectures enforcing on $\mathcal{B}$ the properties Φ_1 and Φ_2 respectively. The composition $A_1 \oplus A_2$ enforces on $\mathcal{B}$ the property $\Phi_1 \wedge \Phi_2$.*

Theorem 1 implies that safe BIP systems can be designed *compositionally*: it is sufficient to verify that (1) the applied architectures do enforce their characteristic properties and (2) they are pairwise upwards compatible. To a large extent, the latter can be carried out syntactically by analysing the structure of the connectors that define the interaction models. The next section is devoted to the encoding of architectures into pNets, addressing item 1 by symbolic verification.

4   Encoding of Architectures into Open pNets

We define the encoding of BIP architectures into pNets by associating to each architecture $A = (\mathcal{C}, V_A, P_A, \varepsilon_A, \Gamma)$ with $C = (Q_C, q_C^0, V_C, \sigma_C^0, P_C, \varepsilon_C, \rightarrow)$, for each $C \in \mathcal{C}$, and a partition $\mathcal{D} \subseteq 2^{P_A}$ of its dangling ports (i.e. $\biguplus_{D \in \mathcal{D}} D = P_A \setminus \bigcup_{C \in \mathcal{C}} P_C$), the corresponding pNet $enc(A, \mathcal{D})$. For the sake of clarity, we define the encoding without any priority model. Then, we provide a brief sketch of the modifications necessary to encode maximal progress (implicitly assumed). Recall that Γ is an interaction model over the interface $(V_A, P_A, \varepsilon_A)$, i.e. these interface elements are implicitly involved in the definition of Γ. We define $enc(A, \mathcal{D}) \overset{def}{=} \langle\!\langle (enc(C))^{C \in \mathcal{C}}, \mathcal{D}, enc(\Gamma) \rangle\!\rangle$, where $enc(C)$ and $enc(\Gamma)$ are the encodings of a coordinator C and the interaction model Γ respectively.

Below, we present both the encodings of coordinators and interaction models. The key constraint is that we encode each connector by one synchronisation vector. This is necessary to (1) preserve the structure of the system and (2) allow the encoding of maximal progress.

Although somewhat technical, the encoding of coordinators is, in fact, pretty straightforward, comprising three key ideas: (1) we introduce an additional transition (hence also an additional state) to explicitly initialise the variables; (2) we introduce additional input variables to manipulate the values provided to the coordinator by the rest of the system for all exported variables; and (3) following the classical technique [35], we simulate the absence of action by an additional loop transition.

The encoding of connectors (interaction models) is more involved. Since a connector represents a set of potential interactions, some ports may not participate in all of them. To encode this possibility, we introduce, for each port, an additional Boolean variable denoting whether the port participates in the interaction or not and, for each connector, a predicate characterising the interaction pattern. Intuitively, the semantics of *flat* BIP connectors [14] depends on the synchron/trigger annotations of ports. If all ports in a connector are synchrons, the only allowed interaction is that comprising all the ports, i.e. they all have to "agree to interact". This case corresponds precisely to the semantics of synchronisation vectors in pNets. If a connector has at least one trigger, then the allowed interactions are those that comprise at least one trigger, i.e. they must be "initiated by a trigger". In a hierarchical connector, these principles are applied recursively. Thus, we observe a "causality" relation among ports of a connector: participation of a synchron in an interaction *implies* that of a trigger. Causal Interaction Trees and Systems of Causal Rules, proposed in [15], formalise this causality relation and provide transformations from connectors to Boolean predicates and back. Since we use SMT techniques for the analysis of the resulting pNet, the encoding presented below is optimised to reduce the number of variables by treating separately the "top-level" triggers (e.g. T.tick in the connector T.tick▶—•(fail▶—•C.fail) in Fig. 1).

Encoding the Coordinators. The encoding of a coordinator C is a pLTS with: (1) an initial state and an init transition that initialises all the variables to those defined by the initial valuation σ_C^0 of C, (2) an action algebra that matches the actions of the coordinator ports but adds, an additional Boolean action parameter, and also, for each exported variable x, a corresponding fresh input variable $?x'$ to allow updates during interactions, (3) pLTS transitions that reflect the original transitions of C with tt as parameter and (4) additional loop transitions marked by ff. Formally, $enc(C) \stackrel{def}{=} \langle\!\langle S, s_0, \xrightarrow[enc(C)]{}\rangle\!\rangle$, such that

- $s_0 \notin Q_C$ is fresh and $S = Q_C \cup \{s_0\}$,
- $vars(s) = V_C \cup \{?x' \mid x \in \varepsilon_C(p), p \in a, s \xrightarrow{a}\}$, for all $s \in Q_C$, and $vars(s_0) = \emptyset$,
- let $uinit \stackrel{def}{=} (x := \sigma_C^0(x))^{x \in V_C}$ and, for all $s \xrightarrow{a,g,u} s'$ with $u = (x := e_x)^{x \in V}$

  (with $V \subseteq V_C$), let $u' \stackrel{def}{=} (x := e_x)^{x \in V \setminus \varepsilon_C(a)} \cup (x := e_x[?x'/x])^{x \in V \cap \varepsilon_C(a)}$, and $\varepsilon'_C(a) \stackrel{def}{=} \{?x' \mid x \in \varepsilon_C(p), p \in a\}$,

$$\xrightarrow[enc(C)]{} \stackrel{def}{=} \Big\{\Big(s, a\big(\varepsilon'_C(a), \varepsilon_C(a), \text{tt}\big), g, u', s'\Big) \,\Big|\, s \xrightarrow{a,g,u} s'\Big\}$$

$$\cup \Big\{\Big(s, a\big(\varepsilon'_C(a), \varepsilon_C(a), \text{ff}\big), \text{tt}, \emptyset, s\Big) \,\Big|\, s \in Q_C, \exists s' \in Q_C : s' \xrightarrow{a}\Big\}$$

$$\cup \big\{(s_0, \text{init}, \text{tt}, uinit, q_C^0)\big\}.$$

The loop transitions marked by ff will be used in the encoding of connectors. Each BIP connector can define several interactions, i.e. ports involved in a connector need not necessarily always participate. On the contrary, each action in a pNet synchronisation vector must participate in the synchronisation. To address this difference, we use the classical approach where non-participation of a port in an interaction is simulated by an additional loop transition [35].

Figure 2 shows the encoding of the Failure Monitor architecture, including the encodings of the two coordinators, i.e. $enc(T)$ and $enc(C)$. Notice that the encoding in the figure is slightly optimised: some of the ports do not have an associated Boolean value, nor the additional loop transitions. We will explain this optimisation after we define the encoding of the interaction model.

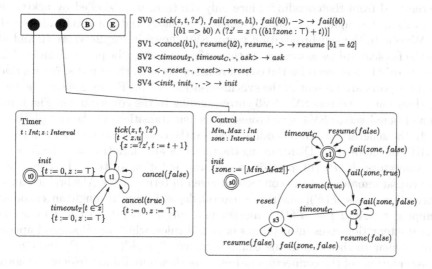

Fig. 2. The open pNet encoding the failure monitor architecture (Fig. 1) without the max progress priority model

Encoding the Interaction Model. The holes in $enc(A, \mathcal{D})$ are indexed by the elements of the partition $\mathcal{D}$. For the encoding of our running example, we take $\mathcal{D} = \{\{\text{fail}, \text{resume}\}, \{\text{ask}, \text{reset}\}\}$. This corresponds to the intuition that the dangling ports fail and resume will be provided by a monitored component, whereas ask and reset correspond to the actions provided by the "environment" (other components of the system) that are invoked in case of a persistent failure. As for the encoding of the coordinators, in the synchronisation vectors of $enc(\Gamma)$, we will associate Boolean values to the actions corresponding to these ports.

The encoding of the interaction model is based on its representation as a set of connectors. Indeed, as illustrated by the Failure Monitor architecture in Fig. 1, each connector can define several allowed interactions, depending on its hierarchical structure and the use of synchrons and triggers.

We encode all interactions of a connector in one synchronisation vector. This will allow us to also encode the maximal progress priority model. We use the additional Boolean values associated to each port by the encoding of coordinator components. For example, observe that the three ports in the connector $T.\text{tick}\blacktriangleright\!\!-\!\!\bullet(\text{fail}\blacktriangleright\!\!-\!\!\bullet C.\text{fail})$ form a "causality chain": $C.\text{fail}$ can only participate in an interaction if the dangling port fail participates, which in turn can only happen if $T.\text{tick}$ does so. These dependencies can be rewritten as Boolean implications $C.\text{fail} \Rightarrow \text{fail}$ and $\text{fail} \Rightarrow T.\text{tick}$. The conjunction of these two implications can be used as a guard for the synchronisation vector encoding this connector.

Within the scope of this connector, the port $T.\text{tick}$ participates in all interactions. Furthermore, it is not involved in any other connector. Hence, the loop transition in $enc(T)$ labelled by $\text{tick}(\text{ff})$ can never be taken and, therefore, can be removed from the encoding. Since only the transition labelled by $\text{tick}(\text{tt})$ is ever taken, the implication $\text{fail} \Rightarrow T.\text{tick}$ is a tautology and can also be discarded.

We obtain the synchronisation vector SV0 shown in Fig. 2, where $b0$ and $b1$ are the Boolean values associated to the actions encoding the ports fail and $C.\text{fail}$. The guard $b1 \Rightarrow b0$ encodes the causal relation between these ports. Notice that all three ports are present in the synchronisation vector. Figure 2 shows the four synchronisation vectors SV0–SV3 corresponding to the connectors in Fig. 1 and an additional vector SV4, synchronising the init transitions of the two pLTSs.

In the general case, the encoding relies on the causal semantics of the algebra of BIP connectors [15]. Disregarding the variables and data transfer, the Algebra of Connectors $\mathcal{AC}(P)$ [13] provides a syntactic notation for the BIP connectors. The causal semantics of the connectors, given in terms of the Algebra of Causal Interaction Trees $\mathcal{T}(P)$, elicits the causal dependencies through an encoding mapping $\tau : \mathcal{AC}(P) \to \mathcal{T}(P)$. Another mapping $R : \mathcal{T}(P) \to \mathcal{CR}(P)$ encodes causal interaction trees into systems of causal rules, which are Boolean implications similar to the ones in the example above. The $\mathcal{AC}(P)$, $\mathcal{T}(P)$ and $\mathcal{CR}(P)$ representations of the connectors in Fig. 1 are shown in Table 1 (elements shown in red can be removed for simplification as described in the example above).

Now we lift this encoding to the data-sensitive case. Below, we assume that, as in Fig. 1, the interaction model is defined by a set of connectors, annotated with Boolean guards and with update assignments. In particular, we assume that the guards and update assignments are well-defined for any interaction allowed by the connector. For example, the choice $C.\text{fail} ? C.\text{zone} : \top$ in the update assignment $T.z := T.z \cap ((C.\text{fail} ? C.\text{zone} : \top) + T.t)$ associated to the connector $T.\text{tick}\blacktriangleright\!\!-\!\!\bullet(\text{fail}\blacktriangleright\!\!-\!\!\bullet C.\text{fail})$ in Fig. 1 ensures that the assignment is well-defined independently of whether $C.\text{fail}$ participates or not. Let us denote by $\gamma \subset \mathcal{AC}(P_A) \times \mathbb{B}_{V_A}^{\leq} \times \mathbb{A}_{V_A}$ the set of connectors in the architecture A and by P_x the set of ports involved in the connector $x \in \gamma$. Then, the interaction model defined by γ is $\Gamma = \{(a, g, u) \mid (x, g, u) \in \gamma, a \in \|x\|\}$ and the set of synchronisation vectors

Table 1. Algebraic representations of the connectors in Fig. 1

Connector	Causal Interaction Tree	System of Causal Rules

T.tick fail C.fail	T.tick
	    ↘
	      fail
	        ↘
	          C.fail
		C.fail $\Rightarrow$ fail $\wedge$ T.tick
		fail $\Rightarrow$ T.tick
		T.tick $\Rightarrow$ tt
		tt $\Rightarrow$ T.tick

resume T.cancel C.resume	resume ↓ T.cancel C.resume	C.resume $\Rightarrow$ resume $\wedge$ T.cancel T.cancel $\Rightarrow$ resume $\wedge$ C.resume resume $\Rightarrow$ tt tt $\Rightarrow$ resume
ask T.timeout$_T$ C.timeout$_C$	ask T.timeout$_T$ C.timeout$_C$	C.timeout$_C$ $\Rightarrow$ ask $\wedge$ T.timeout$_T$ T.timeout$_T$ $\Rightarrow$ ask $\wedge$ C.timeout$_C$ ask $\Rightarrow$ T.timeout$_T$ $\wedge$ C.timeout$_C$ tt $\Rightarrow$ ask $\wedge$ T.timeout$_T$ $\wedge$ C.timeout$_C$
reset C.reset	reset C.reset	C.reset $\Rightarrow$ reset reset $\Rightarrow$ C.reset tt $\Rightarrow$ reset $\wedge$ C.reset

encoding Γ is $enc(\Gamma) \stackrel{def}{=} \{\, enc(x, g, u) \,|\, (x, g, u) \in \gamma \,\}$, with

$$enc(x,g,u) \stackrel{def}{=} \left(\left\{ p\big(\varepsilon_A(p), \varepsilon'_A(p), b_p\big) \,\middle|\, p \in P_x \cap P \right\}^{P \in P_C^{C \in \mathcal{C}} \cup \mathcal{D}} \rightarrow \alpha\big(b_p^{p \in P_x}\big) \right.$$

$$\left. \left[\bigwedge R(\tau(x))\big[b_p/p\big] \wedge \bigwedge_{(x:=e_x) \in u} (?x' = e_x) \wedge \bigwedge_{x \in \varepsilon_A(x), x \notin u} (?x' = x) \right] \right), \quad (3)$$

with $b_p^{p \in P_x}$ fresh Boolean variables, α a fresh name, $\tau : \mathcal{AC}(P_A) \rightarrow \mathcal{T}(P_A)$ and $R : \mathcal{T}(P_A) \rightarrow \mathcal{CR}(P_A)$ the two mappings [15] discussed above and illustrated in Table 1, $\big[b_p/p\big]$ is the substitution that replaces in the expression that precedes it all occurrences of all p by corresponding variables b_p.

For the sake of clarity, we simplify the case study encoding in Fig. 2 by reusing the port names of the original architecture instead of fresh names α. This is made possible by the fact that each synchronisation vector involves at most one action of interest (see the properties in [12]).

In the following theorem, we claim an *isomorphism* between the open automaton semantics of a pNet encoding a BIP architecture and the LTS semantics of this architecture applied to a set of simple components. We omit the formal definition of this isomorphism relation. However, noting that open automata are, essentially, symbolic representations of automata with data, we can summarise it as follows: a transition belongs to the LTS iff a corresponding open transition belongs to the open automaton and the source and target data values of the LTS transition satisfy the predicate and implement the assignments of the open transition.

Theorem 2. *The open automaton* $[enc(A, \mathcal{D})]$ *corresponding to* $enc(A, \mathcal{D})$ *is isomorphic to the LTS* $[\![\Gamma(\mathcal{C}_A, (B_D)^{D \in \mathcal{D}})]\!]$ *(see Definition 6), with, for each* $D \in \mathcal{D}$, *the component* $B_D \overset{def}{=} (\{q\}, q, V_D, \sigma_D^0, D, \varepsilon_D, \rightarrow)$, *with a fresh state* q *and*

$$V_D = \bigcup_{p \in D} \varepsilon_A(p), \qquad\qquad \sigma_D^0(v) = \bot, \text{ for all } v \in V_D,$$

$$\rightarrow = \{(q, p, \text{tt}, \emptyset, q) \mid p \in D\}, \qquad \varepsilon_D(p) = \varepsilon_A(p), \text{ for all } p \in D.$$

Encoding of the Maximal Progress. We only present the key idea, which consists in introducing an additional Boolean variable, for each port, for which we have introduced one in $enc(A, \mathcal{D})$. Intuitively, the Boolean variables introduced for the encoding of interaction models determine whether it is the original transition labeled by the port that is executed (tt), or rather the corresponding self-loop, introduced by the encoding (ff). The new variables determine whether *there is an original transition labelled by p that could be executed from the same state*, i.e., with b_p the variable introduced above for the encoding without maximal progress, $q \xrightarrow{p(\text{tt}, b_p)} q'$ iff $\exists q'' : q \xrightarrow{p(b_p)} q''$ with $b_p = \text{tt}$ in $enc(A, \mathcal{D})$. In the SV guard, we have to check whether *all ports leading to p in the causal interaction tree $\tau(x)$ can be fired* (see the second column of Table 1 for examples). If so, then p must be fired, i.e. $p(\text{ff})$ must be blocked.

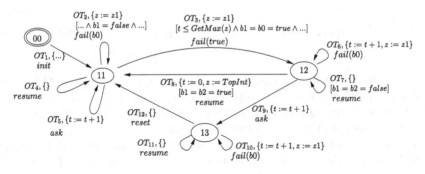

Fig. 3. The open automaton of the failure monitor architecture

Practical Experiments. The above encoding provides a mechanism for the symbolic verification of architectures using our existing tool [36] to compute the open automaton semantics of an open pNet. This tool computes open transitions from pLTS behaviours and synchronisation vectors of the pNet, then uses an SMT engine to check satisfiability of their predicates, minimising the size of the resulting automaton.

In Fig. 3 we show the full open automaton obtained from the pNet in Fig. 2. Due to space limitations, we do not show the details of the open transitions, but only the assignments of state variables, some useful parts of the predicates, and the resulting action; full details can be found in [12]. This automaton has 12 transitions, including those encoding various possible firing of some interactions, e.g. OT_2 and OT_3 for fail. Notice, however, that the global actions of these open transitions have an additional Boolean parameter. In this context, model checking should be understood after application of the encoding, namely here the original fail event must be an effective "fail" of the hole "B", that is a $fail(true)$ action in the open automaton.

Model-checking of open-automaton is out of the scope of this paper, though the resulting automaton here is small enough to observe the kind of properties we can prove. It is clear that our encoding allows to test specific values of state-variables in formulas, like e.g.:

$$A\,[(z = \top)\ \mathsf{W}\ \mathsf{fail}] \quad \wedge \quad \mathsf{AG}\ \big(\mathsf{reset} \to A\,[(z = \top)\ \mathsf{W}\ \mathsf{fail}]\big). \tag{4}$$

that says that *as long as no failure has occured, the z variable of the T component has the value* $\top$.

But we can also (as long as we get a proper axiomatisation of our data operators in the SMT engine) handle more involved data properties, like here the fact that *a reset can only be requested within the specified delay after a failure:*

$$\forall T_0, T_1 \in \mathbb{Z},\ \mathsf{AG}\ \Big((\mathsf{fail} \wedge T.t = T_0) \to$$

$$A\,\big[\big((\mathsf{ask} \wedge T.t = T_1) \to (T_1 - T_0 \in C.zone)\big)\ \mathsf{W}\ (\mathsf{reset} \vee \mathsf{resume})\big]\Big), \tag{5}$$

Last, a detailed study shows that the safety property stated in Definition 12 does not hold, because of the fail loop on state 11. This is because we did not use the maximal progress assumption here. If we do, we get the corrected behaviour where OT_7 disappears, and OT_2 and OT_{10} are restricted to $b0 = \mathtt{ff}$. This one verifies all the properties listed above.

5 Related Work

The design methodology based on BIP architectures is inspired by the notion of design patterns introduced in [24]. It is radically different insofar as BIP architectures posses formal semantics; their composition is well defined and preserves their characteristic properties. This is a relatively novel trend with few comparable works, whereof the most relevant is a theory formalising common architectural styles, such as *publisher-subscriber* or *blackboard*, proposed in [32,33].

Although direct verification of BIP models is possible [4,9–11,37], none of these previous works address compositional verification of parameterised BIP systems with data and maximal progress priorities achieved in the present paper.

From a broader perspective, basic research on behaviour models and verification algorithms for data-sensitive systems started in the nineties, with the seminal work of Hennessy, Lin, and their colleagues on value-passing systems with assignments [26,30,31]. Later, many different works addressing various classes of infinite-state systems and/or parameterised topologies have been published, using combinations of approaches, often including predicate abstraction and SMT satisfiability (e.g. [1,16,20,21,25]). With respect to these, we use symbolic representations not only to get a finite representation of infinite spaces, but also to express the (data-sensitive) synchronisations with the environment, making our models suitable for compositional verification. Among these works, several have shown the capacity of the SMT engines (either Z3 or Yikes) as servers for solving verification conditions of the algorithms, for large case-studies (e.g. [18,22]).

As compositional proof of safety is difficult, some approaches rely on theorem proving to ensure the safety of component operations. Coqots and Pycots [17] even manage to prove the safety of reconfiguration procedures which are known to be highly difficult to verify, and massively parameterised. The approach relies on a high expertise and significant efforts from the user. Here, we rely on automatic verification thanks to the SMT solver but we cannot prove the safety of the reconfiguration procedure.

In [23], the authors propose a compositional proof system for distributed objects that is suitable for implementation within the KeY framework [8] and uses a Hoare logic approach. Compared to this approach, we do not deal with complex history-based specifications and use interaction specification and SMT-reasoning instead of Hoare logic.

6   Conclusion

BIP architectures are composition tools that enforce safety properties; the composition of architectures entails the composition of the associated properties. We have extended architectures with data-sensitive interactions, and proved that this extension still guarantees the preservation of safety properties by architecture composition, under reasonable assumptions. This extends the original compositional methodology offered by BIP architectures. Then we use pNets as a semantic formalism to encode architectures with data. pNet is a low level coordination model for open systems, in which composition preserves bisimulation equivalences. pNet is equipped with tools computing its behavioural semantics in terms of symbolic automata, allowing model-checking and equivalence checking with algorithms relying on SMT engines. As a result, we obtain automatic and compositional guarantees of safety properties with data where compositionality is given by the BIP architectures, and pNet tools provide automatic verification of the properties of each architecture.

The translational approach allows us to benefit from the methods and tools developed separately in BIP and pNets communities, avoiding the additional effort of designing the corresponding tools in both contexts from scratch.

The presented work opens a number of avenues for future work, among which the most immediate ones consist in (1) developing tools that would implement the discussed encoding and verification techniques; (2) studying the preservation of liveness properties by architecture composition under assumptions similar to those discussed in [5] and (3) generalisation to priority models other than maximal progress.

References

1. Alberti, F., Ghilardi, S., Pagani, E., Ranise, S., Rossi, G.P.: Universal guards, relativization of quantifiers, and failure models in model checking modulo theories. JSAT **8**(1/2), 29–61 (2012). https://satassociation.org/jsat/index.php/jsat/article/view/93
2. Ameur-Boulifa, R., Henrio, L., Kulankhina, O., Madelaine, E., Savu, A.: Behavioural semantics for asynchronous components. J. Log. Algebr. Methods Program. **89**, 1–40 (2017). https://doi.org/10.1016/j.jlamp.2017.02.003, http://www.sciencedirect.com/science/article/pii/S2352220817300287
3. Arnold, A.: Synchronised behaviours of processes and rational relations. Acta Inform. **17**, 21–29 (1982)
4. Aştefănoaei, L., Ben Rayana, S., Bensalem, S., Bozga, M., Combaz, J.: Compositional verification of parameterised timed systems. In: Havelund, K., Holzmann, G., Joshi, R. (eds.) NFM 2015. LNCS, vol. 9058, pp. 66–81. Springer, Cham (2015). https://doi.org/10.1007/978-3-319-17524-9_6
5. Attie, P., Baranov, E., Bliudze, S., Jaber, M., Sifakis, J.: A general framework for architecture composability. Form. Asp. Comput. **18**(2), 207–231 (2016)
6. Baranov, E.: A semantic framework for architecture modelling. Ph.D. thesis, EPFL (2017)
7. Basu, A., et al.: Rigorous component-based system design using the BIP framework. IEEE Softw. **28**(3), 41–48 (2011). https://doi.org/10.1109/MS.2011.27
8. Beckert, B., Hähnle, R., Schmitt, P.H.: Verification of Object-Oriented Software: The KeY Approach. Springer, Heidelberg (2007). https://doi.org/10.1007/978-3-540-69061-0
9. Bensalem, S., Bozga, M., Nguyen, T.H., Sifakis, J.: D-finder: a tool for compositional deadlock detection and verification. In: CAV, pp. 614–619 (2009). https://doi.org/10.1007/978-3-642-02658-4_45
10. Bensalem, S., Griesmayer, A., Legay, A., Nguyen, T.-H., Sifakis, J., Yan, R.: D-Finder 2: towards efficient correctness of incremental design. In: Bobaru, M., Havelund, K., Holzmann, G.J., Joshi, R. (eds.) NFM 2011. LNCS, vol. 6617, pp. 453–458. Springer, Heidelberg (2011). https://doi.org/10.1007/978-3-642-20398-5_32
11. Bliudze, S., et al.: Formal verification of infinite-state BIP models. In: Finkbeiner, B., Pu, G., Zhang, L. (eds.) ATVA 2015. LNCS, vol. 9364, pp. 326–343. Springer, Cham (2015). https://doi.org/10.1007/978-3-319-24953-7_25
12. Bliudze, S., Henrio, L., Madelaine, E.: Verification of concurrent design patterns with data. Technical report, Inria (2019, to appear)
13. Bliudze, S., Sifakis, J.: The algebra of connectors–structuring interaction in BIP. In: Proceedings of the 7th ACM & IEEE International Conference on Embedded Software, EMSOFT 2007, pp. 11–20. ACM SigBED, Salzburg, October 2007. https://doi.org/10.1145/1289927.1289935
14. Bliudze, S., Sifakis, J.: The algebra of connectors–structuring interaction in BIP. IEEE Trans. Comput. **57**(10), 1315–1330 (2008). https://doi.org/10.1109/TC.2008.26

15. Bliudze, S., Sifakis, J.: Causal semantics for the algebra of connectors. Form. Methods Syst. Des. **36**(2), 167–194 (2010). https://doi.org/10.1007/s10703-010-0091-z

16. Bruni, R., de Frutos-Escrig, D., Martí-Oliet, N., Montanari, U.: Bisimilarity congruences for open terms and term graphs via tile logic. In: Palamidessi, C. (ed.) CONCUR 2000. LNCS, vol. 1877, pp. 259–274. Springer, Heidelberg (2000). https://doi.org/10.1007/3-540-44618-4_20

17. Buisson, J., Calvacante, E., Dagnat, F., Leroux, E., Martinez, S.: Coqcots & Pycots: non-stopping components for safe dynamic reconfiguration. In: CBSE 2014: proceedings of the 17th International ACM SIGSOFT Symposium on Component-Based Software Engineering, Lille, France, p. 1, June 2014. https://hal.archives-ouvertes.fr/hal-00984365, https://doi.org/10.1145/2602458.2602459

18. Calvanese, D., Ghilardi, S., Gianola, A., Montali, M., Rivkin, A.: Verification of data-aware processes via array-based systems (extended version). CoRR **abs/1806.11459** (2018). http://arxiv.org/abs/1806.11459

19. Cansado, A., Madelaine, E.: Specification and verification for grid component-based applications: from models to tools. In: de Boer, F.S., Bonsangue, M.M., Madelaine, E. (eds.) FMCO 2008. LNCS, vol. 5751, pp. 180–203. Springer, Heidelberg (2009). https://doi.org/10.1007/978-3-642-04167-9_10

20. Cavada, R., et al.: The NUXMV symbolic model checker. In: Biere, A., Bloem, R. (eds.) CAV 2014. LNCS, vol. 8559, pp. 334–342. Springer, Cham (2014). https://doi.org/10.1007/978-3-319-08867-9_22

21. Champion, A., Mebsout, A., Sticksel, C., Tinelli, C.: The KIND 2 model checker. In: Chaudhuri, S., Farzan, A. (eds.) CAV 2016. LNCS, vol. 9780, pp. 510–517. Springer, Cham (2016). https://doi.org/10.1007/978-3-319-41540-6_29

22. Cimatti, A., Griggio, A., Mover, S., Tonetta, S.: IC3 modulo theories via implicit predicate abstraction. CoRR abs/1310.6847 (2013). http://arxiv.org/abs/1310.6847

23. Din, C.C., Dovland, J., Johnsen, E.B., Owe, O.: Observable behavior of distributed systems: component reasoning for concurrent objects. J. Log. Algebr. Program. **81**(3), 227–256 (2012). https://doi.org/10.1016/j.jlap.2012.01.003. The 22nd Nordic Workshop on Programming Theory (NWPT 2010)

24. Gamma, E., Helm, R., Johnson, R., Vlissides, J.: Design Patterns: Elements of Reusable Object-Oriented Software. Addison-Wesley Professional, Boston (1994)

25. Ghilardi, S., Nicolini, E., Ranise, S., Zucchelli, D.: Towards SMT model checking of array-based systems. In: Armando, A., Baumgartner, P., Dowek, G. (eds.) IJCAR 2008. LNCS (LNAI), vol. 5195, pp. 67–82. Springer, Heidelberg (2008). https://doi.org/10.1007/978-3-540-71070-7_6

26. Hennessy, M., Lin, H.: Symbolic bisimulations. Theor. Comput. Sci. **138**(2), 353–389 (1995)

27. Henrio, L., Madelaine, E., Zhang, M.: pNets: an expressive model for parameterised networks of processes. In: 23rd Euromicro International Conference on Parallel, Distributed, and Network-Based Processing (PDP 2015). IEEE (2015)

28. Henrio, L., Kulankhina, O., Li, S., Madelaine, E.: Integrated environment for verifying and running distributed components. In: Stevens, P., Wąsowski, A. (eds.) FASE 2016. LNCS, vol. 9633, pp. 66–83. Springer, Heidelberg (2016). https://doi.org/10.1007/978-3-662-49665-7_5

29. Henrio, L., Madelaine, E., Zhang, M.: A theory for the composition of concurrent processes. In: Albert, E., Lanese, I. (eds.) FORTE 2016. LNCS, vol. 9688, pp. 175–194. Springer, Cham (2016). https://doi.org/10.1007/978-3-319-39570-8_12

30. Lin, H.: Symbolic transition graph with assignment. In: Montanari, U., Sassone, V. (eds.) CONCUR 1996. LNCS, vol. 1119, pp. 50–65. Springer, Heidelberg (1996). https://doi.org/10.1007/3-540-61604-7_47

31. Lin, H.: Model checking value-passing processes. In: 8th Asia-Pacific Software Engineering Conference (APSEC 2001). Macau, December 2001

32. Marmsoler, D.: Towards a theory of architectural styles. In: Proceedings of the 22nd ACM SIGSOFT International Symposium on Foundations of Software Engineering, FSE 2014, pp. 823–825. ACM, New York (2014). https://doi.org/10.1145/2635868. 2661683

33. Marmsoler, D.: Hierarchical specification and verification of architectural design patterns. In: Russo, A., Schürr, A. (eds.) FASE 2018. LNCS, vol. 10802, pp. 149–168. Springer, Cham (2018). https://doi.org/10.1007/978-3-319-89363-1_9

34. Mavridou, A., Stachtiari, E., Bliudze, S., Ivanov, A., Katsaros, P., Sifakis, J.: Architecture-based design: A satellite on-board software case study. In: 13th International Conference on Formal Aspects of Component Software (FACS 2016) (2016)

35. Milner, R.: Calculi for synchrony and asynchrony. TCS **25**(3), 267–310 (1983). https://doi.org/10.1016/0304-3975(83)90114-7

36. Qin, X., Bliudze, S., Madelaine, E., Zhang, M.: Using SMT engine to generate symbolic automata. In: 18th International Workshop on Automated Verification of Critical Systems (AVOCS 2018). Electronic Communications of the EASST (2018)

37. Qiang, W., Bliudze, S.: Verification of component-based systems via predicate abstraction and simultaneous set reduction. In: Ganty, P., Loreti, M. (eds.) TGC 2015. LNCS, vol. 9533, pp. 147–162. Springer, Cham (2016). https://doi.org/10.1007/978-3-319-28766-9_10

Self-organising Coordination Regions: A Pattern for Edge Computing

Roberto Casadei, Danilo Pianini$^{(\boxtimes)}$, Mirko Viroli, and Antonio Natali

Alma Mater Studiorum–Università di Bologna, Cesena, Italy
{roby.casadei,danilo.pianini,mirko.viroli,antonio.natali}@unibo.it

Abstract. Design patterns are key in software engineering, for they capture the knowledge of recurrent problems and associated solutions in specific design contexts. Emerging distributed computing scenarios, such as the Internet of Things, Cyber-Physical Systems, and Edge Computing, define a novel and still largely unexplored application context, where identifying recurrent patterns can be extremely valuable to mainstream development of language mechanisms, algorithms, architectures and supporting platforms—keeping a balanced trade-off between generality, applicability, and guidance. In this work, we present a design pattern, named *Self-organising Coordination Regions* (SCR), which aims to support scalable monitoring and control in distributed systems. Specifically, it is a decentralised coordination pattern for partitioned orchestration of devices (typically on a spatial basis), which provides adaptivity, resilience, and distributed decision-making in large-scale situated systems. It works through a self-organising construction of regions of space, where internal coordination activities are regulated via feedback/control flows among leaders and worker nodes. We present the pattern, provide a template implementation in the Aggregate Computing framework, and evaluate it through simulation of a case study in Edge Computing.

Keywords: Coordination · Distributed systems · Design patterns · Decentralised orchestration · Self-organisation · Edge computing

1 Introduction

Design Patterns are paramount in software engineering. They capture expert knowledge by describing reasoned solution schemas for a well-defined class of repeatedly occurring problems in specific contexts [8]. Patterns help harnessing complexity by characterising systems of forces arising in a context, and strategies to resolve them [1], while abstracting from implementation details, denoting intents and properties of solutions, providing motivated guidance towards desired configurations, and supporting documentation and team communication through a common vocabulary [8]. Over time, several classes of patterns have been discovered to assist designers and implementors of software-based systems, resulting in *catalogues* of patterns, e.g., for object-oriented software [21], concurrency [40],

© IFIP International Federation for Information Processing 2019
Published by Springer Nature Switzerland AG 2019
H. Riis Nielson and E. Tuosto (Eds.): COORDINATION 2019, LNCS 11533, pp. 182–199, 2019.
https://doi.org/10.1007/978-3-030-22397-7_11

messaging [25], reactive systems [44], fault-tolerant software [23] etc. Moreover, patterns can be classified into multiple taxonomies (e.g., by level of abstraction into architectural, design patterns, and idioms [8]), can be related to each other (e.g., by refinement, variance, and combination [8]), and can be presented using different formats (e.g., *Alexandrian* [1], *GoF* [21], and *POSA* [8]).

In this paper, we consider the context of coordination in large-scale distributed systems. Specifically, we focus on scenarios – e.g., pervasive computing, Collective Adaptive Systems (CAS), Internet of Things (IoT), Cyber-Physical Systems (CPS), and Edge Computing – characterised by the following forces:

- *Distribution.* Having distributed components leads to concurrency, lack of global clock, and independent (and often frequent) failure or unavailability of components [14]—with corresponding implications.
- *Situatedness.* Components may be logically or physically immersed into an environment such that their location and context are relevant, since their inputs and outputs may be limited to the surroundings.
- *Heterogeneity.* Components may differ by their computational capabilities, energy requirements, and general dependability.
- *Large scale.* Systems may be too large to be centrally orchestrated or manually operated.

Given the rather intense research ongoing in these contexts, their broad scope, complexity of the challenges, and proliferation of paradigms, some catalogues of design patterns have emerged. Relevant examples include pattern catalogues for multi-agent architectures [24] and ensemble structures [26], bio-inspired computing [20], and decentralised control [49] and coordination [17] in self-adaptive systems. They typically work at different levels of abstractions, from principles and high-level behaviour components to mathematically-defined evolution rules, and do not generally provide complete solutions for the complex problem of scalable coordination of large-scale situated systems.

Accordingly, in this paper we provide three original contributions, namely, we: (*i*) present a general, decentralised coordination design pattern for partitioned orchestration that aims to provide adaptivity and resilience in large-scale situated systems; (*ii*) improve over the existing instances by proposing a feedback loop dynamically resizing partitions, to be used e.g. for load balancing; (*iii*) propose a possible implementation of the pattern in the Aggregate Computing framework [4]; and (*iv*) show an application of the pattern in the context of *edge computing*, through a case study.

The pattern we describe finds application in several scenarios where a sparse set of leaders is expected to collect feedback from and enact decisions for a subset of other participants—examples include distributed sensing [12], target counting [37], group management for target tracking [32], decentralised service orchestration [29], self-adaptative software [49], Wireless Sensor Networks (WSN) [19,31], robot swarm control [48], crowd tracking and steering [4,10], peer-to-peer clouds [13], and coordination in hierarchical thing/edge/fog/cloud environments (as explored in this paper). We call this pattern **Self-organising Coordination Regions (SCR)**, since it works through an internally-regulated, adaptive construction of regions where activity is coordinated via feedback/control flows among master and worker nodes. In other words, it leverages asymmetry in complex coordination scenarios and accordingly proposes a tunable trade-off between centralised and decentralised decision-making.

The rest of this paper is structured as follows, with content following roughly the GoF pattern template form [21]. Section 2 provides context, a motivating example and discusses related work and patterns. Section 3 presents the pattern by providing its intent, synonyms, structure, dynamics as well as known uses, consequences and methodological guidelines of its application. Section 4 shows an implementation in the Aggregate Computing framework, and discusses variants. Section 5 provides empirical evaluation. Finally, Sect. 6 concludes the paper.

2   Motivation

2.1   Motivating Scenario

Background: Edge Computing. Fog and edge computing [7,41,43] are emerging paradigms with the goal of bringing cloud-like functionality at the edge of the network, i.e., close to end users and to where data is generated and used (or, generally, to where computational intelligence is most needed—cf., IoT and CPS). There are at least three cases in which this is highly desirable: (i) *when the cloud is not available*, e.g., because of lack of Internet connectivity; (ii) *when the cloud is available but it cannot satisfy application requirements*, because of data privacy issues or lack of real-time guarantees due to large round-trip time to remote data centres; (iii) *when the cloud is available and suitable but it is costly*, e.g., in terms of subscription or network bandwidth. That is, edge computing is in some cases a necessity, but in general it represents a complementary model to cloud computing which enables a whole new set of possibilities ranging from infrastructure-level optimisations (like exploiting idle edge devices or filtering data before sending it to the cloud) to flexibility in service-level agreements and resilience through decentralisation.

Case Study. As paradigmatic case study, consider a multimedia application that requires computation over user-generated video stream and low-latency communication. Example applications are, e.g., metropolitan collaborative surveillance [16] and multiplayer gaming. For the latter, pervasive usage of multi-view and 360-degree-view video streams is currently limited by delay intolerance and excessive bandwidth usage [5]. Moreover, relevance of low-latency video processing will likely increase in the future with advancements in mobile augmented reality technology [39]. One wants such multimedia application to execute on a smart urban environment, where users, equipped with mobile devices (smartphones, or even augmented-reality equipment) can move. The smart city is populated with a network of static (non-mobile) edge servers, with which mobile devices can communicate. The goal is to adaptively select a subset of edge nodes (enough to sustain the computation) to work as local leaders, gather and redirect the video streams from user devices to one leader edge device, process the data gathered, and finally spread the computation result back to the users.

2.2   Problem and Forces

The SCR pattern addresses the problem of coordination in situations where:

1. heterogeneity creates asymmetry in individual capabilities, or tasks are so complex that *collaboration* is essential;
2. a *locality principle* holds, as context is key and cost is typically proportional to the distance between sources, processes, and users;
3. neither *full centralisation* nor *full decentralisation* in control and decision making is possible or desirable; and
4. the environment and system structure are *dynamic* (e.g., due to mobility or failure).

2.3   Related Work and Patterns

The SCR pattern recurs in a number of scientific works and proposed solutions, and is implemented variously.

Related Patterns and Abstractions. Related catalogues of design pattern and abstractions include [17], addressing decentralised coordination in self-organising emergent systems; [20], covering bio-inspired patterns; [49], focussing on decentralised control in self-adaptive systems; and [45], providing a library of reusable components of distributed behaviour. Some patterns there presented constitute the foundations of the current work. Indeed, the SCR pattern is a combination of three fundamental coordination (sub-)patterns:

- *Multi-leader election.* In distributed systems, it is sometimes useful to break symmetry or introduce multiple local centralisation points to simplify decision making or coordination. This pattern consists in the election of multiple leaders to uniformly cover a logical or physical space.
- *Information propagation.* Communication patterns that abstract from low-level implementation or networking details are essential in distributed systems. This pattern consists of propagating information from one or more sources outward, independently of the underlying system structure.
- *Information collection.* This pattern consists of collecting information from a set of sources into one or more sinks, still abstracting from low-level details.

In order to account for situations where devices can fail or change, coherently to the self-organisation principle, we should consider the above patterns as *continuous processes* (or, at least, as processes that are *reactive* [34] to failure or change). This means that information (updates) must move continuously, as a stream (logically, and despite potential optimisations), as captured by the *information flow* abstraction, defined in [18] as follows:

> An information flow is a stream of information from source localities towards destination localities and this stream is maintained and regularly updated to reflect changes in the system. Between sources and destinations, a flow can pass other localities where new information can be aggregated and combined into the information flow.

A common way to implement information flows is by activating processes that create and maintain structures for the communication paths. One such example is the *gradient* [2,15,17,33], a self-healing distributed data structure mapping any node of the system to its hop-by-hop estimated distance from source points: it provides an underlying carrier for controlling effective directions of propagation/collection of data flows. Information flows can be naturally expressed in the library of [45], which fosters the definition of collective behaviour of an ensemble of devices through a composition of self-organising patterns, drawing inspiration from biology [20]. The aforementioned sub-patterns are "building blocks" in [4], where are respectively called S (for **S***parse-choice*—i.e., a scattered selection from the set of participating devices), G (for **G***radient-cast*—i.e., a multicast diffusing information along a gradient), and C (for **C***onverge-cast*—i.e., a multicast aggregating information to a sink device).

A well-known organisational meta-pattern for self-adaptive systems is MAPE [30]: it suggests structuring the system feedback control loop into four components: Monitor, Analyse, Plan, and Execute. In [49], several MAPE patterns are provided for organising the adaptation logic in decentralised self-adaptive systems. These are related and operate in a similar design context, but their focus is on internal organisation of system adaptivity rather than on external, application design. In particular, the *Regional Planning* pattern [49] consists in distributing *Planning* components to different "software regions" (i.e., loosely coupled software subsystems); there, they collect data from *Analyse* components (which are fed by *Monitoring* components) and command *Execute* components for enaction of planned adaptations. SCR subsumes Regional Planning: it enables the design of self-adaptation control loops but goes beyond that, by covering various assignments of responsibilities to the participants and being directly usable for application logic as well; e.g., leaders in SCR may gather regional data, resolve contention, or propagate events.

Known Uses. Various forms and uses of the SCR pattern can be found in literature. In [29], SCR is used to design a decentralised service orchestration system; there, a workflow specification is split for scalability and performance into sub-workflows executed by multiple collaborating engines that are migrated to different network regions based on placement analysis. In [19], SCR is applied in the design of a WSN middleware, *TCMote*, where the system is organised in (possibly hierarchical) *sensor regions* governed by *leaders* with higher capabilities than the other region nodes (called *motes*); TCMote uses tuple channels for one-to-many and many-to-one communication between region sensors and the region leader in a single-hop. In the WSN middleware *TS-Mid* [31], tuple space-based logical regions are used for power saving; there, regional leaders dispatch operations to normal nodes and transmit results to sink nodes. In [48], the authors leverage dynamically selected, human-controlled leaders to guide robot swarms towards goal regions. Other known uses of the pattern include distributed sensing [12], target counting [37], group management for target tracking [32], design of self-adaptation control loops [49] (as discussed above), crowd tracking and steering [4,10] in opportunistic IoT, as well as peer-to-peer clouds [13].

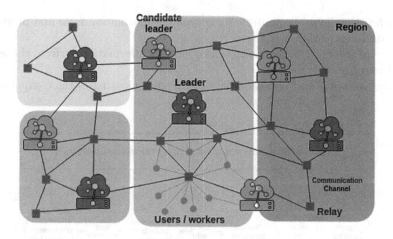

Fig. 1. SCR from a structural perspective—see description in Sect. 3.1. Notation: "gateway-like" nodes denote candidate leaders (red for active ones, grey for unelected ones); small grey squares denote relays; small grey circles denote users/workers (Color figure online)

3 Pattern Description

Intent. Support scalable control and monitoring of a distributed system, with resiliency to failures and dynamicity, and balancing centralisation and decentralisation in decision making.

Name and Synonyms

- *Self-organising Coordination Regions.* This reflects the decentralised nature of this pattern, as well as its support for coordination through scoped, endogenous, emergent structures and dynamics.
- *Decentralised Multi-Orchestration.* This is also a suitable name, as the pattern defines a decentralised coordination strategy for injecting multiple orchestration points into a system, creating corresponding system partitions regulated through feedback loops.
- *SGCG.* This name denotes the chain of aggregate programming blocks that provides a possible implementation schema of the pattern (see Sect. 4).

3.1 Structure and Participants

Structurally, the pattern is organised as of Fig. 1. The system is a network of *nodes* on which spatially extended and dynamic structures, called *regions*, emerge, each "containing" a subset of devices. These components can assume at any time one or more of the following roles:

- *Candidate leader*: a device eligible for leader election—even though the pattern itself makes no assumption on the network structure, on an edge deployment usually candidate leaders correspond to edge servers;

- *Leader*: the device responsible for obtaining information from and propagating decisions within a *region*;
- *User* (or *worker*): device which sends/receives information to/from the leader of the region it is part of;
- *Relay*: non-user and non-candidate device participating in the computation.

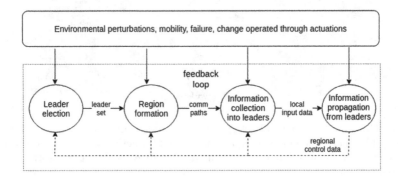

Fig. 2. SCR from a dynamical perspective—see description in Sect. 3.2. Notation: solid arrows represent required inputs or unavoidable perturbations; dashed lines denote possible feedback loops

3.2   Dynamics and Collaborations

The pattern induces a computational behaviour organised in four phases:

1. *Election of leaders.* Leaders are elected from the set of candidates.
2. *Formation of regions.* Structures are created such that each user is assigned to a single leader, and information can flow in both directions through proper communication paths.
3. *Information flow from users to leaders.* User nodes stream data or updates needed by leaders to achieve the system goals, and some processing can occur *en-route*—examples include sensor data, local events, service requests, or feedback information for the assigned tasks.
4. *Information flow from leaders to users.* Leaders stream computation results to all members of their managed region—it may be a decision to be enacted, a collective view to be propagated, instructions to be assigned, and so on.

Note that these phases are only conceptually sequential: they are rather dynamical processes that happen concurrently, are continuously revised, and are related by input/output dependencies (see Fig. 2). Specifically, the leader election phase can be thought as an active process black box that can react to various perturbations to automatically revise the selection of leaders and shape of regions; then, as regions change, the corresponding collection and propagation processes need to adapt. Moreover, the system can be configured with feedback loops: information propagated by leaders may produce an effect on workers that can subsequently get perceived by leaders through collected data.

Variants and Extensions

- *Leader election with pre-established regions.* In some cases, the regions must be decided before the corresponding leaders are elected.
- *Connected leaders.* In some scenario, communication between leaders is desired to allow for global, system-wide coordination that goes beyond the needs of individual regions.
- *Hierarchical organisation.* The pattern can be applied recursively: a region can be split into sub-regions governed by sub-leaders, and so on.
- *Overlapping regions.* Multiple instances of the pattern may be concurrently spawned with different regions, in order to provide in each device a superimposed view of its various "localities". This requires the capability to execute some parts of the distributed coordination algorithm concurrently.

3.3   Applicability

When to Apply. Use of the SCR pattern is encouraged in any of the following:

- A large-scale situated system needs to self-organise in such a way that its components can be monitored and coordinated according to a view larger than local, such as in complex situation recognition.
- A balance between centralisation and decentralisation is required to support effective decision making in large-scale, dynamic contexts.
- All or part of the information should be processed nearby the users, because of resource constraints like bandwidth, storage, energy, and so on.
- The underlying network structure is unknown, the system is open (new relays, leader candidates and users can join and leave the system dynamically), failures are possible, or other events can dynamically change the network structure.

When Not to Apply. Adoption of the SCR pattern is discouraged (or would lead to degenerate cases) in the following circumstances:

- Decision making can be carried out in a fully local way.
- Decision making must be entirely centralised (actually, this could be tackled by electing a single leader, but more efficient solutions may exist for less dynamic scenarios).
- The network structure is statically defined.

3.4 Consequences

The SCR pattern has the following consequences:

- *Hybrid decision making.* Decisions are taken considering a tunable subset of the whole system, de-facto creating a hybrid between centralised and decentralised decision making.
- *Sub-network isolation.* Unless an extended version of the pattern is deployed, users belonging to different regions do not participate in the same sub-system (i.e., they do not exchange data).
- *Reduced dependence from deployment and network structure.* SCR creates a sort of dynamic, adaptive network overlay structure on top of the existing communication infrastructure. By merely organising application logic on that overlay, the specific shape of the underlying network can be abstracted away, allowing for easier porting to diverse setups (e.g. cloud, edge, purely P2P).
- *Eventual consistency.* Temporal mobility, loss of messages, and device failures, only temporarily affect the values collected in leaders, and hence, deviation from the actual global view.

4   Implementation

In this section, we describe some possible variants in the implementation strategy of the four phases described in previous section (Sect. 4.1), and then provide an example specification in the framework of Aggregate Computing (Sect. 4.2).

4.1   Implementation Issues

Election of Leaders and Formation of Regions

- *Consensus strategy.* Consensus on leadership may involve centralised algorithms, or resort to (more challenging) algorithms for distributed and asynchronous systems [42].
- *Candidate leaders.* In general, there could be constraints or preferences concerning which nodes can be selected as leaders: coordinators are usually preferably static, dependable nodes with significant computational and network resources, and little or no power saving concern—such as edge gateways or fog nodes. Trust could also be used to rate and therefore include/exclude nodes from the candidate set based on observed activity [9].
- *Time of election.* Leaders can be elected statically (i.e., before system execution) or be dynamically reconsidered, continuously or after a delay.

- *Objectives.* The goal is usually a configuration of leaders that must be valid or optimised with respect to a particular property—e.g., uniformity in spatial coverage (as of a smart city environment) or balancing of load (tasks, workers).
- *Adaptivity and resilience.* A new leader election process must be activated when the current leader configuration gets invalidated. E.g., this could happen due to mobility, change of load, or failure of some leader.

Information Spreading

- *Gossip.* One way to implement spreading of information is through gossip protocols [6], which are suitable for letting information flow from leaders to users under the condition that the generated information is monotonic (namely, it can only change in a single direction). Whenever such an assumption does not hold, gossip algorithms should get periodically reset (or overlapping replicates of the algorithm should execute in parallel [36]).
- *Gradient-based information cast.* A class of algorithms for distributed information spreading is rooted on the idea of carrying information along with a monotonically-increasing (logical or physical) distance from the information source. This is suitable both for generating regions once leaders are elected (by selecting the closest leader) and for propagating information from leaders to users. Several implementations of the algorithm exist, ranging from distributed adaptive Bellman-Ford [15] to advanced versions and compound algorithms taking into account aspects like time, speed, and acceleration of devices [2].

Information Accumulation

- *Gossip.* Information accumulation is generally a tougher task than information spreading. As for spreading, accumulation can be realised by gossiping information such that the leader is reached with messages from all nodes in the region: however, this effectively works only in the case of small regions.
- *Spanning tree techniques.* A more scalable technique is based on building a spanning tree over the network (locally selecting as parent the closest neighbour to the source), then accumulating along such tree towards the leader. Spanning trees, however, are highly fragile to changes in the network: disruption and creation of links may lead to different configurations, making naive versions of this algorithm unsuitable for mobile scenarios.
- *Multi-path techniques.* Multi-path techniques aggregate information along the source using multiple spanning trees rather than a single one. They are usually more robust to changes in the network structure, but take more time to converge in case of stable networks [45].

4.2   Sample Code

We propose an implementation draft for the pattern in the paradigm of aggregate computing [4,46]—used in next section as a basis for evaluating a smart city case study. The reason for this choice is rooted in the rather straightforward mapping between the sub-patterns of SCR and the building blocks available in existing aggregate computing languages, which allow for a concise implementation.

Background: Computational Fields and Aggregate Computing [4,46]. Aggregate computing is founded on the idea of programming systems from a global perspective, declaratively [47], by functional manipulation of *(computational) fields* data structures—time-evolving maps from devices to values. The *field calculus* [3,46] is the formal, universal, minimal language for functionally composing and manipulating fields, based on which domain-specific languages (DSL) like ScaFi [12] and Protelis [38] have been introduced to specify, simulate and run self-organising behaviours and collective coordination logic.

In the field calculus, a program describes a collective behaviour by neglecting the single-device viewpoint. However, the operational semantics [3] defines how the single device can "continuously" process the program and sustain the overall system behaviour, by cyclic steps encompassing: *(i)* assessment of a local context (previous state, environment perception, collection of input messages received so far); *(ii)* interpretation of the aggregate program against such a context (producing a new state, messages to be sent, and actions to be executed); *(iii)* execution of actions and spread of messages to neighbours.

Pattern Implementation Schema. In ScaFi, a Scala-internal DSL for aggregate programming, the pattern can be encoded as follows[1] (for the implementation of the sub-patterns in ScaFi and details on the syntax, refer to [11]) (Fig. 3):

```
class SCR extends AggregateProgram with BlockG with BlockC with BlockS {
  def main = {
    // selects a field of leaders, with at least grain distance
    val leader = branch(isCandidate) { S(grain) } { false }
    // creates a gradient from leaders based on a given metric
    val potential = distanceTo(leader, metric)
    // gathers localInput values towards leaders by aggregation
    val convergeCast = C(potential, localInput, aggregationFun)
    // on leaders, takes a local decision based on received data
    val decision = decisionMaking(leader, convergeCast)
    // broadcast decisions and take action
    val divergeCast = G(leader, metric, decision)
    localAction(divergeCast)
  }
}
```

---

[1] Purple symbols are non-primitive aggregate building blocks, grey symbols are configuration parameters, and bold symbols denote methods for local activity to be tailored to the application.

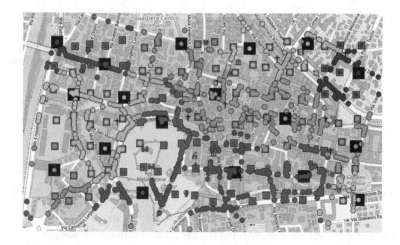

Fig. 3. A snapshot of the simulation in execution. Edge servers are depicted as square nodes, users as circular nodes. Leaders are black, big squares; unelected leaders (working as relays) are smaller, greyed squares. The colour of the circular dot identifies the id of the region assigned to that node (Color figure online)

5 Evaluation

In this section, we present an example implementation of the pattern in the context of smart cities and edge computing (as introduced in Sect. 2.1) and evaluate it by simulation to reveal its intrinsic self-organisation character.

5.1 Scenario Description

We consider a scenario of multiple edge servers (specifically, 126) in the centre of the Italian city of Cesena, all participating in the system as leader candidates. Their positions form an irregular grid, and vary on different simulation runs. We dynamically select a subset of these leader candidates to work as leaders, and let the others participate in the system as relays. More precisely, the edge servers elect a leader for every region of 200 m in radius, competing using the S building block (namely, breaking symmetry using a device local id, and favouring already established leaders if in a proper range).

The goal of the system is to collect data streams generated by users, aggregate it, and diffuse to the whole region the number of streams being processed. Users are modelled as devices moving along roads open to pedestrian traffic (data obtained from OpenStreetMap [22]) at a constant speed of $1.4\frac{m}{s}$. Bidirectional communication is considered established between users and edge servers, and among edge servers, if physical distance is within WiFi range (100 m). Users do not directly communicate with each other. In our experiment, we let the system run for 10 simulated minutes, then we simulate a disruptive event: elected leaders fail with probability ρ—e.g. as would happen due to a city-wise power shortage. After this event, we simulate 10 further minutes of system evolution.

Table 1. Free variables for the scenario in exam

Name	Description	Values
u	Active user devices count	[50, 100, 200, 500, 1000]
α	Backoff algorithm parameter	$[0, 10^{-3}, 10^{-2}, 10^{-1}, 1]$
ρ	Probability for a leader to shut down after 10 min	[0, 0.25, 0.5, 0.75, 1]
fb	Determines whether the feedback loop is enabled	[true, false]

Table 2. Measures for the case study

Name	Description	Unit
E of feedback adjustment	Mean of the feedback adjustment for every leader. It measures how much the radius of the coordinated region is extended. Lower values indicate bigger regions	m
σ of feedback adjustment	Standard deviation of the feedback adjustment for every leader. It is an indication of how much the radius of the coordinated region varies among leaders. Higher values indicate higher disparity in such values, meaning that the feedback system is altering the region sizes more intensively	m
$\sum$ of clients per edge server	Overall number of users served. The value should ideally match the number of users in the system. Higher values indicate streams being processed by multiple leaders (due to users changing region), lower values indicate non-served users	users
σ of clients per edge server	Standard deviation of number of users served by each leader. Indication of load balancing. Higher values indicate that more computational capacity is required for some leaders w.r.t. others. The lower, the better balanced is the load	users

We compare two implementations of the SCR pattern, a classic one (as described in Sect. 4) and a version with a feedback loop. In the latter, leaders try to coordinate and resize their regions in the attempt to cover approximately the same number of users, so as to reduce disparities in elaboration load that would cause slowdowns on overloaded edge servers. We implement self-organising adaptation of region size by feeding the information on the number of served users back to the leader, and using it to dynamically change the region size (the more users, the smaller the region), competing with other leaders. In order to prevent sharp oscillations of the region sizes, with possible resonance phenomena, we don't feed the served user count back to the algorithm input directly, but we filter it using an exponential backoff (a low pass filter), namely, the feedback value is $\alpha u_t + (1 - \alpha)u_{t-1}$, where u_t is the count of served users at time t.

We first evaluate good values for α in our scenario, by looking at how different values affect the size of regions and their stability. We then measure performance and resilience for both the base and the optimal-α versions of the SCR pattern varying the number of users and ρ, and observe the number of users served in total and by each edge server. A summary of the free variables for the case study is given in Table 1; measures are instead summarised and explained in Table 2.

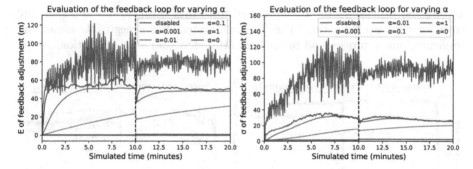

Fig. 4. Evaluation of the backoff parameter. Values are averaged along all values of u and ρ. Not considering new values ($\alpha = 0$) has a similar effect to disabling feedback entirely. Plugging the feedback directly, without filtering, makes the system oscillate. Other values show how α tunes the trade-off between reactivity and stability, with $\alpha = 0.01$ both smooth and with an impact on the system comparable to $\alpha = 0.1$

The pattern has been implemented in Protelis [38], and simulations have been performed using Alchemist [35]. We executed 100 replicas of the experiment for each configuration in the cartesian product of the parameters values, varying displacement of edge devices, initial position of users and their waypoints, and execution times of devices. Data has been processed using Python xarray [27] and matplotlib [28]. The experiments include a reference implementation of the SCR pattern, they are entirely open-sourced, automated, and reproducible using the instructions provided in a publicly accessible repository[2]. Confidence intervals are not pictured in charts reported on this paper, but can be obtained by using the full data and processing tools available in the aforementioned repository.

5.2   Results

We initially measure the benefits of using the feedback system and the impact of different values for α. Results are depicted and described in Fig. 4, and show how $\alpha = 10^{-2}$ is the best choice among the analysed values.

We then evaluate correctness and performance of the algorithm both without and with feedback enabled ($\alpha = 10^{-2}$). Results presented in Fig. 5 show that the system is able to serve all the users, actually serving some users twice at the moment they cross the boundary between neighbouring regions.

Finally, we study resilience of the system to failures by analysing its behaviour with different sudden disruptions hitting the leaders. Figure 6 shows the pattern reaches stability in few seconds even when disruption is large, and regardless of the feedback system. At disruption time, several nodes are not served and several others get instead apparently overserved, as they are in an inconsistent state and participating in multiple, quickly changing regions, with their streams

---

[2] https://bitbucket.org/danysk/experiment-2019-coordination-dynamic-orchestration.

getting lost because of the time required to recover both regions and spanning trees for data accumulation. The feedback system has a negligible impact on resilience, but improves load balancing both before and after disruption.

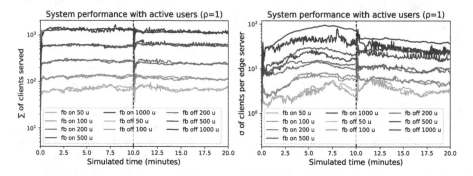

Fig. 5. System correctness. Warm colours are results with feedback system disabled, cold colours are results with feedback system enabled and $\alpha = 10^{-2}$. Both configurations serve all the users, and actually slightly "overserve" them. This is due to the fact that users joining a different region, have, for some time, their streams counted also in the region they left due to network propagation and elaboration times. The feedback system provides benefits in terms of load balancing, as depicted in the right chart: the lower σ means lower disparity among leaders in the number of served users (Color figure online)

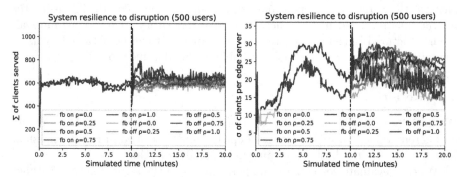

Fig. 6. System resilience to disruption. Both the pattern configurations provide resilience to disruptions. The system is able to find new leaders in few seconds even if the whole set of previously selected leaders is shut off. The feedbacked system seems to achieve slightly better performance for smaller disruptions, but takes more time to stabilise in the worst case. As seen in Fig. 5, the feedbacked system achieves visible better performance in terms of load balancing, both before and after the disruptive event, regardless of its entity

6   Conclusion

In this paper, we introduce *Self-organising Coordination Regions*, an adaptive coordination pattern for dynamic, opportunistic scenarios where neither complete centralisation nor full decentralisation of control and decision making are possible or desirable. The pattern fits a problem of potentially growing relevance, and it is particularly suitable for edge systems and for deploying a coordination stance that covers more than pure locality yet without requiring any global coordinator. To show applicability and benefits, we also present a case study in edge computing, showing that the pattern is able to create semi independent coordination regions, aggregate information, and propagate results to region members. The pattern is also easily extensible: we show, e.g., how a simple feedback mechanism could be devised to improve the load balancing across different leaders. We believe the presented pattern, along with easy implementation on the Aggregate Computing framework and its library of reusable blocks, can streamline prototype and development of a wide class of advanced coordination mechanisms, especially in the context of edge computing.

References

1. Alexander, C.: A Pattern Language: Towns, Buildings, Construction. OUP, Oxford (1977)
2. Audrito, G., Casadei, R., Damiani, F., Viroli, M.: Compositional blocks for optimal self-healing gradients. In: IEEE SASO (2017)
3. Audrito, G., Viroli, M., Damiani, F., Pianini, D., Beal, J.: A higher-order calculus of computational fields. ACM Trans. Comput. Log. **20**(1), 5:1–5:55 (2019)
4. Beal, J., Pianini, D., Viroli, M.: Aggregate programming for the internet of things. IEEE Comput. **48**(9), 22–30 (2015)
5. Bilal, K., Erbad, A.: Edge computing for interactive media and video streaming. In: 2nd International Conference on Fog and Mobile Edge Computing (FMEC). IEEE, May 2017
6. Birman, K.: The promise, and limitations, of gossip protocols. ACM SIGOPS Oper. Syst. Rev. **41**(5), 8 (2007)
7. Bonomi, F., Milito, R., Zhu, J., Addepalli, S.: Fog computing and its role in the internet of things. In: 1st Workshop on MCC, pp. 13–16. ACM (2012)
8. Buschmann, F., Meunier, R., Rohnert, H., Sommerlad, P., Stal, M.: Pattern-Oriented Software Architecture, Volume 1: A System of Patterns. Wiley, Hoboken (1996)
9. Casadei, R., Aldini, A., Viroli, M.: Towards attack-resistant aggregate computing using trust mechanisms. Sci. Comput. Program. **167**, 114–137 (2018)
10. Casadei, R., Fortino, G., Pianini, D., Russo, W., Savaglio, C., Viroli, M.: Modelling and simulation of opportunistic IoT services with aggregate computing. Futur. Gener. Comput. Syst. **91**, 252–262 (2019)
11. Casadei, R., Pianini, D., Viroli, M.: Simulating large-scale aggregate MASs with Alchemist and Scala. In: FedCSIS Proceedings, pp. 1495–1504. IEEE (2016)
12. Casadei, R., Viroli, M.: Programming actor-based collective adaptive systems. In: Ricci, A., Haller, P. (eds.) Programming with Actors. LNCS, vol. 10789, pp. 94–122. Springer, Cham (2018). https://doi.org/10.1007/978-3-030-00302-9_4

13. Casadei, R., Viroli, M.: Coordinating computation at the edge: a decentralized, self-organizing, spatial approach. In: Proceedings of 4th IEEE Fog and Mobile Edge Computing Conference (2019, to appear)
14. Coulouris, G.F., Dollimore, J., Kindberg, T.: Distributed Systems: Concepts and Design. Pearson Education, London (2005)
15. Dasgupta, S., Beal, J.: A Lyapunov analysis for the robust stability of an adaptive bellman-ford algorithm. In: 55th Conference on Decision & Control (CDC). IEEE (2016)
16. Dautov, R., Distefano, S., Bruneo, D., Longo, F., Merlino, G., et al.: Metropolitan intelligent surveillance systems for urban areas by harnessing IoT and edge computing paradigms. Softw.: Pract. Exp. **48**(8), 1475–1492 (2018)
17. De Wolf, T., Holvoet, T.: Design patterns for decentralised coordination in self-organising emergent systems. In: Brueckner, S.A., Hassas, S., Jelasity, M., Yamins, D. (eds.) ESOA 2006. LNCS (LNAI), vol. 4335, pp. 28–49. Springer, Heidelberg (2007). https://doi.org/10.1007/978-3-540-69868-5_3
18. De Wolf, T., Holvoet, T.: Designing self-organising emergent systems based on information flows and feedback-loops. In: 1st SASO Conference, pp. 295–298. IEEE (2007)
19. Diaz, M., Rubio, B., Troya, J.M.: A coordination middleware for wireless sensor networks. In: Systems Communications, pp. 377–382. IEEE (2005)
20. Fernandez-Marquez, J.L., Serugendo, G.D.M., Montagna, S., Viroli, M., Arcos, J.L.: Description and composition of bio-inspired design patterns: a complete overview. Nat. Comput. **12**(1), 43–67 (2013)
21. Gamma, E., Helm, R., Johnson, R., Vlissides, J.M.: Design Patterns: Elements of Reusable Object-Oriented Software, 1st edn. Addison-Wesley Professional, Boston (1994)
22. Haklay, M., Weber, P.: OpenStreetMap: user-generated street maps. IEEE Pervasive Comput. **7**(4), 12–18 (2008)
23. Hanmer, R.S.: Patterns for Fault Tolerant Software. Wiley, Hoboken (2013)
24. Hayden, S., Carrick, C., Yang, Q., et al.: Architectural design patterns for multiagent coordination. In: International Conference on Agent Systems, vol. 99 (1999)
25. Hohpe, G., Woolf, B.: Enterprise Integration Patterns. Prentice Hall, Upper Saddle River (2004)
26. Horling, B., Lesser, V.: A survey of multi-agent organizational paradigms. Knowl. Eng. Rev. **19**(4), 281–316 (2004)
27. Hoyer, S., Hamman, J.: xarray: N-D labeled arrays and datasets in Python. J. Open Res. Softw. **5**(1), 1–6 (2017)
28. Hunter, J.D.: Matplotlib: a 2D graphics environment. J. Open Res. Softw. **9**(3), 90–95 (2007). https://doi.org/10.1109/MCSE.2007.55
29. Jaradat, W., Dearle, A., Barker, A.: Towards an autonomous decentralized orchestration system. Concurr. Computat. Pract. Exper. **28**(11), 3164–3179 (2016)
30. Kephart, J.O., Chess, D.M.: The vision of autonomic computing. Computer **1**, 41–50 (2003)
31. Lima, R., Rosa, N., Marques, I.: Ts-Mid: middleware for wireless sensor networks based on tuple space. In: 22nd AINA Workshops, pp. 886–891. IEEE (2008)
32. Liu, J., Liu, J., Reich, J., Cheung, P., Zhao, F.: Distributed group management in sensor networks: algorithms and applications to localization and tracking. Telecommun. Syst. **26**(2–4), 235–251 (2004)
33. Lluch-Lafuente, A., Loreti, M., Montanari, U.: Asynchronous distributed execution of fixpoint-based computational fields. Log. Methods Comput. Sci. **13**(1) (2017)

34. Magnaudet, M., Chatty, S.: What should adaptivity mean to interactive software programmers? In: Symposium on Engineering Interactive Computing Systems, pp. 13–22. ACM (2014)
35. Pianini, D., Montagna, S., Viroli, M.: Chemical-oriented simulation of computational systems with ALCHEMIST. J. Simul. **7**(3), 202–215 (2013)
36. Pianini, D., Beal, J., Viroli, M.: Improving gossip dynamics through overlapping replicates. In: Lluch Lafuente, A., Proença, J. (eds.) COORDINATION 2016. LNCS, vol. 9686, pp. 192–207. Springer, Cham (2016). https://doi.org/10.1007/978-3-319-39519-7_12
37. Pianini, D., Dobson, S., Viroli, M.: Self-stabilising target counting in wireless sensor networks using Euler integration. In: 11th SASO Conference. IEEE (2017)
38. Pianini, D., Viroli, M., Beal, J.: Protelis: practical aggregate programming. In: ACM Symposium on Applied Computing (2015)
39. de Sá, M., Churchill, E.F.: Mobile augmented reality: a design perspective. In: Huang, W., Alem, L., Livingston, M. (eds.) Human Factors in Augmented Reality Environments, pp. 139–164. Springer, Heidelberg (2012). https://doi.org/10.1007/978-1-4614-4205-9_6
40. Schmidt, D.C., Stal, M., Rohnert, H., Buschmann, F.: Pattern-Oriented Software Architecture, Volume 2: Patterns for Concurrent and Networked Objects. Wiley, Hoboken (2000)
41. Shi, W., Cao, J., Zhang, Q., Li, Y., Xu, L.: Edge computing: vision and challenges. IEEE Internet Things J. **3**(5), 637–646 (2016)
42. Stoller, S.: Leader election in asynchronous distributed systems. IEEE Trans. Comput. **49**(3), 283–284 (2000)
43. Vaquero, L., Rodero-Merino, L.: Finding your way in the fog: towards a comprehensive definition of fog computing. ACM CCR **44**(5), 27–32 (2014)
44. Vernon, V.: Reactive Messaging Patterns with the Actor Model: Applications and Integration in Scala and Akka, 1st edn. Addison-Wesley Professional, Boston (2015)
45. Viroli, M., Audrito, G., Beal, J., Damiani, F., Pianini, D.: Engineering resilient collective adaptive systems by self-stabilisation. ACM Trans. Model. Comput. Simul. **28**(2), 1–28 (2018)
46. Viroli, M., Beal, J., Damiani, F., Audrito, G., Casadei, R., Pianini, D.: From field-based coordination to aggregate computing. In: Di Marzo Serugendo, G., Loreti, M. (eds.) COORDINATION 2018. LNCS, vol. 10852, pp. 252–279. Springer, Heidelberg (2018). https://doi.org/10.1007/978-3-319-92408-3_12
47. Viroli, M., Casadei, R., Pianini, D.: On execution platforms for large-scale aggregate computing. In: ACM Conference on Pervasive and Ubiquitous Computing, pp. 1321–1326 (2016)
48. Walker, P., Amraii, S.A., Chakraborty, N., et al.: Human control of robot swarms with dynamic leaders. In: Conference on Intelligent Robots and Systems, pp. 1108–1113. IEEE (2014)
49. Weyns, D., et al.: On patterns for decentralized control in self-adaptive systems. In: de Lemos, R., Giese, H., Müller, H.A., Shaw, M. (eds.) Software Engineering for Self-Adaptive Systems II. LNCS, vol. 7475, pp. 76–107. Springer, Heidelberg (2013). https://doi.org/10.1007/978-3-642-35813-5_4

Aggregate Processes in Field Calculus

Roberto Casadei[1]([✉])[iD], Mirko Viroli[1][iD], Giorgio Audrito[2][iD],
Danilo Pianini[1][iD], and Ferruccio Damiani[2][iD]

[1] Alma Mater Studiorum–Università di Bologna, Cesena, Italy
{roby.casadei,mirko.viroli,danilo.pianini}@unibo.it
[2] Università di Torino, Turin, Italy
{giorgio.audrito,ferruccio.damiani}@unito.it

Abstract. Engineering distributed applications and services in emerging and open computing scenarios like the Internet of Things, cyber-physical systems and pervasive computing, calls for identifying proper abstractions to smoothly capture collective behaviour, adaptivity, and dynamic injection and execution of concurrent distributed activities. Accordingly, we introduce a notion of "aggregate process" as a concurrent field computation whose execution and interactions are sustained by a dynamic team of devices, and whose spatial region can opportunistically vary over time. We formalise this notion by extending the Field Calculus with a new primitive construct, spawn, used to instantiate a set of field computations and regulate key aspects of their life-cycle. By virtue of an open-source implementation in the SCAFI framework, we show basic programming examples and benefits via two case studies of mobile ad-hoc networks and drone swarm scenarios, evaluated by simulation.

Keywords: Aggregate processes · Computational fields ·
Distributed computing · Collective coordination · Dynamic ensembles ·
Self-*

1 Introduction

Emerging scenarios like pervasive computing, Internet of Things (IoT), cyber-physical systems (CPS) and edge computing, are leading towards a new reference computational *fabric* made of dense, large-scale networks of heterogeneous devices. New opportunities for developing software services naturally arise that fully leverage the pervasive availability of sensing, actuation, storage, computational power and networking. To help unveiling the true potentials of such digitally empowered ecosystems, proper abstractions and development techniques are needed to smoothly express *collective* coordination and computation activities that can be transparently executed on opportunistic formations of devices [10].

This work has been partially supported by Ateneo/CSP project "AP: Aggregate Programming" (http://ap-project.di.unito.it/).

H. Riis Nielson and E. Tuosto (Eds.): COORDINATION 2019, LNCS 11533, pp. 200–217, 2019.
https://doi.org/10.1007/978-3-030-22397-7_12

In such contexts, computational events might trigger multiple distributed activities that are highly contextual and hence fundamentally related to their space-time situation and physical environment. Openness and dynamism, then, require such activities to be dependable, self-adaptive and self-organising in order to maintain coherence and functionality across unpredictable and inevitable context changes and adversary events, and to opportunistically activate wherever and whenever their existence conditions hold—whether they are by-design or emergent. For instance, for collaborative smartphone-based applications in a smart city, such activities may include: a gossip process by which people in a plaza share comments, a guidance process to make a group of friends gather in a convenient point, a dispersal process for people creating bloat, a process to advertise one's presence to nearby users for the next minute, a process to provide crowd-aware directions towards a point of interest, and so on [5,8,25,31,38].

According to this vision, we present the concept of *aggregate process*, denoting a distributed computation sustained by a dynamic aggregation of devices—hence using the term *aggregate* with the meaning of "pertaining to a collective", i.e., in the sense of [5,35]. This abstraction can be useful to model transient collective activities, which may concurrently span and overlap over the fabric created by a mobile, large-scale deployment of devices; it is aimed to capture: *(i) aggregate stance*, to promote pervasive adaptation, by abstracting the individual device and seamlessly regulating the behaviour of an ensemble across scales, density, and heterogeneity; *(ii) dynamicity and context-orientation*, to conveniently support the implementation of dynamic, distributed, spatio-temporal activities where locality and context play a major role, and continuous change is the norm; *(iii) intrinsic resiliency*, to specify and execute collective (inter-)actions independently of large classes of environmental dynamics and faults. This notion, hence, fosters a broader view of programming smart distributed environments like sorts of *distributed virtual machines* for aggregate processes, supporting the dynamic injection and execution of collective computations, their diffusion over an opportunistically selected region of space-time, and their inherent self-adaptation to changes and faults by full abstraction over individual behaviours of devices.

To formally capture the features of aggregate processes, and experiment with mechanisms to handle their life-cycle (process creation, disposal, logic and interaction), we adopt as basis framework the *field calculus* [4,35]—a coordination model based on the notion of *(computational) field* (a time-evolving distributed structure mapping devices to computational values) where coordination policies are declaratively and compositionally expressed as pure functions from fields to fields. As key contribution, aggregate processes are supported in the field calculus by a new primitive construct, spawn, yielding a field that, across space and time, combines several independent but interacting "computational bubbles" (process instances). Programming constructs to work with aggregate processes are implemented in SCAFI [9,11] (https://github.com/scafi/scafi), a Scala-based incarnation of field calculus: this is used to showcase the expressiveness of the notion and to empirically evaluate the proposed abstraction through simulation of two paradigmatic case studies of mobile ad-hoc networks and drone swarms.

The remainder of this paper is organised as follows. Section 2 presents field calculus and its extension to support aggregate processes. Section 3 describes implementation in SCAFI along with examples and programming techniques. Section 4 provides evaluation of aggregate processes through synthetic experiments. Section 5 concludes the paper with discussion of related and future work.

2   Founding Aggregate Processes by the Field Calculus

Founding the notion of aggregate processes requires a coordination model with the power to declaratively express complex spatio-temporal behaviour possibly involving large sets of networked devices. Among the various frameworks enabling such a "macro-programming" paradigm, reviewed in Sect. 5, we consider the field calculus [4] (FC). This is a minimal functional language that captures the foundational mechanisms for compositionally expressing the emergent behaviour of a collective system by a global perspective. It provides constructs to represent and manipulate *(computational) fields*, i.e., distributed and time-evolving data structures that map device identities to computational values.

Arguably, FC represents a natural basis for technically developing a notion of aggregate process—which in fact somewhat emerged from technical issues about field computations. Indeed, FC enables an *aggregate stance* to programming: field computations target a collective of devices as a whole, and the field semantics formally provides a bridge from global behaviour to local activity of individual devices. *Dynamicity and context-orientation* are also directly supported: a system is modelled as a logical network of devices connected through a neighbouring relationship; devices can sample their portion of the environment and communicate with neighbours to infer/propagate context and react to changes in their surroundings. Moreover, the model also provides *inherent resiliency*, by abstracting from networking issues and adopting an execution model where computations are "continuously" re-evaluated in order to sustain field evolution in spite of individual failures and outages.

In this section, we briefly introduce FC (Sect. 2.1—the reader interested in full technical details should refer to [4]); then, we motivate the need for specific mechanisms to support a true notion of "process" (Sect. 2.2); finally, we conclude with the formalisation of a new primitive construct spawn (Sect. 2.3), responsible for managing (i.e., activating, executing, closing) a dynamic number of field computations (i.e., process instances).

2.1   Overview of Field Calculus

Figure 1 (first frame) presents the syntax and device semantics of FC, where the grey-boxed parts correspond to the new spawn construct and will be explained in Sect. 2.3. Following [24], the overbar notation denotes metavariables over sequences and the empty sequence is denoted by "•": e.g., for expressions, we let $\bar{e}$ range over sequences of expressions, written $e_1, e_2, \ldots e_n$ ($n \geq 0$). A program P consists of a sequence of function declarations and of a main expression e.

Syntax:

$P ::= \overline{F}\ e$ program $\qquad \mid F ::= \textbf{def}\ d(\overline{x})\ \{e\}$ function declaration

$e ::= x \mid v \mid (\overline{x}) \overset{\tau}{=>} e \mid e(\overline{e}) \mid \textbf{rep}(e)\{(x) => e\} \mid \textbf{nbr}\{e\} \mid \boxed{\textbf{spawn}(e, e, e)}$ expression

$v ::= \phi \mid \ell$ value $\qquad \mid \phi ::= \overline{\delta} \mapsto \overline{\ell}$ neighbouring field value

$\ell ::= f \mid c(\overline{\ell})$ local value $\qquad \mid f ::= b \mid d \mid (\overline{x}) \overset{\tau}{=>} e$ function value

---

Value-trees and value-tree environments:

$\theta ::= v \mid v\langle\overline{\theta}\rangle \mid \overline{v} \mapsto \overline{\theta}$ value-tree

$\Theta ::= \overline{\delta} \mapsto \overline{\theta}$ value-tree environment

---

Auxiliary functions:

$args((\overline{x}) \overset{\tau}{=>} e) = \overline{x}$ $\qquad body((\overline{x}) \overset{\tau}{=>} e) = e$ $\qquad name((\overline{x}) \overset{\tau}{=>} e) = \tau$

$args(d) = \overline{x}$ if $\textbf{def}\ d(\overline{x})\{e\}$ $\quad body(d) = e$ if $\textbf{def}\ d(\overline{x})\{e\}$ $\quad name(d) = d$

$\rho(v\langle\overline{\theta}\rangle) = v$ $\qquad\qquad\qquad\qquad\qquad\qquad\qquad\qquad name(b) = b$

$\pi_i(v\langle\theta_1, \ldots, \theta_n\rangle) = \theta_i$ $\qquad$ if $1 \leq i \leq n$ $\qquad\qquad$ else $\bullet$

$\pi^f(v\langle\theta_1, \ldots, \theta_n\rangle) = \theta_n$ $\qquad$ if $name(\rho(\theta_1)) = name(f)$ $\quad$ else $\bullet$

$\pi^k(\overline{v} \mapsto \overline{\theta}) = \theta_i$ $\qquad\qquad$ s.t. $v_i = k$ if it exists $\qquad$ else $\bullet$

$F(\theta) = v\langle\overline{\theta}\rangle$ $\qquad\qquad$ if $\theta = \textbf{pair}(v, \textbf{True})\langle\overline{\theta}\rangle$ $\quad$ else $\bullet$

For $aux \in \rho, \pi_i, \pi^f, \pi^k, F :$ $\begin{cases} aux(\bullet) = \bullet \\ aux(\delta \mapsto \theta, \Theta) = aux(\Theta) & \text{if } aux(\theta) = \bullet \\ aux(\delta \mapsto \theta, \Theta) = \delta \mapsto aux(\theta), aux(\Theta) & \text{if } aux(\theta) \neq \bullet \end{cases}$

Rules for expression evaluation: $\qquad\qquad\qquad\boxed{\delta; \Theta; \sigma \vdash e \Downarrow \theta}$

[E-APP] $\dfrac{\delta; \pi_1(\Theta); \sigma \vdash e \Downarrow \theta \quad \delta; \pi_{i+1}(\Theta); \sigma \vdash e_i \Downarrow \theta_i \text{ for } i = 1 \ldots n \quad f = \rho(\theta)}{\begin{array}{c} \theta' = (\!|f|\!)_{\delta,\sigma}^{\pi^f(\Theta)}(\rho(\overline{\theta})) \text{ if } f \text{ built-in else } \delta; \pi^f(\Theta); \sigma \vdash body(f)[args(f) := \rho(\overline{\theta})] \Downarrow \theta' \\ \delta; \Theta; \sigma \vdash e(\overline{e}) \Downarrow \rho(\theta')\langle\theta, \overline{\theta}, \theta'\rangle \end{array}}$

[E-LOC] $\dfrac{}{\delta; \Theta; \sigma \vdash \ell \Downarrow \ell\langle\rangle}$ $\quad$ [E-FLD] $\dfrac{\phi' = \phi|_{\textbf{dom}(\Theta) \cup \{\delta\}}}{\delta; \Theta; \sigma \vdash \phi \Downarrow \phi'\langle\rangle}$ $\quad$ [E-NBR] $\dfrac{\Theta_1 = \pi_1(\Theta) \quad \delta; \Theta_1; \sigma \vdash e \Downarrow \theta_1}{\delta; \Theta; \sigma \vdash \textbf{nbr}\{e\} \Downarrow \rho(\theta_1)[\delta \mapsto \rho(\theta_1)]\langle\theta_1\rangle}$

[E-REP] $\dfrac{\delta; \pi_1(\Theta); \sigma \vdash e_1 \Downarrow \theta_1 \quad \ell_1 = \rho(\theta_1) \qquad \ell_0 = \begin{cases} \rho(\pi_2(\Theta))(\delta) \text{ if } \delta \in \textbf{dom}(\Theta) \\ \ell_1 \qquad\qquad \text{otherwise} \end{cases}}{\delta; \pi_2(\Theta); \sigma \vdash e_2[x := \ell_0] \Downarrow \theta_2 \quad \ell_2 = \rho(\theta_2)}{\delta; \Theta; \sigma \vdash \textbf{rep}(e_1)\{(x) => e_2\} \Downarrow \ell_2\langle\theta_1, \theta_2\rangle}$

[E-SPAWN] $\dfrac{\delta; \pi_i(\Theta); \sigma \vdash e_i \Downarrow \theta^i \qquad\qquad \text{for } i \in 1, 2, 3 \quad k_1, \ldots, k_n = \rho(\theta^2) \cup \bigcup\{\textbf{dom}(\pi_4(\Theta(\delta'))) \text{ for } \delta' \in \textbf{dom}(\Theta)\}}{\delta; \pi^{k_i}(\pi_4(\Theta)); \sigma \vdash \rho(\theta_1)(k_i, \rho(\theta_3)) \Downarrow \theta_i \quad \text{for } i \in 1, \ldots, n}{\delta; \Theta; \sigma \vdash \textbf{spawn}(e_1, e_2, e_3) \Downarrow F(\overline{k} \mapsto \rho(\overline{\theta}))\langle\theta^1, \theta^2, \theta^3, F(\overline{k} \mapsto \theta)\rangle}$

Fig. 1. Syntax and device semantics for the field calculus (extended part in grey)

A function declaration F defines a (possibly recursive) function. It consists of the name of the function d, of $n \geq 0$ variable names $\overline{x}$ representing the formal parameters, and of an expression e representing the body of the function. Expressions e are the main entities of the calculus, and will evaluate to a whole field, understood at the macro-level as a space/time-wide data structure, mapping *computational events* (i.e., when and where a device executes a computation) to values: the set of such computational events is called *field domain*. Expressions include rather standard functional constructs, like: *variables* x, used as function formal parameters; *values* v (described below); and *anonymous func-*

tion expressions $(\bar{x}) \overset{\tau}{=}> e$, where $\bar{x}$ are the formal parameters, e is the body and τ is a *tag*[1]. A value can be either a *neighbouring value* ϕ or a *local value* ℓ. Technically, a neighbouring value is a mapping from device identifiers (corresponding to a device's neighbourhood including the device itself) to local values, while a local value can be: *(i)* a *data value* $c(\bar{\ell})$, consisting of a data-constructor applied to local value arguments (true, false, 0, 1, pair(1,2) and so on); or *(ii)* a *function value* f, consisting of either a declared function name d, a closed anonymous function, or a built-in function name b always working locally—used to denote usual mathematical/logical operators (e.g., +, -, or), 0-ary sensors (e.g., temperature, pressure, sns), or functions to turn neighbouring values to local values (e.g. minimisation of values by minHood, or minimisation excluding the device itself by minHoodPlus).

We model the computation of a device at each event by a big-step operational semantics where the result of evaluation is a *value-tree (vtree)* θ, i.e., an ordered tree of values that tracks the results of all evaluated subexpressions. The vtrees produced by an evaluation are made available to neighbours (including the device itself) for their forthcoming event through a broadcast. The evaluation of an expression at a given time in a device is thus performed "against" the recently-received vtrees of neighbours, as collected into a *vtree environment* Θ, mapping device identifiers to vtrees. The syntax of vtrees and vtree environments is given in Fig. 1 (second frame). The operational semantics judgement is of the form $\delta; \Theta; \sigma \vdash e \Downarrow \theta$, to be read "expression e evaluates to vtree θ on device δ w.r.t. the vtree environment Θ and sensor state σ", where: *(i)* δ is the identifier of the current device; *(ii)* Θ is the neighbouring field of the vtrees produced by the most recent evaluation of (an expression corresponding to) e on δ's neighbours; *(iii)* σ is a data structure containing enough sensor information to allow each non-pure built-in to be computed; *(iv)* e is an expression; *(v)* the vtree θ represents the values computed for all the expressions encountered during the evaluation of e—in particular $\rho(\theta)$ is the resulting value of e.

Expressions include also constructs that are tailored to field computations. A *function call* $e_f(\bar{e})$ adapts the standard call notion with the fact that e_f is a field and hence could evaluate to different functions at different events, in which case it provides an advanced branching mechanism: the domain is partitioned in regions by the identity of such functions (determined by tag τ for anonymous functions, and by name for other functions), function application in each region applies the single function being there, and finally juxtaposition is applied to all regions. The function call mechanism is used to implement conventional branching, which also splits the domain of computation into two non-overlapping regions defined by where e evaluates to true or false (e_1 is executed in isolation in the former, e_2 is in the latter, and the juxtaposition of the two sub-fields defines the overall result). Namely, if(e){e_1}{e_2} is syntactic sugar for mux(e, () $\overset{\tau_1}{=}> e_1$, () $\overset{\tau_2}{=}> e_2$)(), where

---

[1] Tags τ do not appear in source programs: when the evaluation starts, each anonymous function expression $(\bar{x})$ => e occurring in the program is converted into a tagged anonymous function expression by giving it a tag that is uniquely determined by its syntactical representation—see [4] for a detailed explanation.

the built-in mux is simply a multiplexer (it takes three arguments, evaluates all of them, and returns the second if the first has value true ot the third otherwise). A rep-*expression* rep(e_0){(x) = > e_1} models fields evolving over time: the result field is initially e_0, and iteratively at each device function (x) = > e_1 is applied to obtain the value at an event based on the value at previous one—e.g., rep(0){(x) = > x + 1} is the field that counts the number of occurred events at each device. Finally, a nbr-*expression* nbr{e} is used to model device-to-neighbourhood interaction: at each device, it gives a local map from neighbours to values (a so-called *neighbouring value*) filled with the most recent results of evaluating e at each neighbour.

A key aspect of how the operational semantics is developed is called "alignment" [3,4]: to implement coherent sharing of values, an instance of operator nbr (say it is localised in position p of the vtree), is such that it gathers values from neighbours by retrieving them in the same position (p) of all vtrees contained in Θ. This is the cornerstone technique to support a declarative and compositional specification of interactions, and hence, of global level coordination.

2.2 On "Multiple Alignments"

Conceptually, and technically, FC is used to specify a "single field computation" working on the entire available domain. As a paradigmatic example, consider a gradient [2,25,34], namely, a field of hop-by-hop distances based on local estimates metric (a field of neighbouring real values) from the closest node in *source* (a field of boolean values):

```
def gradient(source, metric) {
  rep(infinity)(distance =>
    mux(source, 0, minHoodPlus( nbr{distance} + metric ))) }

def limitedGradient(source, metric, area) {
  if (area) {gradient(source, metric)} {infinity} }
```

If sns is a sensor giving true only at a device s (and false everywhere else) and nbrRange is a sensor giving local estimate distances from neighbours (as a range detector would support), then the main expression gradient(sns,nbrRange) gives a field stabilising to a situation where each device is mapped to its (hop-by-hop, nearest) distance to s [2,4,16,25,34]. If multiple devices are sources, estimated distance considers the nearest source.

There are mechanisms in FC to tweak this "single field computation" model. First of all, one could realise two computations by a field of pairs of values, say pair(v1,v2): e.g., expression pair(gradient(sns1,nbrRange), gradient(sns2,nbrRange)) would actually generate two completely independent gradient computations. The same approach is applicable to realise an arbitrary number of computations, but this practically works only if the number of such computations is small, known, and uniform across space and time, otherwise, FC has no mechanism to capture the abstraction of "aligned iteration" over a collection of values conceptually belonging to different computations.

A second key aspect involves the ability to restrict the domain of a computation. It is true that, by branching, one can prevent evaluation of some subexpressions—e.g., in function `limitedGradient`, if `area` is a boolean field giving `true` to a small subdomain, then computation of `gradient` is limited there. However, this approach has limitations as well: if one wants to limit a gradient to span the ball-like area where distances from the source are smaller than a given value, hence setting `area` to "`gradient(source,metric) < range`", there would be no direct way of avoiding computation of `gradient` outside that limited ball, because the decision on whether an event is inside or outside the ball has to be reconsidered everywhere and everytime.

So, technically, in FC there are no constructs to directly model, e.g., a reusable function that turns a field of boolean `sources` into a collection of independent gradients, one per source: that would require to create a field of lists of reals, of arbitrary size across space-time, but crucially this would not correctly support alignment. More generally, and although being universal [1], FC falls short in expressing the situation in which a field computation is composed of a set of subcomputations that is dynamic in the sense that has changing size over space and time. But this is precisely what is needed to support aggregate processes.

2.3   The spawn Construct Extension

We formalise our notion of *aggregate process* by extending FC with a `spawn` mechanism essentially carrying on a multiple aligned execution of concurrent computations, managing their life-cycle (i.e., activation, execution, disposal). Syntactically (see Fig. 1), this is formed by a **spawn**-*expression* $\mathsf{spawn}(\mathsf{e}_b, \mathsf{e}_k, \mathsf{e}_i)$, modelling a collection of aggregate processes. Expression e_b models process behaviour: it is a function (of informal type $k \rightarrow a \rightarrow \langle v, \mathit{bool} \rangle$) taking a process key (i.e., an identifier) and an input argument, and returning a pair of an output value and a boolean stating whether the process should be maintained alive or not. Expression e_k defines a field of process keysets to add at each location (device); and e_i is the input field to feed processes. The result of **spawn** is a field of maps from process keys to values. As a result, we can precisely define an *aggregate process with key* k as the projection to k of the field of maps resulting from **spawn**, that is, the computational field associating each event to the value corresponding to k at that event—as this may simply be absent at an event, aggregate processes are to be considered partial fields over the whole domain.

The semantic details of **spawn** are presented in grey in Fig. 1. On the second frame, we allow to express vtrees also as $\overline{\mathsf{v}} \mapsto \overline{\theta}$, i.e., as a map from keys to vtrees. On the third frame, we define auxiliary functions ρ, π_i, π^k for extracting from a vtree respectively: its root value, an ordered subtree by its index i, and an unordered subtree by its key k. It also defines a *filtering* function F which selects vtrees whose root is a pair $\mathsf{pair}(\mathsf{v}, \mathsf{True})$, collapsing the root into v. All of these functions can be extended to maps (see *aux*), which are intended to be unordered vtree nodes for F, and vtree environments for ρ, π_i and π^k.

Finally, in fourth frame, we define the behaviour of construct spawn, formalised by the big-step operational semantics rule [E-SPAWN]: the sub-expressions e_1, e_2 and e_3 are evaluated and their results stored in vtrees θ^1, θ^2, θ^3 forming the first branches of the final result. Then, a list of *process keys* $\overline{k}$ is computed by adjoining *(i)* the keys currently present in the result $\rho(\theta^2)$ of e_2; *(ii)* the keys that any neighbour δ' broadcast in their last unordered sub-branch $\pi_4(\Theta(\delta'))$. To realise "multiple alignment", for each key k_i, the process $\rho(\theta^1)$ resulting from evaluation of e_1 is applied to k_i and the result $\rho(\theta^3)$ of e_3, producing θ_i as a result. The map $\overline{k} \mapsto \overline{\theta}$ is then filtered by F, discarding evaluations resulting in a pair(v, False), before being made available to neighbours. The same results $F(\overline{k} \mapsto \rho(\overline{\theta}))$ are also returned as the root of the resulting vtree.

3 Programming with Aggregate Processes

In this section, we show how the spawn construct formalised in Sect. 2.3 is implemented in SCAFI [9,11], and describe, through examples, how aggregate processes based on spawn can be programmed in practice.

Background: ScaFi—Field Calculus in Scala. SCAFI (Scala Fields) is a development toolkit for aggregate systems in the Scala programming language. It provides a Scala-internal domain-specific language (DSL) – i.e., an API masked as an "embedded language"– and library of functions for programming with fields, as well as other development tools (e.g., for simulation). In SCAFI, the field constructs introduced in Sect. 2.1 are captured by the following interface:

```
trait Constructs {
  def rep[A](init: => A)(fun: A => A): A
  def nbr[A](expr: => A): A
  def foldhood[A](init: => A)(acc: (A, A) => A)(expr: => A): A
  def branch[A](cond: => Boolean)(th: => A)(el: => A)
  def mid: ID
  ...
}
```

Method branch stands for field construct if (as the latter is a reserved keyword in Scala), nbr expressions are to be used within the expr passed to foldhood (used to aggregate over neighbours), and mid is a sensor giving the local device identifier. By SCAFI expressions one essentially defines "scripts" that specify whole fields at the macro-level: then, such scripts will be properly executed by each node/actor [11], following FC's operational semantics. A full introduction of SCAFI is outside the scope of this paper: it is deeply covered, e.g., in [9].

3.1 Aggregate Processes in ScaFi

The spawn primitive supports our notion of aggregate processes by handling activation, propagation, merging, and disposal of process instances (for a specified kind of process). Coherently with the formalisation in Sect. 2, it has signature:

```
def spawn[K,A,R](process: K => A => (R,Boolean),
                 newKeys: Set[K],
                 args: A): Map[K,R]
```

It is a generic function, parametrised by three types: *(i)* K, the type of process *keys*; *(ii)* A, the type of process *arguments* (or inputs); *(iii)* R, the type of process *result*. The function accepts three formal parameters and works as formalised in previous section. Note that a process key has a twofold role: it works both as a *process identifier* (PID) and as *initialisation* or *construction parameter*. When different construction parameters should result in different process instances, it is sufficient to instantiate type K with a data structure type including both pieces of information and with proper equality semantics. Function **spawn** accepts a *set* of keys to allow *generation* of zero or more process instances in the current round. Notice that if a new key already belongs to the set of active processes, there will be no actual generation (or restart) but *merging* instead, since identity is the same as an existing process instance. Finally, note also that the outcome of **spawn** (a map from process keys to process result values) can in turn be used to fork other process instances or as input for other processes; i.e., the basic means for processes to interact is to connect the corresponding **spawns** with data.

In the following, we discuss programming and management of aggregate processes activated through **spawn**.

3.2   Process Generation, Expansion/Shrinking, and Termination

Generating process instances is just a matter of creating a field of keysets that become non-empty as soon as the proper space-time event has been recognised (e.g., spatial conditions on sensors data and computation, or timers firing) [34]. Then, by **spawn**, every process instance is *automatically propagated by all the participating devices to their neighbours*. However, it is possible to regulate the shape of such "computational bubble" by dictating conditions by which a device must return status **false** (i.e., meaning *external* to the bubble)—as mentioned, this indicates the willingness to *stop* computing (i.e., participate in) the process. That is, only devices that return status **true** (i.e., *internal*) will propagate the process. Moreover, such a propagation happens continuously: so, a device that exited from a process may execute it again in the future. In particular, the *border* (or *fence*) of a process bubble is given by the set of all the devices that are external but have at least one neighbour which is internal. As long as a node is in the fence, it continuously re-acquires and immediately quits from the process instance: this repeated evaluation of the border is what ultimately enables a spatial extension of the process bubble (*expansion*). Conversely, a process bubble gets restricted (*shrinking*) when internal nodes become external.

A process instance *terminates* when all the devices quit by returning status **false**. Implementing process termination may not be trivial, since proper (local or global) conditions must be defined so that the "collapsing force" can overtake the "propagation force"; i.e., precautions should be taken so that external devices do not re-acquire the process: the border should steadily shrink, also considering temporary network partitions and transient recoverable failures from devices.

Example: Time Replication. In [29], a technique based on time replication for improving the dynamics of gossip is presented. It works by keeping k running replicates of a gossip computation executing concurrently, each alive for a certain amount of time. New instances are activated with interval p, staggered in time. The whole computation always returns the result of the oldest active replicate. This is intended to improve the dynamics of algorithms, providing an intrinsic refresh mechanism that smoothly propagates to the output. With spawn, it is trivial to design a replicated function that provides process replication in time.

```
def replicated[A,R](proc: A => R)(argument: A, p: Double, k: Int) = {
  val lastPid = clock(p, dt())
  spawn[Long,A,R](pid => arg => (proc(arg), pid > lastPid+k),
            Set(lastPid), argument)
}
```

clock is a distributed time-aware counter [29] (whose synchronicity depends on the implementation) yielding an increasing number i at each interval p that represents the PID of the i-th replica. Notably, in this case, every device can locally determine when it must quit a process instance; moreover, the exit condition based on PID numbering (pid > lastPid+k) prevents process reentrance. Section 4.2 provides an empirical evaluation of the behaviour of function replicated.

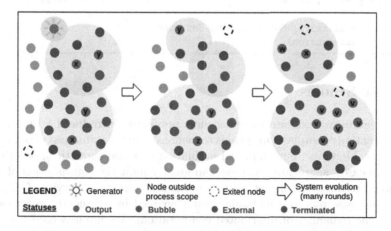

Fig. 2. Graphical example of the evolution of a system of processes and the role of statuses in statusSpawn. The green bubble springs into existence; the blue bubble dissolves after termination is initiated by a node; the orange bubble expands. Only output nodes will yield a value. Bubbles may of course overlap (i.e., a node may participate, with different statuses, to multiple processes) and the dynamics can be arbitrarily complex (because of mobility, failures, and local decisions) (Color figure online)

3.3   More Expressive Process Definitions

Managing processes upon `spawn` revolves around specifying the logic for input/output, creation, evolution, and termination of processes instances. One approach to make such code more declarative consists of programming process behaviour so as to specify additional information w.r.t. just a boolean status/flag: more expressive `Statuses` can be mapped to the flag and can be used to activate advanced behaviours. To do so, a higher-level function `statusSpawn` can be considered, based on a `Status` value that indicates the "stance" of the current device w.r.t. the process instances at hand (see Fig. 2): `Output` corresponds to flag `true` in `spawn`; `External` corresponds to flag `false` in `spawn`; `Bubble` means the device participates to the process but is not interested in the output (i.e., the process entry can be discarded); and `Terminated` means the device is willing to close the process instance (i.e., it triggers a shutdown behaviour).

Example: Multi-gradient. The problem described in Sect. 2.2 of activating a spatially-limited gradient computation for each device where sensor `isSrc` gives true, and deactivating it when it stops doing so, can be solved as follows:

```
statusSpawn[ID,Double,Double](src => limit =>
  gradient(src==mid,nbrRange) match { // consider the usual gradient
    case g if src==mid && !isSrc => (g, Terminated) // close if src quits
    case g if g>limit => (g, External)              // out of bubble
    case g => (g, Output)                           // in bubble
  },
  newKeys = if(isSrc) Set(mid) else Set.empty,
  args = maxExtension)
```

4   Case Studies

In this section, we exercise the constructs previously introduced by presenting two application examples. One goal is to demonstrate the soundness of our implementation. Moreover, our empirical evaluation will also show that, orderly: *(i)* in certain cases, aggregate processes can greatly limit the consumption of computational resources while retaining a reasonable quality of service (QoS); *(ii)* in certain cases, powerful meta-algorithms enabled by aggregate processes can improve the dynamics of distributed computations. We implemented both scenarios with the Alchemist simulator [30], which already provides SCAFI support [9]; the results are the average over 101 runs. For the sake of reproducibility, the source code and instructions for running experiments are publicly available (https://bitbucket.org/metaphori/experiment-spawn).

4.1   Opportunistic Instant Messaging

Motivation. The possibility of communicating by delivering messages regardless the presence of a conventional Internet access has recently gained attention as a mean to work around censorship (http://archive.is/C3niO) as well as in situations with limited access to the global network—e.g., in rural areas, or during urban events when the network capability is overtaken. We here consider a simple messaging application where a source device (aka *sender*) wants to deliver a payload to a peer device (aka *recipient, target,* or *destination*) in a hop-by-hop fashion by exploiting nearby devices as relays. The source device only knows the identifier of its recipient: it is not aware of its physical location, nor of viable routes. Our goal is to show how aggregate processes can support this kind of application (with multiple concurrent messages) while limiting the number of devices involved in message delivery, leading to bandwidth savings (and energy savings in turn).

Setup. We compare two aggregate implementations of such messaging system. The first implementation, called *flood chat*, simply broadcasts the payload to all neighbours. In spite of an in-place garbage collection system, however, this strategy may end up dispatching the message towards directions far-off the optimal path, burdening the network. The second implementation, *spawn chat*, leverages spawn in order to reduce the impact on the network infrastructure by electing a node as coordinator, then creating an aggregate process connecting the source and the coordinator and the coordinator and the destination, and finally delivering the message along such support. In this experiment, we naively choose a coordinator randomly, but better strategies could be deployed to improve over this configuration. The experiment is simulated on a mesh network of one thousand devices randomly deployed in the urban area of Cesena, in Italy. We simulate the creation and delivery of messages among randomly chosen nodes, with one message per second generated on average by the whole network in time window $[0, 250]$; devices execute rounds asynchronously at an average of 1 Hz. We gather a measure of QoS and a measure of resource usage. We use the probability of delivering a message with time as a QoS measure, and we measure the number of payloads sent by each node as a measure of impact on performance. In doing so, we suppose payload makes up for the largest part of the communication (as is typically the case when multimedia data are exchanged).

Results. Figure 3 shows experimental results. The two implementations achieve a very similar QoS, with the flood implementation being faster on average. This is expected, as flooding the whole network also implies sending through the fastest path. The difference, however, is relatively small and, on the contrary, we see the *spawn chat* affords a dramatic decrease in bandwidth usage (by properly constraining the expansion of message delivery bubbles), despite the simplistic selection of the coordinating device.

4.2 Reconnaissance with a Drone Swarm

Motivation. Performing reconnaissance of areas with hindrances to access and movement such as forests, steep climbs, or dangerous conditions (e.g. extreme weather and fire) can be a very difficult task for ground-based teams. In those

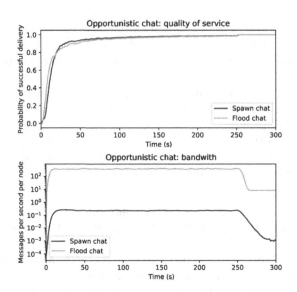

Fig. 3. Evaluation of the opportunistic chat algorithms. The figure on top shows similar performance for the two algorithms, with the *flood chat* featuring a slightly better delivery time for the payloads (as it intercepts the optimal path among others). However, as the bottom figure depicts, *spawn chat* requires orders of magnitude less resources due to the algorithm executing on a bounded area (i.e., by involving only a subset of system devices for each message delivery process).

```
def gossipNaive[T](value: T)(implicit ev: Bounded[T]) = rep(value)(max =>
    ev.max(value, maxHoodPlus(nbr(ev.max(max, value)))))

def gossipReplicated[T:Bounded](value: T, p: Double, k: Int) =
    (replicated{ gossipNaive[T] }(value,p,k) // returns a Map[Long,Double]
    + (Long.MaxValue -> value) // default, lowest-priority entry of the map
    ).minBy[Long](_._1)._2 // projects the value of instance with min PID
```

Fig. 4. Code of the gossip algorithms used in the reconnaissance case study

cases, swarms of unmanned airborne vehicles (UAVs) could be deployed to quickly gather information [6]. One scenario in which such systems are particularly interesting is fire monitoring [12]. With this case study, we show how aggregate processes enable easy programming of a form of gossip that supports a precise collective estimation of risk in dynamic scenarios.

Setup. We simulate a swarm of 200 UAVs in charge of monitoring the area of Mount Vesuvius in Italy, which has been heavily hit by wildfires in 2017 (http://archive.is/j3lsm). UAVs follow a simple exploration strategy: they all start from the same base station on the southern side of the volcano, they visit a randomly generated sequence of ten waypoints, and once done they come back to the station for refuelling and maintenance. UAVs sense their surroundings once per

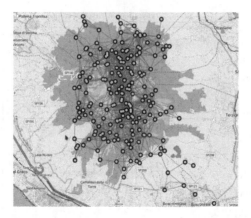

Fig. 5. Snapshot of the UAV swarm surveying the Vesuvius area as simulated in Alchemist. Yellow dots are UAVs. Grey lines depict direct drone-to-drone communication. Drones travel at an average speed of $130\frac{km}{h}$, in line with the cruise speed performance of existing military-grade UAVs (see http://archive.is/8zar5), and communicate with other drones within 1 km distance in line-of-sight. Forming a dynamic mesh network using UAV-to-UAV communication is feasible [19], although challenging [22] (Color figure online)

second and assess the local situation by measuring the risk of fire. The goal of the swarm is to agree on the area with the highest risk of fire and report the information back to the station for deployment of ground intervention. A snapshot of the drones performing the reconnaissance is provided in Fig. 5. In this paper, we are not concerned with realistic modelling of fire dynamics: we designed the risk of fire to be maximum in a random point of the surveyed area for 20 min; the risk then drops (e.g. due to a successful fire-fighting operation), with the new maximum (lower than the previous) being in another randomly generated coordinate; after further 20 min the risk sharply increases again to on a third random coordinate. We compare three approaches: *(i) naive gossip*, a simple implementation of a gossip protocol; *(ii) S+C+G*, a more elaborated algorithm – based on self-stabilising building blocks [34] – that elects a leader, aggregates the information towards it, then spreads it to the whole network by broadcast; *(iii) replicated gossip*, which replicates the first algorithm over time (as per [29]) and whose implementation, shown in Fig. 4, uses function `replicated` (defined in Sect. 3 upon `spawn`).

Results. Results are shown in Fig. 6. The naive gossip algorithm quickly converges to the correct value, but then fails at detecting the conclusion of the dangerous situation: it is bound to the highest peak detected, and so it is unsuitable for evolving scenarios. S+C+G can adapt to changes, but it is very sensitive to changes in the network structure: data gets aggregated along a spanning tree generated from the dynamically chosen coordinator, but in a network of fast-moving airborne drones such structure gets continuously disrupted. Here the `spawn`-based replicated gossip performs best, as it conjugates the stability of the

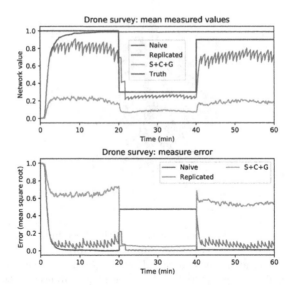

Fig. 6. Evaluation of the gossip algorithms in the UAV reconnaissance scenario. The figure on top shows expected values and measures performed by the competing algorithms. The bottom figure measures the error as root mean square: $\sqrt{\frac{\sum_n (v_n - a)^2}{n}}$ where n device count, a actual value, and v_n value at the n-th device. The naive gossip cannot cope with danger reduction, S+C+G cannot cope with the volatility of the network, while replicated gossip provides a good estimate while being to cope with changes.

naive gossip algorithm with the ability to cope with reductions in the sensed values. The algorithm in this case provides underestimates, as it reports the highest peak sensed in the time span of validity of a replicate, and drones rarely explore the exact spot where the problem is located, but rather get in its proximity.

5   Conclusions, Related and Future Work

In this paper, we have proposed and implemented a notion of aggregate processes to model dynamic, concurrent collective adaptive behaviours carried out by dynamic formations of devices—hence extending over field calculus and SCAFI.

Various spacetime- and macro-programming models have been developed across a wide variety of applications, which can potentially support mechanisms of aggregate processes. The survey [35] describes the historical evolution of "aggregate computing" from research in distributed systems, coordination languages, and spatial computing. In particular, four main clusters of approaches can be identified: (i) "bottom-up" approaches, such as TOTA [26], and Hood [37], that abstract individual networked devices; (ii) languages for expressing spatial and geometric patterns, such as GPL [14] and OSL [27]; (iii) languages for streaming and summarising information over space-time regions, such as Regiment [28] and TinyLime [15] and (iv) general purpose space-time computing models, such as MGS [20], the field calculus [4], and the Soft Mu-calculus for Computational fields (SMuC) [25]. Other works, often more generic and less operational, include models and languages for programming ensembles, such as SCEL [17], and process algebras (cf., the SAPERE approach [39]).

Multi-agent systems can bring agents together according to multiple organisational paradigms [23]. With aggregate processes, it is possible to program the logic of group formation so as to implement various grouping strategies. In the messaging case study, e.g., a dynamic, goal-directed *team* of devices is formed just to to connect senders with recipients, dissolving when the task is completed.

Related to the specifics of process execution, there are different models which aims at simplifying programming of multiple computing nodes as well as analysis of resulting programs. For instance, in the Bulk Synchronous Parallel (BSP) model [33], computations are structured as sequences of rounds followed by synchronisation steps; large-scale graph processing frameworks such as Apache Giraph [13] are inspired by BSP. Modern distributed data processing models (e.g., MapReduce [18] and derived ones) also abstract away network structure and trade performance for constrained programming schemas. By another perspective, works on service computing [7] tailored to dynamic ad-hoc environments [21] are also relevant but usually neglect the collective dimension and rarely consider open-ended situated activities. The service perspective connects also to utility computing and related efforts for abstracting and automatically managing networking and hardware infrastructure [32]—aggregate processes, by admitting diverse computation partitioning schemas [36], foster this vision.

In future work, we would like to use processes for advanced distributed coordination scenarios and implement a support for dynamic relocation of aggregate processes across a full IoT/Edge/Fog/Cloud stack. Further experimentation will be key to fully develop a theory of aggregate processes (e.g. in the style of π-calculus and its derivatives) as well as fully-fledged API and platform support.

Acknowledgements. We thank the anonymous COORDINATION referees for their comments and suggestions on improving the presentation of the paper.

References

1. Audrito, G., Beal, J., Damiani, F., Viroli, M.: Space-time universality of field calculus. In: Di Marzo Serugendo, G., Loreti, M. (eds.) 20th International Conference on Coordination Models and Languages. LNCS, vol. 10852, pp. 1–20. Springer, Heidelberg (2018). https://doi.org/10.1007/978-3-319-92408-3_1
2. Audrito, G., Casadei, R., Damiani, F., Viroli, M.: Compositional blocks for optimal self-healing gradients. In: 11th International Conference on Self-adaptive and Self-organizing Systems (SASO 2017), pp. 91–100. IEEE (2017)
3. Audrito, G., Damiani, F., Viroli, M., Casadei, R.: Run-time management of computation domains in field calculus. In: 1st International Workshops on Foundations and Applications of Self* Systems (FAS*W), pp. 192–197. IEEE (2016)
4. Audrito, G., Viroli, M., Damiani, F., Pianini, D., Beal, J.: A higher-order calculus of computational fields. ACM Trans. Comput. Log. **20**(1), 51–555 (2019)

5. Beal, J., Pianini, D., Viroli, M.: Aggregate programming for the internet of things. IEEE Comput. **48**(9), 22–30 (2015)
6. Beal, J., Usbeck, K., Loyall, J., Rowe, M., Metzler, J.: Adaptive opportunistic airborne sensor sharing. ACM Trans. Auton. Adapt. Syst. **13**(1), 6 (2018)
7. Bouguettaya, A., Singh, M., Huhns, M., Sheng, Q.Z., et al.: A service computing manifesto: the next 10 years. Commun. ACM **60**(4), 64–72 (2017)
8. Casadei, R., Fortino, G., Pianini, D., Russo, W., Savaglio, C., Viroli, M.: Modelling and simulation of opportunistic IoT services with aggregate computing. Futur. Gener. Comput. Syst. **91**, 252–262 (2018)
9. Casadei, R., Pianini, D., Viroli, M.: Simulating large-scale aggregate MASs with Alchemist and Scala. In: FedCSIS Proceedings, pp. 1495–1504. IEEE (2016)
10. Casadei, R., Viroli, M.: Collective abstractions and platforms for large-scale self-adaptive IoT. In: 3rd International Workshops on Foundations and Applications of Self* Systems (FAS*W), pp. 106–111. IEEE (2018)
11. Casadei, R., Viroli, M.: Programming actor-based collective adaptive systems. In: Ricci, A., Haller, P. (eds.) Programming with Actors. LNCS, vol. 10789, pp. 94–122. Springer, Cham (2018). https://doi.org/10.1007/978-3-030-00302-9_4
12. Casbeer, D.W., Kingston, D.B., Beard, R.W., McLain, T.W.: Cooperative forest fire surveillance using a team of small unmanned air vehicles. Int. J. Syst. Sci. **37**(6), 351–360 (2006)
13. Ching, A., Edunov, S., Kabiljo, M., et al.: One trillion edges: graph processing at facebook-scale. VLDB Endow. Proc. **8**(12), 1804–1815 (2015)
14. Coore, D.: Botanical computing: a developmental approach to generating inter connect topologies on an amorphous computer. Ph.D. thesis, MIT (1999)
15. Curino, C., Giani, M., Giorgetta, M., Giusti, A., et al.: Mobile data collection in sensor networks: the TinyLime middleware. Pervasive Mob. Comput. **4**, 446–469 (2005)
16. Viroli, M., Damiani, F.: Type-based self-stabilisation for computational fields. Log. Methods Comput. Sci. **11**(4), 1–53 (2015)
17. De Nicola, R., et al.: The SCEL language: design, implementation, verification. In: Wirsing, M., Hölzl, M., Koch, N., Mayer, P. (eds.) Software Engineering for Collective Autonomic Systems. LNCS, vol. 8998, pp. 3–71. Springer, Cham (2015). https://doi.org/10.1007/978-3-319-16310-9_1
18. Dean, J., Ghemawat, S.: MapReduce: simplified data processing on large clusters. Commun. ACM **51**(1), 107–113 (2008)
19. Frew, E., Brown, T.: Airborne communication networks for small unmanned aircraft systems. Proc. IEEE **96**(12), 2008–2027 (2008)
20. Giavitto, J.-L., Michel, O., Cohen, J., Spicher, A.: Computations in space and space in computations. In: Banâtre, J.-P., Fradet, P., Giavitto, J.-L., Michel, O. (eds.) UPP 2004. LNCS, vol. 3566, pp. 137–152. Springer, Heidelberg (2005). https://doi.org/10.1007/11527800_11
21. Groba, C., Clarke, S.: Opportunistic service composition in dynamic ad hoc environments. IEEE Trans. Serv. Comput. **7**(4), 642–653 (2014)
22. Gupta, L., Jain, R., Vaszkun, G.: Survey of important issues in UAV communication networks. IEEE Commun. Surv. Tutor. **18**(2), 1123–1152 (2016)
23. Horling, B., Lesser, V.: A survey of multi-agent organizational paradigms. Knowl. Eng. Rev. **19**(4), 281–316 (2004)
24. Igarashi, A., Pierce, B.C., Wadler, P.: Featherweight Java: a minimal core calculus for Java and GJ. ACM Trans. Program. Lang. Syst. **23**(3), 396–450 (2001)

25. Montanari, U., Loreti, M., Lafuente, A.L.: Asynchronous distributed execution of fixpoint-based computational fields. Log. Methods Comput. Sci. **13**(1:13), 1–46 (2017)
26. Mamei, M., Zambonelli, F.: Programming pervasive and mobile computing applications: the TOTA approach. ACM Trans. Softw. Eng. Methodol. **18**(4), 1–56 (2009)
27. Nagpal, R.: Programmable self-assembly: constructing global shape using biologically-inspired local interactions and origami mathematics. Ph.D. thesis, MIT, Cambridge, MA, USA (2001)
28. Newton, R., Welsh, M.: Region streams: functional macroprogramming for sensor networks. In: WS on Data Management for Sensor Nets, pp. 78–87 (2004)
29. Pianini, D., Beal, J., Viroli, M.: Improving gossip dynamics through overlapping replicates. In: Lluch Lafuente, A., Proença, J. (eds.) COORDINATION 2016. LNCS, vol. 9686, pp. 192–207. Springer, Cham (2016). https://doi.org/10.1007/978-3-319-39519-7_12
30. Pianini, D., Montagna, S., Viroli, M.: Chemical-oriented simulation of computational systems with ALCHEMIST. J. Simul. **7**(3), 202–215 (2013)
31. Shi, W., Dustdar, S.: The promise of edge computing. IEEE Comput. **49**(5), 78–81 (2016)
32. Truong, H.L., Dustdar, S.: Principles for engineering IoT cloud systems. IEEE Cloud Comput. **2**(2), 68–76 (2015)
33. Valiant, L.: A bridging model for parallel computation. Commun. ACM **33**(8), 103–111 (1990)
34. Viroli, M., Audrito, G., Beal, J., Damiani, F., Pianini, D.: Engineering resilient collective adaptive systems by self-stabilisation. ACM Trans. Model. Comput. Simul. **28**(2), 16 (2018)
35. Viroli, M., Beal, J., Damiani, F., Audrito, G., Casadei, R., Pianini, D.: From field-based coordination to aggregate computing. In: Di Marzo Serugendo, G., Loreti, M. (eds.) 20th International Conference on Coordination Models and Languages. LNCS, vol. 10852, pp. 252–279. Springer, Heidelberg (2018). https://doi.org/10.1007/978-3-319-92408-3_12
36. Viroli, M., Casadei, R., Pianini, D.: On execution platforms for large-scale aggregate computing. In: ACM UbiComp: Adjunct, pp. 1321–1326. ACM (2016)
37. Whitehouse, K., Sharp, C., Brewer, E., Culler, D.: Hood: a neighborhood abstraction for sensor networks. In: Conference on Mobile Systems, Applications, and Services. ACM (2004)
38. Zambonelli, F.: Toward sociotechnical urban superorganisms. IEEE Comput. **45**(8), 76–78 (2012)
39. Zambonelli, F., et al.: Developing pervasive multi-agent systems with nature-inspired coordination. Pervasive Mob. Comput. **17**, 236–252 (2015)

Tools (2)

Automatic Quality-of-Service Evaluation in Service-Oriented Computing

Agustín E. Martinez Suñé[1] and Carlos G. Lopez Pombo[1,2]([✉])

[1] Facultad de Ciencias Exactas y Naturales, Department of Computing,
Universidad de Buenos Aires, Buenos Aires, Argentina
aemartinez@dc.uba.ar
[2] Instituto de Investigación en Ciencias de la Computación,
CONICET–Universidad de Buenos Aires, Buenos Aires, Argentina
clpombo@dc.uba.edu.ar

Abstract. Formally describing and analysing quantitative requirements of software components might be important in software engineering; in the paradigm of API-based software systems might be vital. Quantitative requirements can be thought as characterising the *Quality of Service – QoS* provided by a service thus, useful as a way of classifying and ranking them according to specific needs. An efficient and automatic analysis of this type of requirements could provide the means for enabling dynamic establishing of *Service Level Agreements – SLA*, allowing for the automatisation of the *Service Broker*.

In this paper we propose the use of a language for describing QoS contracts based on convex specification, and a two-phase analysis procedure for evaluating contract satisfaction based on the state of the art techniques used for hybrid system verification. The first phase of the procedure responds to the observation that when services are registered in repositories, their contracts are stored for subsequent use in negotiating SLAs. In such a context, a process phase of contract minimisation might lead to great efficiency gain when the second, and recurrent, phase of determining QoS compliance is run.

1 Introduction

Distributed software resulting from paradigms like *Service-oriented Computing – SOC*, and emerging ones like Cloud/Fog computing and the Internet of Things are transforming the world of software systems in order to support applications able to respond and adapt to the changes of their execution environment, giving impulse to what is called the API's economy. The underlying idea of the

C.G. Lopez Pombo's—Research is supported by Universidad de Buenos Aires by grant UBACyT 20020170100544BA, and Consejo Nacional de Investigaciones Científicas y Técnicas by grant PIP 11220130100148CO. The authors want to thank to Marie Skłodowska-Curie Research and Innovation Staff Exchange BehAPI – *Behavioural Application Program Interfaces*.

© IFIP International Federation for Information Processing 2019
Published by Springer Nature Switzerland AG 2019
H. Riis Nielson and E. Tuosto (Eds.): COORDINATION 2019, LNCS 11533, pp. 221–236, 2019.
https://doi.org/10.1007/978-3-030-22397-7_13

API's economy is that it is possible to construct software artifacts by composing services provided by third parties and previously registered in repositories. This envisages a generation of applications running over globally available computational resources and communication infrastructure, which, at run-time, are dynamically and transparently reconfigured by the intervention of a dedicated *Middleware* with the capability to discover and bind a running application with a certain requirement, to a service capable of fulfilling it, subject to the negotiation of a *Service Level Agreement* – SLA, so they can collectively fulfill certain business goals [4].

Requirements have usually been classified in functional and non-functional depending on the nature of the attributes they capture. Functional requirements are usually understood as those describing what the system has to do, while non-functional ones generally express attributes that do not prescribe a particular behaviour but characterise how the system carries out the behaviour described by the functional ones. From non-functional requirements, we propose a further classification by identifying a subset referred to as *quantitative attributes*. We understand quantitative attributes as those that can be interpreted over a particular metric space [1]. This characteristic carries the potential of admitting some form of formal analysis, depending on the expressive power of the language used in specifying requirements over them. The reader shall note that not every metric space has associated formal methods of analysis but, from both practical and theoretical point of view, the real numbers constitute a natural candidate over which many quantitative attributes can be interpreted. As usual, requirements can be used as contracts between software components and satisfaction of such contracts is dealt with by checking whether certain judgement of the form $Pr \vdash Rq$ holds or not, where Pr is the provision contract and Rq is the requirement contract.

From this perspective, those quantitative non-functional requirements formalised over attributes interpreted as real variables might be used to classify functionally equivalent services by the *Quality of Service* – QoS they provide. This means that while services might have the same functional behavior, they could differ on their non-functional one (for example, a service may offer low speed computation at a very low cost while another, functionally equivalent one, might be faster but more onerous), a phenomena that could be useful as a way of classifying and ranking them according to specific needs; a motivation shared with other works like [14].

Identifying and formally describing quantitative properties of a system is not novel, examples of this range from the well known formalisation of the time/space required by an algorithm by means of the asymptotic growth of functions [2, Part. I, Chap. 2], to a very prolific research field dedicated to the verification of hybrid systems. Hybrid systems [6] are dynamic artifacts exhibiting both discrete and continuous behaviour. In general, the continuous aspects of such systems are formalised as constraints over variables taking their values from the real numbers. There is a plethora of analysis techniques that have been proposed for this type of systems, with the vast majority focussing on those aspects laying within the boundary of what is decidable [8]. A relatively new approach to the analysis of hybrid systems' specification, due to Pappas et al. [13], integrates SMT-solving [10] with convex constraints [5], under the name of *SMC – Satisfiability Modulo Convex Optimization.*

In this work we developed an efficient two phase procedure for evaluating quantitative SLA based on SMC, but adapted to profit from the fact that contracts (both provision Pr and requirement Rq) can be minimised in a preprocessing phase, referred to as *Minimisation through Convex Optimisation – MCO*, when the service is registered in the repository. The expectation is that such preprocessing might produce an efficiency gain when $Pr \vdash Rq$ is checked to evaluate if an SLA is met. Moreover, as finding the minimum size contract requires, at least, enumerating all boolean assignments satisfying a SAT problem, we propose an approach in which contract minimisation can be performed as semantics preserving incremental partial minimizations.

The paper is organised as follows: in Sect. 2 we concentrate both the definition of the formal framework we will use to specify QoS contracts as quantitative requirements, and present our proposal for its analysis, at the same time we state the research questions we want to answer; in Sect. 3 we present the experimental design and results supporting the answers to each of the research questions. Finally in Sect. 4 we draw some conclusions and point out some further lines of research.

2   Formalisation and Analysis of QoS Contracts

In this section we concentrate on formalising QoS contracts by identifying quantitative non-functional requirements and, in analogy to the continuous elements in hybrid system specification, by interpreting each of the attributes as a real variable. Thereafter, we present state of the art analysis techniques for this kind of formal specifications and our proposal for the optimisation of the procedure based on a preprocess of contract minimisation.

In [13], Pappas et al. adopt *monotone SMC formulae* as specification language; we will refer to this specifications as *convex specification*. Monotone SMC formulae are defined as quantifier-free formulae in conjunctive normal form, with atomic propositions ranging over a subset of the propositional variables and convex constraints.

Definition 1 (Convex specification, *Sect. 3.2, [13]).* *Let $\mathcal{X}$ be a set of real variables and $\mathcal{P}$ a set of propositional variables, then a* monotone SMC formula *is any formula that can be produced by the following grammar:*

$$formula ::= \{clause \wedge\}^* clause$$
$$clause ::= (\{literal \vee\}^* literal)$$
$$literal ::= p \mid \neg p \mid \top \mid \bot \mid conv\_constraint, \text{ where } p \in \mathcal{P}$$
$$conv\_constraint ::= equation \mid inequality$$
$$equation ::= f(x_0, \ldots, x_{arity(f)}) = 0$$
$$\text{, where } f \text{ is an affine function and } x_0, \ldots, x_{arity(f)} \in \mathcal{X}.$$
$$inequality ::= f(x_0, \ldots, x_{arity(f)}) \text{ relation } 0$$
$$\text{, where } f \text{ is a convex function and } x_0, \ldots, x_{arity(f)} \in \mathcal{X}.$$
$$relation ::= < \mid \leq$$

Then a convex specification *over $\mathcal{X}$ and $\mathcal{P}$ is a tuple $\langle\langle \mathcal{X}, \mathcal{P}\rangle, \alpha\rangle$, where α is a monotone SMC formula over $\mathcal{X}$ and $\mathcal{P}$.*

In the grammar above, *affine_function* and *convex_function* denote, as one could guess, affine and convex functions, respectively. Monotone SMC formulae only admit convex constraints as atoms, in contrast to generic SMC formulae over convex constraints [11], reverse convex constraints are not allowed[1]. As it is mentioned in [13], monotonicity (i.e. the lack of negation to convex constraints) is key to guarantee that whenever a convex specification has a model, it is found by solving one (or more) convex optimization problems.

The following example illustrates a specification written in the language presented in Definition 1.

Example 1 (Service requirement). Let us consider a context of an API-based software application requiring a service accessed and paid for, for the time it is used. In that context we consider as relevant quantitative attributes the cost (formed by: *a. perSec*: the cost (in a given currency) of the service per second elapsed while the communication session is open, and *b. costMb*: the cost (in the same currency) per megabyte of information processed); and execution time (formed by: *a. maxWait*: the maximum waiting time in seconds for the server to effectively attend a request, *b. maxTimeGb*: the maximum amount of time in seconds the service will execute for processing one gigabyte, and *c. netSpeedMb*: an upper bound in seconds for transferring one megabyte). Additionally, costs may change if the system requiring the service has some kind of *promotional code*. Then, such attributes can be formalised by a convex specification $\langle\langle \mathcal{X}, \mathcal{P}\rangle, \alpha\rangle$ where $\mathcal{X} = \{perSec, costMb, maxWait, maxTimexGb, netSpeedMb\}$, $\mathcal{P} = \{promotionMode\}$, and where α is the conjunction of the following formulae[2]:

$$0 < maxWait \leq 100$$
$$(1000 \leq maxTimexGb \leq 3000) \wedge (0.05 \leq netSpeedMb \leq 0.15)$$
$$promotionMode \implies 0.0 \leq perSec < 0.1$$
$$\neg promotionMode \implies 0.1 \leq perSec \leq 0.3$$
$$costMb < 0.5$$

---

[1] Note that linear convex constraints could admit negations but, as the negation of a linear convex constraints can be rewritten as a linear convex constraint itself, there is no need for any special treatment.

[2] The reader shall note that there is no impediment in translating the specification below to a formula recognisable by the grammar presented in Definition 1.

In [13, Definition 3.4] the authors define the *monotone convex expansion* of a convex specification $\langle\langle\mathcal{X}, \mathcal{P}\rangle, \alpha\rangle$ as a new convex specification $\langle\langle\mathcal{X}, \widehat{\mathcal{P}}\rangle, \widehat{\alpha}\rangle$ where:

- $\widehat{\mathcal{P}} = \mathcal{P} \cup \mathcal{V}$, where $\mathcal{V} = \left\{ v_{f(\vec{x})\ \mathcal{R}\ 0} \mid f(\vec{x})\ \mathcal{R}\ 0 \text{ appears in } \alpha \right\}$ and
- $\widehat{\alpha} = \alpha_B \wedge \left[\bigwedge_{v_C \in \mathcal{V}} (\neg v_C \vee C) \right]$, where $\alpha_B = \alpha \vert_C^{v_C}$, the result of substituting every occurrence of an affine/convex constraint C in the monotone SMC formula α by the fresh new propositional variable $v_C \in \mathcal{V}$ associated to C, called the *propositional abstraction* of α.

Thereafter, in [13, Proposition 3.5], the authors prove that: 1. α and $\widehat{\alpha}$ are equi-satisfiable (i.e. for every satisfying assignment for $\widehat{\alpha}$, there exists a satisfying assignment for α) and if $\widehat{\alpha}$ is unsatisfiable, then so is α, 2. any satisfying boolean assignment for α_B reduces the satisfiability problem of $\widehat{\alpha}$ to a conjunction of convex constraints, and 3. the satisfiability problem of $\widehat{\alpha}$ reduces to a finite disjunction (one for every satisfying boolean assignment for α_B) of finite conjunctions of convex constraints.

Roughly speaking, the analysis method proposed by Pappas et al. in [13], sketched in Fig. 1, reduces to enumerating every possible satisfying boolean assignments $\gamma : \widehat{\mathcal{P}} \to \{0, 1\}$ for α_B, and then using a convex constraint solver for testing the feasibility of the set of convex constraints $\{C \mid \gamma(v_C) = 1\}$.

1. Let $\langle\langle\mathcal{X}, \mathcal{P}\rangle, \alpha\rangle$ be a convex specification and α_B the propositional abstraction of α, and a function δ mapping variables in $\mathcal{V}$ to their corresponding convex or affine constraint appearing in α,
2. Feed an SAT-solver with α_B,
3. **if** there exists a satisfying assignment γ, **then**
   1. Feed a convex solver with $\{f(\vec{x})\ \mathcal{R}\ 0 \mid (\exists v \in \mathcal{V})(\delta(v) = f(\vec{x})\ \mathcal{R}\ 0 \wedge \gamma(v) = 1)\}$
   2. **if** it is feasible **then**
      1. α **is satisfiable**
      else
      2. Update the SAT-solver information with $\neg minimise(\gamma_\delta)$
      3. **goto** 3,
4. α **is unsatisfiable**

Fig. 1. SMCO analysis procedure

Updating the SAT-solver's clause database by injecting a new clause, as it is done in Line 3(2)2 requires the next assignment to satisfy the clauses in SAT-solver database, plus the new one. Minimising an assignment $\gamma_\mathcal{V}$ (the subassignment of γ considering only variables in $\mathcal{V}$), as stated also in Line 3(2)2, produces a clause $\gamma_\mathcal{V}^{min}$ (subassignment of $\gamma_\mathcal{V}$ such that $\{C \mid \gamma_{min}(v_C) = 1\}$) which is (potentially) smaller that $\gamma_\mathcal{V}$, minimal and still unfeasible. It is reasonably evident that the smaller the amount of variables involved in $\gamma_\mathcal{V}^{min}$, the bigger the pruning of the search space, because no boolean assignment containing such partial assignment will be considered further in the enumeration of satisfying boolean assignments. We will return to this point in Sect. 3 where we discuss some implementation notes. It is worth noting that clause minimisation, used to produce more efficient unsatisfiability certificates during the enumeration of satisfying boolean assignments, is orthogonal to the main contribution of this work on the minimisation of QoS contracts.

This type of automatic analysis is usually understood as a refutation method aiming at finding counterexamples to properties. Assume $\langle\langle \mathcal{X}, \mathcal{P}\rangle, \alpha\rangle$ is a satisfiable[3] convex specification of a system and β a desirable property written in the same language then, if $\alpha \wedge \neg\beta$ (a formula equivalent to $\neg(\alpha \implies \beta)$) is satisfiable, one can conclude that β does not follows from α, and the satisfying assignment constitutes a counterexample.

2.1   From QoS Contracts to an Efficient Determination of SLA

Service-Oriented Computing relies on a notion of software system as a dynamic entity built up from services discovered and bound in run-time. To make this possible, services must be previously registered in public repositories from where they can be procured by a *Service broker* as required by a dedicated *Middleware* who dynamically reconfigures the executing application by binding it to the service. This process of dynamic reconfiguration is triggered automatically by an application reaching a point in its execution where a continuation depends exclusively on the intervention of an external service.

Consider the case of a (satisfiable) QoS requirement contract Rq. A service with a (satisfiable) QoS provision contract Pr will be a good candidate only if $Pr \implies Rq$ holds; or equivalently, the formula $Pr \wedge \neg Rq$ is not satisfiable. Assuming that such a formula can be seen as a convex specification (i.e. a formula that can be produced by the grammar in Definition 1), then it is possible to perform the interoperability check by executing the algorithm of Fig. 1 to determine compliance between the application's QoS requirement contract and the service's QoS provision contract. Although from a theoretical point of view there is no objection to applying this procedure for determining SLA, from a practical perspective, this interoperability check is expected to be performed over many candidates, in order to guarantee that the service chosen by the service broker is the optimum according to the status of the repository.

Such a use context imposes strong efficiency considerations over this type of analysis, and coping with them requires reducing the execution time for performing the analysis as much as possible, even at the expense of investing a bigger amount of time preprocessing the contracts in advance when the services are registered in the repository. Returning to our example, assume that Pr and $\neg Rq$ are satisfiable convex specifications denoting provision QoS contract and the negation of a requirement QoS contract, respectively; both Pr_B and $\neg Rq_B$ might have

---

[3] It is important for the specification to be satisfiable in order to ensure the existence of logical models, which in the case of this particular language, are boolean assignments. The existence of a model can be interpreted as the existence of a concrete implementations of the system satisfying the specification.

plenty of satisfying boolean assignments γ_{Pr} (resp. $\gamma_{\neg Rq}$) leading to non-feasible sets of convex constraints $\{C \mid \gamma_{Pr}(v_C) = 1\}$ (resp. $\{C \mid \gamma_{\neg Rq}(v_C) = 1\}$), suggesting that contracts admit some relative minimisation that can be performed by updating the solver's clause database by injecting a new clause characterising such unfeasibility information. Ideally this process of *Minimisation through Convex Optimisation* – MCO must traverse the whole space of boolean assignments of the propositional abstraction of the contract, determining which of them leads to a feasible set of convex constraints. This observation motivates the idea of a two phase analysis approach based on the algorithm of Fig. 1, in which the first phase aims at the minimisation of QoS contracts, performed only once when a service is registered in a repository, and the second phase is the analysis of QoS contract compliance, executed for SLA negotiation.

A Two Phase Analysis Algorithm of Convex Specifications. Our proposal for the analysis of QoS contract compliance is motivated by the specific usage scenario of SOC, where specifications are expected to be reused in many analysis. Such a context imposes that time consumption to check whether $Pr \wedge \neg Rq$ is satisfiable or not, has to be as tight as possible due to the fact that such a check has to be performed over every candidate satisfying the functional requirements. To cope with such demand, we devised a preprocess (referred to as *minimisation phase*) aiming at the minimisation of QoS contracts, represented by a convex specification, and a second phase (referred to as *check phase*) that implements the exact same analysis than the algorithm of Fig. 1.

Our first research questions aims at relating the performance of the algorithm in Fig. 1 as distributed by Pappas et al. and our reimplementation when satisfying boolean assignments are iterated by using Z3 and Minisat as SAT-solvers.

RQ1: Is there any performance gain in a Z3-based implementation of the check phase with respect to that of the algorithm shown in Fig. 1? What about between a Minisat-based implementation with respect to the Z3-based implementation of the check phase?

Next we present and evaluate the main contribution of the paper, being the implementation of a QoS contract MCO procedure, aiming at preprocessing QoS contracts in order to prune a significant portion of the space of satisfying boolean assignments of its propositional abstraction. Such minimisation procedure is motivated by two observations about the algorithm of Fig. 1: 1. the analysis procedure relies on enumerating all possible models of the propositional abstraction of the QoS contract, and 2. line 3(2)2 of the algorithm of Fig. 1 alters the enumeration process by using the unfeasibility information obtained from the convex analysis, transformed into a minimal boolean clause, acting as an unfeasibility certificate. The algorithm for QoS contract MCO is based on performing convex analysis to test the feasibility of the set of convex constraints determined by each satisfying boolean assignment. The single difference with SMCO analysis procedure is that, while in Line 3(2)1 of the algorithm of Fig. 1 the problem is reported as satisfiable and the search for more satisfying assignments ends, MCO discards that satisfying boolean assignment to return to the enumeration and continue the search for boolean assignments that lead to non-feasible sets of constraints.

Given a QoS contract, consisting of a monotone SMC formula α, the reader might note that the minimisation process visits all satisfying boolean assignments of the propositional abstraction α_B in order to determine which of them are declared feasible by the convex solver so they must remain as satisfying boolean assignments, and which of them must be pruned from the space of models of the specification. Then we can design a two phase convex analysis algorithm by considering: 1. a single time application of the process of QoS contract MCO phase of both, a provision contract Pr, and the negation of a requirement contract $\neg Rq$, yielding $\widehat{Pr}$ and $\widehat{\neg Rq}$ respectively, and 2. a second phase of searching for a satisfying boolean assignment for the propositional abstraction of $\widehat{Pr} \wedge \neg \widehat{Rq}$ that leads to feasible set of convex constraints (i.e. the result of applying the algorithm shown in Fig. 1).

An important concern regarding the MCO procedure, is that, as we mentioned before, minimising a QoS contract requires visiting all possible boolean assignments satisfying the propositional abstraction of the formula $\widehat{Pr} \wedge \neg \widehat{Rq}$. It is trivial to see that this procedure is of an exponential nature due to the fact that the size of the space of satisfying boolean assignments of a boolean formula is (potentially) exponential with respect to the amount of boolean variables[4]. Having said that, efficiency improvement resulting from potential optimisations of the process cannot change such a high complexity bound. A direct consequence of this observation is that, even if minimisation is considered as a one time preprocess, full scalability is, by any means, unreachable.

The remaining research questions aims at evaluating the performance of our proposal of a two phase procedure for checking QoS contract compliance. To accomplish that, the comparison of the three different implementations of the SMCO analysis procedure done to answer **RQ1** will serve to set a baseline for the experimental evaluation of the main contribution of this work, being the comparison of the time required for checking QoS contract after performing a *Minimization Through Convex Optimisation* phase.

The second research question aims at identifying whether there is a bound to the size of the QoS contracts that can be fully minimised.

RQ2: What is the size of QoS contracts that can be fully minimised in 3 h?

A close look to the proposed minimisation procedure exposes that if it were stopped at any iteration, right before continuing the enumeration of satisfying boolean assignments, the resulting QoS contract shares every feasible model with the original one.

Proposition 1. *Let $\langle\langle \mathcal{X}, \mathcal{P}\rangle, \alpha\rangle$ be a convex specification, α_B the propositional abstraction of α and δ a function mapping variables in $\mathcal{V}$ to their corresponding convex or affine constraint appearing in α. Let $[\alpha_{Bi}]_{0 \leq i \leq n}$ be a sequence of boolean formulae where $\alpha_{B0} = \alpha_B$, α_{Bi+1}, for all $i < n - \overline{1}$, is the result of a*

---

[4] To be precise, the problem of enumerating all possible satisfying assignment of a SAT-formula is, at least, in the complexity class **#P**.

single iteration of the minimisation algorithm to α_{Bi} and α_{Bn} is the result at the end of the algorithm.

Then, every convex specification $\langle\langle \mathcal{X}, \mathcal{P} \rangle, \alpha_{Bi} \rangle$, where $0 \leq i \leq n$, share the same feasible models.

An interesting fact derived from the previous proposition is that the process of QoS contract minimisation can be performed incrementally, one iteration at a time, leading to a succession of partially minimised QoS contracts, leading us to our third research question.

RQ3: How does the nature of the problem change considering successive partial minimisations of a given specification?

3 Implementation and Experimental Results

In this section we present the answers to the research questions posed in Sect. 2 through experimental evaluation. First we will provide some details about the implementation of the algorithms, the hardware configuration of the experimental setup and the dataset used for the experimental evaluation.

Notes on the Implementation. In this section we will briefly discuss some aspects of the implementation of the algorithms presented in the paper. The implementation developed by Pappas et al. in [13] of the algorithm of Fig. 1 uses Z3 [12] as SAT-solver. Having said that, we developed two versions of our algorithms, one also using Z3 to check wheter the reimplementation of the algorithm does not introduce any significant difference in performance, a second one resorting to Minisat [3], a well-known SAT-solver whose minimality has made it one of the most efficient ones available.

Checking feasibility of sets of constraints was implemented using IBM ILOG CPLEX Optimization Studio [9] since it is one of the most powerful convex optimization softwares that is available for research and educational purposes.

The algorithm orchestrating the enumeration of satisfying boolean assignments of the propositional abstraction of the contracts with the convex solving of the set of convex constraints determined by corresponding assignment, as well as all the framework needed for the generation of instances according to the experimental design and their systematic execution were developed in Python 2.7 (https://www.python.org) resorting to the existent libraries needed to integrate the various tools mentioned above.

Hardware Configuration. Experiments were run over an x86_64 architecture processor Intel(R) Core(TM) i5 CPU 750 at 2.67GHz (CPU MHz: 2661 – CPU max MHz: 2661 – CPU min MHz: 1197) with 3 level cache (L1d cache: 32K, L1i cache: 32K – L2 cache: 256K – L3 cache: 8192K), 8 Gb of SDRAM at 1333 MHz, and running SMP Debian Linux 4.9.88-1+deb9u1 (2018-05-07). Each individual instance was run for at most 3 h, unless it is noted, as we believe that what is feasible within that time frame provides enough information to validate our answers. Whenever the analysis of a problem instance, or the construction of the solving infrastructure, exceded the time limit, the corresponding cell in the tables was marked with "TO" denoting that the process reached the timeout, and whenever the limit was a consequence of the exhaustion of the system memory leading the machine to a sate of trashing was marked with "OoM" denoting the system run out of memory.

Notes on the Experimental Setting. A first note on the experimental designs we need to put forward is that we did not use the experimental setting distributed by the authors of [13] for the following reasons: (1) specifications are constructed hardcoding the solver instance and not providing any interface allowing users to feed a specification in any standard language, making very difficult to test the tool over different data sets, and (2) there is no report on the time needed to construct the solver instance which, after profiling the implementations based on Z3, are proven to be not negligible due to the fact that part of the solving is performed during the addition of the clauses, sometimes consuming more time than the invocation of the solve itself (see column "Initialisation time" of Table 1).

3.1 Experimental Evaluation

In this section we evaluate the research questions posed previously and show experimental data supporting our answers.

RQ1: Is there any performance gain in a Z3-based implementation of the check phase with respect to that of the algorithm shown in Fig. 1? What about between a Minisat-based implementation with respect to the Z3-based implementation of the check phase?

Experimental Design: QoS provision contracts were obtained by first generating random SAT instances of satisfiable provision contracts, Pr_B using the number of boolean and real variables as parameters. The dataset is formed by QoS contracts with boolean variables ranging from 50 to 350, stepping every 50 variables. The number of clauses is 80 times the number of boolean variables. From the total amount of variables we randomly choose 50% to which we associated randomly generated linear convex constraints. Convex constraints were considered to apply over 5 to 30 real variables stepping every 5 variables. Satisfiable contracts $\neg Rq_B$ are obtained from: (1) negating Pr_B, (2) pushing negations to the atoms, and (3) reversing the linear constraints (producing also linear constraints). In this way, $Pr_B \wedge \neg Rq_B$ results satisfiable from the boolean point of view, but having no feasible convex model. This lack of counterexamples for $Pr \implies Rq$ aims at stressing the checking procedure forcing it to traverse the whole space of solutions.

The upper limit in the number of boolean variables respond to the fact that generating a CNF boolean formula $\neg Pr_B$ as a QoS requirement contract, using Tseitin's transformation [15], yields a boolean formula quadratically bigger than Pr_B, both in the number of clauses and variables. If we consider that a propositional abstraction of a provides contract Pr_B of 400 boolean variables and 32000 clauses results in a 35 Mb file, the construction of a QoS contract equivalent to $\neg Pr_B$ yields a CNF formula of approximately 30000 boolean variables and 9500000 clauses, consuming approximately 1 Gb. The analysis was performed over 8 instances of each combination of boolean variables and real variables to try palliating the variance among cases. The time was split in two, the time needed to setup the checking infrastructure, and the analysis time itself, as the use of Z3 showed that a significant part of the analysis takes place during the initialisation of the SMT-solver with the clauses.

Table 1. Comparison of different implementations of algorithm for checking an unsatisfiable formula

# bool. vars in provides	Solver	Initialisation time (approx.)	# real variables					
			5	10	15	20	25	30
50	SMC	150	157.48	176.71	176.71	178.28	176.86	178.22
	Z3 check	170	167.82	177.82	177.55	177.01	176.84	177.55
	Minisat check	4	3.21	2.23	2.13	2.12	2.12	2.12
100	SMC	630	1575.70	1802.20	1756.17	1812.62	1854.42	1852.64
	Z3 check	640	1589.20	1819.81	1843.83	1954.84	1925.89	1931.48
	Minisat check	17	16.47	19.89	11.90	10.01	9.11	8.70
150	SMC	1680	4243.10	TO	TO	TO	TO	TO
	Z3 check	1820	4580.25	TO	TO	TO	TO	TO
	Minisat check	45	21.32	174.12	79.92	47.76	26.66	23.60
200	SMC	3100	TO	TO	TO	TO	TO	TO
	Z3 check	3120	TO	TO	TO	TO	TO	TO
	Minisat check	77	35.53	236.32	906.17	488.88	102.78	60.34
250	SMC	4920	TO	TO	TO	TO	TO	TO
	Z3 check	5010	TO	TO	TO	TO	TO	TO
	Minisat check	127	45.93	321.73	1231.22	2929.81	1052.29	405.59
300	SMC	OoM	–	–	–	–	–	–
	Z3 check	7300	TO	TO	TO	TO	TO	TO
	Minisat check	186	60.05	431.87	1714.84	4423.42	8259.39	4720.92
350	SMC	OoM	–	–	–	–	–	–
	Z3 check	OoM	–	–	–	–	–	–
	Minisat check	OoM	–	–	–	–	–	–

Experimental Results: Table 1 shows the running time comparison between the original implementation of SMCO algorithm presented in [13], reviewed in Fig. 1, and the implementations of the check phase based on Z3 and Minisat. The layout of the table is: 1. the first column shows the amount of boolean variables in the provision contract, 2. the second one shows the solver used to solve the problem, 3. the third column shows the time required for initialising the solver until the exact moment before it is ready to solve the problem, and 4. columns fourth to nine show the average time required to solve the instances of the corresponding number of real variables. Figure 2 shows boxplots graphs containing the run-time information for the first two rows of Table 1 exposing the relative stability of the algorithms. Figure 2a and b show the running time of the tool using the algorithm in Fig. 1 and the Z3-based implementation of the check phase algorithm, while Fig. 2c and d show the running time using the Minisat-based implementation.

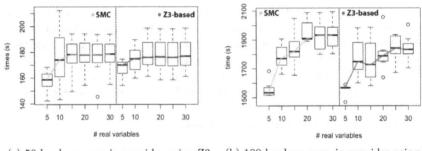

(a) 50 boolean vars. in provides using Z3   (b) 100 boolean vars. in provides using Z3

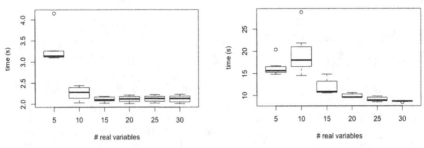

(c) 50 bool. vars. in provides using Minisat (d) 100 bool. vars. in provides using Minisat

Fig. 2. Compliance analysis of QoS contracts over 50 and 100 boolean variables in provides (total problem size of +4000 and +8000 bool. vars. respectively)

Conclusions and Discussion: Observing the running times obtained from executing the three implementations of SMCP algorithm for checking an unsatisfiable formula shown in Table 1 we derive the following conclusions: 1. running time grows exponentially at a rate of 2.37 on the number of boolean variables, 2. observing the rows it is possible to appreciate that the time required to analyse the satisfiability of the instances grows until it finds a maximum, then decrease until it stabilises in what seems to be a plateau. As for every row the CNF used is the same, also prescribing the amount of convex constraints, this phenomenon seems to expose a relation between the number of constraints and the number of real variables over which those constraints are expressed. It is also observable that decrease, and further stabilisation, of the time is mimicked by the number of iterations of the algorithm. Having said this, we believe that understanding this particular phenomenon has no impact on the experiment conducted to answer this research question, 3. there is no consistent and significant difference between the performance of the SMCP original implementation by Pappas et al. and our implementation based on Z3 as boolean solver. The experimental data shows a running time difference no bigger than 10%. This difference might be a byproduct of having developed a more abstract implementation of the convex specification encapsulating an iterator for the satisfying boolean assignments of the propositional abstraction, 4. the Minisat-based implementation greatly outperforms both Z3-based implementations taking only approximately 2% of the time required by the latter, considering setting up the analysis infrastructure and analysing compliance altogether.

An important observation about the answer given to **RQ1**, is that only the Minisat-based implementation of the check phase algorithm can produce a significant amount of experimental data useful enough to evaluate our proposal of a two phase QoS contract compliance analysis procedure; thus **RQ2** and **RQ3** will be answered only evaluating the performance of the Minisat-based implementation of both phases of the procedure.

RQ2: What is the size of QoS contracts that can be fully minimised in 3 h?

Experimental Design: The dataset used to run the experiment was generated using the same criteria used for generating the dataset used to run the experiment performed to answer **RQ1** but considering a finer granularity in the axis of boolean variables (stepping every 5) and starting from 30 variables, as the running time of the minimisation phase of instances with less than 30 was negligible. In those cases in which the minimisation process did not find any unfeasible convex model thus, not producing any minimisation, the running time is reported tagged with **(nm)**, indicating "no minimisation".

Experimental Results: Table 2 shows the running time of the minimisation phase. A side by side comparison of the time required by the analysis algorithm, over minimised and not minimised instances, is of no interest in this case as the cost associated to the process of full minimisation of QoS contracts is so high that even the smaller instance of Table 1 of 50 boolean variables and 5 real variables could not be minimised within the time bound of 3 h.

Conclusions and Discussion: Results shown in Table 2 expose that a naïve approach to minimisation is not viable as the cost of full minimisation might be too high, even for very small contracts.

RQ3: How does the nature of the problem change considering successive partial minimisations of a given specification?

Experimental Design: To provide an answer to this research question we performed partial minimisations (from 0 min to 3 h stepping every 30 min) of every pair of QoS contracts of those cells of rows 200, 250 and 300 of Table 1 where the

Table 2. Running time of the Minisat-based minimisation algorithm

# boolean vars	# real variables					
	5	10	15	20	25	30
30	186.68	(nm) 200.40	(nm) 203.18	(nm) 206.43	(nm) 209.94	(nm) 212.82
35	691.26	(nm) 852.93	(nm) 921.20	(nm) 930.37	(nm) 944.27	(nm) 953.85
40	5606.34	(nm) 9519.08	(nm) 9682.34	(nm) 9814.39	(nm) 10004.27	(nm) 7234.67
45	TO	TO	TO	TO	TO	TO

number of real variables ranges between 5% and 10% of the number of boolean variables. Then, we performed the compliance analysis in order to identify how analysis time decreases while more time is invested in the minimisation procedure.

Results: Figure 3 show graphs of the evolution of time required by the check phase over partially minimised QoS contracts, considering the snapshots taken every 30 min of minimisation. Table 3 shows the comparison of the solving time required by partially minimised QoS contracts up to 3 h.

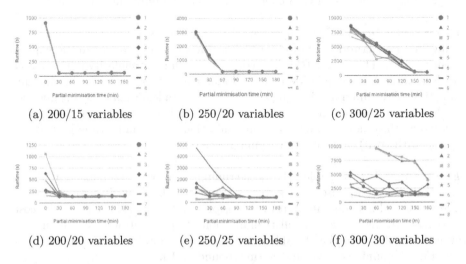

(a) 200/15 variables   (b) 250/20 variables   (c) 300/25 variables

(d) 200/20 variables   (e) 250/25 variables   (f) 300/30 variables

Fig. 3. Solving times for partial minimisations (from 0 min to 3 h stepping every 30 min) of provides and requires QoS contracts

Conclusions and Discussion: Observing the graphs in Fig. 3 we derive the following conclusions: 1. the running time required by the check phase decreases while the amount of time invested in minimisation grows. For QoS contracts over 200 boolean variables, the time required by the check phase drops dramatically to a plateau after only 30 min. of minimisation. In the case of QoS contracts over 250 boolean variables, the pattern is exactly the same but requiring between 60 to 90 min. of minimisation. Finally, for QoS contracts over 300 boolean variables, this phenomenon can be seen only for instances over 25 real variables after 150 min. but in the case of 30 real variables we can witness cases that cannot be checked within 3 h time when QoS contracts are not minimised, that can be checked after 60 min. of minimisation phase, 2. the growth on the number of real variables for instances over the same number of boolean variables shows more dispersion (in the time required for the check phase) over instances minimised for short periods of time, but rapidly collapsing to the plateau,

Table 3. Comparison of solving time required between not minimised and minimised contracs (3 h)

# bool. vars in provides		Initialisation time (approx.)	# real variables				
			10	15	20	25	30
150	not minimised	43	171.35	94.01	–	–	–
	minimised	44	15.13	38.59	–	–	–
	percentage	102.3	8.8	41	–	–	–
200	not minimised	77	–	896.46	444.53	–	–
	minimised	80	–	50.31	139.34	–	–
	percentage	103.90	–	5.6	31.3	–	–
250	not minimised	127	–	–	2930.41	1310.06	–
	minimised	130	–	–	173.81	429.67	–
	percentage	102.36	–	–	5.9	32.7	–
300	not minimised	186	–	–	–	8083.04	3400.33 / **TO**
	minimised	189	–	–	–	560.94	2265.39
	percentage	101.61	–	–	–	6.9	66.6

The results in Table 3 show how 3 h of minimisation phase dramatically reduce the cost of the check phase. The reduction naturally depends on the size of the problem under analysis; it is easy to see that bigger problems show smaller reductions over the same amount of time invested in the minimisation phase.

4   Conclusions

We proposed the use of a formal language for QoS contract specification together with an associated two phase compliance checking procedure, based on the algorithm proposed by Pappas et al. in [13] for hybrid system verification, adapted to the concrete scenario of SLA negotiation for the automatic reconfiguration of software systems found in distributed environments such as SOC.

Research questions were posed and experiments were conducted to answer them. The dataset was designed in order to stress the technique by forcing the problem instances to be unsatisfiable thus, requiring the exhaustion of the space of potential solutions; the evaluation of the tool under satisfiable instances remains to be addressed. The experimental results shown in the answering of **RQ2** evidenced that full minimisation of contracts might be unreachable as time and memory consumption, even for small case studies, result too high. To mitigate such demand we proposed the use of incremental minimisation and the experimental results shown in the answering of **RQ3** evidenced that a relatively small amount of time invested in a first phase of QoS contract MCO dramatically reduces the time required by a second phase dedicated to check compliance of minimised versions of the QoS contracts.

References

1. Bryant, V.: Metric Spaces: Iteration and Application. Mathematical Systems Theory. Cambridge University Press, Cambridge (1985)
2. Cormen, T.H., Clifford, S., Leiserson, C.E., Rivest, R.L., Stein, C.: Introduction to algorithms. MIT Press, Cambridge (2001)
3. Eén, N., Sörensson, N.: An extensible SAT-solver. In: Giunchiglia, E., Tacchella, A. (eds.) SAT 2003. LNCS, vol. 2919, pp. 502–518. Springer, Heidelberg (2004). https://doi.org/10.1007/978-3-540-24605-3_37
4. Fiadeiro, J.L., Lopes, A., Bocchi, L.: An abstract model of service discovery and binding. Formal Aspects Comput. **23**(4), 433–463 (2011)
5. Grünbaum, B.: Convex polytopes, Graduate Texts in Mathematics, vol. 221. Springer, Berlin, Germany (1967). https://doi.org/10.1007/978-1-4613-0019-9
6. Henzinger, T.A.: The theory of hybrid automata. In: Vardi, M.Y., Clarke, E.M. (eds.) Proceedings of Eleventh Annual IEEE Symposium on Logic in Computer Science, 1996. LICS 1996, pp. 278–292. IEEE Computer Society, July 1996. see also [7]
7. Henzinger, T.A.: The theory of hybrid automata. In: Inan, M.K., Kurshan, R.P. (eds.) Verification of Digital and Hybrid Systems. NATO ASI Series (Series F: Computer and Systems Sciences), vol. 170, pp. 265–292. Springer, Heidelberg (2000). https://doi.org/10.1007/978-3-642-59615-5_13. see also [6]
8. Henzinger, T.A., Kopke, P.W., Puri, A., Varaiya, P.: What's decidable about hybrid automata? J. Comput. Syst. Sci. **57**(1), 94–124 (1998)
9. IBM: IBM ILOG CPLEX Optimization Studio (2004). https://www.ibm.com/analytics/data-science/prescriptive-analytics/cplex-optimizer
10. de Moura, L.M., Bjørner, N.: Satisfiability modulo theories: introduction and applications. Commun. ACM **54**(9), 69–77 (2011)
11. Nuzzo, P., Puggelli, A., Seshia, S.A., Sangiovanni-Vincentelli, A.L.: CalCS: SMT solving for non-linear convex constraints. In: Bloem, R., Sharygina, N. (eds.) International Conference on Formal Methods in Computer-Aided Design, FMCAD 2010, pp. 71–79. IEEE, October 2010
12. Microsoft Research: Z3: An efficient SMT solver. http://research.microsoft.com/projects/z3/
13. Shoukry, Y., Nuzzo, P., Sangiovanni-Vincentelli, A.L., Seshia, S.A., Pappas, G.J., Tabuada, P.: SMC: satisfiability modulo convex optimization. In: Proceedings of the 20th International Conference on Hybrid Systems: Computation and Control, pp. 19–28. ACM Press, New York (2017)
14. Strunk, A.: QoS-aware service composition: a survey. In: Brogi, A., Pautasso, C., Papadopoulos, G.A. (eds.) Proceedings of 8th IEEE European Conference on Web Services (ECOWS 2010), pp. 67–74. IEEE Computer Society, December 2010
15. Tseitin, G.S.: On the complexity of derivation in propositional calculus. In: Siekmann, J.H., Wrightson, G. (eds.) Automation of Reasoning. Symbolic Computation (Artificial Intelligence), pp. 466–483. Springer, Heidelberg (1983). https://doi.org/10.1007/978-3-642-81955-1_28

DiRPOMS: Automatic Checker
of Distributed Realizability of POMSets

Roberto Guanciale$^{(\boxtimes)}$

KTH, Stockholm, Sweden
`robertog@kth.se`

Abstract. DiRPOMS permits to verify if the specification of a distributed system can be faithfully realised via distributed agents that communicate using asynchronous message passing. A distinguishing feature of DiRPOMS is the usage of set of pomsets to specify the distributed system. This provides two benefits: syntax obliviousness and efficiency. By defining the semantics of a coordination language in term of pomsets, it is possible to use DiRPOMS for several coordination models. Also, DiRPOMS can analyze pomsets extracted by system logs, when the coordination model is unknown, and therefore can support coordination mining activities. Finally, by using sets of pomsets in place of flat languages, DiRPOMS can reduce exponential blows of analysis that is typical in case of multiple threads due to interleaving. (Demo video available at https://youtu.be/ISYdBNMxEDY. Tool available at https://bitbucket. org/guancio/chosem-tools/).

Keywords: Pomsets · Choreography · Realisability · CFSMs

1 Introduction

Choreographic approaches advocate two views of the same distributed system: a *global view* that describes ordering conditions and constraints under which messages are exchanged, and *local views* that are used by each party to build their components. Here, the global view is a specification that is realised by combination of the local systems. As observed in [1], a source of problems is that there are some global specifications that are impossible to implement using distributed agents in a given communication model.

DiRPOMS is a tool designed to analyze realisability of choreographies. A choreography is formalized as a set of pomsets, were each pomset represents the causalities of events in one single branch of execution. Local views are modeled via finite state machines that communicate via asynchronous message passing. DiRPOMS checks realizability by verifying two closure conditions of the input pomsets and outputs the corresponding counterexamples:

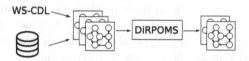

Published by Springer Nature Switzerland AG 2019
H. Riis Nielson and E. Tuosto (Eds.): COORDINATION 2019, LNCS 11533, pp. 237–249, 2019.
https://doi.org/10.1007/978-3-030-22397-7_14

The first use case of our tool is design time analysis, where an architect checks if a choreography is realizable. In this case, violations of the closure conditions (i.e. the counterexamples) enable to identify behaviors that are not included in the choreography but are necessary in any distributed system that implements it (using finite state machines and asynchronous message passing). The usage of set of pomsets allows this analysis to be syntax oblivious, since the semantics of several existing choreographic models (i.e. [6,8,11]) can be expressed using set of pomsets.

The second use case is choreography mining. In this case an analyst extracts a hypotheses choreography from (partial) execution logs of a distributed system. Here, violations of the closure conditions enable to identify behaviors of the distributed system that are not included in the logs, so supplementing partial information regarding the system under test and reducing the number of executions needed to extract a model of the system.

The paper is organized as follows. In Sect. 2 we present the models for local and global views and in Sect. 3 we briefly recall the theory supporting our tool. Section 4 presents some examples of faulty choreographies, which cannot be implemented using communicating finite state machines. Section 5 shows an example of choreography mining, where the tool is used to identify missing traces from a partial execution log. Usage, implementation, and evaluation of the tool are presented in Sects. 6, 7, and 8.

2   Local and Global Views of Choreographies

We assume a set $\mathcal{P}$ of distributed *participants* (ranged over by A, B, etc.) and a set $\mathcal{M}$ of *messages* (ranged over by m, x, etc.). Participants communicate by exchanging messages over *channels*, that are elements of the set $C = (\mathcal{P} \times \mathcal{P})$. The set of *(communication) labels* L, ranged over by l and l', is defined by

$$L = L^! \cup L^? \quad \text{where (outputs) } L^! = C \times \{!\} \times \mathcal{M} \quad \text{and (inputs) } L^? = C \times \{?\} \times \mathcal{M}$$

we shorten $(A, B, !, m)$ as $A\,B!m$ and $(A, B, ?, m)$ as $A\,B?m$. The *subject* of output and input are the sender $(sbj(A\,B!m) = A)$ and receiver $(sbj(A\,B?m) = B)$ respectively.

Local systems are modeled in terms of *communicating fine state machines* [1].

Definition 1. *An* A-communicating finite state machine (A-CFSM) $M = (Q, q_0, F, \rightarrow)$ *is a finite-state automaton on the alphabet* $\{l \in L \mid sbj(l) = A\}$ *such that,* $q_0 \in Q$ *is the initial state, and* $F \subseteq Q$ *are the accepting states. A* (communicating) system *is a map* S *assigning an* A-*CFSM to each participant* $A \in \mathcal{P}$.

Figure 1 presents a system with three participants: A, B, and C. Participant C always sends message x to B. Participant A sends two messages to B: the first message is x or y; the second message is always z. Participant B receives the first message from A and C in any order, then it receives the second message of A.

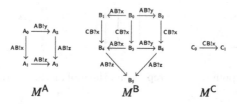

Fig. 1. A system consisting of CMFSs. Initial states are A_0, B_0, and C_0. Accepting states are A_3, B_5, and C_1.

A *configuration* of a communicating system consists of a state-map $\vec{q}$, which maps each participant to its local state, and buffer-map $\vec{b}$, which maps each channel and message to the number of outputs that have been consumed. A configuration is *accepting* if all buffers are empty and the local state of each participant is accepting while it is a *deadlock* if no accepting configuration is reachable from it. The *initial* configuration is the one where, for all $A \in \mathcal{P}$, $\vec{q}(A)$ is the initial state of the corresponding CFSM and all buffers are empty.

The semantics of communicating systems is defined in terms of a labeled transition relation between configurations. Each transition models one action performed by one machine: an output, which adds a message to a channel, or an input, which consumed a pending message from a channel. Formally $\langle \vec{q}; \vec{b} \rangle \overset{l}{\Longrightarrow} \langle \vec{q}'; \vec{b}' \rangle$ if there is a message $m \in \mathcal{M}$ such that either (1) or (2) below holds:

1. $l = A\,B!m$, $q(A) \overset{l}{\to} q'(A)$, $q'(C) = q(C)$ for all $C \neq A \in \mathcal{P}$, and $\vec{b}'(A\,B) = \vec{b}(A\,B)[m \mapsto \vec{b}(A\,B)(m) + 1]$
2. $l = A\,B?m$, $q(B) \overset{l}{\to} q'(B)$, $q'(C) = q(C)$ for all $C \neq B \in \mathcal{P}$, $\vec{b}(A\,B)(m) > 0$ and $b'(A\,B) = b(A\,B)[m \mapsto b(A\,B)(m) - 1]$

where, $f[x \mapsto y]$ represents updating of a function f in x with a value y.

Definition 2. *The* language *of a communicating system S is the set $\mathbb{L}(S) \in \mathcal{L}^*$ of sequences $l_0 \ldots l_{n-1}$ such that exist a trace labeled with $l_0 \ldots l_{n-1}$ that start in the initial configuration and ends in an accepting configuration.*

The notion of *realisability* is given in terms of the relation between the *language* of the global view and the one of a system of local views "implementing" it [1].

Definition 3 (Realisability). *A language $L \subseteq \mathcal{L}^*$ is weakly realisable if there is a communicating system S such that $L = \mathbb{L}(S)$; when S is deadlock-free we say that L is safely realisable.*

We model the global views in terms of sets of pomsets, where each pomset models one branch of execution.

Definition 4 (Pomsets [4]). *A labelled partially-ordered set (lposet) is a triple $(\mathcal{E}, \leq, \lambda)$, with $\mathcal{E}$ a set of events, $\leq \subseteq \mathcal{E} \times \mathcal{E}$ a reflexive, anti-symmetric, and*

Fig. 2. A set of two pomsets that represents the global view of the system of Fig. 1

transitive relation on $\mathcal{E}$, and $\lambda : \mathcal{E} \to \mathcal{L}$ a labelling function mapping events in $\mathcal{E}$ to labels in $\mathcal{L}$.

A partially-ordered multi-set (of actions), pomset for short, is an isomorphism class of lposets, where $(\mathcal{E}, \leq, \lambda)$ and $(\mathcal{E}', \leq', \lambda')$ are isomorphic if there is a bijection $\phi : \mathcal{E} \to \mathcal{E}'$ such that $e \leq e' \iff \phi(e) \leq' \phi(e')$ and $\lambda = \lambda' \circ \phi$.

Pomsets allow to represent scenarios where the same communication occurs multiple times. Intuitively, $\leq$ represents causality; if $e < e'$ then e' is caused by e. Note that λ is not required to be injective: $\lambda(e) = \lambda(e')$ means that e and e' model different occurrences of the same action. In the following, $[\mathcal{E}, \leq, \lambda]$ denotes the isomorphism class of $(\mathcal{E}, \leq, \lambda)$, symbols $r, r', \dots$ (resp. $R, R', \dots$) range over (resp. sets of) pomsets, and we assume that pomsets r contain at least one lposet which will possibly be referred to as $(\mathcal{E}_r, \leq_r, \lambda_r)$. The *projection* $r|_A$ *of a pomset* r *on a participant* $A \in \mathcal{P}$ is obtained by restricting r to the events having subject A. We will represent pomsets as (a variant of) Hasse diagrams of the immediate predecessor relation.

A pomset is *well-formed* if (1) for every output $A\,B!m$ there is at most one immediate successor input $A\,B?m$, (2) for every input $A\,B?m$ there exists exactly one immediate predecessor output $A\,B!m$, (3) if an event immediately precedes an event having different subjects then these events are matching output and input respectively, (4) ordered output events with the same label cannot be matched by inputs that have opposite order. A pomset is *complete* if there is no output event in without a matching input event.

Definition 5. *Given a pomset $r = [\mathcal{E}, \leq, \lambda]$, a linearization of r is a string in $\mathcal{L}^*$ obtained by considering a total ordering of the events $\mathcal{E}$ that is consistent with the partial order $\leq$, and then replacing each event by its label. The language of a pomset ($\mathbb{L}(r)$) the set of all linearizations of r. The language of a set of pomsets R is simply defined as $\mathbb{L}(R) = \bigcup_{r \in R} \mathbb{L}(r)$.*

The set of pomsets of Fig. 2 represents the global view of the system of Fig. 1, i.e. the two views have the same language. The two pomsets represents two different scenarios (i.e. branches): in the left scenario A sends x, in the right scenario A sends y.

3   Realisability Conditions

Our tool uses the verification conditions for realisability identified in [5]. These conditions requires to introduce the following definitions.

Definition 6 (Inter-participant Closure). *Let $(r^A)_{A \in \mathcal{P}}$ be the tuple where $r^A = r^A \lfloor_A$ for all $A \in \mathcal{P}$. The inter-participant closure $\Box((r^A)_{A \in \mathcal{P}})$ is the set of all well-formed pomsets $[\bigcup_{A \in \mathcal{P}} \mathcal{E}_{r^A}, \ \leq_I \cup \bigcup_{A \in \mathcal{P}} \leq_{r^A}, \ \bigcup_{A \in \mathcal{P}} \lambda_{r^A}]$ where $\leq_I \subseteq \{(e^A, e^B) \in \mathcal{E}_{r^A} \times \mathcal{E}_{r^B}, A, B \in \mathcal{P} \mid \lambda_{r^A}(e^A) = AB!m, \lambda_{r^B}(e^B) = AB?m\}$.*

The inter-participant closure takes one pomset for every participant and generates all "acceptable" matches between output and input events. We use the following tuple of pomsets (r^A, r^B) to illustrate the inter-participant closure.

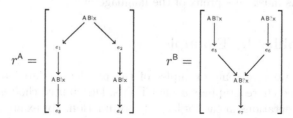

Pomset r^A represents a fork while pomset r^B represents a join. The inter-participant closure of (r^A, r^B) consists of four well-formed pomsets:

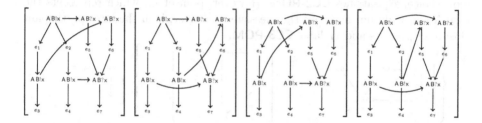

Definition 7 (More permissive relation). *A pomset r' is more permissive than pomset r, written $r \sqsubseteq r'$, when $\mathcal{E}_r = \mathcal{E}_{r'}$, $\lambda_r = \lambda_{r'}$, and $\leq_r \supseteq \leq_{r'}$.*

The more permissive relation guarantees language inclusion, i.e. if $r \sqsubseteq r'$ then $\mathbb{L}(r) \subseteq \mathbb{L}(r')$.

Definition 8 (Prefix pomsets). *A pomset $r' = [\mathcal{E}', \leq', \lambda']$ is a prefix of pomset $r = [\mathcal{E}, \leq, \lambda]$ if there exists a label preserving injection $\phi : \mathcal{E}' \to \mathcal{E}$ such that $\phi(\leq') = \leq \cap (\mathcal{E} \times \phi(\mathcal{E}'))$.*

A *prefix* of a pomset r is a pomset on a subset of the events of r that preserves the order and labelling of r.

The realisability conditions presented in [5] are two closure conditions, which are formalized by the following theorem.

Theorem 1. *If R satisfies* **CC2-POM** *then $\mathbb{L}(R)$ is weak realisable, if R also satisfies* **CC3-POM** *then its language is safe realisable, where*

- **CC2-POM**$(R) \triangleq$ *for all tuples $(r^A)_{A \in \mathcal{P}}$ of pomsets of R, for every pomset $r \in \Box((r^A \lfloor_A)_{A \in \mathcal{P}})$, there exists $r' \in R$ such that $r \sqsubseteq r'$.*

- **CC3-POM**$(R) \triangleq$ *for all tuples of pomsets* $(\bar{r}^A)_{A \in \mathcal{P}}$ *such that* $\bar{r}^A$ *is a prefix of a pomset* $r^A \in R$ *for every* A, *and for every pomset* $\bar{r} \in \square((\bar{r}^A|_A)_{A \in \mathcal{P}})$ *there is a pomset* $r' \in R$ *and a prefix* $\bar{r}'$ *of* r' *such that* $\bar{r} \sqsubseteq \bar{r}'$.

Intuitively **CC2-POM** requires that if all the possible executions of a pomset cannot be distinguished by any of the participants of R, then those executions must be part of the language of R. Similarly, **CC3-POM** requires that if all partial executions cannot be distinguished by any of the participants of R, then those executions must be a prefix of the language of R.

4   Realisability by Examples

In this section we give some examples of the problems related to implementing pomset-based choreographers using CFSMs. Distributed choices can prevent faithful implementations in case of lack of coordination. For example, the set R_1 models two branches. Participants A and C should both send the message x or both send the message y. However, A and C do not coordinate to achieve this behaviour; this makes it impossible for them to distributively commit to a common choice. R_1 satisfies **CC2-POM**. However, pomset r_1, which represents the case A and C do not agree on the message to deliver, is in the inter-participant closure of prefixes and violates **CC3-POM**.

A different problem affects R_2. Here the two branches describe different orders of the same set of events. The behaviour of A (and D) is the same in both branches: A (resp. D) concurrently sends message x (resp. y) to B and C. The behaviours of B and C differ: in the left branch they first receive the message from A then the one from D, in the right branch, they have the same interactions but in opposite order. This choreography cannot be realised since, intuitively, it requires B and C to commit on the same order of reception without communicating with each other. Pomset r_2, which captures the case when B and C do not agree on the order of message reception, is in the inter-participant closure and violates **CC2-POM**.

The last example demonstrates problems led by the usage of the same message in the concurrent threads. The set R_3: consists of a single pomset, which represents two concurrent sub-choreographies. The usage of message x in both threads can cause the following problem: (1) the left thread of A executes $A\,C!l_1$ and $A\,B!x$; (2) after the output $B\,C!r_2$, the right thread of B executes the input $A\,B?x$, so "stealing" the message x generated by the left thread of A and meant for the left thread of B; (3) the right thread of B executes $B\,C!r_3$. Pomset r_3, which represents this case, is in the inter-participant closure and violates **CC2-POM**.

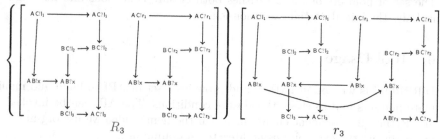

$$R_3 \qquad\qquad\qquad r_3$$

5 Identifying Missing Execution Logs for Choreography Mining

Choreography (and process) mining [10] consists of extracting a hypothesis choreography from a partial execution log of a distributed system. In this section we show that violations of the closure conditions can be used to identify behaviors of the distributed system that are not included in the log. Therefore the closure conditions can support the mining and testing activities.

Let the partial execution log of the system of Fig. 1 contains the following traces

A log	B log	C log
AB!x; AB!z	AB?x;CB?x;AB?z	CB!x
AB!x; AB!z	CB?x;AB?x;AB?z	CB!x
AB!y; AB!z	AB?y;CB?x;AB?z	CB!x

A choreography that precisely represents these traces is the following set of pomsets:

$$\left\{ \left[\begin{array}{c} A B!x \rightarrow A B?x \quad C B?x \leftarrow C B!x \\ \downarrow \qquad\qquad \searrow \nearrow \\ A B!z \longrightarrow A B?z \end{array} \right], \left[\begin{array}{c} A B!y \rightarrow A B?y \longrightarrow C B?x \leftarrow C B!x \\ \downarrow \qquad\qquad \nearrow \\ A B!z \longrightarrow A B?z \end{array} \right] \right\}$$

This set of pomsets satisfies **CC2-POM**, but it does not satisfy **CC3-POM**. The following pomset is in the inter-participant closure of prefixes and violates **CC3-POM**:

$$\left[\begin{array}{c} A B!y \quad C B?x \leftarrow C B!x \\ \downarrow \\ A B!z \end{array} \right]$$

This pomset represents the fact that there must be an execution of the system where A sends y and B receives the first message from C, i.e.:

```
A  log           | B  log           | C  log
─────────────────┼──────────────────┼─────────────
AB!y;  AB!z  | CB?x ;...        | CB!x
```

This information can be used to fix the hypothesis choreography, by enabling the traces that are necessarily part of the behaviors of the distributed system. The set of pomsets of Fig. 2 satisfies both closure conditions and its language includes the initial partial execution log.

6   Tool Usage

DiRPROM is written in Python and provides a set of API to build and manipulate pomsets and to check the closure conditions. The API can be invoked by any Python development environment (in the demo video we use org-mode [9] for analyzing the examples using literate programming).

A typical DiRPOM session starts by defining the set of pomsets modeling the choreography. Pomsets can be loaded using the existing formats (including GEXF, GraphML, and JSON), be generated by translating other choreography models, or be dynamically generated. For example, the following snippet creates R_1 as input choreography:

```python
# a choreography is a list of pomsets
global_view = []

# a pomset is a defined using a directed graph
# left pomset of R1
gr1 = nx.DiGraph()
# add_pair(gr1, A, B, n, m) creates two node "out-n" and "in-n"
# labeled with AB!m and AB?m, connects the two events and returns
# the pair (out-n, in-n)
abx = add_pair(gr1, "a", "b", 1, "x")
cby = add_pair(gr1, "c", "b", 2, "x")
abz = add_pair(gr1, "a", "b", 3, "z")
# Input pomsets do not need to be transitive (transitive closure
# is done internally)
gr1.add_edge(abx[1], abz[1])
gr1.add_edge(cby[1], abz[1])
gr1.add_edge(abx[0], abz[0])
global_view.append(gr1)

# right pomset of R2
gr2 = nx.DiGraph()
abx = add_pair(gr2, "a", "b", 1, "y")
cby = add_pair(gr2, "c", "b", 2, "y")
abz = add_pair(gr2, "a", "b", 3, "z")
gr2.add_edge(abx[1], cby[1])
gr2.add_edge(cby[1], abz[1])
gr2.add_edge(abx[0], abz[0])
global_view.append(gr2)
```

The closure condition **CC2-POM** can be checked using

```
cc2c = cc2closure(global_view)          # cc2c is the list of pomsets
cc2res = cc2pom(cc2c, global_view)
```

The result `cc2res` is a map that yields for each index i of `cc2c` the index of `global_view` matching it or `None` if `cc2c[i]` is a counterexample. Similarly closure condition **CC3-POM** can be checked using

```
(cc3c, pref) = cc3closure(global_view) # cc3c and prefix are lists
cc3res = cc3pom(cc3c, pref)
```

The list `pref` contains the list of prefixes of the input choreography, and the result `cc3res` maps each index of `cc3c` to an index of `pref` or `None`. The counter examples can be rendered using:

```
errors = counterexamples(cc3c, cc3res)
debug_graphs(errors, "output−folder")  # generates pictures of errors
```

DiRPOM also provides a command line utility, which uses GraphML format for input and output of pomsets. The left pomset of R_1 can be defined by the following GraphML file:

```xml
<?xml version='1.0' encoding='utf−8'?>
<graphml>
  <key attr.name="label" attr.type="string" for="node" id="d0" />
  <graph edgedefault="directed">
    <node id="b−2"><data key="d0">CB?x</data></node>
    <node id="b−3"><data key="d0">AB?z</data></node>
    <node id="b−1"><data key="d0">AB?x</data></node>
    <node id="a−1"><data key="d0">AB!x</data></node>
    <node id="a−3"><data key="d0">AB!z</data></node>
    <node id="c−2"><data key="d0">CB!x</data></node>
    <edge source="b−2" target="b−3" />
    <edge source="b−1" target="b−3" />
    <edge source="a−1" target="a−3" />
    <edge source="a−1" target="b−1" />
    <edge source="a−3" target="b−3" />
    <edge source="c−2" target="b−2" />
  </graph>
</graphml>
```

Each GraphML must contain a **key** element, specifying the existence of the node attribute **label** of type **string**. Each node has a unique identifier and a data sub-element, which defines the node label. The following command executes the analysis of a choreography:

```
dirpom [input] [output1] [output2] −−draw −−graphml
```

The parameter **input** specifies the path of a directory that contains one GraphML file for each pomset of the choreography. The tool produces one GraphML file in the **output1** and **output2** for each violation of **CC2-POM** and **CC3-POM** respectively. Additionally, if the **--draw** option is specified, the tool renders the counterexamples as .png in the same directories.

7   Tool Implementation

DiRPROM relies on the NetworkX package for graph operations. In fact, pomsets are represented as direct labelled acyclic graphs. The tool consists of five modules:

- `utils`: provides export of pomsets to png and utilities to build pomsets
- `pomset`: provides functions to process pomsets, e.g. query lists of participants and messages, projections per participant or message, transitive closure and reduction, enumeration of prefixes, enumeration of linearizations
- `inter_closure`: implements inter-participant closure
- `ccpom`: generates the two closure sets and verifies the closure conditions
- `dirpom`: provides the command line utility

dirpom		
utils	ccpom	
	pomsets	inter_closure
NetworkX		

In order to demonstrate the implementation of the analyses and the internal API, we report the implementation of **CC3-POM**:

```python
def cc3closure(graphs):
    # retrieves the list of principals in graphs
    principals = pomset.get_all_principals(graphs)
    # projects the input graphs on principals and yields a map mapping
    # principals to list of "local" pomsets (avoids duplicates)
    local_threads = pomset.get_principal_threads(graphs, principals)
    local_prefixes = {}
    for p in principals:
        # computes all prefixes of all graphs in local_threads[p]
        # (avoids duplicates)
        local_prefixes[p] = pomset.get_prefixes(local_threads[p])
    # generates all tuples in the product of local_prefixes
    tuples = inter_closure.make_tuples(local_prefixes)
    # computes the inter-participant closure of all the tuples
    # (avoids duplicates)
    ipc = inter_closure.inter_process_closure(tuples)
    # computes all prefixes of the input graphs (avoids duplicates)
    prefixes = pomset.get_prefixes(graphs)
    return (ipc, prefixes)

def cc3pom(ipc, prefixes):
    matches = {}
    for i in range(len(ipc)):
        matches[i] = None
        for j in range(len(graphs)):
            # checks if graph[j] is more permissive than ipc[i]
            if (pomset.is_more_permissive(graph[j], ipc[i])):
                matches[i] = j
                break
    return matches
```

8   Tool Evaluation

The main primitive of NetworkX used by the tool is `subgraph_is_ismorphic`, which returns true iff r_1 is (label-preserving) isomorphic to a subgraph of r_2. If r_1 and r_2 have the same number of nodes and the predicates holds then $r_2 \sqsubseteq r_1$.

```
import networkx.algorithms.isomorphism as iso
nm = iso.categorical_node_match('label', '')

def is_more_permissive(g1, g2):
    if len(g1.nodes()) != len(g2.nodes()):
        return False
    m = iso.GraphMatcher(g1, g2, nm)
    return m.subgraph_is_isomorphic()
```

The complexity of finding a label-preserving graph isomorphism is in general exponential in the number of events. However, since the graphs are acyclic, the complexity can be bound to the number of *concurrently-repeated actions*: i.e. events that have the same label, are unordered, and have the same number of predecessor with the same label (e.g. A B!x in R_3). If there are no concurrently repeated actions then isomorphism of pomsetes can be checked in polynomial time with respect to the number of events.

We report the performance of our tool for the examples. The experiments have been executed on a Intel 2.2 GHz i7 with 16 GB of RAM. The table reports the size of the closures, the number of counterexamples, and the processing time in milliseconds.

	CC2-POM	errors	ms	CC3-POM	errors	ms
R_1	2	0	3	38	10	64
R_2	2	1	9	100	18	340
R_3	2	1	16	668	258	9297

In general the evaluation of closure conditions is fast for simple examples. However, the number of prefixes to check in **CC3-POM** can be large when participant have several concurrent threads.

One of the advantages of checking **CC⋆-POM** with respect to previous work [1] is that the former does not require the explicit computation of the language of the family of pomsets, which can lead to combinatorial explosion due to interleavings. In fact, in case of concurrency, the number of prefixes is usually smaller than the number of possible linearizations of a pomset. For example, the following pomset consists of two independent threads, each one consisting of n sequential and distinguished events

$$\begin{bmatrix} e_1 \longrightarrow e_2 \longrightarrow \cdots \longrightarrow e_n \\ e'_1 \longrightarrow e'_2 \longrightarrow \cdots \longrightarrow e'_n \end{bmatrix}$$

The closure condition in [1] requires to directly compute the language of the pomset, which has 2^n words. Instead, the prefix of the pomset are $(n+1)^2$.

As a further example, the set of pomsets R_3 contains one pomset and has two actions that occur in both threads: $A\,B!x$ and $A\,B?x$. The inter-participant closure has exactly two pomsets: the element of R_3 itself and r_3. The left and right subpomsets of R_3, which represent the two threads, have 32 different linearizations, each one consisting of 8 events. Therefore the language of R_3 consists of $32 * 32 * 2^8 = 2^{18}$ words. On the other hand, analyzing **CC3-POM** for R_3 requires to check 668 prefixes.

9   Concluding Remarks

Realisability of specifications is of concern for both practical and theoretical reasons. Several works (e.g., [2,3,7]) defined constraints to guarantee soundness of the implementation of choreographies. These approaches address the problem for specific languages and use conditions that rely on the syntactical structure of the specification. DiRPOMS provides a language independent tool to check realisability of choreographies. Therefore, it can be used for several choreographic models, as long as their semantics can be expressed via set of partial orders.

There two main limitations of DiRPOMS that we plan to address. First, our tool cannot analyze recursive choreographies, since their pomset based semantics is infinite. Even if loops are bounded, naive loop unrolling can easily generate large sets of pomsets which are intractable. Secondly, **CC⋆-POM** conditions are sufficient but not necessary conditions for realisability. In fact, the same set of traces can be expressed using different sets of pomsets by exploring different interleavings. We are currently investigating a notion of normal forms for families of pomsets that can be used to guarantee that our conditions are necessary.

We are also working on optimizing our tool. In particular we think that it is possible to demonstrate equivalence between **CC3-POM** and a different formulation, which requires to check only a subset of prefixes. For instance, in verifying **CC3-POM** for R_3, the analysis of the prefix $\left[\,_{AC!l_i}\quad _{AC!r_i}\right]$ covers also the cases of the prefixes $\left[\,_{AC!l_i}\right]$ and $\left[\,_{AC!r_i}\right]$.

References

1. Alur, R., Etessami, K., Yannakakis, M.: Inference of message sequence charts. IEEE Trans. Softw. Eng. **29**(7), 623–633 (2003). https://doi.org/10.1109/TSE. 2003.1214326
2. Bocchi, L., Melgratti, H., Tuosto, E.: Resolving non-determinism in choreographies. In: Shao, Z. (ed.) ESOP 2014. LNCS, vol. 8410, pp. 493–512. Springer, Heidelberg (2014). https://doi.org/10.1007/978-3-642-54833-8_26
3. Carbone, M., Honda, K., Yoshida, N.: A calculus of global interaction based on session types. Electron Notes Theor. Comput. Sci. **171**(3), 127–151 (2007). https://doi.org/10.1016/j.entcs.2006.12.041
4. Gaifman, H., Pratt, V.R.: Partial order models of concurrency and the computation of functions. In: LICS, pp. 72–85 (1987)
5. Guanciale, R., Tuosto, E.: Realisability of pomsets via communicating automata. CoRR abs/1810.02469 (2018). http://arxiv.org/abs/1810.02469

6. Gunter, E.L., Muscholl, A., Peled, D.A.: Compositional message sequence charts. In: Margaria, T., Yi, W. (eds.) TACAS 2001. LNCS, vol. 2031, pp. 496–511. Springer, Heidelberg (2001). https://doi.org/10.1007/3-540-45319-9_34

7. Honda, K., Yoshida, N., Carbone, M.: Multiparty asynchronous session types. J. ACM **63**(1), 9:1–9:67 (2016). https://doi.org/10.1145/2827695. Extended version of a paper presented at POPL08

8. Lange, J., Tuosto, E., Yoshida, N.: From communicating machines to graphical choreographies. In: POPL 2015, pp. 221–232 (2015)

9. Schulte, E., Davison, D., Dye, T., Dominik, C., et al.: A multi-language computing environment for literate programming and reproducible research. J. Stat. Softw. **46**(3), 1–24 (2012)

10. Van Der Aalst, W.: Process Mining: Discovery, Conformance and Enhancement of Business Processes, vol. 2. Springer, Heidelberg (2011). https://doi.org/10.1007/978-3-642-19345-3

11. WSCDL Version 1.0 (2005). https://www.w3.org/TR/ws-cdl-10/

Coordination of Tasks on a Real-Time OS

Guillermina Cledou[1(✉)], José Proença[1,2(✉)], Bernhard H. C. Sputh[3],
and Eric Verhulst[3]

[1] HASLab/INESC TEC, Universidade do Minho, Braga, Portugal
mgc@inesctec.pt
[2] CISTER, ISEP, Porto, Portugal
pro@isep.ipp.pt
[3] Altreonic NV, Lubbeek, Belgium
{bernhard.sputh,eric.verhulst}@altreonic.com

Abstract. VirtuosoNext™ is a distributed real-time operating system (RTOS) featuring a generic programming model dubbed *Interacting Entities*. This paper focuses on these interactions, implemented as so-called *Hubs*. Hubs act as synchronisation and communication mechanisms between the application tasks and implement the services provided by the kernel as a kind of Guarded Protected Action with a well defined semantics. While the kernel provides the most basic services, each carefully designed, tested and optimised, tasks are limited to this handful of basic hubs, leaving the development of more complex synchronization and communication mechanisms up to application specific implementations. In this work we investigate how to support a programming paradigm to compositionally build new services, using notions borrowed from the Reo coordination language, and relieving tasks from coordination aspects while delegating them to the hubs. We formalise the semantics of hubs using an automata model, identify the behaviour of existing hubs, and propose an approach to build new hubs by composing simpler ones. We also provide tools and methods to analyse and simplify hubs under our automata interpretation. In a first experiment several hub interactions are combined into a single more complex hub, which raises the level of abstraction and contributes to a higher productivity for the programmer. Finally, we investigate the impact on the performance by comparing different implementations on an embedded board.

1 Introduction

When developing software for resource-constrained embedded systems, optimising the utilization of the available resources is a priority. In such systems, many system-level details can influence time and performance in the execution, such as interactions with the cache, mismatches between CPU clock speed, the speed of the external memory, and connected peripherals, leading to unpredictable execution times. VirtuosoNext [16] is a Real Time operating system developed by the company Altreonic that runs efficiently on a range of small embedded devices, and is accompanied by a set of visual development tools – Visual Designer –

© IFIP International Federation for Information Processing 2019
Published by Springer Nature Switzerland AG 2019
H. Riis Nielson and E. Tuosto (Eds.): COORDINATION 2019, LNCS 11533, pp. 250–266, 2019.
https://doi.org/10.1007/978-3-030-22397-7_15

that generates the application framework from a visual description and provides tools to analyse the timing behaviour in detail.

The developer is able to organise a program into a set of individual tasks, scheduled and coordinated by the VirtuosoNext kernel. The coordination of tasks is a non-trivial process. A kernel process uses a priority-based preemptive scheduler deciding which task to run at each time, with hub services used to synchronise and pass data between tasks. A fixed set of hubs is made available by the Visual Designer, which are used to coordinate the tasks. For example, a FIFO hub allows one or more values to be buffered and consumed exactly once, a Semaphore hub uses a counter to synchronise tasks based on counting events, and a Port hub synchronises two tasks, allowing data to be copied between the tasks without being buffered. However, the set of available hubs is limited. Creating new hubs to be included in the mainline distribution is difficult since each hub must be carefully designed, model checked, implemented and tested. It is still possible for users to create specific hubs in their installations, however they would need to fully implement them, losing the assurances of existing hubs.

This paper starts by formalising hubs using an automata model, which we call Hub Automata, inspired in Reo's parametrised constraint automata semantics [1]. This formalism brings several advantages. On the one hand, it brings a generic language to specify hubs, which can be interpreted by VirtuosoNext's kernel task. New hubs can be built by specifying new Hub Automata, or by composing the Hub Automata from existing hubs. On the other hand, it allows existing (and new) hubs to be formally analysed, estimating performance and memory consumption, and verifying desired properties upfront. Furthermore, we show that by using more specific hubs one can shift some of the coordination burden from the tasks to the hubs, leading to easier and less error prone programming of complex protocols, as well as leaving room for optimizations. In some cases it can also reduce the amount of context switches between application tasks and the kernel task of VirtuosoNext, improving performance.

We implemented a prototype implementation, available online,[1] to compose hubs based on our Hub Automata semantics, and to analyse and simplify them. We also compared the execution times on an embedded system between different orchestration scenarios of tasks, one using existing hubs and another using a more refined hub built out of the composition of hubs, evidencing the performance gains and overheads of using composed hubs.

Summarising, our key contributions are the formalisation of coordinating hubs in VirtuosoNext (Sect. 3), a compositional semantics of hubs (Sect. 4), and a set of tools to compose and analyse hubs, together with a short evaluation of the execution times of a given scenario using composed hubs (Sect. 5).

2   Distributed Tasks in VirtuosoNext

A VirtuosoNext *system* is executed on a target system, composed of processing *nodes* and communication *links*. Orthogonally, an *application* consists of a

---

[1] http://github.com/arcalab/hubAutomata.

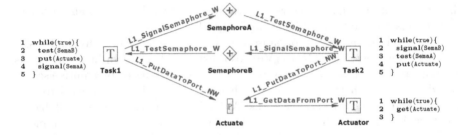

Fig. 1. Example architecture in VirtuosoNext, where two tasks communicate with an actuator in a round robin sequence through two semaphores and a port.

number of *tasks* coordinated by *hubs*. Unlike links, hubs are independent of the hardware topology. When building application images, the code generators of VirtuosoNext map tasks and hubs onto specific nodes, taking into account the target platforms. A special *kernel task*, running on each node, controls the scheduler of tasks, the hub services, and the internode communication and routing.

This section starts by giving a small overview of how tasks are built and composed, followed by a more detailed description over existing hubs.

2.1   Example of an Architecture

A program in VirtuosoNext is a fixed set of tasks, each running on a given computational node, and interacting with each other via dedicated interaction entities, called hubs. Consider the example architecture in Fig. 1, where tasks Task1 and Task2 send instructions to an Actuator task in a round robin sequence. SemaphoreA tracks the end of Task1 and the beginning of Task2, while SemaphoreB does the reverse, and port Actuate forwards the instructions from each task to the Actuator. In this case two Semaphore hubs were used, depicted by the diamond shape with a '+', and a Port hub, depicted by a box with a 'P'. Tasks and hubs can be deployed on different processing nodes, but this paper will consider only programs deployed in the same node, and hence omit references to nodes. This and similar examples can be found in the VirtuosoNext's manual [13].

2.2   Task Coordination via Hubs

Hubs are coordination mechanisms between tasks, which can be interacted with via *put* and *get* service requests to transfer information from one task to another. This can be a data element, the notification of an event occurrence, or some logical entity that needs to be protected for atomic access. A call to a hub constitutes a descheduling point in the tasks' execution. The behaviour depends on which hub is selected, e.g. tasks can simply synchronise (with no data being transferred) or synchronise while transferring data (either buffered or non-buffered). Other hubs include the Resource hub, often used to request atomic access to a resource, and hubs that act as gateways to peripheral hardware.

Table 1. Examples of existing Hubs in VirtuosoNext

Hub	Waiting Lists for Service Requests
P Port	**put** – signals some data entering the port; and **get** – signals some data leaving the port. Both must synchronize to succeed.
◇ Event	**raise** – sets an event. Succeeds if not set yet; and **test** – checks if an event happened, in which case succeeds, and clears the event.
◌ DataEvent	**update** – sets an event and buffers some data, overriding any previous data. Always succeeds; **read** – reads the data. Succeeds if the event is set; and **clear** – clears the buffer and the event.
⊕ Semaphore	**signal** – signals the semaphore, incrementing an internal counter c. Succeeds if $c < MAX$;[a] and **test** – checks if $c > 0$, in which case succeeds, and decrements c.
🔒 Resource	**lock** – locks a logical resource and buffers the **id** of the requesting task. Succeeds only if the resource is free; and **unlock** – unlocks the resource. Succeeds only if locked by the same task.
⊞⊞ FIFO	**enqueue** – buffers some data in the queue. Succeeds if the queue is not full; and **dequeue** – gets data from the queue. Succeeds if the queue is not empty.
BB Blackboard	**update** – buffers some data, overriding any previews data, incrementing a sequence number. Always succeeds; **read** – reads the data and the sequence number. Succeeds if not empty. Reader tasks can use the sequence number to attest the freshness of the data; and **wipe** – clears the buffer.

[a] Here, MAX represents L1_UINT32_MAX in VirtuosoNext[TM], which is $2^{32} - 1$.

Any number of tasks can make put or get requests to a given hub. Such requests will be queued in waiting lists (at each corresponding hub) until they can be served. Waiting lists are ordered by task priority – requests get served by following such an order. In addition, requests can use different interaction semantics. As such, the interaction can be *blocking, non-blocking* or *blocking with a time-out*, which will determine how much time, if any, a task will wait on a request to succeed – indefinitely, none, or a certain amount of time, respectively.

There are various hubs available, each with its predefined semantics [13]. Table 1 describes some of them and their put and get service request methods.

3   Deconstructing Hubs

This section formalises *hubs*, using an automata model with variables, providing a syntax (Sect. 3.1) and a semantics (Sect. 3.2).

3.1   Syntax

We formalise the behavioural semantics of a hub using an automata model, which we call *Hub Automata*. We start by introducing some preliminary concepts.

Definition 1 (Guard). *A guard $\phi \in \Phi$ is a logical formula given by the grammar below, where $x \in \mathcal{X}$ is a variable, $\overline{x}$ denotes a sequence of variables, and pred $\in \mathcal{P}$red is a predicate.*

$$\phi \; := \; \top \mid \bot \mid pred(\overline{x}) \mid \phi \vee \phi \mid \phi \wedge \phi \mid \neg\phi$$

We say $\Phi(\mathcal{X})$ is the set of all possible guards over variables in $\mathcal{X}$.

Definition 2 (Update). *An update $u \in \mathcal{U}$ is an assignment of variables $x \in \mathcal{X}$ to expressions $e \in \mathcal{E}$, a sequence of updates, or updates in parallel, given by the grammar below, where $d \in \mathcal{D}$ is a data value, and $f \in \mathcal{F}$ is a deterministic function without side-effects.*

$$u \; := \; x \leftarrow e \mid u; u \mid u|u \qquad\qquad (update)$$

$$e \; := \; d \mid x \mid f(\overline{x}) \qquad\qquad (expression)$$

We write $\mathcal{U}(\mathcal{X})$ to denote the set of all updates over variables in $\mathcal{X}$.

For example, the update $a \leftarrow 2; (b \leftarrow c + 1 \mid c \leftarrow \mathtt{getData}())$ is an update that starts by setting a to 2, and then sets b to $c + 1$ and c to $\mathtt{getData}()$ in some (a-priori unknown) order. Note that the order of evaluation of the parallel assignments will affect the final result. We avoid non-determinism by following up dependencies (e.g., $c \leftarrow \mathtt{getData}()$ should be executed before $b \leftarrow c+1$) and by requiring that the order of executing any two independent assignments does not affect the result. This will be formalised later in the paper.

Hubs interact with the environment through ports that represent actions. Let $\mathcal{P}$ be the set of all possible ports uniquely identified. For a $p \in \mathcal{P}$, $\hat{p}$ is a variable holding a data value flowing through port p. We use $\hat{\mathcal{P}}$ to represent the set of all data variables associated to ports in $\mathcal{P}$.

Definition 3 (Hub Automata). *A Hub Automaton is a tuple $H = (L, \ell_0, P, \mathcal{X}, v_0, \rightarrow)$ where L is a finite set of locations, ℓ_0 is the initial location, $P = P_I \uplus P_O$, is a finite set of ports, with P_I and P_O representing the disjoint sets of input and output ports, respectively, $\mathcal{X}$ is a finite set of internal variables, $v_0 : \mathcal{X} \rightarrow \mathcal{D}$ is the initial valuation that maps variables in $\mathcal{X}$ to a value in $\mathcal{D}$, and $\rightarrow \subseteq L \times \Phi(\mathcal{X} \cup \hat{\mathcal{P}}) \times 2^P \times \mathcal{U}(\mathcal{X} \cup \hat{\mathcal{P}}) \times L$ is the transition relation.*

For a given transition $(l, g, \omega, u, l') \in \rightarrow$, also written $l \xrightarrow{g,\omega,u} l'$, l is the source location, g is the guard defining the enabling condition, ω is the set of ports triggering the transition, u is the update triggered, and l' is the target location.

Informally, a Hub Automaton is a finite automaton enriched with *variables* and an *initial valuation* of such variables; and where transitions are enriched with *multi-action* transitions, and *logic guards* and *updates* over variables. A transition $l \xrightarrow{g,\omega,u} l'$ is enabled only if (1) all of its ports ω are ready to be executed simultaneously, and (2) the current valuation satisfies the associated guard g. Performing this transition means applying the update u to the current valuation, and moving to location l'. This is formalised in the following section.

Figure 2 depicts the Hub Automata for each of the hubs described in Sect. 2.2, except the Resource hub (for space restrictions). Consider, for example, the Hub Automaton for the FIFO hub, implemented using an internal circular queue, with size N and with elements of type T. Initially, the FIFO is at location *idle* and its internal variables are assigned as follows: $c \mapsto 0$, $f \mapsto 0$, $p \mapsto 0$, and $bf_i \mapsto null$ for all $i \in \{0 \ldots N-1\}$. Here c is the current number of elements in the queue, f and p are the pointers to the front and last empty place of the queue, respectively, and each bf_i holds the value of the i-th position in the queue. The FIFO can *enqueue* an element —if the queue is not full $(c < N)$—storing the incoming data value in bf_p, and increasing the c and p counters; or it can *dequeue* an element—if the queue is not empty $(c \geq 1)$, updating the corresponding variables.

Note that more than one task can be using the same port of a given hub. In these cases VirtuosoNext selects one of the tasks to be executed, using its scheduling algorithm. The semantics of this behaviour is illustrated in the automaton of Port†, that uses multiple incoming and outgoing ports, denoting all possible combinations of inputs and outputs. This exercise can be applied to any other hub other than the Port hub.

Hub Automata can be used to describe new hubs to restrict synchronous interactions between tasks. Figure 2 includes two hubs that do not exist in VirtuosoNext (hubs with *): a Duplicator broadcasts a given input to two outputs atomically, and a Drain receives two inputs synchronously without storing any value.

3.2 Semantics

We start by defining guard satisfaction, used by the semantics of Hub Automata.

Definition 4 (Guard Satisfaction). *The satisfaction of a guard g by a variable valuation v, written $v \models g$, is defined as*

$$
\begin{aligned}
&v \models \top &&\text{always} &\qquad& v \models \phi_1 \wedge \phi_2 &&\text{if } v \models \phi_1 \text{ and } v \models \phi_2 \\
&v \models \bot &&\text{never} && v \models \phi_1 \vee \phi_2 &&\text{if } v \models \phi_1 \text{ or } v \models \phi_2 \\
&v \models \neg\phi &&\text{if } v \not\models \phi && v \models pred(\overline{x}) &&\text{if } pred(v(\overline{x})) \text{ evaluates to } \mathsf{true}
\end{aligned}
$$

Definition 5 (Update application). *Given a serialisation function σ that converts general updates into sequences of assignments, the application of an update u to a valuation v is given by $v[\sigma(u)]$, where $v[-]$ is defined below.*

$$
\begin{aligned}
&v[x \leftarrow e](x) = e \\
&v[x \leftarrow e](y) = v(y) \text{ if } x \neq y
\end{aligned}
\qquad\qquad
v[u_1; u_2](x) = (v[u_1])[u_2](x)
$$

The serialisation function σ is formalised in Sect. 4.3, after describing how to compose Hub Automata. We will omit σ when not relevant. The execution of an automaton is defined as sequences of steps that do not violate the guards, and such that each step updates the current variable valuation according to the corresponding update.

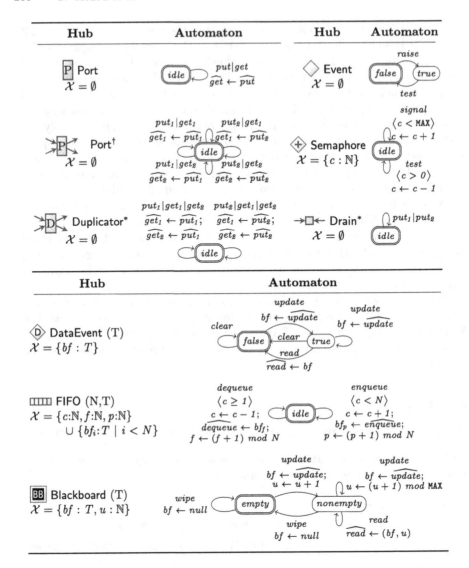

Fig. 2. Automata semantics of hubs – from VirtuosoNext except those with *. Port[†] captures how VirtuosoNext interprets multiple calls to the same port.

Definition 6 (Semantics of Hubs). *The semantics of a Hub Automaton* $H = (L, \ell_0, P, \mathcal{X}, v_0, \rightarrow)$ *is given by the rule below, starting on configuration* (ℓ_0, v_0).

$$\frac{\ell \xrightarrow{g,p,u} \ell' \quad v \models g \quad v' = v[u]}{(\ell, v) \xrightarrow{p} (\ell', v')} \quad \text{(seq)}$$

For example, the following is a valid trace of a Fifo hub with size 3 (Fig. 2).

$$(idle, \{c \mapsto 0, f \mapsto 0, p \mapsto 0, bf_0 \mapsto null, bf_1 \mapsto null, bf_2 \mapsto null\})$$
$$\xrightarrow{enqueue} (idle, \{c \mapsto 1, f \mapsto 0, p \mapsto 1, bf_0 \mapsto 42, \quad bf_1 \mapsto null, bf_2 \mapsto null\})$$
$$\xrightarrow{dequeue} (idle, \{c \mapsto 0, f \mapsto 1, p \mapsto 1, bf_0 \mapsto 42, \quad bf_1 \mapsto null, bf_2 \mapsto null\})$$

4 Reconstructing Hubs

Two hubs can be composed to form a more complex one, following the same ideas as in Reo [1]. The composition is done on top of two simpler operations: *product* and *synchronisation*. This section starts by defining these two operations, followed by an example and by a suitable definition of serialisation of updates.

4.1 Hub Composition

The *product* takes two hubs with disjoint ports and variables, and produces a new hub where they behave in an interleaving or synchronous fashion, i.e. fully concurrent. The *synchronisation* operation is conducted over a Hub Automaton H and it links two ports a and b in P such that they can only operate in a synchronous manner.

Definition 7 (Product of Hub Automata). *Let H_1 and H_2 be two Hub Automata with disjoint sets of ports and variables. The product of H_1 and H_2, written $H_1 \times H_2$, is a new Hub Automaton defined as*

$$H = (L_1 \times L_2, (l_{0_1}, l_{0_2}), P_1 \cup P_2, \mathcal{X}_1 \cup \mathcal{X}_2, v_{0_1} \cup v_{0_2}, \rightarrow)$$

where $\rightarrow$ is defined as follows:

$$\frac{l_1 \xrightarrow{g_1, \omega_1, u_1} l_1'}{(l_1, l_2) \xrightarrow{g_1, \omega_1, u_1} (l_1', l_2)} \qquad \frac{l_2 \xrightarrow{g_2, \omega_2, u_2} l_2'}{(l_1, l_2) \xrightarrow{g_2, \omega_2, u_2} (l_1, l_2')} \qquad \frac{l_1 \xrightarrow{g_1, \omega_1, u_1} l_1' \quad l_2 \xrightarrow{g_2, \omega_2, u_2} l_2'}{(l_1, l_2) \xrightarrow{g_1 \wedge g_2, \omega_1 \cup \omega_2, u_1 | u_2} (l_1', l_2')}$$

Definition 8 (Synchronisation of Hub Automata). *Let H be a Hub Automaton, a and b two ports in P, and x_{ab} a fresh variable. The synchronisation of a and b is given by $\Delta_{a,b}(H)$, defined below.*

$$\Delta_{a,b}(H) = (L, l_0, (P \backslash \{a, b\}), \mathcal{X} \cup \{x_{ab}\}, v_0, \rightarrow')$$
$$\rightarrow' = \{l \xrightarrow{g, \omega, u} l' \mid a \notin \omega \text{ and } b \notin \omega\} \cup$$
$$\{l \xrightarrow{g', \omega', u'} l' \mid l \xrightarrow{g, \omega, u} l', a \in \omega, b \in \omega, \omega' = \omega \backslash \{a, b\},$$
$$g' = g[x_{ab}/\hat{a}][x_{ab}/\hat{b}], \ u' = u[x_{ab}/\hat{a}][x_{ab}/\hat{b}]\}$$

where $g[x/y]$ and $u[x/y]$, are the logic guard and the update that result from replacing all appearances of variable y with x, respectively.

The composition of two Hub Automata consists of their product followed by the synchronisation of their shared ports.

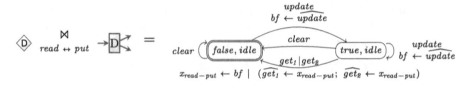

Fig. 3. Example of composition between two Hub Automata, where a DataEvent automaton is composed with a Duplicator automaton by synchronising on actions *read* and *put* (left), resulting in the composed automaton on the right.

Definition 9 (Composition of Hub Automata). *Let H_1 and H_2 be two Hub Automata with disjoint sets of ports and variables, and let $\{(a_0, b_0), \ldots, (a_n, b_n)\}$ be a finite (possibly empty) set of ports bindings, such that for each pair (a_i, b_i) for $0 \le i \le n$ we have that $(a_i, b_i) \in P_{I_{H_1}} \times P_{O_{H_2}}$ or $(a_i, b_i) \in P_{O_{H_1}} \times P_{I_{H_2}}$. The composition of H_1 and H_2 over such a set is defined as follows.*

$$H_1 \bowtie_{(a_0, b_0), \ldots, (a_n, b_n)} H_2 = \Delta_{a_0, b_0} \ldots \Delta_{a_n, b_n} (H_1 \times H_2)$$

Intuitively, composing two automata means putting them in parallel ($\times$), and then restrict their behaviour by forcing shared ports to go together (Δ). The first step joins concurrent transition into new transitions, placing updates in parallel. This emphasises the need for a serialisation process that guarantees a correct evaluation order of values to data in ports, which is the focus of Sect. 4.3.

Figure 3 shows the composition of two Hub Automaton: a DataEvent, and a Duplicator with two output points. The composed automaton (right) illustrates the behaviour of the two hubs when synchronised over the actions *read* and *put*: whenever a data event is raised and the buffer updated, the hub can be tested simultaneously by two tasks through get_1 and get_2. Both tasks will receive the stored data in the DataEvent Hub, before setting the event to false. Synchronised ports are removed from the composed model, and variables associated to such ports are renamed accordingly, i.e. $\widehat{read}$ and $\widehat{put}$, are both renamed to $x_{read\text{-}put}$.

4.2 Example: Round Robin Tasks

Consider the example architecture in Fig. 1, consisting of 3 independent hubs. Such architectures with independent hubs can be combined into a single hub, but it brings little or no advantage because it will produce all possible interleavings and state combinations. In this case, the joint automaton has 1 state and 26 transitions, representing the possible non-empty combinations of transitions from the 3 hubs. More concretely, the set of transitions is the union of the 5 sets below, abstracting away data, where p_i, s_i and t_i denote the *put*, *signal* and *test* actions of task i, respectively, and g denotes the *get* action of the actuator.

$$P = \{p_1 | g\,, \; p_2 | get\}$$
$$A \| B = \{s_1, s_2, t_1, t_2\}$$
$$A\&B = \{x_1 | x_2 \;\; | \;\; x_1 \in \{s_1, t_1\}\,, x_2 \in \{s_2, t_2\}\}$$
$$P\&A \| B = \{p_i | g | x \;\; | \;\; i \in \{1, 2\}, x \in A \| B\}$$
$$P\&A\&B = \{p_i | g | x \;\; | \;\; i \in \{1, 2\}, x \in A\&B\}$$

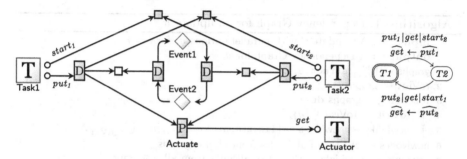

Fig. 4. Alternative architecture for the example in Fig. 1 – Reo connector (left) and its Hub Automaton (right) after updates have been serialised and simplified.

We propose an alternative hub that exploits shared ports (Fig. 4), built by composing a set of primitives from Fig. 2, which further restricts the behaviour of the coordinator. More specifically, when a task sends a data value to the actuator, the coordinator interprets it as the end of its round. Furthermore, it requires each task to send only when the other is ready to start – a different behaviour could be implemented to buffer the end of a task round (as in Fig. 1).

4.3   Serialisation of Updates

Recall that the application of an update u (Definition 5) requires a serialisation function σ that converts an update with parallel constructs into a sequence of assignments. This subsection proposes a serialisation algorithm that preserves dependencies between variables, and rejects updates that have variables with circular dependencies. It uses an intermediate dependency graph that is traversed based on Kahn's algorithm [9], and later discards intermediate assignments.

Consider the transition $(true, idle) \xrightarrow{get_1 \mid get_2, u_1 \mid u_2} (false, idle)$ from Fig. 3, where $u_1 = x_{read\text{-}put} \leftarrow bf$ and $u_2 = \widehat{get_1} \leftarrow x_{read\text{-}put};\ \widehat{get_2} \leftarrow x_{read\text{-}put}$. Here, u_2 depends on a variable produced by u_1. Thus, a serialisation of $u_1 \mid u_2$ is $u_s = u_1; u_2$. Once serialised, u_s has an intermediate assignment, $x_{read\text{-}put} \leftarrow bf$, which can be removed by replacing appearances of $x_{read\text{-}put}$ with bf, leading to $\widehat{get_1} \leftarrow bf;\ \widehat{get_2} \leftarrow bf$, reducing the number of assignments and variables needed.

Building Dependency Graphs. A dependency graph is a directed graph $D = (N, L)$, where N is a set of nodes, each representing an update of the form $x \leftarrow e$, and $L \subseteq N \times N$ is a set of links between nodes, where a link (n, m) indicates that n must appear before m in a sequence of assignments. Given D_1 and D_2, their composition, $D_1 \bowtie D_2 = (N_1 \cup N_2, L_1 \cup L_2)$ is a new dependency graph.

Given a dependency graph $D = (N, L)$, we say a node n is a *leaf* ($\mathtt{leaf}_L(n)$) if $\nexists_{(m,o) \in L} \cdot o = n$, or a a *root* ($\mathtt{root}_L(n)$) if $\nexists_{(o,m) \in L} \cdot o = m$. We first define $\mathtt{struct}(u)$ recursively to consider dependencies between assignments imposed by the structure of the update (i.e., imposed by ; and |), defined as follows.

Algorithm 1. Dependency Graph for an update u

---
    input   : An update u with parallel options u_i for $i = 1..n$
    output : A Dependency Graph for u
1 graphs $\leftarrow \bigcup_{i=1}^{n}$ struct(u_i);
2 toVisit $\leftarrow$ graphs;
3 **foreach** $g \in$ graphs **do**
4 | toVisit $\leftarrow$ toVisit $\setminus \{g\}$;
5 | newLinks $\leftarrow$ newLinks $\cup \{$links$(n, m) \mid n \in N_g, m \in \bigcup_{v \in \text{toVisit}} N_v\}$;
6 newNodes $\leftarrow$ the set of all nodes from all $g \in$ graphs;
7 newLinks $\leftarrow$ newLinks $\cup$ the set of all links from all $g \in$ graphs;
8 **return** *A dependency graph with* newNodes *and* newLinks;

$$\frac{\text{struct}(x \leftarrow e)}{(\{x \leftarrow e\}, \{\})} \qquad \frac{\text{struct}(u_1 \mid u_2)}{\text{struct}(u_1) \bowtie \text{struct}(u_2)}$$

$$\frac{\text{struct}(u_1 \; ; \; u_2), \ \text{struct}(u_1) = (N_1, L_1), \ \text{struct}(u_2) = (N_2, L_2)}{(N_1 \cup N_2, L_1 \cup L_2 \cup \{(n, m) \mid n \in N_1, \text{leaf}_{L_1}(n), m \in N_2, \text{root}_{L_2}(m)\})}$$

Secondly, we create dependency links between nodes of different subgraphs of u (generated by |) based on their dependency on variables. These links between two nodes n and m, noted as links(n, m), are created as follows: from n to m if m depends on a variable produced by n; from m to n if n depends on a variable produced by m; and both ways if both conditions apply.

The complete algorithm to build a dependency graph is given in Algorithm 1. If the graph is not acyclic, Kahn's algorithm will return a topological order.

Simplification of Updates. This step considers all transitions of the automaton to find and remove unnecessary and intermediate assignments. We consider *unnecessary assignments*: assignments to internal variables that are never used on the right-hand side (RHS) of an assignment nor on a guard; and assignments that depend only of internal variables that are never assigned (undefined variables). We consider *intermediate assignments*, assignments to internal variables that are followed by (eventually in the same sequence) an assignment where the variable is used on the RHS, and such that the variable is never used on guards.

5 Evaluation

We compare the two architectures from Sect. 4.2, using a variation of these, and provide both an analytical comparison, using different metrics, and a performance comparison, executing them in an embedded board.

Scenarios. We compare four different scenarios in our evaluation, using the architectures from Sect. 4.2, and compile and execute them on a TI Launchpad EK-TM4C1294XL[2] board with a 120 MHz 32-bit ARM Cortex-M4 CPU.

---
[2] http://www.ti.com/tool/EK-TM4C1294XL.

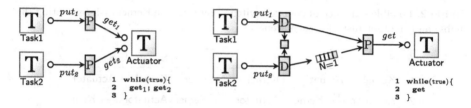

Fig. 5. Architectural view of scenarios $S_{2\text{-}ports}$ (left) and S_{altern} (right).

- S_{orig} the initial architecture as in Fig. 1;
- S_{custom} using a custom-made hub that follows the automaton in Fig. 4 without any data transfer;
- S_{altern} using a custom-made hub that acts as S_{custom}, but discarding the **start** queues, and assuming that tasks start as soon as possible (Fig. 5 right); and
- $S_{2\text{-}ports}$ simple architecture with two ports, each connecting a task to the actuator, also discarding the **start** queue, whereas the actuator is responsible to impose the alternating behaviour (Fig. 5 left).

Observe that S_{altern} and $S_{2\text{-}ports}$ are meant to produce the same behaviour, but only the latter is compiled and executed. While S_{altern} assumes that the actuator is oblivious of who sends the instructions, $S_{2\text{-}ports}$ relies on the actuator to perform the coordination task.

Analytic Comparison. We claim that the alternative architecture requires less memory and requires less context switches (and hence is expected to execute faster). Memory can be approximated by adding up the number of variables and states. The original example uses a stateless hub (a Port) and two Semaphores, each also stateless but with an integer variable each—hence requiring the storage of 2 integers. The refined example requires 2 states and no variables (after simplification), hence a single bit is enough to encode its state.

Table 2 lists possible sequence of context switches for each of the 4 proposed scenarios, for each round where both tasks send an instruction to the actuator. Observe that S_{orig} requires the most context switches for each pair of values sent (17), while $S_{2\text{-}ports}$ and S_{altern} require the least (9).

Note that conceptually the original architecture further requires the tasks to be well behaved, in the sense that a task should not signal/test a semaphore more times than the other task tests/signals it. In the refined architecture functionality is better encapsulated: tasks abstract from implementing coordination behaviour and focus only on sending data to the actuator, while the coordinator handles the order in which tasks are enabled to send the data. This contributes to a better understanding of the behaviour of both the tasks and the coordination mechanism. In addition, by knowing the semantics of each hub and by looking at the architecture in Fig. 1 is not enough to determine the behaviour of the composed architecture, but it requires to look at the implementation of the

Table 2. Possible sequence of context switches between the Kernel task (executing the hubs) and the user tasks for each scenario.

#	S_{orig}	S_{custom}	$S_{2\text{-}ports}$ & S_{altern}
1	Kernel → Actuator	Kernel → Actuator	Kernel → Actuator
2	Actuator $\xrightarrow{get}$ Kernel	Actuator $\xrightarrow{get}$ Kernel	Actuator $\xrightarrow{get}$ Kernel
3	Kernel → Task2	Kernel → Task1	Kernel → Task1
4	Task2 $\xrightarrow{signalB}$ Kernel	Task1 $\xrightarrow{put}$ Kernel	Task1 $\xrightarrow{put}$ Kernel
5	Kernel → Task1	Kernel → Task2	Kernel → Actuator
6	Task1 $\xrightarrow{testB}$ Kernel	Task2 $\xrightarrow{start}$ Kernel	Actuator $\xrightarrow{get}$ Kernel
7	Kernel → Task1	Kernel → Actuator	Kernel → Task2
8	Task1 $\xrightarrow{put}$ Kernel	Actuator $\xrightarrow{get}$ Kernel	Task2 $\xrightarrow{put}$ Kernel
9	Kernel → Actuator	Kernel → Task2	Kernel → Actuator
10	Actuator $\xrightarrow{get}$ Kernel	Task2 $\xrightarrow{put}$ Kernel	(Repeat from #2)
11	Kernel → Task1	Kernel → Task1	
12	Task1 $\xrightarrow{signalA}$ Kernel	Task1 $\xrightarrow{start}$ Kernel	
13	Kernel → Task2	Kernel → Actuator	
14	Task2 $\xrightarrow{testA}$ Kernel	(Repeat from #2)	
15	Kernel → Task2		
16	Task2 $\xrightarrow{put}$ Kernel		
17	Kernel → Actuator		
18	(Repeat from #2)		

tasks to get a better understanding of what happens. However, in Fig. 4 these two premises are sufficient to understand the composed behaviour.

Measuring Execution Times on the Target Processor. We compiled, executed, and measured the execution of 4 systems: (1) S_{orig}, (2) a variation of S_{custom} implemented as a dedicated task, which we call $Task[S_{custom}]$, (3) a variation of S_{custom} that abstracts away from the actual instructions (implemented as a native hub, which we call $NoData[S_{custom}]$)!b, and (4) $S_{2\text{-}ports}$. The results of executing 1000 rounds using our TI Launchpad board are presented below, whereas the end of each round consists of the actuator receiving an instruction from both tasks (i.e., 500 values from each task).

	S_{orig}	$Task[S_{custom}]$	$NoData[S_{custom}]$	$S_{2\text{-}ports}$
Time (ms)	41.88	64.27	32.19	21.16

These numbers provide some insight regarding the cost of coordination. On one hand, avoiding the loop of semaphores can double the performance (S_{orig} vs. $S_{2\text{-}ports}$). On the other hand, replacing the loop of semaphores by a dedicated hub that includes interactions with the actuator can reduce the execution time to around 75% (S_{orig} vs. $NoData[S_{custom}]$). Note that this dedicated hub does not perform data communication, and the tasks do not send any data in any of the scenarios. Finally, $Task[S_{custom}]$ reflects the cost of building a custom hub as a user task, connected to the coordinated tasks using extra (basic) hubs, which can be seen as the price for the flexibility of complex hubs without the burden of implementing a dedicated hub.

Online Analysis Tools. We implemented a prototype that composes, simplifies, and analyses Hub Automata, available online,[3] and depicted in Fig. 6. The generated automata can be used to produce either new hubs or dedicated tasks that perform coordination. These generated automata can also be formally analysed to provide key insight information regarding the usefulness and drawbacks of such a hub. Our current implementation allows specifications of composed hubs using a textual representation based on ReoLive [3,14], and produces (1) the architectural view of the hub, (2) the simplified automaton of the hub, and (3) a summary of some properties of the automaton, such as required memory, size estimation of the code, information about which hubs' ports are always ready to synchronise, and minimum number of context switches for a given trace.

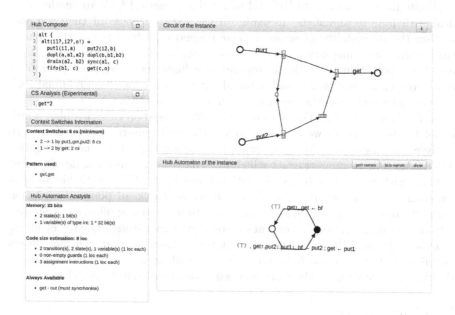

Fig. 6. Screenshot of the online analyser for VirtuosoNext's hubs.

---

[3] http://github.com/arcalab/hubAutomata

6   Related Work

The global architecture of VirtuosoNext RTOS, including the interaction with hubs, has been formally analysed using TLA+ by Verhulst et al. [16]. More concretely, the authors specify a set of concrete hubs, their waiting lists, and the priority of requests, and use the TLC model checker to verify a set of safety properties over these. Our approach uses a formalism focused on the interactions, abstracting away waiting lists, and aims at the analysis and code generation of more complex hubs built compositionally.

The automata model proposed here is mainly inspired by Reo's paramiterised constraint automata [1] and constraint automata with memory cells [8], both used to reason about data-dependent coordination mechanism. In the former states can store variables which are updated or initialised when transiting, while the latter treats variables as first-class objects, as in here, allowing to efficiently deal with infinite data domains. Both approaches use data constraints as a way to assign values to ports, and define updates as a way to modify internal variables. Here, we treat both variables more uniformly, requiring a serialization method, and postponing it until obtaining the final composed automaton.

The composition and the restrictions imposed here on the input and output ports are similar to those introduced by Interface Automata [4] to deal with the composition of open systems. However, [4] imposes additional restrictions to ensure automata compatibility, i.e. whenever an automaton is ready to send an output, which is an input of the other, the latter should be able to receive it.

Finite-memory automata [10] and nominal automata [12,15] are models that deal with infinite alphabets, focusing on the expressiveness of their variants and on the decidability of some of their properties, which is not the goal of this paper. Finite-memory automata uses substitution instead of equality tests over the input alphabet with the support of a finite set of registers (variables) associated to the automata, and nominal automata are based on nominal sets, which can be seen as infinite sets with a finite representation.

Formal analysis of RTOS are more typically focused on the scheduler, which is not the focus of this work. For example, theorem provers have been used to analyse schedulers for avionics software [7]. Carnevali et al. [2] use preemptive Time Petri Nets to support exact scheduling analysis and guide the development of tasks with non-deterministic execution times in an RTOS with hierarchical scheduling. Dietrich et al. [5] analyse and model check all possible execution paths of a real-time system to tailor the kernel to particular application scenarios, resulting in optimisations in execution speed and robustness. Dokter et al. [6] propose a framework to synthesise optimised schedulers that consider delays introduced by interaction between tasks. Scheduling is interpreted as a game that requires minimising the time between subsequent context switches.

7   Conclusions

This paper proposes an approach to build and analyse hubs in VirtuosoNext, which are services used to orchestrate interacting tasks in a Real Time OS that runs on embedded devices. In VirtuosoNext, complex coordination mechanisms are the responsibility of the programmer, who can use a set of fundamental hubs to coordinate tasks, but have to implement more complex interaction mechanisms as application specific code, deteriorating readability and maintainability.

Our proposed formal framework provides mechanisms to design and implement complex hubs that can be formally analysed to provide the same level of assurance that predefined hubs provide. Currently, the framework allows to build complex hubs out of simpler ones, and analyse some aspects of the hubs such as: memory used, estimated lines of codes, and always available ports.

Preliminary tests on a typical set of scenarios have confirmed our hypothesis that using dedicated hubs to perform custom coordination can result in performance improvements. In addition, we claim that moving coordination aspects away from tasks enables a better understanding of the tasks and hubs behaviour, and provides better visual feedback regarding the semantics of the system.

Ongoing work to extend our formal framework includes: **runtime behaviour analysis,** by taking into account the time-sensitive requests made to hubs and some contracts that tasks are expected to obey; **variability support** to analyse and improve the development of families of systems in VirtuosoNext, since VirtuosoNext provides a simple and error-prone mechanism to allow topologies to be applied to the same set of tasks; **code refactoring and generation** applied to existing (on-production) VirtuosoNext programs, probably adding new primitive hubs, by extracting the coordination logic from tasks and into new complex hubs; and **analysis extension** to support a wider range of analysis to Hub Automata, such as the number of context switches required to perform certain behaviour, or the model checking of liveness and safety properties using mCRL2 (c.f. [3,11]).

Acknowledgements. This work is financed by the ERDF – European Regional Development Fund through the Operational Programme for Competitiveness and Internationalisation – COMPETE 2020 Programme and by National Funds through the Portuguese funding agency, FCT – Fundação para a Ciência e a Tecnologia, within project POCI-01-0145-FEDER-029946 (DaVinci). This work is also partially supported by National Funds through FCT, within the CISTER Research Unit (UID/CEC/04234); also by the Norte Portugal Regional Operational Programme (NORTE 2020) under the Portugal 2020 Partnership Agreement, through ERDF and also by national funds through the FCT, within project NORTE-01-0145-FEDER-028550 (REASSURE).

References

1. Baier, C., Sirjani, M., Arbab, F., Rutten, J.J.M.M.: Modeling component connectors in Reo by constraint automata. Sci. Comput. Program. **61**(2), 75–113 (2006)
2. Carnevali, L., Lipari, G., Pinzuti, A., Vicario, E.: A formal approach to design and verification of two-level hierarchical scheduling systems. In: Romanovsky, A., Vardanega, T. (eds.) Ada-Europe 2011. LNCS, vol. 6652, pp. 118–131. Springer, Heidelberg (2011). https://doi.org/10.1007/978-3-642-21338-0_9

3. Cruz, R., Proença, J.: ReoLive: analysing connectors in your browser. In: Mazzara, M., Ober, I., Salaün, G. (eds.) STAF 2018. LNCS, vol. 11176, pp. 336–350. Springer, Cham (2018). https://doi.org/10.1007/978-3-030-04771-9_25

4. de Alfaro, L., Henzinger, T.A.: Interface-based design. In: Broy, M., Grünbauer, J., Harel, D., Hoare, T. (eds.) Engineering Theories of Software Intensive Systems. NSS, vol. 195, pp. 83–104. Springer, Dordrecht (2005). https://doi.org/10.1007/1-4020-3532-2_3

5. Dietrich, C., Hoffmann, M., Lohmann, D.: Global optimization of fixed-priority real-time systems by rtos-aware control-flow analysis. ACM Trans. Embed. Comput. Syst. **16**(2), 35:1–35:25 (2017). https://doi.org/10.1145/2950053

6. Dokter, K., Jongmans, S.-S., Arbab, F.: Scheduling games for concurrent systems. In: Lluch Lafuente, A., Proença, J. (eds.) COORDINATION 2016. LNCS, vol. 9686, pp. 84–100. Springer, Cham (2016). https://doi.org/10.1007/978-3-319-39519-7_6

7. Ha, V., Rangarajan, M., Cofer, D., Rues, H., Dutertre, B.: Feature-based decomposition of inductive proofs applied to real-time avionics software: an experience report. In: Proceedings of the 26th International Conference on Software Engineering. ICSE 2004. pp. 304–313. IEEE Computer Society, Washington (2004). http://dl.acm.org/citation.cfm?id=998675.999435

8. Jongmans, S.S., Kappé, T., Arbab, F.: Constraint automata with memory cells and their composition. Sci. Comput. Prog. **146**, 50–86 (2017). https://doi.org/10.1016/j.scico.2017.03.006, http://www.sciencedirect.com/science/article/pii/S0167642317300552. special issue with extended selected papers from FACS 2015

9. Kahn, A.B.: Topological sorting of large networks. Commun. ACM **5**(11), 558–562 (1962). https://doi.org/10.1145/368996.369025

10. Kaminski, M., Francez, N.: Finite-memory automata. Theor. Comput. Sci. **134**(2), 329–363 (1994). https://doi.org/10.1016/0304-3975(94)90242-9

11. Kokash, N., Krause, C., de Vink, E.P.: Reo+ mCRL2: a framework for model-checking dataflow in service compositions. FAC **24**(2), 187–216 (2012)

12. Kurz, A., Suzuki, T., Tuosto, E.: On nominal regular languages with binders. In: Birkedal, L. (ed.) FoSSaCS 2012. LNCS, vol. 7213, pp. 255–269. Springer, Heidelberg (2012). https://doi.org/10.1007/978-3-642-28729-9_17

13. NV, A.: OpenComRTOS-Suite Manual and API Manual (1.4.3.3). http://www.altreonic.com/sites/default/files/OpenComRTOS_API-Manual.pdf

14. Proença, J., Madeira, A.: Taming hierarchical connectors. In: Fundamentals of Software Engineering - 8th International Conference, FSEN 2019. LNCS, Tehran, Iran (2019, to appear)

15. Schröder, L., Kozen, D., Milius, S., Wißmann, T.: Nominal automata with name binding. In: Esparza, J., Murawski, A.S. (eds.) FoSSaCS 2017. LNCS, vol. 10203, pp. 124–142. Springer, Heidelberg (2017). https://doi.org/10.1007/978-3-662-54458-7_8

16. Verhulst, E., Boute, R.T., Faria, J.M.S., Sputh, B.H., Mezhuyev, V.: Formal Development of a Network-Centric RTOS: software engineering for reliable embedded systems. Springer Science & Business Media (2011). https://doi.org/10.1007/978-1-4419-9736-4

Author Index

Printed in the United States
By Bookmasters